A HISTORY OF HUMANITARIAN INTERVENTION

The question of 'humanitarian intervention' has been a staple of international law for around 200 years, with a renewed interest in the history of the subject emerging in the last twenty years. This book provides a chronological account of the evolution of the discussion and uncovers the fictional narrative provided by international lawyers to support their conclusions on the subject, from justifications and arguments for 'humanitarian intervention', the misrepresentation of Great Power involvement in the Greek War of Independence in 1827, to the 'humanitarian intervention that never was', India's war with Pakistan in 1971. Relying on a variety of sources, some of them made available in English for the first time, the book provides an undogmatic, alternative history of the fight for the protection of human rights in international law.

MARK SWATEK-EVENSTEIN is a scholar and lawyer specialising in criminal law, immigration, and refugee law. He is a member of the International Network of Genocide Scholars and has taught courses on 'The Holocaust and The Law'. His current research focuses on the minority experience in international law.

A History of Humanitarian Intervention

MARK SWATEK-EVENSTEIN

CAMBRIDGE
UNIVERSITY PRESS

CAMBRIDGE
UNIVERSITY PRESS

University Printing House, Cambridge CB2 8BS, United Kingdom

One Liberty Plaza, 20th Floor, New York, NY 10006, USA

477 Williamstown Road, Port Melbourne, VIC 3207, Australia

314–321, 3rd Floor, Plot 3, Splendor Forum, Jasola District Centre, New Delhi – 110025, India

79 Anson Road, #06–04/06, Singapore 079906

Cambridge University Press is part of the University of Cambridge.

It furthers the University's mission by disseminating knowledge in the pursuit of education, learning, and research at the highest international levels of excellence.

www.cambridge.org
Information on this title: www.cambridge.org/9781107061927
DOI: 10.1017/9781107449459

© Mark Swatek-Evenstein 2020

An early version of this book was published in German by Nomos, as *Geschichte der "Humanitären Intervention"*, 2008.

First published 2020

Printed in the United Kingdom by TJ International Ltd., Padstow Cornwall

A catalogue record for this publication is available from the British Library.

Library of Congress Cataloging-in-Publication Data
NAMES: Swatek-Evenstein, Mark, author.
TITLE: A history of humanitarian intervention / Mark Swatek-Evenstein, Touro College, Berlin.
Other titles: Geschichte der "Humanitären Intervention". English.
DESCRIPTION: Cambridge, United Kingdom ; New York, NY, USA Cambridge University Press, 2020. | Based on author's thesis (doctoral - Universität Bonn, 2008) issued under title: Geschichte der "Humanitären Intervention". | Includes bibliographical references and index.
IDENTIFIERS: LCCN 2019040877 (print) | LCCN 2019040878 (ebook) | ISBN 9781107061927 (hardback) | ISBN 9781107695863 (paperback) | ISBN 9781107449459 (epub)
SUBJECTS: LCSH: Humanitarian intervention–History–19th century. | Humanitarian intervention–History–20th century.
CLASSIFICATION: LCC KZ6369 .S92813 2020 (print) | LCC KZ6369 (ebook) | DDC 341.5/84–dc23
LC record available at https://lccn.loc.gov/2019040877
LC ebook record available at https://lccn.loc.gov/2019040878

ISBN 978-1-107-06192-7 Hardback

Because night has fallen and the barbarians haven't come.

And some of our men just in from the border say there are no barbarians any longer.

Now what's going to happen to us without barbarians?

Those people were a kind of solution.

(C. P. Cavafy, *Waiting for the Barbarians*)

Contents

Acknowledgements

This book is the updated and expanded version of my German-language book *Geschichte der 'Humanitären Intervention'*, published roughly ten years ago. What began as a relatively straightforward intention to translate the book into English so it could reach a wider audience ultimately grew in scope. At the same time, progress on this project was hampered by my ongoing work outside academia as a lawyer for refugees and other migrants. My experience working with people who came to Europe and, more specifically to Germany, not only during the so-called migration crisis of 2015, but also before and after, has significantly informed the content of this book. To paraphrase a political pop song from the 1980s, 'we can talk of humanitarian intervention all day long, but if we fail to organise, we'll waste our lives on protest songs'.

In the following pages, I hope to show that talk of 'humanitarian intervention' has always been disproportionate to any meaningful 'humanitarian' action in the face of man-made disasters, civil wars, state brutality and oppression. And to this day, the victims of such atrocities face major obstacles in their efforts to gain international protection. How meaningful is our discussion about the legality of potential efforts to use force to prevent people from becoming victims if our record of helping actual victims of these atrocities is what it is?

All the mistakes and inaccuracies in this book are my own, but a number of people helped to turn the manuscript into its final form and I would like to express my gratitude to them, in no particular order: Marianna Evenstein, Anja Henebury, Paul Hockenos, Jenny Kohn, Sam Reid, Lisa Rosson, Michelle Standley, Aderet Furer, and everybody at Cambridge University Press. My work also greatly benefitted from the opportunity to attend a conference organised by Professor Dr. André Nollkaemper and participate in a panel organised by Professor Dr. Jessica Gienow-Hecht. This book would never have been possible without the support of Elizabeth Spicer. Thank you very much.

Introduction

In 2014, when the Syrian Civil War was in its third year, an early episode of the successful American television series *Madam Secretary* revolved around events in the fictitious 'Republic of West Africa', where 50,000 innocent civilians faced a campaign of ethnic cleansing by their government. Convinced that it was America's duty to help, the show's main character, a woman named Elizabeth McCord (played by Téa Leoni) as the Secretary of State, in her first few weeks in office, faces an administration convinced that saving the lives of thousands of people in Africa is nothing that would be in the national interest of the United States of America. Over the course of this episode of *Madam Secretary*, the protagonists discuss the political and moral implications of a military intervention to stop a possible genocide taking place on their watch. But for a popular show engaging with national and international events, it is remarkably silent about the law on such international operations. While the situation is eventually resolved through a military operation by the African Union, an organisation arguably capable of engaging in legal military 'humanitarian interventions',[1] this seems like a major gap in the storyline – the question of the legality of such operations under international law, particularly in light of the ongoing conflict in Syria and its rising death toll.

Several years later, the conflict in Syria continues without any coordinated military attempt to intervene to stop a humanitarian crisis that has global repercussions on an unprecedented scale. Red lines have been drawn, but crossed without consequence. While international military intervention does happen, it is not with the intention to stop the humanitarian crises, but to prop up a regime at least partly responsible for many of the atrocities that have caused millions to flee their home country. As the conflict continues, the framework of international law is

---

[1] E.g. Ben Kioko, 'The Right of Intervention under the African Union's Constitutive Act: From Non-interference to Non-intervention', *International Review of the Red Cross* 2003, 85(852), pp. 807–825.

employed by a growing number of academics in the language of 'humanitarian intervention', the language also used in the episode of *Madam Secretary*. Human rights, ethnic cleansing, genocide, these are all relatively new concepts in international law; 'humanitarian intervention', however, is not. It is a concept with a long history, a history that goes back at least to the nineteenth century, if not to antiquity. While this history has become more of a focus of attention since the German edition of this book was published in 2008, it is still a history very much used rather than studied. Recent attempts by some historians have taken an even wider approach to the question of 'humanitarian intervention' and understand 'intervention' not in the legal sense it has traditionally taken on in international law[2]. This book, however, is concerned with international law, as this is where the concept of 'humanitarian intervention' in the sense widely understood today originates.

Like the TV show, accounts of 'humanitarian intervention' in international law revolve around 'trigger' situations, the moment at which an already grave violation of human rights turns into an 'event' or 'international incident'[3] and international law is invoked to resolve the situation, usually through a justification for the use of military force 'when a State mistreated its own nationals in a way so far below international minimum standards "as to shock the conscience of mankind"'.[4] The connection between the legal justification and the historic event, however, is rarely as straightforward as in 1999, when the Kingdom of Belgium argued before the International Court of Justice on the Use of Force during Operation Allied Force that it took 'the view that this is an armed humanitarian intervention, compatible with Article 2, paragraph 4, of the Charter [of the United Nations], which covers only interventions against the territorial integrity or political independence of a State'.[5] This statement is the culmination of developments in international law that are concerned with the protection of values not originally associated with international law, namely human life and human dignity. Historically speaking, the individual, both as a person with feelings and a life to lose, as well as a member of the populace, has no place in international law, concerned as it originally was with the relations between royals and nations, not people. It will be shown that it takes

---

[2] E.g. some contributions in Brendan Simms and D. J. B. Trim (eds.), *Humanitarian Intervention – A History*, Cambridge University Press 2011.

[3] W. Michael Reisman and Andrew R. Willard (eds.), *International Incidents*, Princeton University Press 1988; Fleur Johns, Richard Joyce, and Sundhya Pahuja, *Events: The Force of International Law*, Abingdon: Routledge 2011.

[4] Richard B. Lillich, 'Humanitarian Intervention through the United Nations: Towards the Development of Criteria', *Zeitschrift für ausländisches öffentliches Recht und Völkerrecht* 1993, p. 559, quoting the classic formulation by Hersch Lauterpacht, in: Lassa Oppenheim, *International Law: A Treatise, Vol. I, Peace*, 8th ed, edited by H. Lauterpacht, London: Longmans, Green and Co, 1955, p. 312.

[5] Legality of Use of Force Case [Interim Measures], ICJ 1999, Federal Republic of Yugoslavia vs. 10 NATO member states [Belgium, Germany, France, Italy, Canada, the Netherlands, Portugal, Spain, United Kingdom, United States of America], www.icj-cij.org/docket/files/105/4515.pdf – Oral Arguments, 10 May 1999, CR 99/15.

quite a stretch of the imagination to invoke international law for the protection of the 'conscience of mankind'.

This book is a book about the history of international law, about the history in international law and about the stories we tell us when we talk about international law, about the histories constructed to fit a certain understanding of international law and about the history made by international law. It is just as much a book about history in international law as it is a book about current international law, because the histories and narratives constructed for international law live on in the memory and in the present of international law: The idea that international law may be able (or might need) to provide a legal justification for something intuitively considered 'moral' continues to fascinate lawyers and the wider general public alike. The question of the legality or legitimacy of so-called 'humanitarian intervention', the use of military force by one state or a group of states to protect the citizens of a third state from the violent oppression exercised by that third state's government, has entered popular culture, it is the subject of demonstrations, television series, and widespread international debate in academic and popular and political fora.

The purpose of this book is not to attempt to provide the definitive answer to this question, but to uncover some of the underlying narratives, hidden in the legal construct of 'humanitarian intervention', or, as it was known in its original manifestation in the nineteenth century, 'intervention d'humanité'. For what was not as widely known when the discussion over the legality of the use of force by NATO in the Kosovo case erupted in the late 1990s/early twenty-first century, has since become abundantly clear: 'Humanitarian intervention' is not a new idea. As this book argues, it is an idea that was developed as a legal doctrine under the very specific characteristics of nineteenth century law and evolved through a discussion in most of the important writings on international law in the nineteenth and early twentieth century, which – despite all the factual and legal changes since – already covered most of the problematic issues revolving around the legitimacy and legality of this type of intervention.[6] Throughout its history, the term 'humanitarian intervention' has developed a strong 'pull' towards legitimacy (though not necessary legality)[7] with relatively widespread consensus on its definition[8] and no consensus

---

[6] Doubts about the relevance of the historical development are expressed, for example, by Otto Kimminich, 'Der Mythos der humanitären Intervention', *Archiv des Völkerrechts* 1995, p. 431; Karl Doehring, 'Die Humanitäre Intervention – Überlegungen zu ihrer Rechtfertigung', in: Antonio Augusto Cançado Trindade (Ed.), *The Modern World of Human Rights*, Essays in honour of Thomas Buergenthal, San José, Costa Rica: Inter-American Institute of Human Rights 1996, p. 549; Shand J. Watson, *Theory and Reality in the International Protection of Human Rights*, New York: Transnational Publishers 1999, p. 245. But as is evidenced by, among many others, Christian J. Tams, *Enforcing Obligations* Erga Omnes *in International Law*, Cambridge University Press 2005, p. 93, the claimed historical narrative is part of the fabric of international law.

[7] Thomas Franck, *The Power of Legitimacy among Nations*, Oxford University Press 1990.

[8] A number of authors do not even provide any definition anymore, e.g. Michael J. Bazyler, 'Reexamining the Doctrine of Humanitarian Intervention in Light of the Atrocities in

on its legal standing. The term's pull towards legitimacy has had a tendency to overshadow the relevant legal and factual questions relevant to the application of the doctrine in practice, a trend that continues today.

The question of the legality of the use of force to save lives and to stop the use of force to destroy lives has troubled writers on international law for centuries and the founding fathers of international law discussed similar issues when asking under what conditions war could be considered just. Yet at some point in the historical evolution of international law, these questions came into a certain focus that is not only markedly different from the focus of previous centuries, but that also continues to shape the outlines of the current discussion of the legality of 'humanitarian intervention' and the so-called Responsibility to Protect. For all the uncertainties over the details of these questions, the core concept has always been clear: That international law should pass judgement on the use of (military) force by one state or a group of states for the purpose of stopping mass atrocities in a different country. Over the course of the centuries, not only has the language employed to describe the situations in which the question of whether there should be or was a legal justification for such use of force been remarkably consistent, the belief that this question was more than theoretical has also hardly waned.

An earlier version of this book appeared in German in 2008,[9] and first attempted an investigation into the historical legal evolution of the doctrine that takes into account the constructive nature of this evolution. The few enquiries into the history of 'humanitarian intervention' that have been published since have either focused on re-discovering that previous writers on international law had already discussed the question of 'humanitarian intervention' in the nineteenth century[10] or they have attempted to re-create an understanding of the interventions that brought forward this discussion in the first place.[11] A book making the connection between these two strands of enquiry for the English reader is still missing. This book aims to fill that gap by discussing the evolution of the doctrine of 'humanitarian intervention' in the context of the evolution of the international legal system in which the doctrine operates. It seeks to contribute to an understanding of the intellectual history of international law by recalling the histories that are told in international law. It is an updated and expanded version of the German book.

Kampuchea and Ethiopia', *Stanford Journal of International Law* 1987, p. 547, fn 1: 'There is little use in defining the doctrine of humanitarian intervention'.
9 Mark Swatek-Evenstein, *Geschichte der 'Humanitären Intervention'*, Baden-Baden: Nomos 2008.
10 Alexis Heraclidis, 'Humanitarian Intervention in International Law 1830–1939 – The Debate', *Journal of the History of International Law* 2014, 16, pp. 26–62. This applies, to a lesser extent, also to Alexis Heraclidis and Ada Dialla, *Humanitarian Intervention in the Long Nineteenth Century – Setting the Precedent*, Manchester University Press 2015.
11 Gary J. Bass, *Freedom's Battle*, New York: Alfred A. Knopf 2008; Davide Rodogno, *Against Massacre: Humanitarian Interventions in the Ottoman Empire, 1815–1914*, Princeton University Press 2012.

The reason that the question of the legality of 'humanitarian intervention' has troubled writers on international law for centuries is not because of its immense practical relevance. Those familiar with the realities on our planet are mostly aware that it usually is less a question of normative uncertainties than the lack of political will that prevents decisive action in the face of mass atrocities like the genocide in Rwanda or the civil war currently raging in Syria. As its absence from the story arch of the aforementioned TV episode indicates, the rules of international law on the use of force may not be the significant factor they are sometimes made out to be. This is not to state that these rules may be losing significance, but to state that 'paramount' amongst the multifarious reasons why the United Nations 'finds it so difficult to intervene effectively for humanitarian purposes' are 'the inviolability accorded state boundaries and the consequent failure to agree to any legal right of humanitarian intervention', as some do,[12] is to blame the international system for – apparently: unwanted? – consequences. This explains why, despite the reluctance of some international lawyers to continue the discussion over 'humanitarian intervention',[13] it remains, as others claim, 'the most controversial issue in the whole of international law'.[14] Again, this is not for its practical relevance, but because the issues discussed under the rubric of 'humanitarian intervention' cut through the fundamental layers of international law in different and opposing ways.

As political scientist Robert H. Jackson has correctly pointed out:

> The debate on humanitarian intervention is not a debate between those who are concerned about human rights and those who [are] indifferent or callous about human suffering. Every decent person has these concerns. It is not even a debate about how to best go about preventing human suffering. That is an important question. But it is of secondary importance. It is a debate about the basic values of international society. Issues of justifiable armed intervention and justifiable warfare are being raised that are at the very foundations of international society.[15]

The enquiry into the historical evolution of this debate will show just how fundamentally the values at hand cut through the cornerstones of international law and, how, in fact, the *construction* of the legal arguments on 'humanitarian interventions' is inherently tied to the construction of a system of international law around the model of the (Western) European nation state. Consequently, this book is not interested in the question of whether or not 'humanitarian intervention' is or at some point in history was legal under international law. It does not seek to count the number of authorities writing on international law to come to a definitive

---

[12] David Fisher, 'Humanitarian Intervention', in Charles Reed and David Ryall (eds.), *The Price of Peace*, Cambridge University Press 2007, p. 105.

[13] E.g. Stephan Oeter, 'Humanitäre Intervention und Gewaltverbot: Wie handlungsfähig ist die Staatengemeinschaft?', in Hauke Brunkhorst (ed.), *Einmischung erwünscht?*, Frankfurt am Main: S. Fischer 1998, p. 37.

[14] Stephen C. Neff, *War and the Law of Nations*, Cambridge University Press 2005, p. 362.

[15] Robert Jackson, *The Global Covenant*, Oxford University Press 2000, p. 291.

conclusion, but instead seeks to de-construct the conditions under which 'humanitarian intervention' was considered by some renowned authorities on international law to be legal.

The history of 'humanitarian intervention' in general and especially its legal dimension is usually told in the language of humanitarianism and situated within the history of the evolution of international human rights protection. In recent years, in particular, historians and political scientists have turned their attention to the subject, which previously mainly received attention within the field of international law, and, again, the narrative places 'humanitarian intervention' in the context of human rights and humanitarianism, as embodied in the iconic title of Nicolas Wheeler's book *Saving Strangers*.[16] One of the purposes of this book is to challenge these narratives, for a close reading of nineteenth-century discourse in international law on the origins of what is now commonly referred to as 'humanitarian intervention' suggests that a more appropriate setting might be the history of 'imagined communities' (Benedict Anderson), the invention of tradition of the nation state for the purpose of establishing the nation state as defined by the European experience of the nineteenth century as the principal actor of international law. In a sense, the original project of 'humanitarian intervention' can be seen as a part of the 'constitutionalisation' or, in fact, the 'Europeanisation' of 'Europe'. The 'Europe' that we know today constituted itself in the wars and skirmishes that are part of the history of 'humanitarian intervention', by rearranging the borders of 'Europe' as was necessary to reaffirm a secular Christian identity as authentically *European*. In these conflicts, potentially multi-cultural societies with sizeable Muslim populations were – with the approval of writers on the international law of 'humanitarian intervention' – turned into predominantly Christian nation-states, creating national identities that mirrored their Western counterparts.

'Humanitarian intervention' is, in fact, a euphemism for violence, the use of military force for a specific aim. As the Australian philosopher C. A. J. Coady has forcefully pointed out: It needs to be insisted that invasion is what military intervention, in the strict sense, standardly involves.'[17] For all the talk of humanitarianism and human rights cannot conceal the fact that 'humanitarian intervention' favours one type of violence over another; favours the violence of one side over the violence of the other. Kofi Annan, in his role as Secretary General of the Security Council of the United Nations, once famously said:

> Of course military intervention can be undertaken for humanitarian motives. There are times when the use of force may be legitimate and necessary because there is no other way to save masses of people from extreme violence and slaughter. [But] let's get right away from using the term 'humanitarian' to describe military operations.

[16] Nicolas J. Wheeler, *Saving Strangers*, Oxford University Press 2000.
[17] C. A. J. Coady, *Morality and Political Violence*, Cambridge University Press 2008, p. 76.

Otherwise, we will find ourselves using phrases like 'humanitarian bombing', and people will soon get very cynical about the whole idea.[18]

This book hopes to show that while there need not be anything cynical about the idea of 'humanitarian intervention' as such, the application of the idea may be a very different matter. It is one thing to consider the Allied war effort in World War II justified, but quite another to present it as a 'humanitarian intervention'.

This book is interested in the way the doctrine of 'humanitarian intervention' evolved to justify the violence of military force and how this violence was portrayed in the narratives created to justify the existence of the doctrine. Violence is usually portrayed as an aberration, a mistake, a plan gone wrong or a type of illness, to be healed one day.'[19] In the narrative of 'humanitarian intervention', however, the violence of the intervention is the violence which brings peace, uncharacteristically, not the violence of destruction, but 'therapeutic violence', the violence to end violence. Generations of jurists and writers engaged with the subject of 'humanitarian intervention' have been operating under the assumption that – in the words of one of the fiercest current critics of the instrument of 'humanitarian intervention' as an 'elite assault on sovereignty' – in the nineteenth century the European Great Powers 'dispatched troops abroad to stop mass killings in the Ottoman Empire' in (at least) 'three instances'.[20] But, as this books seeks to demonstrate, such simple causal connections only exist as narratives constructed by international lawyers with an agenda. This agenda might simply be the idealist belief that international law has something meaningful to say about the way to deal with the sometimes 'unimaginable atrocities' that give rise to the question whether or not to intervene. But that is precisely why this book does not claim to understand 'how international law works' or to understand 'humanitarian interventions' as cases of 'when international law works', but instead seeks to demonstrate what happens when international law is applied to 'make international law work' as an example of the use of the legal doctrine of 'humanitarian intervention'. Accordingly, while this is a book about the history of international law, it situates its topic at the crossroads between international history, legal history, and genocide studies, hoping to reconnect narratives that exist in international law almost in isolation to a broader history of international responses to atrocities since the nineteenth century.

---

[18] Remarks made by Secretary-General Kofi Annan to an International Peace Academy Symposium on Humanitarian Action, November 20, 2000 – available at www.un.org/press/en/2000/20001120.sgsm7632.doc.html, last accessed 6 October 2018.

[19] Jörg Baberowski, *Räume der Gewalt*, Frankfurt am Main: S. Fischer Verlag 2015, p. 25.

[20] Rajan Menon, *The Conceit of Humanitarian Intervention*, Oxford University Press 2016, p. 26, 78.

1

The Battlegrounds of a History of 'Humanitarian Intervention'

1.1 INTRODUCTION

In April 1917, Warren Harding, at the time a US Senator and later the twenty-ninth President of the United States, declared in a speech that eighteen years prior, the United States had 'unsheathed the sword [. . .] for the first time in the history of the world in the name of humanity', and had thus given 'proof to the world at the time of an unselfish nation'.[1] Harding was referring to the American intervention in the Cuban struggle for independence from Spanish colonial rule, which eventually culminated in the Spanish–American War of 1898. In the preceding years, American public opinion had long been in favour of action against Spanish mis-rule, which had included brutal policies of 'reconcentración', the forced relocation of more than 400,000 people to the vicinity of the ports, and their internment in camps.[2] The situation had eventually led to an intervention by the United States, declared in a resolution by Congress as the reaction to the 'abhorrent' conditions in Cuba, which had 'shocked the moral sense of the people of the United States' and had been considered 'a disgrace to the Christian civilisation'.[3] William McKinley, then President of the United States, had then told the world that it had been necessary 'in the cause of humanity' to put an end 'to the barbarities, bloodshed, starvation and horrible miseries' in Cuba: 'It is no answer to say this is all in another

---

[1] Quoted in Wilhelm G. Grewe, *The Epochs of International Law*, trans. by Michael Byers, De Gruyter: Berlin 2000, p. 490, fn 24.
[2] For details see Section 2.8.
[3] 'Whereas the abhorrent conditions which have existed for more than three years on the island of Cuba, so near to our borders, have shocked the moral sense of the people of the Unites States and have been a disgrace to Christian civilisation . . . and can no longer be endured. . .'. Joint Resolution of the US Congresses, in: John Bassett Moore (ed.), *A Digest of International Law*, Vol. VI, Washington: Government Printing Office 1906, p. 226.

country, belonging to another nation, and is therefore none of our business. It is our special duty, for it is right at our door'.[4]

At first glance, this historical episode meets all the international law criteria for a 'humanitarian' intervention. There was a 'trigger situation', because certainly at some point there had been a widespread violation of fundamental human rights in Cuba; there was the military intervention by a third state to end such violations; and there was an official justification for this action on the grounds of 'humanity', the combination of moral reasoning and a claim to know what (according to 'Christian civilisation') was right or necessary in the face of 'abhorrent', or 'barbaric' behaviour by a third state. It purports to carry the 'right' answer to conditions so 'wrong' that only outside interference could correct them. But this is only the surface. At the same time, this official justification – by claiming it was a state of affairs that could no longer be endured because it was a 'disgrace to Christian civilisation' – exposes the underlying values behind such claims: The 'humanitarian intervention' brought into effect here is a civilising mission, based on Christian values, and, as such, it is not meant to uphold the law as much as it is meant to develop the law; to use the law as an educational tool. This is particularly evident in the case of Cuba, where 'Christian' values are used to justify an intervention in a fight *between* Christians (Cubans and their Spanish colonial rulers). It is, therefore, hardly surprising that the contemporary European powers were more or less dismissive of the American intervention.[5] Contrary to Harding's claim, the American intervention was not the first intervention to have been undertaken in the 'cause of humanity', at least not according to the contemporary literature on international law. Even current writing on international law and 'humanitarian intervention' is more likely to cite the intervention of the European powers Russia, Great Britain, and France in the Greek struggle for independence in first half of the nineteenth century as a 'first precedent' of a 'humanitarian' intervention.[6] But while Greek rebellion against the Ottoman Empire – the 'Sick Man of Europe' – may be compared to Cuban rebellion against a weakened and declining Spanish empire, there was more at stake in this case than the slow death of a former major power: In the Greek case,[7] the 'interests of humanity' were pitted against 'inhuman

---

[4] Special Message by US President McKinley, 11 April 1898, in: Moore 1906, pp. 219–220: 'First. In the cause of humanity and to put an end to the barbarities, bloodshed, starvation and horrible miseries now existing there, and which the parties to the conflict are either unable or unwilling to stop or to mitigate. It is no answer to say this is all in another country, belonging to another nation, and is therefore none of our business. It is our special duty, for it is right at our door'.

[5] For details, see Section 2.8.2.

[6] Christian Hillgruber, 'Humanitäre Intervention, Großmachtpolitik und Völkerrecht', *Der Staat* 2001, 40(2), p. 169.

[7] See Section 2.2.

barbarism' – and it was seen as such from both sides.[8] In the case of the American intervention in the Cuban struggle for independence, the roles are less clearly defined. For a history of the legal instrument of 'humanitarian intervention', the salient point is the historical context of Spain and the Ottoman Empire: two former major powers operating outside or at the outskirts of their historic spheres of influence. Almost all 'humanitarian' interventions discussed in the literature on the subject take place in this setting of 'unequal sovereigns'[9] on the borderlines of the world normally inhabited by a nineteenth-century European understanding of international law. These particular circumstances provide the original framework for a history of 'humanitarian intervention'.

Early theorists of a right of 'humanitarian intervention' operated with an underlying and often invisible assumption of an international law of unequal sovereigns. They would stress that the question of 'humanitarian intervention' might in fact only arise where different religions clashed, but this was not to change the unique, 'humanitarian' character of the legal instrument.[10] As such, the legal understanding of 'humanitarian intervention' was only fully conceptualised in the nineteenth century once Christianity had ceased to openly be the foundation of international law, then commonly referred to as the law of 'civilised' nations. It was replaced by the idea of 'civilisation', as expressed by the guarantees of freedom of religion and protection of minorities in the countries of the European Great Powers. The concept of 'civilisation', especially insofar as it rested upon a guarantee of freedom of religion, was largely theoretical. Gerrit Gong has shown that there is no indication in British state practice or published documents on international law that the Treaty of Paris, which 'admitted' the Ottoman Empire 'to participate in the advantages of the Public Law and System (Concert) of Europe', had any effect on the British position on the legal status of the Ottoman Empire,[11] and, indeed, the Treaty seems to have had little effect on the treatment of the Empire by the European Great Powers.[12] The replacement of religion with civilisation was a conceptual

---

[8] Richard Bonney, *Jihad: From Qur'an to bin Laden*, Basingstoke, Hampshire: Palgrave Macmillan 2004, p. 146: '[T]he Greek revolution was a war "against the enemies of Our Lord", defensive in character, of justice against injustice, of "reason against the senselessness and ferocity of tyranny", a true war of the Christian religion against the Qur'an'.

[9] On the subject of 'unequal sovereigns', see Gerry Simpson, *Great Powers and Outlaw States*, Cambridge University Press 2004.

[10] Antoine Rougier, 'La Théorie de l'Intervention de Humanité', *Revue générale de droit international public* 1910, p. 472: 'L'intervention en matière de religion est chose nettement différente de l'intervention d'humanité'. Antoine Pillet, 'Le Droit International Public', *Revue générale de droit international public* 1894, p. 16. For a different opinion, see: Andre Mandelstam, *La Société des Nations et les puissances devant le problème Arménien*, Paris: Pédone 1925, p. 6 with fn (I).

[11] Gerrit W. Gong, *The Standard of 'Civilization' in International Society*, Oxford: Clarendon Press 1984, p. 112.

[12] Alexander Orakhelashvili, 'The Idea of European International Law', *European Journal of International* 2006, 17(2), p. 337.

change only; the leading powers in international law remained the same.[13] The civilised/uncivilised dichotomy only gradually established itself as conceptually different from the original Christian/non-Christian dichotomy, but whether this is a meaningful difference remains in question. At the same time, the institutionalisation of the Great Powers as the 'leading nations' (or 'Wortführer')[14] of an international society of nations, though unclear as to its legal effect, corresponds to a subordination of smaller states and the stigmatisation of certain states as (unequal) 'pariah states'.[15] The Ottoman Empire was the state most visibly affected by this development. The Empire's status in both political and legal terms changed significantly during the course of the nineteenth century, and this is the context in which 'humanitarian intervention' as a legal instrument begins to take on its own specific shape.

At the beginning of the nineteenth century, the Ottoman Empire could still be considered as one of the states of Europe.[16] While there may have been doubts as to the legal relevance of this assessment,[17] it is clear that relations with the Ottoman

---

[13] Dietrich Schindler, 'Völkerrecht und Zivilisation', *Schweizerisches Jahrbuch für internationales Recht* 1956, p. 82.

[14] Friedrich August Freiherr von der Heydte, 'Ein Betrag zum Problem der Macht im "klassischen" und im "neuen" Völkerrecht', in: Walter Schätzel and Hans-Jürgen Schlochauer (eds.), *Rechtsfragen der Internationalen Organisation*, Festschrift für Hans Wehberg, Frankfurt a.M.: Vittorio Klostermann 1956, p. 176.

[15] See: Petra Minnerop, *Paria-Staaten im Völkerrecht?*, Berlin: Springer 2004; Simpson 2004.

[16] Johann Jacob Moser, *Grundsätze des jetzt üblichen Europäischen Völcker-Rechts in Friedenszeiten*, Hanau 1750, p. 20, § 16; Karl Gottlob Günther, *Europäisches Völkerrecht in Friedenszeiten nach Vernunft, Verträgen und Herkommen*, Altenburg: Richtersche Buchhandlung 1787, pp. 109, 247; Georg Friedrich von Martens, *Einleitung in das positive Europäische Völkerrecht auf Verträge und Herkommen gegründet*, Göttingen: Dieterich 1796, p. 29, § 15; Julius Schmelzing, *Systematischer Grundriß des praktischen Europäischen Völker-Rechts*, Band I, Rudolfstadt: Verlag der Hof-Buch- und Kunsthandlung 1818, p. 5; Friedrich Saalfeld, *Handbuch des positiven Völkerrechts*, Tübingen: Verlag von C. F. Osiander 1833, p. 29, § 15, p. 50, § 24. For a different opinion, see Theodor Schmalz, *Das europäische Völker-Recht in acht Büchern*, Berlin: Duncker und Humblot 1817, p. 41, considering only 'alle christlichen Völker von Europa' bound through their shared international law.

[17] Early writers on international law like Georg Friedrich von Martens conceded that 'the Turks' did not observe international law 'on many occasions' ('in vielen Punkten', my translation), see: von Martens 1796, p. 6, fn. a. This passage remained essentially unchanged over the years. The English language translation from 1829 reads as follows: 'I thought it necessary to confine my title to the *nations of Europe*; although, *in* Europe, the Turks have, in many respects, rejected the positive law of nations of which I here treat; [. . .]', Georg Friedrich von Martens, *The Law of Nations*, 4th ed., trans. by D. B. Cobbett, London: Cobbett 1829, p. 5. von Martens was of the opinion that the Ottoman Empire never completely joined the bond of 'political and legal mutual respect' (von Martens 1796, pp. 26–27). The English translation speaks of a 'connexion' between the states of Europe, based on the 'resemblance in manners and religion, the intercourse of commerce, the frequency of treaties of all sorts, and the ties of blood between sovereigns' that allowed one to 'consider Europe (particularly the Christian states of it) as a society of nations and states' and went to point that the 'connexion between the Ottoman Empire and the Christian states of Europe is much less general' (von Martens 1829, p. 27). The work of von Martens stands for the emergence of a new tradition in international law,

Empire during the course of the nineteenth century were guided by rules that cannot be classified as anything but rules of law.[18] This did not stop authors well into the twentieth century from claiming that the Ottoman Empire deserved no place among the nations ruled and protected by international law. Even the decision in state practice to 'admit' the Empire to participate in the advantages of the *'droit public et du concert européens'*, as evidenced by the Paris Treaty of 1856,[19] had little to no effect on such an assessment.[20] This friction between a more general state practice and interpretations of specific events of state practice in relation to alleged cases of 'humanitarian interventions' will be the focus of the coming pages.

1.2 THE DEFINITION OF 'HUMANITARIAN INTERVENTION'

Current legal scholarship on international law generally agrees on the basics of a definition of 'humanitarian intervention'. The term refers to the qualified threat or the use of force, i.e. military measures, by one or more states aimed at protecting citizens of another state against massive human rights violations in their home state, without the consent of their government.[21] It is used to describe coercive measures aimed at changing political policy decisions in another state with the intention of ensuring respect for the most fundamental human rights.[22]

overcoming eighteenth century concepts, see Karl Heinz Ziegler, *Völkerrechtsgeschichte*, 2nd ed., Munich: C. H. Beck 2007, p. 163. He was among the first 'internationalistes', Emmanuelle Jouannet, *The Liberal-Welfarist Law of Nations*, Cambridge University Press 2011, p. 19. However, this passage also makes it clear that the separation between the 'states of Europe' and the Ottoman Empire was not necessarily a legal one.

[18] See: Gong 1984, p. 66; Thomas Naff, 'The Ottoman Empire and the European State System', in: Hedley Bull and Adam Watson (eds.), *The Expansion of International Society*, Oxford University Press 1984, p. 169. Ziegler 2007, pp. 163–165.

[19] Traité générale de Paris, 30 March 1856, between the Russian Empire and an alliance of the Ottoman Empire, the British Empire, the Second French Empire, the Austrian Empire, the Kingdom of Prussia, and the Kingdom of Sardinia – Art. VII: '. . . déclarent la Sublime Porte admise à participer aux avantages du droit public et du concert européens'. Georg Friedrich von Martens and Charles Samwer, *Nouveau Recueil Général des Traités*, Vol. XV, Göttingen: Dieterich 1857, p. 774 ff. The exact legal effect of this passage remains in doubt, see Section 2.3.3.

[20] E.g. Adolph Hartmann, *Institutionen des praktischen Völkerrechts in Friedenszeiten, mit Rücksicht auf die Verfassung, die Verträge und die Gesetzgebung des Deutschen Reichs*, 2nd ed., Hannover: C. Meyer 1878, pp. 6–7; James Lorimer, *The Institutes of the Law of Nations*, Vol. I, Edinburgh and London: William Blackwood & Sons 1883, p. 102; Peter Resch, *Das Völkerrecht der heutigen Staatenwelt europäischer Gesittung*, 2nd. ed., Graz and Leipzig: Verlag von Ulr. Mosers Buchhandlung (J. Meyerhoff) 1890, p. 3; Alfred von Wachter, *Die völkerrechtliche Intervention als Mittel der Selbsthilfe*, Munich: Krämer 1911, pp. 50–52.

[21] E.g. J. L. Holzgrefe, 'The Humanitarian Intervention Debate', in: J. L. Holzgrefe and Robert O. Keohane (eds.), *Humanitarian Intervention*, Cambridge University Press 2003, p. 18. Further references for similar definitions can be found in Swatek-Evenstein 2008, pp. 53–54, fn. 252.

[22] The German language discussion over the threshold for a (justified) 'humanitarian intervention' regularly employs the term 'humanitärer Mindeststandard', e.g. Alexander Pauer, *Die humanitäre Intervention*, Basel: Helbing & Lichtenhahn 1985, p. 23, Malte Wellhausen,

This definition excludes interventions undertaken exclusively for the protection or rescue of the intervening state's own nationals. Some writers also include interventions of this type in their treatment of 'humanitarian intervention'.[23] But a state acting to save its own nationals effectively reinforces the justification of its existence,[24] fulfilling its traditional role and, at least in some sense, acts in *self-defence*.[25] Interventions of such a nature could rely on their own justification, especially under nineteenth-century international law. The real value of 'humanitarian intervention', its defining moment even, is alluded to in the title of Nicolas Wheeler's book *Saving Strangers* – the idea that the intervention is, at least, in some way, 'selfless'.[26] From an international law perspective, excluding interventions undertaken with the sole purpose of protecting a state's *own* nationals is justified, even if – from a human rights perspective – atrocities committed against *foreigners* in another country are equally serious human rights violations. Conceptually, the situation is not necessarily different in cases of interventions in civil wars, or wars of 'national liberation',[27] and for interventions undertaken at the request or with the consent of the government of the target state. In the latter case, there may be doubts as to the validity of such consent or whether the 'request' was the result of – maybe

Humanitäre Intervention, Baden-Baden: Nomos 2002, pp. 47–48. The best translation for this term would probably be a 'minimum standard of human rights', though the terminology seems to link the concept to international humanitarian law rather than human rights law.

[23] See the statements made by Thomas Franck (pp. 12–13), Ellen Frey Wouters (pp. 22–23) and Richard Baxter (pp. 53–54) in Richard B. Lillich (ed.), *Humanitarian Intervention and the United Nations*, Charlottesville: University of Virginia Press 1973; H. Scott Fairley, 'State Actors, Humanitarian Intervention and International Law: Reopening Pandora's Box', *Georgia Journal of International and Comparative Law* 1980, 10(1), p. 35; Francis Kofi Abiew, *The Evolution of the Doctrine and Practice of Humanitarian Intervention*, The Hague: Kluwer Law International 1999, p. 32, fn. 39. According to the International Commission on Intervention and State Sovereignty, *The Responsibility to Protect*, Ottawa: International Development Research Centre 2001, Suppl. Vol., p. 16, this is supposed to be due to developments up until the 1920s, though no further information is given. Some German authors also include these cases in discussions on 'humanitarian intervention', e.g. Ulrich Beyerlin, 'Humanitarian Intervention', in: Rudolf Bernhardt (ed.), *Encyclopaedia of Public International Law*, Vol. 2, Amsterdam: North-Holland Publishing 1995, p. 926.

[24] A point well made and traced back to Aristotle by Josef Isensee, 'Die alte Frage nach der Rechtfertigung des Staates', *Juristenzeitung* 1999, pp. 265–278.

[25] Cf. Jack Donnelly, *Universal Human Rights in Theory and Practice*, 2nd ed., Ithaca: Cornell University Press 2003, p. 243; Theodor Schweisfurth, *Völkerrecht*, Tübingen: UTB 2006, pp. 366–367, IX/297. This does not imply the technical sense of Art. 51 UN-Charter (Schweisfurth 2006, p. 367, IX/300).

[26] This is not to say that such interventions can only be termed 'humanitarian' if they are 'purely humanitarian', see Thomas Franck, *Recourse to Force*, Cambridge University Press 2002, p. 138.

[27] Edward Gordon, Article 2(4) in Historical Context, *Yale Journal of International Law* 1985, 10, available at: https://digitalcommons.law.yale.edu/yjil/vol10/iss2/4at, discusses three different types of interventions as 'humanitarian interventions': 'first, where a state uses force to protect the lives or property of its own nationals abroad when a host government is unwilling or unable to provide such protection, second, where the use of force serves to prevent a foreign government from initiating or perpetuating a massive and gross violation of the human rights of its own or a third state's nationals, third, where a state intervenes in a foreign state's civil war or so-called war of national liberation'.

more subtle – coercion, but interventions based on such grounds are substantially different from interventions based on the claim that massive human rights violations *themselves* carry the potential to serve as the legal basis for a justification. Interventions in civil wars, on the other hand, typically involve a sense of partisanship that may offer its own justification: In these situations, modern international law will focus on questions connected to a people's right of self-determination.[28] Indeed, some earlier writers on international law had already made this connection.[29] Yet, while the conceptual exclusion of corresponding interventions can easily be defended, a history of 'humanitarian intervention' in international law would be incomplete if it did not cover such cases as well. The evolution of 'humanitarian intervention' as a legal concept and as developed by writers in international law has included historic interventions which, strictly speaking, would be better understood as interventions in wars of national liberation or interventions authorised by consent.

The definition offered here is generally accepted in current international law. However, the legal content of the components of this definition is much less clear: The definition's central term (human rights) only came to take on its specific legal meaning in present day international law, and its precise scope and content is still the subject of much debate. At the same time, it is used to define a legal instrument, a doctrine, which began to develop in the nineteenth century under the very different conditions of the law of those times, when human rights were not unheard of, but had very little, if any, doctrinal (legal) content. At the same time, there is little reason to suspect that international lawyers then, insofar as they recognised a right of 'humanitarian intervention', had different *motives* for doing so than their counterparts today:[30] A belief in international law as a means to contribute to a solution of the types of situations that might warrant a 'humanitarian' intervention.

Contrary to most readings of nineteenth-century international law,[31] the idea that humans have rights because they are human can already be found in writings on international law from that century's first half.[32] While such acknowledgements

---

[28] See C. G. Roelofsen, 'The Right to National Self-determination in the 18th and 19th Century, an emerging Principle of Public International Law?', in: Nerl Sybesma-Knol and Jef van Bellingen (eds.), *Naar een nieuwe interpretatie van het Recht of Zelfbeschikking*, Brussels: VUB Press 1995, on the evolution of the legal concept.

[29] E.g. Henry Wheaton, *Elements of International Law*, 3rd ed., Philadelphia: Lea & Blanchard 1846, p. 112 ff.; Edward S. Creasy, *First Platform of International Law*, London: John Van Voorst 1874, pp. 299–300; Ellery C. Stowell, *Intervention in International Law*, Washington: John Byrne & Co 1921, p. 126.

[30] For a more skeptical reading, see: Kimminich 1995, p. 431 f.

[31] Christian Tomuschat, *Human Rights – Between Idealism and Realism*, 2nd ed., Oxford University Press, 2008, p. 16, suggests that most authors, Heffter among them, simply ignored the term, and considered this 'quite understandable, given the absence of any practice to substantiate the concept'.

[32] E.g. August Wilhelm Heffter, *Das Europäische Völkerrecht der Gegenwart*, Berlin: Verlag von E. H. Schröder 1844, p. 27, § 13; Heinrich Bernhard Oppenheim, *System des Völkerrechts*, 2nd ed., Stuttgart and Leipzig: Kröner 1866, p. 3.

rarely yielded specific legal results,[33] the language used to describe the conditions of 'humanitarian intervention' by the mid-nineteenth century[34] already mirrored current usage with references to a 'droit humain' or 'the law of humanity'[35] and '(so-called) human rights' ('sog. Menschenrechte')[36] or the 'inhumanity' of a government[37] to describe reasons for intervention. It may therefore be said that general respect for human rights simply reinstates the common foundation of 'civilisation', which was a self-evident prerequisite of nineteenth-century international law.[38] Just as today an 'international crime' – for instance a crime committed against all states – is now considered to be a sufficient reason to trigger a *legal* 'humanitarian intervention',[39] in the nineteenth century, the 'crime of a government against its subjects' was considered a sufficient justification for intervention[40] – even if there was no 'crime' to speak of in any technical sense, given the absence of any accepted form of international criminal law. Even the claim that there is a 'legal' minimum standard of behaviour applicable to the community of nations,[41] was already made well before

---

[33] Heffter 1844, pp. 1–2, § 1.

[34] Ian Brownlie, *International Law and the Use of Force by States*, Oxford: Clarendon Press 1963, p. 338, note 2, states that Stowell considered 'a work by von Rotteck, published in 1845, as the first to establish a theory of intervention on the ground of humanity'. Stowell himself only wrote that von Rotteck's study 'Das Recht der Einmischung in die inneren Angelegenheiten eines fremden Staates' 'seems to be the first to undertake a systematic and comprehensive study of intervention', and did not mention the question of the grounds of humanity in this context, see Stowell 1921, p. 525. In the German edition of this book, I mistakenly attributed this study to Karl von Rotteck, when it was, in fact, written by his son, Hermann von Rotteck. It was, in any case, preceded by the 1821 study by Carl Christoph von Kamptz, which already included vague references to 'national unrest' as legitimate grounds for intervention, for details see Section 2.2.3. The report of the International Commission on Intervention and State Sovereignty states the '[r]eferences to humanitarian intervention first began to appear in the international legal literature after 1840', see International Commission on Intervention and State Sovereignty 2001, Suppl. Vol., p. 16, mentioning Augustus Granville Stapleton, *Intervention and Non-intervention, or the Foreign Policy of Great Britain from 1790 to 1865*, London: John Murray 1866, Stowell 1921, and Brownlie 1963, but none of these references explains the year 1840.

[35] Gustave Rolin-Jaequemyns, 'Note sur la théorie du droit d'intervention, a propos d'une lettre de M. le Professeur Arntz', *Revue de droit international et de législation comparée* 1876, 8, p. 673, as translated in Grewe 2000, p. 495.

[36] Hermann Strauch, *Zur Interventionslehre – Eine völkerrechtliche Studie*, Heidelberg: Carl Winter's Universitätsbuchhandlung 1879, p. 13.

[37] Hermann von Rotteck, *Das Recht der Einmischung in die inneren Angelegenheiten eines fremden Staates*, Freiburg: Adolph Emmerling 1845, p. 11: 'Wenn die Einmischung als moralischer Verpflichtung erscheint, z.B. wegen eines bis zur Unmenschlichkeit gesteigerten Missbrauchs der Staatsgewalt[...]'.

[38] Schindler 1956, p. 93.

[39] E.g. Karl Doehring, *Völkerrecht*, Heidelberg: C. F. Müller Verlag 2004, p. 447, no. 1014.

[40] Theodore Woolsey, *Introduction to the Study of International Law*, 2nd ed., New York: Charles Scribner 1864, p. 57.

[41] André Mandelstam, 'Der internationale Schutz der Menschenrechte und die New Yorker Erklärung des Instituts für Völkerrecht', *Zeitschrift für ausländisches öffentliches Recht und Völkerrecht* 1931, p. 366: 'Es scheint nun, daß für jede Epoche der Weltgeschichte ein *rechtliches Minimum* existiert, unter dessen Niveau herabzusinken es keinem Staate von der Völkergemeinschaft gestattet werden darf'. ('It appears that for every epoch of history there

the events of World War II, and the Shoah spurred efforts to put this 'legal minimum' into more precise and binding terms. Since then, more binding international human rights protection rests on the development of a legal regime originally aimed at protecting foreign nationals only.[42] Arguably, the transformation of these rules to a general customary international obligation by states to guarantee their *own* nationals a certain 'humanitarian minimum' is still awaiting completion. A 'human rights revolution' is yet to occur in international law, and the developments relating to the civil war in Syria have shown that there is little reason to believe that it will come anytime soon.[43]

Ultimately, efforts to define the requirements for an intervention to be deemed 'humanitarian' say relatively little about the normative content of the legal instrument 'humanitarian intervention'. Stating that massive violations of fundamental human rights are a prerequisite for any intervention to be classified as 'humanitarian' is purely descriptive: This observation alone says nothing about the legal character of an intervention thus undertaken, let alone its legality. International law knows of no right of states to vindicate international law by virtue of the law's violation. In fact, the absence of such a right is one of the defining features (or shortcomings) of international law. While current international law has evolved to include high standards of human rights protection, no corresponding right to 'check' violations of this standard exists. Nor is there any guarantee that states might not abandon those high standards in the face of domestic opposition to the consequences of a support for international human rights protection. The protection awarded to the vulnerable in international society by human rights is still extremely ineffective, especially when the law of human rights alone is the last layer of protection.[44] In that respect, we have not moved on very far from the time of Hannah Arendt's observation.

Violations of human rights can be – and often are – identified without any further legal consequences. This follows from their specific status as rights of a distinct category, as 'human' rights.[45] Their legal status or their level of acceptance in social

exists a *legal minimum* under which no state can be allowed to slip by the international community'.)

[42] See Knut Ipsen, *Völkerrecht*, 4th. ed., Munich: C. H. Beck 1999, pp. 703–705, § 50; Walter Kälin and Jörg Künzli, *Universeller Menschenrechtsschutz*, Basel: Helbig & Lichtenhan 2005, pp. 7–8.

[43] But see Akira Iriye, Petra Goedde, and William I. Hitchcock (eds.), *The Human Rights Revolution*, Oxford University Press 2012.

[44] Hannah Arendt, *The Origins of Totalitarianism*, New York: Harcourt Brace Jovanovich 1951. See also: Ian Clark, *The Vulnerable in International Society*, Oxford University Press 2013; Alison Kesby, *The Right to Have Rights*, Oxford University Press 2012.

[45] The distinction between 'human rights' (as moral rights) and 'human rights law' might be generally accepted in the Anglo-American literature, but, in the German philosophical tradition, the idea that 'human rights' are 'moral rights' is not as common, see for details, Stefan Gosepath and Georg Lohmann (eds.), *Philosophie der Menschenrechte*, Frankfurt am Main: Suhrkamp 1998.

terms is not relevant to the question of their existence: That human beings are imprisoned or their lives are being threatened is something that can be observed irrespective of whether there exists a positive right to liberty or a right to life.[46] One may reasonably suggest that an intervention undertaken for humanitarian purposes ought to be justified on the basis of the current stage of development of human rights protection in international law. But the specific legal character of both human rights law and international law does not allow for an easy answer to the question of who is (or should be) authorised to protect human rights on the international level.[47]

The American diplomat Henry Wheaton was the first English-language writer[48] on international law to explicitly refer to 'humanity' as a possible justification for intervention.[49] In his discussion of an 'interference when the general interests of humanity are infringed by the excesses of barbarous and despotic governments'[50], he focused on the 'general interests of humanity' as the object of protection. At the heart of the first theory of 'humanitarian intervention', developed by the Belgian international lawyer Egide Arntz in 1876,[51] was a prohibition against violating the 'laws of humanity', the 'laws of human society'. This 'humanity' was constituted through 'our morals and our civilization', limiting 'the rights of sovereignty and independence of States' by the laws of a 'société humaine'.[52] As the century progressed, the expressions used included 'intervention on the ground of humanity'[53] and 'intervention on behalf of the interest of humanity'.[54] By the end of the nineteenth century, the term 'humanitarian intervention' began to be the

---

[46] Donnelly 2003, p. 13: 'Human rights ground moral claims to strengthen or add to existing legal entitlements. That does not make human rights stronger or weaker, just different. They are human (rather than legal) rights. If they did not function differently, there would be no need for them'.

[47] See James Pattison, *Humanitarian Intervention and the Responsibility to Protect – Who Should Intervene*, Oxford University Press 2010.

[48] Lillich 1973, p. 25. On Wheaton and 'humanitarian intervention': see Nicolas Onuf, 'Henry Wheaton and "The Golden Age of International Law"', *International Legal Theory* 2000, 6, pp. 2–9.

[49] Wheaton talks of 'interference', not 'intervention', but Richard Lillich has attributed this to the common usage of the time, see Lillich 1973, p. 25. One glance at the contemporary literature confirms this, e.g. James Kent and J. T. Abdy, *Kent's Commentary on International Law*, 2nd ed., Cambridge: Deighton, Bell & Co. 1866, pp. 48–49.

[50] Wheaton 1846, p. 112.

[51] Rougier 1910, p. 490, fn. 3. The same claim is made by André Mandelstam, 'La Protection des Minorités', Recueil de Cours, Collected Courses of the Hague Academy of International Law, The Hague Academy of International Law 1923, pp. 389–390.

[52] Rolin-Jaequemyns 1876, p. 675. English language translation according to Grewe 2000, p. 495.

[53] Henry W. Halleck, *International Law; or: Rules Regulating the Intercourse of States in Peace and War*, New York: Van Nostrand 1861, p. 54: 'Another ground of foreign interference, in the internal affairs of a sovereign state, is that of humanity, it being done for the alleged purpose of stopping the effusion of blood caused by a protracted and desolating civil war in the bosom of the state so interfered with'.

[54] Creasy 1874, p. 300.

established term[55] for interventions against 'gross tyranny'.[56] The exact words may have kept on changing, but the subject under discussion was not in doubt. The legal evaluation, however, differed considerably.[57]

In French, the traditional language of diplomacy and early nineteenth-century international law, the term for 'humanitarian intervention' originally was not 'intervention humanitaire', but 'intervention d'humanité'.[58] The latter expression has also been used in German language academic literature.[59] In current discussions on the subject among French speaking international lawyers, both expressions seem to be used interchangeably.[60] Conceptually – and historically – there are reasons to believe that the different terms denote different meanings. The original version, 'intervention d'humanité', shows most clearly the importance of the term

[55] Simon Chesterman, *Just War or Just Peace*, Oxford University Press 2001, p. 24, referencing William Edward Hall, *International Law*, Oxford: Clarendon Press 1880, p. 247, fn I. Malbone W. Graham, 'Humanitarian Intervention in International Law as Related to the Practice of the United States', *Michigan Law Review* 1924, 22, p. 314.

[56] William Edward Hall, *International Law*, 3rd. ed., Oxford: Clarendon Press 1890, pp. 287–288, § 92: 'While however it is settled that as a general rule a state must be allowed to work out its internal changes in its own fashion, so long as its struggles do not actually degenerate into internecine war, and intervention to put down a popular movement or the uprising of a subject race is wholly forbidden, intervention for the purpose of checking gross tyranny or of helping the efforts of a people to free itself is very commonly regarded without disfavour'.

[57] Wheaton generally was in favour of such interventions, cf. Wheaton 1846, p. 112. Halleck 1861, p. 54, only approved the legality of 'such interference [. . .] in the nature of a pacific mediation, one state merely proposing its good offices for the settlement of the intestine dissensions of another state'. Creasy 1874, p. 301, was rather skeptical; 'This last is a justification, which commends itself to our feelings, but [. . .] will not bear the test of reasoning. Chancellor Kent, although he is willing to admit it in this case, accompanies his admission of it by observations which show how dangerous a precedent it may be rendered'. The nature of Hall's opinion is discussed in Section 2.7.2.

[58] Rougier 1910, pp. 489–490.

[59] e.g. Friedrich August Freiherr von der Heydte, *Völkerrecht*, Cologne: Verlag für Politik und Wirtschaft 1958, p. 266; Ignaz Seidl-Hohenveldern and Torsten Stein, *Völkerrecht*, 10th ed., Cologne: Heymanns 2000, p. 299, no. 1586.

[60] Compare Djamchid Momtaz, 'L'intervention d'humanité' de l'OTAN au Kosovo et la règle du non-recours à la force. *Revue Internationale De La Croix-Rouge/International Review of the Red Cross* 2000, pp. 89–102, and Anne Ryniker, 'Position du Comité international de la Croix-Rouge sur l'"intervention humanitaire"', *Revue Internationale De La Croix-Rouge/ International Review of the Red Cross* 2001, pp. 521–526. However, Robert Kolb considers 'intervention d'humanité' differently and defines this concept as 'forcible intervention in order to protect one's own nationals abroad if they are in a situation of imminent peril jeopardizing life or limb (but not property)', comparing this concept to the principle of passive personality, whereas 'humanitarian intervention can be compared intellectually to the principle of universal jurisdiction in criminal matters', see Robert Kolb, 'Note on Humanitarian Intervention', *Revue Internationale De La Croix-Rouge/International Review of the Red Cross* 2003, pp. 120–121. This distinction, however, does not seem to be particularly widespread. For a more extensive discussion, see: Katia Boustany, 'Intervention humanitaire et intervention d'humanité – évolution ou mutation en Droit International?', *Revue québécoise de droit international* 1993–1994, 8, pp. 103–111.

'humanité', or 'humanity' for the understanding of the legal concept 'humanitarian intervention': An intervention in line with this concept is an intervention 'of humanity', for instance it is an intervention undertaken with the purpose of protecting 'humanity', but it can also be understood as an intervention undertaken *by* 'humanity'. In other words, the term not only refers to the object of a 'humanitarian intervention', but also serves to connect to its (legal) justification: Those authorised to act on behalf of 'humanity' may do so when 'humanitarian' interests are at stake – and have 'humanity's law' on their side. In this context, 'humanity' is less an expression referring to the 'humanitarian' concerns or catastrophes making intervention *necessary* or *justifiable*, but the term that carries the intervenor's claim of moral superiority: The intervention is undertaken – as the official justification of the American intervention on Cuba explicitly states – in the name of 'humanity', not in the national interest. The term 'humanité' was a relatively common term in treaties agreed to by the Great Powers in the nineteenth century, sometimes appearing as a reference to the 'demands of humanity', but also to the 'laws of humanity' or the 'wishes of humanity'.[61] Arguably the 'demands' (or 'wishes') of humanity are of a more moral claim than the 'laws of humanity', which would suggest a more binding legal character.[62] It is precisely for this reason that the idea of 'humanitarian intervention' is both so exceptional for and representative not only of nineteenth-century international law: it functions to demonstrate the progressive character of the law of 'civilised nations'. Under current international law, very little has changed in this regard.

The status of 'humanity' with respect to international law is ambiguous at best, even today.[63] Both the English and the French term can be understood in two very different and distinct ways, as evidenced by the fact that they both can be translated into German as either 'Menschlichkeit' or 'Menschheit', where 'Menschlichkeit' refers to a feeling of compassion towards other human beings – and 'Menschheit' stands for the whole of humanity, or even humanity as a whole, that is, humankind. The subtle and not so subtle differences in meaning have lead some writers in English or French to use the German expressions to describe the scope of meaning contained in just one word.[64] Other writers distinguish between

---

[61] E.g. Treaty of the Quadripartite Alliance of the Great Powers, November 20, 1815, Preamble, in: Wilhelm G. Grewe (ed.), *Fontes Historiae Iuris Gentium* – Sources Relating to the History of the Law of Nations, Vol. 3/1, Berlin: De Gruyter 1992, p. 101; Declaration of the eight European Courts on the Abolition of the Slave Trade, Vienna, February 8, 1815, in: Grewe 1992, pp. 376–377; Declaration Renouncing the the Use in Time of War of Explosive Projectiles Under 400 Grammes Weight, St. Petersburg, December 11, 1868, in: Grewe 1992, p. 557.

[62] See: Egon Schwelb, 'Crimes against Humanity', *British Yearbook of International Law* 1947, 23, p. 180.

[63] Robin Coupland, 'Humanity: What Is It and How Does It Influence International Law?', *Revue Internationale De La Croix-Rouge/International Review of the Red Cross* 2001, p. 971.

[64] e.g. René Provost, *International Human Rights and Humanitarian Law*, Cambridge University Press 2002, p. 5.

'humanity-humankind' and 'humanity-sentiment', with the latter referring to 'a form of behaviour or disposition'.[65] The matter is further complicated by the fact that 'humanity' may also be understood as a 'moral principle intrinsic to international law',[66] an 'ethical idea', and as such a 'defining feature of world conscience'.[67] It is a term that is capable not only of expressing a certain demand (to be humane), but also of representing the bearer of this demand (humanity itself).[68] And while it may be now said that 'of course, humanity is not a club',[69] it will be shown that, at least to nineteenth-century international law, 'humanity' was precisely that: a club with strict rules for admission. In his *Empire of Humanity*, Michael Barnett has claimed that, beginning in the nineteenth century, 'a more inclusive view of humanity slowly evolved, extending the boundaries of the community and expanding the number of people who were viewed as worthy of assistance'.[70] In international law, however, the sphere of 'humanity' actually shrank during the course of the nineteenth century, while the power of legitimacy attributed to the concept only grew. Here, the term referred to the moral idea that others ought to be treated in the way we wish to be treated ourselves, but only with the important modification that this idea is a product of 'our civilisation'.[71] The way the word 'humanity' was understood by international lawyers in the nineteenth century was not uniform and ranged from 'concerns arising *from* humanity-sentiment' to 'concerns *for* humanity-humankind',[72] but it remained exclusive throughout, even if there was no consensus as to how exclusive it was. At the end of World War I, the only consensus to be found was that there was no fixed and universal 'standard of humanity', rather, that it varied with time, place, and circumstance.[73] Whether this at any point transformed into legal obligations is far from certain.

The justification for 'humanitarian intervention' as expressed by nineteenth-century international lawyers did not rest on the idea that states were violating their obligations under international law. On the contrary, the theory of 'humanitarian intervention' expressly stipulated that a government might well act 'within the limits of its sovereign rights', but violate the 'laws of humanity, either by measures contrary

---

[65] Coupland 2001, p. 972.

[66] Alfred Verdross and Bruno Simma, *Universelles Völkerrecht*, 3rd. ed. Berlin: Duncker & Humblot 1984, p. 48, § 63, ein 'dem Völkerrecht immanenter moralischer Grundsatz' (my translation).

[67] Ernst Sauer, *Der Welthilfsverband und seine Rechtsstellung*, Göttingen: Vandenhoeck & Ruprecht 1932, p. 13.

[68] The difficulty of distinguishing between these meanings has led to harsh criticism for the German translation of 'Crimes against humanity' as 'Verbrechen gegen die Menschlichkeit', most notably by Hannah Arendt.

[69] Larry May, *Crimes against Humanity*, Cambridge University Press 2005, p. 82.

[70] Michael Barnett, *Empire of Humanity*, Ithaca: Cornell University Press 2011, p. 36.

[71] Fritz Wust, *Der gewohnheitsrechtliche Humanitätsgrundsatz im Völkerrecht*, Dissertation, Nuremberg 1968, p. 3: 'bedeutsamste[n] Kulturerbe[s] des Abendlandes'.

[72] Coupland 2001, p. 975.

[73] Schwelb 1947, p. 182.

to the interest of other States, or by excesses of injustice and cruelty which profoundly injure our morals and our civilisation', so that 'the right of intervention is legitimate'.[74] This right of intervention was therefore understood as arising from the exercise of rights awarded by the law in a manner inconsistent with the foundations of this very law. In other words, 'the law' had granted rights which were then being used in a way 'the law' did not approve, which in turn gave rise to a right of intervention, also granted by 'the law', but, in fact, not reciprocally enjoyed by all states.

Theories such as these have been appraised by current writers on international law as overcoming purely natural law-based approaches to a justification of 'humanitarian intervention'.[75] Indeed, one of the first theorists of 'humanitarian intervention' in the twentieth century explicitly considered the idea of the 'droit humain', the 'laws of humanity', a step towards a more formal law and progress away from natural law.[76] But this progress was based on the commitment to understand international law in accordance with the demands of the 'conscience of the civilised world', a very European conscience.[77] To better understand the 'nature' of this progress, it is necessary to take a closer look at the meaning of 'humanity' within the context of nineteenth century international law.

1.3 'HUMANITY' IN NINETEENTH-CENTURY INTERNATIONAL LAW

International law, understood as a universal body of law that applies to all states regardless of their specific cultures, belief systems, and political organisations, is a relatively recent development.[78] In the nineteenth century, international law theory was dominated by European thinkers, and most writers agreed that international law was not the body of law under which all nations were united, but a law that applied only to a certain family of nations already sharing similar values. In the years following the beginning of the 'Concert of Europe' in 1815, relations between European powers (or the United States of America) and other possible subjects of

---

[74] Rolin-Jaequemyns 1876, p. 675. English language translation according to Grewe 2000, p. 495. See also: John Westlake, *International Law, Part I – Peace*, 2nd ed., Cambridge University Press 1910, p. 320: 'Laws are made for men and not for creatures of the imagination, and they must not create or tolerate for them situations which are beyond their endurance, we will not say of average human nature, since law may fairly expect to raise standard by their operation, but of the best human nature at the time and place they can hope to meet with'.

[75] Norman Paech, '"Humanitäre Intervention" und Völkerrecht', in: Ulrich Albrecht and Paul Schäfer (eds.), *Der Kosovo-Krieg*, 2nd ed., Cologne: Papyrossa 1999, p. 87; Wellhausen 2002, p. 76.

[76] Rougier 1910, p. 490: 'A la conception du droit naturel succéda la conception plus juridique du droit humain'.

[77] Martti Koskenniemi, *The Gentle Civilizer of Nations: The Rise and Fall of International Law 1870–1960*, Cambridge University Press 2002, p. 51.

[78] Antony Anghie, 'Finding the Peripheries: Sovereignty and Colonialism in Nineteenth-Century International Law', *Harvard International Law Journal* 1999, 40, p. 1.

international law – in particular those not yet belonging to the society of the 'family' of (civilised) nations, for instance the 'uncivilised' states and 'tribes'[79] – were only of indirect interest to most writers.[80] Questions of 'membership' in the 'family' or 'society of nations' were questions of the (territorial) 'spheres of validity of international law',[81] and some states were simply (and strategically) excluded from these spheres.[82]

In the sixteenth and seventeenth centuries, international law had been a 'Law of Nations and of Nature'[83] (or naturalist international law) and existed as a universal international law deriving from human reason, applying – though not necessarily equally – to all peoples, whether European or non-European.[84] Positive international law, as it developed during the nineteenth century, (re-)created an international order based on state practice as observed between only a limited number of states. It was essentially a procedural law,[85] a 'family law' as it applied to European

---

[79] See Paul Heilborn, 'Subjekte des Völkerrechts', in: Karl Strupp (ed.), *Wörterbuch des Völkerrechts*, Vol. II, Berlin: De Gruyter 1925, pp. 684–685.

[80] See Anghie 1999, p. 7; Yasuki Onuma, 'International Law in and with International Politics: The Functions of International Law in International Society', *European Journal of International Law* 2003, 14, p. 121.

[81] Early international law theory discussed the question of limited or unlimited 'spheres (of validity) of international law', cf. Hans Kelsen, *Principles of International Law*, New York: Rinehart & Company 1952, pp. 92–301, as questions of the membership to the 'community' of nations under international law, e.g. Fritz Stier-Somlo, 'Völkerrechtsgemeinschaft', in: Karl Strupp (ed.), *Wörterbuch des Völkerrechts und der Diplomatie*, Vol. 3, De Gruyter: Berlin 1929, pp. 187–189.

[82] See Antony Anghie, *Imperialism, Sovereignty and the Making of International Law*, Cambridge University Press 2005, p. 99.

[83] Travers Twiss, *Two Introductory Lectures on the Sciences of International Law*, London: Longman, Brown, Green, and Longmans 1856, p. 2.

[84] Anghie 2005, p. 35. However, even according to that 'natural' international law, the same rules did not apply to all peoples, with the 'community of nations under international law' often restricted to Christianity. At the same time, there was an expectation that this law would provide answers on how to deal with the 'Barbarians', 'Infidels' or 'recently discovered Indians', cf. Ziegler 2007, pp. 120–132.

[85] Cf. Otto Kimminich and Stephan Hobe, *Einführung in das Völkerrecht*, 7th ed., Tübingen: A. Francke 2000, p. 42, claim that 'classic international law' was an 'impartial system of norms for the interactions of sovereigns and states in times of both war and peace'. Otto Kimminich was professor of international law at the University of Regensburg for most of his life, and his prolific publications show his intense involvement with, among others, issues of asylum and refugee law, minority rights, religious freedom, and humanitarian intervention. His writings are remarkable for connecting modern human rights concepts with right-wing traditions, cf. Lora Wildenthal, 'Human Rights Advocacy and National Identity in West Germany', *Human Rights Quarterly* 2000, 22, pp. 1051–1059. His view of nineteenth century international law was accordingly ideological and the impartiality of the system he described may well be doubted. The quoted passage was reworked by the next edition, see: Stephan Hobe and Otto Kimminich, *Einführung in das Völkerrecht*, 8th ed., Tübingen: A. Francke 2004, p. 38, though the 'impartiality' of nineteenth century international law is still praised here.

heads of state who in those times were more often than not literally members of one family.[86] It was also a particular law, applicable *only* to a 'distinct set or family of nations'.[87] Today, the question of whether the recognition of state has a legal effect is considered by most writers to be merely of academic relevance. In nineteenth century international law, however, a doctrine of recognition was developed, as part of a *positivist* theory of international law, that re-constructed international law as the law of an exclusive 'society', the 'positive law of nations'.[88] The assumption that all existing states were subject to *one* international law was rejected well into the twentieth century as an idea belonging to natural law, but wrong from the point of view of the 'positive, that is, truly legal understanding' of the law.[89]

In continental Europe, the new focus of international law thinking at the turn of the nineteenth century was evident in textbooks on the subject published at the time. Where these books had previously treated the 'natural law' or the 'law of nature and nations' ('Natur- und Völkerrecht'), such terms as the 'Law of Nations, or the Principles of the Law of Nature' ('Le Droit des Gens ou Principes de la Loi Naturelle')[90] were replaced by the 'now customary European law of nations' ('jetzt übliche Europäische Völkerecht')[91] or the 'European and American public international law' ('Droit International Public Européen & Américain').[92] In the English language tradition, the development from a 'law of nations' to Jeremy Bentham's (positive) 'international law' might be considered a similar phenomenon.[93] Both the positivism of this international law and its 'European' character were ideological concepts.[94] It was not a law for 'mankind' but a law of 'humanity', that is the part of 'mankind' (explicitly) recognised as 'human'. As a result of this development, massacres of Christians were relevant to nineteenth century international law as

---

[86] Rolf Knieper, *Nationale Souveränität – Versuch über Anfang und Ende einer Weltordnung*, Frankfurt: Fischer Taschenbuch 1991, p. 71.

[87] Wheaton 1846, p. 40, § 9: 'International law is only a particular law, applicable to a distinct set or family of nations, varying at different times with the change in religion, manners, government, and other institutions, among every class of nations'.

[88] Anghie 2005, pp. 98–114; Alexis Keller, 'Justice, Peace, and History: A Reappraisal', in: Pierre Allan and Alexis Keller (eds.), *What Is a Just Peace?*, Oxford University Press 2006, pp. 49–50; Turan Kayaoglu, *Legal Imperialism*, Cambridge University Press 2010.

[89] Josef L. Kunz, 'Zum Begriff der "nation civilisée" im modernen Völkerrecht', in: *Zeitschrift für öffentliches Recht* 1927–1928, pp. 89–90: 'vom positivistischen, will sagen, allein wirklich juristischen Standpunkt abzulehnen'.

[90] The title of the classic treatise by Vattel. A similar point is made by Jouannet 2011, p. 137.

[91] For example, compare the titles of Johann Jacob Moser, *Grundsätze des jetzt üblichen Europäischen Völcker-Rechts in Friedenszeiten*, Hanau 1750; 2nd. ed. Frankfurt a.M.: Johann August Raspe 1763; von Martens 1796; Schmelzing 1818, to Johann Heinrich Abicht, *Kurze Darstellung des Natur-und Völkerrechts zum Gebrauch bey Vorlesungen*, Bayreuth: Johan Andreas Lubers Erben 1795.

[92] Paul Pradier-Fodéré, *Traité de Droit International Public Européen & Américain*, Vol. I, Paris: A. Pedone 1885.

[93] See Mark Weston Janis, *The American Tradition of International Law*, Cambridge University Press 2004, pp. 1–24.

[94] Orakhelashvili 2006.

'humanitarian' catastrophes, but massacres of Muslims were not.[95] Muslims committing heinous crimes against Christians lost any status as members of 'humanity', if they ever had one.[96] In his famous pamphlet on the atrocities committed in the Ottoman Empire in 1876, later known as the 'Bulgarian Horrors' or the 'Bulgarian Atrocities', the British statesman William E. Gladstone described the 'Turks' as 'the one great anti-human specimen of humanity'.[97] Gladstone only knew about these 'horrors' from the newspapers, so he might not have known that they were part of a large succession of uprisings and (civil) war in which tens of thousands of lives were lost. But it is hardly a surprise that only the Christian, and therefore 'European', victims were recognised as such in international law. European 'civilisation' was seen as superior to other 'civilisations', and this superiority justified any measure taken, especially if directed against a people 'who possibly do not even belong to the progressive races of mankind'.[98]

While European international law applied in its own legal sphere from which nations might be 'expelled' or to which they might gain access, its 'Europe' was an ideological space, not a geographical one.[99] The United States of America participated in this law almost immediately after gaining independence.[100] The states of Latin America were gradually allowed to join, too. In some areas, the practice of Latin American states mirrored the principles of a modern international law based on sovereign equality already at a time when the European Powers still considered themselves legally superior to other states,[101] and European authors still clung to an idea of international law that reflected this view. The Europe of the 'European law of nations' expanded its 'sphere of validity' in the nineteenth century, that is, the Europe of an 'imaginative geography'[102] extended its identity

---

[95] Martha Finnemore, *The Purpose of Intervention – Changing Beliefs about the Use of Force*, Ithaca: Cornell University Press 2004, p. 59.

[96] In the early stages of the Greek struggle for independence, Russia had apparently argued that the Ottoman Empire could no longer be considered one of the civilized states of Europe on account of the treatment of the insurgents, see Section 2.2.2.

[97] William Ewart Gladstone, *Bulgarian Horrors and the Question of the East*, London: Murray, 1876, pp. 12–13: 'They were, upon the whole, from the black day when they first entered Europe, the one great anti-human specimen of humanity . . .'.

[98] Lorimer 1883, p. 102: The international jurist is 'bound to ascertain the points at which, and the directions in which, barbarians or savages come within the scope of partial recognition. In the case of the Turks we have had the bitter experience of the consequences of extending the rights of civilisation to barbarians who have proved to be incapable of performing its duties, and who possibly do not even belong to the progressive races of man-kind'.

[99] John M. Hobson, *The Eastern Origins of Western Civilisation*, Cambridge University Press 2004, p. 111: 'Europe has always been an idea'.

[100] Grewe 2000, pp. 343–348.

[101] Antonio Truyol Y Serra, 'History of International Law – Latin America', in: Rudolf Bernhardt (ed.) *Encyclopedia of Public International Law*, Vol. 2, Amsterdam: North-Holland Publishing 1995, p. 822.

[102] See Edward Said, *Orientalism*, New York: Pantheon Books 1978; Anne Orford, *Reading Humanitarian Intervention*, Cambridge University Press 2003.

in its own image.[103] International law offered no legal tools for *this* development.[104] Instead of providing guidelines for the project of European expansion of power and influence, international law served as its justification.[105] The development from the 'Christian' foundations of a 'Natural Law of Nations' to a 'Law of Civilised Nations' corresponds to the European idea of defining its territory through law.[106] This Europe created itself by reference to the non-European 'other', constructing itself an identity the 'other' should aspire to, but would never be able to make its own. The exclusion manifested itself in guarantees for foreign nationals imposed on 'uncivilised states' in international treaties.[107]

This is the tradition that also informs the justification cited above for the intervention in Cuba. American international law theory in the nineteenth century was concerned with a law necessarily limited to a circle of like-minded states bound by a common tradition of culture, law, and morals and without rules governing interaction with entities outside of this circle. Through its superiority, resting upon 'the brighter light' enshrined in 'their' international law, it allowed for the expansion of its sphere, without setting *legal* standards for this procedure.[108] The conditions existing in Cuba are said to have been 'a disgrace to Christian civilisation', and thus intervention was justified, but at the same time there can be no doubt that 'civilised Christians' – the Spanish colonial rulers – were responsible for these conditions. This view of Cuba, which places the island outside of the 'Christian' and thus the

---

[103] Westlake 1910, pp. 14–16, cited according to Koskenniemi 2002, p. 52: 'What one needed to show when showing custom was "that the general consensus of opinion within the limits of European civilisation is in favor of the rule". And there was the liberal assumption: "The consent of the international society … is the consent of the men who are the ultimate members of that society". In practice, such consent could be found in the writings of jurists "especially when the writer's reputation proves that he represents many persons beside himself"'.

[104] The most striking example is the treatment of Australia as *terra nullius*, see Peter H. Russell, *Recognizing Aboriginal Title*, Toronto: University of Toronto Press 2005, for the genesis and consequences.

[105] Jörg Fisch, *Die europäische Expansion und das Völkerrecht*, Stuttgart: Steiner 1984, p. VI.

[106] See Yannis A. Stivachtis, *The Enlargement of International Society*, Basingstoke, Hampshire: Palgrave Macmillan 1998, p. 30. The term 'civilisation' may be more abstract than any foundation of international law in shared religious traditions, but ultimately, its use only signified an intensification of the missionary zeal of progress, see Gong 1984, pp. 51–53. Even though current historiography of international law identifies the expansion of international law to include non-Christian states as a defining feature of late nineteenth century international law, contemporary international law was still more exclusive. For example, in Resch 1890, p. 3, it is still the 'European, or, Christian morality' ('europäische, bzw. christliche Gesittung') that connects states in international law. See also: Hartmann 1878, pp. 6–7; Lorimer 1883, p. 102.

[107] See: Schindler 1956, p. 87.

[108] See: Janis 2004, pp. 24–50, the quote used is on p. 29 from James Kent, *Commentaries upon International Law*, 2nd ed., New York: Halstead 1832, p. 3.

'civilised' world, follows the conceptual 'expulsion' of the world not yet adhering to 'European' standards from the sphere of international law.[109] It is a result of the reconstruction of international law as a law of 'civilised nations', a particular law that extends rights, though not duties ranging beyond its sphere of validity.

In this 'border' area of international law, between the 'civilised' and as yet 'uncivilised', the history of 'humanitarian intervention' unfolded throughout the nineteenth century, across its fluid boundaries, its territorial and material 'spheres'.[110] These boundaries gain their prominence only in retrospect. The leading role of the 'civilised' nations in determining the future of the world was a given,[111] not a case for legal reflection. The existence of 'new' states was not of concern to international law, but their perspective of gaining access to the 'Family of Nations' was. In current international law, the idea of a 'society of a family of nations', or its German language counterpart 'Völkerrechtsgemeinschaft',[112] is not a contentious point of discussion for international law theory as such, as international law is now (maybe) universal.[113] The terms have retained their relevance in discussions *within* international law, in that the question arises whether international law protects 'common values' (and not mainly the traditional 'state values' like sovereignty and non-intervention),[114] and how far today's states are organised in an 'international society' or an 'international system'. Additionally, there is the question of whether such a 'society' would be closer to a 'community' (a 'Gemeinschaft') or an 'association' (a 'Gesellschaft').[115] In nineteenth century international law, the idea that a 'community' existed – a 'family of nations' or a group of states sharing enough common values to allow them to have their relationships be governed by one law – was the very idea that made international law possible: The 'international society' of

[109] Anghie 1999, p. 34: '. . . [T]he positivists purported to expel the non-European world from the realm of legality . . .'.
[110] These are 'spheres of justice', as well as territorial and temporal spheres of validity of the law, see: Michael Walzer, *Spheres of Justice*, New York: Basic Books 1983; Kelsen 1952.
[111] See sources cited in Koskenniemi 2002, pp. 129–130.
[112] Stier-Somlo 1929, pp. 187–189; Theo Kordt, 'Völkerrechtsgemeinschaft', in: Hans-Jürgen Schlochauer (ed.), *Wörterbuch des Völkerrechts*, Vol. 3, De Gruyter: Berlin 1962, pp. 677–680.
[113] Or is it? See: Anthea Roberts, *Is International Law International?*, Oxford University Press 2017.
[114] On 'common values' in international law, see: Andreas Paulus, *Die internationale Gemeinschaft im Völkerrecht*, Munich: C. H. Beck 2001, pp. 250–284. These can be contrasted with 'state values' (or states' interests) like sovereignty and non-intervention, cf. Louis Henkin, *International Law: Politics, Values and Functions*, General Course on Public International Law, Recueil des Cours Collected Courses of the Hague Academy of International Law, The Hague Academy of International Law 1989 IV, pp. 9–416. However, it may not be necessary to perceive a contrast between these, see: Carlo Focarelli, *International Law as a Social Construct*, Oxford University Press 2012, pp. 356–461.
[115] The terms are borrowed from Hedley Bull, *The Anarchical Society*, 3rd ed., Basingstoke, Hampshire: Palgrave Macmillan 2002. The question of whether the term 'society' represents a 'Gemeinschaft' or a 'Gesellschaft' in international law is discussed employing the German terms, e.g. Stivachtis 1998. For a discussion of the meaning of the terms in international law, see Paulus 2001.

the nineteenth century was the aforementioned exclusive 'club' of states within which 'humanity' was situated. The importance of understanding 'humanity' as constituted through 'civilisation' becomes evident, when recognising that under nineteenth century international law, 'humanitarian intervention' was hardly conceivable between 'civilised' states.[116]

To nineteenth century international law, 'humanity' is the sphere in which the law fully applies. Contrary to current understanding, the term is an exclusionary one that has an 'inhuman-humanitarian' discriminatory potential – as Carl Schmitt, of all people, acknowledged.[117] But this is not necessarily the 'betrayal' one might think of when considering Schmitt in this context.[118] Rather, it makes clear the self-perception of the international lawyers of this time, who perceived 'their' international law as progressive and open to the option of welcoming previously 'uncivilised' states as new and improvable, if not necessarily equal members. Some current treatments of the question of 'humanitarian intervention' seem to follow a similar belief.

1.4 THE 'HUMANITY' OF 'HUMANITARIAN INTERVENTION'

The modifier 'humanitarian' is often used in current international law to connect legal issues in international law to human rights law, even if 'international humanitarian law' might be considered its own distinctive field of international law. To some, 'humanitarian intervention' then is the question of the enforcement of human rights, pure and simple.[119] Human rights, on the other hand, can be seen as representing the core of theories about justice through law. It is precisely for these reasons that claims of or calls for the legality of 'humanitarian intervention' are so closely connected to claims of or calls for (more) justice in international law.[120] The

---

[116] cf. Frederik A. C. van Lynden van Sandenberg, *Eenige Beschouwingen over Interventie in het Internationaal Recht*, Utrecht: P. Den Boer 1899, pp. 180–187 ('Staten, die op dezelfde hoogte van beschaving staan, hebben dergelijk interventie-recht niet noodig'); Friedrich Martens, *Völkerrecht – Das internationale Recht der civilisierten Nationen*, German edition translated by Carl Bergbohm, Vol. I, Berlin: Weidmannsche Buchhandlung 1883, pp. 301–302. See also: Schindler 1956, pp. 86–87.

[117] Carl Schmitt, *Der Nomos der Erde*, Berlin: Duncker & Humblot, reprint of the 1950 edition, 1997, p. 73, my translation. The English language version available translates this passage as an 'inhuman-humanitarian power to divide', see, Carl Schmitt, *The Nomos of the Earth*, trans. by G. L. Ulmen, New York: Telos Press 2004, p. 104.

[118] Carl Schmitt, *Der Begriff des Politischen*, Berlin: Duncker & Humblot, text from 1932, reprint of the 3rd ed. 1963, 1991, p. 55.

[119] Watson 1999, p. 243: '. . . humanitarian intervention should not be viewed as a tangential issue but rather as the enforcement of human rights, pure and simple'.

[120] E.g. Fernando R. Tesón, 'The liberal case for humanitarian intervention', in: J. L. Holzgrefe and Robert O. Keohane (eds.), *Humanitarian Intervention*, Cambridge University Press 2003, pp. 93–129; Allen Buchanan, *Justice, Legitimacy, and Self-determination*, Oxford University Press 2004; Steven R. Ratner, *The Thin Justice of International Law*, Oxford University Press 2015, pp. 292–312; Wilfried Hinsch, *Die Moral des Krieges*, Munich: Piper 2017.

question of whether an understanding of justice based on human rights can be incorporated into international law, a distinct system with its own historical evolution, is not easy to answer.[121] Attempts to re-ascertain the validity of the rules of a 'humane' international law in the face of morally questionable resistance by some states, has in the past lead to the not entirely convincing claim that 'civilised' states have always agreed on the prohibition of genocide.[122]

In its 1951 Advisory Opinion Concerning Reservations to the Genocide Convention, the International Court of Justice did not rest its arguments on the scope of the prohibition of genocide only on the positive and conventional treaty statement of genocide as a crime,[123] but declared that 'the principles underlying the Convention are principles which are recognized by civilized nations as binding on States, even without any conventional obligation'.[124] The reference to the term 'civilised states', also contained in Art. 38 I (c) of the Statute of the International Court of Justice (ICJ Statute) and its reference to the 'general principles of law recognized by civilized nations', suggests that the International Court of Justice referred to the prohibition of genocide as 'a norm derived from general principles of law rather than a component of customary international law'.[125] In the same sense, one might say that a recognition of these principles is an expression of civilisation and a necessary precondition for establishing a system of international law as a legal order.[126] The historical record, however, leaves no doubt that the 'confirmation' of the prohibition of genocide and the (explicit) incorporation of this prohibition into international law came about only *after* one of the 'original' 'civilised nations' of international law[127]

---

[121] See: Thomas M. Franck, 'Is Justice Relevant to the International Legal System?', *Notre Dame Law Review* 1989, 64, pp. 945–963, Franck 1990, pp. 208–246.

[122] E.g. Henry Shue, 'Limiting Sovereignty', in Jennifer M. Walsh (ed.), *Humanitarian Intervention and International Relations*, Oxford University Press 2004, p. 18: '[I]t would be preposterous to suggest that there is a universal negative duty not to commit genocide but that there is no positive duty to protect intended victims. The twentieth century made it clear that significant numbers of people are willing to violate their negative duty not to commit genocide, and to do so with unyielding determination'.

[123] Art. I of the 1948 Convention on the Prevention and Punishment of the Crime of Genocide has the Contracting Parties 'confirm' that genocide 'is a crime under international law' – this statement has been called 'explanatory rather than operational', Christian Tams, Lars Berster, and Björn Schiffbauer, *Convention on the Prevention and Punishment of the Crime of Genocide: A Commentary*, Munich: C. H. Beck 2014, p. 39.

[124] International Court of Justice, Advisory Opinion of 28 May 1951, Reservations to the Convention on the Prevention and Punishment of the Crime of Genocide, available at www.icj-cij.org/files/case-related/12/012-19510528-ADV-01-00-EN.pdf, last accessed 25 January 2019.

[125] William A. Schabas, *Genocide in International Law*, 2nd. ed., Cambridge University Press 2009, p. 4.

[126] As does Wolfgang Graf Vitzthum (ed.), *Völkerrecht*, 4th ed., Berlin: De Gruyter 2007, p.72. For an argument in favour of the legality of 'humanitarian intervention' on the basis of the illegality of genocide, see Tomuschat 2008, pp. 278–280.

[127] Schweisfurth 2006, p. 77, II/106, argues that Nazi Germany robbed itself of the status of a 'civilized' nation, however, during the reign of the Third Reich, that claim was made not nearly often enough. See: Schindler 1956, p. 90.

had committed the crime of genocide by systematically killing not only the majority of European Jewry, and causing, as Dan Diner termed it, a 'rupture in civilisation'.[128] The Shoah arguably challenges conceptions of (one) morality[129] and can be seen as the ultimate attack on 'humanity',[130] which went ahead almost unchallenged as it was taking place.[131] Indeed, at least until early 1942, there is some evidence to suggest that some international lawyers considered the systematic persecution of Jews 'legal' under international law.[132]

The assumption that genocide might not have been prohibited, or could even have been considered 'legal', prior to the entry into force of the Genocide Convention, is difficult to stomach[133] – but so too is the knowledge that the majority of the Jews of Europe and tens of thousands of Sinti and Roma were killed without anyone coming to their rescue, and that approximately 500,000 lives were lost in Rwanda in only 100 days,[134] while calls on an 'international community' to intervene lead to some surreal 'semantic squirming'[135] but little else. In the present day, the plight of the Syrian population seems more likely to provoke lawmakers to reform asylum procedures and interventions against 'people-smuggling' than a military intervention to stop a civil war that has killed hundreds of thousands of civilians.

The idea of the legality of 'humanitarian intervention' corresponds to an international law that *would* have legitimised interventions in this and other comparable cases as justified and 'humanitarian'. The tension between the prohibition of genocide derived from the general principles of law and the necessity to 'confirm' such a prohibition only a few short years after one of the 'founding' nations of this law had violated these very principles extends to the legal instrument of 'humanitarian intervention'. Resorting to the 'typical fiction of the problematical doctrine

---

[128] Dan Diner (ed.), *Zivilisationsbruch: Denken nach Auschwitz*, Munich: Fischer Taschenbuch 1988; Dan Diner, *Gegenläufige Gedächtnisse. Über Geltung und Wirkung des Holocaust*, Göttingen: Vandenhoeck & Ruprecht 2007.

[129] Rolf Zimmermann, *Philosophie nach Auschwitz*, Reinbek: rororo Taschenbuch 2005, p. 26. See also: Robert Meister, *After Evil*, New York: Columbia University Press 2011.

[130] Jonathan Glover, *Humanity: A Moral History of the Twentieth Century*. London: Jonathan Cape 1999. pp. 337–340.

[131] See Section 3.3.3.

[132] Christopher Simpson, 'Die seinerzeitige Diskussion über die in Nürnberg zu verhandelnden Delikte', in: Gerd Hankel and Gerhard Stuby (eds.), *Strafgerichte gegen Menschheitsverbrechen*, Hamburg: Hamburger Edition 1995, pp. 52–53. See also Arieh J. Kochavi, *Prelude to Nuremberg*, Chapel Hill: University of North Carolina Press 1998, pp. 138–171; Philipp Caspar Mohr, *Kein Recht zur Einmischung?*, Tübingen: Mohr Siebeck 2002.

[133] See Rosalyn Higgins, *Problems & Process – International Law and How We Use It*, Oxford: Clarendon Press 1994, pp. 20–22 for a discussion of the legal standing of the prohibition of torture in light of the fact that a great majority of states systematically engaged in torture.

[134] Alison Des Forges, *Leave None to Tell the Story*, Human Rights Watch Report, New York: Human Rights Watch 1999, p. 17, also discussing other estimates.

[135] Payam Akhavan, *Reducing Genocide to Law*, Cambridge University Press 2012, p. 3 and 138.

whose purpose is to veil the arbitrary character of the acts of a sovereign law-maker"[136] by 'confirming' a law that previously did not exist (or did not exist with such clarity) may not be unusual in international law, but the mythical element contained in this technique is fundamental to the origins of international law: As the law made by states, it must conform to standards of justice, lest it legitimise injustice committed by states.[137]

The possible repercussions of a law based *only* on what 'really' happened and happens, may it be legal or illegal according to other systems of law ('was würcklich geschehen ist und zu geschehen pfleget, es mag nun nach denen Göttlichen geschribenen und natürlichen auch menschlichen Rechten recht oder unrecht seyn')[138] are so far-reaching as to require a corrective of *international law*, if the law is to retain its legitimacy. The need for rules of international law to conform to individual ideas of justice is at its most prominent when state practice in international affairs is in violation of these ideas. This might be seen as an example of the dilemma identified by Koskenniemi as the 'descending and ascending patterns of justification', the question of the relationship between (legal) order and obligation in international relations: Judging state practice against a legal order based on state practice and therefore prone to change *through* state practice may lead to contradictory results, neither of them fully corresponding to the necessities of international legal discourse.[139] A tendency to idealise the order created by state practice competes with the desire to subjugate states to an ideal order. The legal instrument 'humanitarian intervention' combines these contradictory approaches when considered as a part of international law, since it can be viewed as the manifestation of a certain vision of an 'ideal' system of law.

It can be argued that the paradigm underlying the claim of the legality of 'humanitarian intervention' has shifted over the course of its evolution, so that what once was a general appeal to humanity-sentiment became an instrument of Great Power politics in the nineteenth century and then an instrument of international human rights protection towards the end of the twentieth century.[140] Others claim that 'the rendition of the nineteenth century as a golden age of humanitarian intervention and a wellspring of the norms that motivate military missions of rescue rests on romanticization and a few decidedly ambiguous cases'.[141] But such dismissals, while reaffirming an alleged impartiality of international law, miss the point.

---

[136] Hans Kelsen, 'Will the Judgement in the Nuremberg Trial Constitute a Precedent?', *International Law Quarterly* 1947, pp. 153–171, cited here after the reprint in: Guenual Mettraux (ed.), *Perspectives on the Nuremberg Trial*, Oxford University Press 2008, p. 281, discussing the similar wording in the Charter of the International Military Tribunal.

[137] See generally: Martti Koskenniemi, *From Apology to Utopia*, Reissue, Cambridge University Press 2005.

[138] Moser 1750, preface without page number, no. 3.

[139] Koskenniemi, *From Apology to Utopia* 2005, pp. 58–70.

[140] E.g., by Kimminich 1995, p. 432.

[141] Menon 2016, p. 82.

At the core of the question of 'humanitarian intervention' is not a shifting paradigm or a romanticisation of past actions, but the very basic question of the values and foundations of international society.

Asserting the value or legitimacy of 'humanitarian intervention' re-affirms the value of the project of international law altogether. If the historical development of international law can serve as a justification for 'humanitarian intervention', such a law would immediately appear to be more 'humane' and certainly more legitimate than a law that developed *not* to include this option. This is international law's claim to the 'humanity' (in the humanity-sentiment sense of the word) of the order it has created. Viewed as such, international law is committed to 'humanity' as presented in the history of international law by Grewe: 'the humanitarian ideal' in this perspective appears as 'the moral and ideological substance of the society of civilised nations'.[142] The corresponding law of this society in the nineteenth century is an expression of culture and of civilisation and therefore leaves no room for genocide, displacement, or confiscation of private property.[143] This is not to say that such things did not occur – violence at the level required to invoke a right of 'humanitarian intervention' in the nineteenth century was a regular feature of colonialism as practised by the European powers outside the 'society of civilized nations'. But this violence was not perceived to be the threat to a 'humanity' that must be reaffirmed and protected through 'humanitarian intervention'.

1.5 THE LAW ON INTERVENTION AND 'HUMANITARIAN INTERVENTION'

In the nineteenth century, international relations and international law did not view intervention in that 'almost wholly pejorative sense' the term has taken on in most usages today.[144] For most of the nineteenth century, the term referred to daily political activities, and described an international law-phenomenon essentially unknown until that century.[145] Whereas twentieth century concepts of international law, at least until the end of the Cold War, traditionally followed the idea that a prohibition of intervention – the territorial inviolability of the state – is one of the law's 'original' and 'constitutional' principles, inherited at birth and resting on centuries of practice,[146] it was the right of the European Powers to intervene in other states that was, at the beginning of the nineteenth century, considered a

---

[142] Grewe 2000, p. 490.
[143] Hobe and Kimminich 2004, p. 39.
[144] Neff 2005, p. 217.
[145] R. J. Vincent, *Nonintervention and International Order*, Princeton University Press 1974; Finnemore 2004, p. 10; Neff 2005, pp. 215–216.
[146] Henkin 1989, pp. 51–52. 51 f. A similar claim is made by Brun-Otto Bryde, 'Die Intervention mit wirtschaftlichen Mitteln', in: Ingo von Münch (ed.), *Staatsrecht – Europarecht – Völkerrecht – Festschrift für Hans-Jürgen Schlochauer zum 75. Geburtstag*, Berlin: De Gruyter 1981, p. 228, referring to a 'constituting principle' ('konstitutives Grundprinzip').

'generally accepted, undisputed principle of European international law, adhered to for centuries'.[147]

International laws on intervention historically originate not from conceptualisations of a society *between* states in mutual *independence*, but of states existing *together* in *interdependence* in a society based on shared values.[148] Today, intervention is considered something like the 'opposite' of sovereignty – its 'logical correlation'[149] – so that international law's principle of the guarantee of the sovereign equality of states leads to a prohibition of intervention, and the subsequent need to reconceptualise sovereignty as a 'responsibility to protect'. In historic international law, intervention and sovereignty were far less incompatible than current views on the evolution of international law would suggest. Sovereignty refers first and foremost to the relationship between international law and the states subject to international law. It can be defined negatively to mean that, under international law, sovereign states are subject to no other higher authority than international law itself. But sovereignty is an abstraction and exists to the extent that we believe it exists – and its meaning depends on how we define the term.[150] Only once the meaning of sovereignty acquires the meaning of a guarantee of sovereign equality does the variable 'sovereignty' shed its limitations imposed by international law and becomes a constitutive principle of international law, which then in turn limits the scope of international law.[151] This step is not a necessary one.

It is obvious that early treatments of the subject of intervention in international law were quite aware of the fact that 'interventions'were potentially problematic in a world of formally equal sovereigns, but these treatments still rested on the assumption that states had to be treated like human beings and therefore 'naturally' had equal rights. State practice did not reflect such assumptions. From the beginning of the nineteenth century at the very least, state practice duly accepted the Great Powers' claim to a leading role in determining the future of the society of the 'family of nations', that is, not only their power to do so, but also their *right*. The idea that international law could somehow prohibit intervention categorically only developed during the course of the nineteenth century, as early twentieth century international lawyers were still very much aware.[152] This development saw the right to intervene,

---

[147] Carl Christoph A. H. von Kamptz, *Völkerrechtliche Erörterung des Rechts der Europäischen Mächte in die Verfassung eines einzelnen Staates sich einzumischen*, Berlin: Nicolaische Buchhandlung 1821, p. XVI. A similar claim was made by Schmelzing 1818, p. 133.

[148] The theoretical origin of the principle of non-intervention in international law may be deduced from the concept of the ideal society organised in the 'civitas maximas' of Christian Wolff, e.g. Arthur Nussbaum, *A Concise History of the Law of Nations*, London: Macmillan 1950, p. 151.

[149] Bryde 1981, p. 228.

[150] John Kuhn Bleimaier, 'The Future of Sovereignty in the 21st Century', *Hague Yearbook of International Law* 1993, 6, p. 17; Nico Schrijver. 'The Changing Nature of State Sovereignty', in *British Yearbook of International Law* 2000, 70, pp. 69–70.

[151] Cf. Ipsen 1999, pp. 37–38, § 2/66–67.

[152] Franz von Liszt, *Das Völkerrecht*, 9th ed., Berlin: Verlag von O. Häring 1913, p. 64.

that aforementioned 'old principle of European international law', be gradually reduced to a right *of* intervention, that could be invoked under certain conditions,[153] and then replaced by the end of the nineteenth century by the claim, championed most clearly in the French and Italian traditions of international law, that there could not be a 'right to intervene', as such a right would contradict the 'right of sovereignty'.[154] The European Great Powers for their part only formally rescinded certain rights of intervention at the beginning of the twentieth century.[155]

The European international order of the nineteenth century was created in the name of the balance of power and was considered to have resulted in a 'moral equilibrium', where power and justice were 'in substantial harmony'.[156] Johann Jacob Moser (1701–1785), one of the founders of positive international law,[157] defined this balance of power as the condition in which the European Powers face each other on equal ground, with each of them existing side by side without fear of being unjustly suppressed or ousted by another power ('Europäische Potenzien in einer solchen Verfassung gegen einander anstehen, dass jeder freyer Staat neben dem anderen bestehen kann und keiner besorgen darff, von dem anderen verschlungen oder wider die Gebühr bedrückt zu werden').[158] This principle governed

---

[153] This position was championed by a number of German authors, e.g. Heinrich Geffcken, 'Das Recht der Intervention', in: Franz von Holtzendorff, (ed.), *Handbuch des Völkerrechts*, Vol. IV, Berlin: Verlag von Carl Habel 1889, p. 134. Strauch 1879, p. 5 and passim; Paul Heilborn, *Das System des Völkerrechts entwickelt aus den völkerrechtlichen Begriffen*, Berlin: J. Springer, 1896, pp. 354–356. It was, however, not held by Germans only, see: Edwin DeWitt Dickinson, *The Equality of States in International Law*, Cambridge: Harvard University Press 1920, pp. 260–264 and sources quoted therein.

[154] See: Theophile Funck-Brentano and Albert Sorel, *Précis du Droit des Gens*, 2nd ed., Paris: Libraire Plon 1887, pp. 214–215: 'Quand on parle du droit d'intervention, soit pour revendiquer, soit pour le contester, on abuse du mot *droit* et l'on se méprend sur le sens qu'il convient d'y attacher dans les relations de États. À l'intérieur des États, les individus possèdent deux sortes de droit (...). Il n'en pas de même dans les rapports des États; ils sont souverains, il n'y a pas d'autorité qui leur soit supérieure, et les seuls droits qu'ils se reconnaissent sont des droits coutumiers dont l'existence repose sur des obligations réciproques et des intérêts communs (...). Les actes qui sont dans la coutume des États, mais qui ne reposent pas sur ce fondement, sont des faits politiques qui résultent de la souveraineté des États, ils ne sont pas des droits: telle est l'intervention. (...) L'intervention n'est donc pas un droit, car il n'y a pas un droit contre le droit; et la souveraineté des États es un principe essentiel du droit des gens. (...) En tout cas gouvernement qui intervient fait un acte de politique plus ou moins intelligent (...). (...) Ce sont des questions de fait et non des questions de droit; elles appartiennent à la critique de l'histoire et non au droit des gens'. Also see Terenzio Count Mamiani, *Rights of Nations, or the New Law of European States*, trans. by Roger Acton, London: W. Jeffs 1860.

[155] See Hans Frisch, 'Drago-Porter-Konvention', in: Karl Strupp (ed.), *Wörterbuch des Völkerrechts und der Diplomatie*, Vol. I, Berlin: De Gruyter 1924, pp. 253–254; Hans-Joachim Hallier, 'Drago-Porter-Konvention von 1907', in: Hans-Jürgen Schlochauer (ed.), *Wörterbuch des Völkerrechts*, Vol. I, Berlin: De Gruyter 1960, pp. 399–400.

[156] Henry Kissinger, *Diplomacy*, New York: Simon & Schuster 1994, p. 79.

[157] Twiss 1856, '[Moser] may be said to have constructed a science, hitherto unknown, of the *positive* Law of Nations'. A similar claim is made by Dickinson 1920, p. 93.

[158] Moser 1763, p. 49, § 3.

European politics for most of the nineteenth century and authorised interventions to uphold the balance of power, or, as some would have it, to protect secondary interests protected by the status quo. The stabilising character of this system, famed for keeping a 'long peace', has since been challenged as a myth.[159] Some 'just' suppression (or intervention) was obviously compatible with it. The question whether such interventions were justified under international law was asked by the earliest theorists of the discipline,[160] even as they admitted that, whether lawfully or not, the Great Powers exercised such rights.[161] The early textbooks reflected this dilemma until well into the twentieth century.[162]

In considering the legality of intervention according to their personal understanding of international law, writers on the subject originally paid little attention to attempts to define the term. In the English-speaking world, 'intervention' and 'interference' were used interchangeably. German writers spoke of 'Intervention', but also of 'Dazwischenkunft'[163] and 'Einmischung'[164] or 'thätiger Einmischung',[165] the latter probably best translated as 'forcible intervention'. Emer de Vattel (1714–1767), sometimes considered the 'inventor' of the principle of non-intervention,[166] did not employ the term 'intervention' in any technical sense, using forms of the verb 'intervenir' 'to signify both meddling in the internal disputes of another state and mediation by a third power between belligerent states'.[167] The rules applied to these scenarios could lead to diverging results, sometimes using the same words. International lawyers could classify 'friendly advice' without any open or indirect threats as 'intercession'[168] or 'diplomatic intervention', but they might have also discussed 'forcible' intervention[169] as belonging to the same category of action under international law.[170] What characterised these different types of intervention was that

---

[159] See: Sheldon Anderson, 'Metternich, Bismarck and the Myth of the "Long Peace," 1815–1914', *Peace & Change* 2007, 32, pp. 301–328.

[160] Moser 1763, pp. 58–60, §§ 32 ff.

[161] See: von Martens 1796, p. 145, § 121.

[162] E.g. Lassa Oppenheim, *International Law – A Treatise*, Vol. I – Peace, London: Longmans, Green and Co 1905, p. 185, § 136.

[163] von Kamptz 1821, p. XVI.

[164] Moser 1763, p. 520, book 10, chapter 4.

[165] von Martens 1796, p. 90, § 72.

[166] E.g. by Albert Bleckmann, *Völkerrecht*, Baden-Baden: Nomos 2001, p. 184, rn 550. At the same time, others consider Vattel to be the 'father of humanitarian intervention', see: Wellhausen 2002, p. 57.

[167] Chesterman 2001, p. 18, and sources quoted therein.

[168] E.g. Oppenheim 1905, p. 182, § 134: 'Intercession is the name for the interference consisting in friendly advice given or friendly offers made with the regard to the domestic affairs of another state'.

[169] Stapleton 1866, p. 6. S.a. Leo Strisower, 'Intervention', in: Karl Strupp (ed.), *Wörterbuch des Völkerrechts und der Diplomatie*, Vol. I, Berlin: De Gruyter 1924, p. 582.

[170] Percy H. Winfield, 'The History of Intervention in International Law', *British Yearbook of International Law* 1922–1923, 3, p. 130: 'A reader, after perusing Phillimore's chapter upon intervention, might close the book with the impression that intervention may be anything from a speech of Lord Palmerston's in the House of Commons to the partition of Poland'.

they did not constitute a threat to the sovereignty of the target state, because by definition they were not aimed at undermining the status quo.[171] The difference between the legal concepts of 'war' and 'intervention' was relevant to nineteenth century international law for the same reasons it is relevant today: the purpose of intervention is *limited* by its objectives.[172] This distinction is the defining moment of the meaning of intervention under nineteenth century international law. It allowed intervention to exist as a feature of international law, rather than a violation of the law.[173] The right to wage war, as an expression of sovereignty, was not contested under this version of international law – but this right was essentially aimed at the liberty to *declare* war, or, more precisely, to declare a *state of war*.[174] War was treated as a separate legal condition, governed by a separate set of rules (the Laws of War) and seen as, in a manner of speaking, the 'inverse legal world' of peace.[175] The right to wage war therefore could not render legal all other forms of the use of force.[176] Intervention in nineteenth century international law belonged to the realm of the law in times of peace, and was specifically intended *not* to introduce a state of war between the parties.[177] In other words, the function of 'intervention' in nineteenth century international law was to provide a term for a widely exercised state practice, using force or demonstrations of force in times of legal peace.

[171] See: Finnemore 2004, pp. 1–51. The point is made clearly by Ian Brownlie, 'International Law and the Use of Force by States Revisited', *Australian Year Book of International Law* 1993, 21, 21–37: '[N]o change of sovereignty could result'.

[172] J. E. S. Fawcett, Intervention in International Law, *Recueil de Cours Collected Courses of the Hague Academy of International Law*, The Hague Academy of International Law 1961, p. 348: 'The purpose of intervention in force, which is not defensive, is commonly limited to the attainment of a few specific objectives, and it is this limitation of purpose which might be said to differentiate intervention and war: for the purposes of war are unlimited in the sense that, subject to the rules of war which may be applicable and observed, a belligerent regards every point in the enemy's position, political, economic for military, as an object for attack. Though intervention may well initiate war, its objects normally fall short of the larger objectives of war'.

[173] See: Neff 2005, pp. 217–225.

[174] See: Johann Caspar Bluntschli, *Das moderne Völkerrecht der civilisirten Staten*, 3rd ed., Nördlingen: C. H. Beck 1878, p. 292, § 521: 'Wenn ein Stat [sic] einen Angriffskrieg beginnt, so ist er schuldig, vorerst den Versuch zu machen, ob nicht seine Forderungen ohne Krieg anerkannt und erfüllt werden und ebenso verbunden, bevor er seinen Entschluss zum Krieg zur Eröffnung der Feindseligkeiten anzukünden. (...) Wird ein Angriffskrieg ohne Kriegsdrohung und ohne vorherige Kriegserklärung lediglich durch thatsächliche Ueberraschung mit Feindseligkeiten begonnen, so wird diese Handlung vor dem civilisirten Völkerrecht gemissbilligt (...)'. A similar position is taken by Halleck 1861, p. 343.

[175] Neff 2005, p. 177.

[176] Kimminich 1995, pp. 430–485 seems to take this position at p. 431.

[177] For nineteenth century international law, the 'law of peace' and the 'law of war' were two distinct separate areas of law. Intervention could lead to war, however it was a 'one-sided' act against another state, that could turn to a state of war when the target state of the intervention responded with the use of force, as Geffcken put it, see Heinrich Geffcken, 'Das Recht der Intervention', in: Franz von Holtzendorff (ed.), *Handbuch des Völkerrechts*, Vol. IV, Berlin: C. Habel 1889, p. 132.

The international law on intervention developed not from a right to intervene, but as the 'law of intervention'. There was no consensus on what the law was, but little doubt that it existed. It was considered 'one of the vaguest branches of international law'.[178] The interpretation that reduced the term to the meaning most familiar to today's usage, that is intervention in that sense only meant 'forcible' (or 'dictatorial') intervention, is itself a product of the late nineteenth century.[179] For the international lawyers of the nineteenth century, the modality of intervention was only one factor to consider when assessing the legality of any given intervention. A law that authorised war as a means to further national interests would have to be understood as also authorising forcible measures falling short of war to that effect.[180] The real question therefore was, which *other* interests might justify intervention, or rather how to define the 'national' interest.[181] There is less room for extensive interpretation of such interests when international law is based on the principle that 'all those actions of a State which are internal, are free',[182] and more if the interest of some states, rightfully on their 'guard', in situations bearing 'immediate reference to the society of nations' has legal relevance.[183]

Contemporary nineteenth century international law theory developed a wide range of opinions related to these issues, which in turn led to a wide range of opinions related to 'humanitarian intervention'.[184] In particular the existing

---

[178] Winfield 1922–1923, p. 130.

[179] Bleckmann 2001, p. 183, no. 546. See Heilborn 1896, p. 353, for a historical perspective. The classic statement is by Hersch Lauterpacht, *International Law and Human Rights*, 2nd ed., London: Stevens & Sons 1951, p. 168, referencing Lassa Oppenheim, *International Law, Vol. I – Peace*, 2nd ed., London: Longmans, Green & Co. 1912, § 134: 'intervention is dictatorial interference by a State in the affairs of another State, intervention proper is always *dictatorial* interference, not interference pure and simple'.

[180] For a clear early expression of this point, see: Heilborn 1896, pp. 354–356.

[181] Karl Hettlage, 'Die Intervention in der Geschichte der Völkerrechtswissenschaft, und im System der modernen Völkerrechtslehre', *Niemeyers Zeitschrift für Internationales Recht* 1927, p. 16. Also see: von Liszt 1913, p. 63, defining intervention as the 'Einmischung in die inneren oder äußeren Angelegenheiten eines anderen Staates'. Strauch 1879, p. 2: 'Intervention – im völkerrechtlichen Sinne – ist die Mitentscheidung von Rechtsstreitigkeiten internationaler Bedeutung durch ursprünglich nicht an demselben betheiligt gewesene souveräne Staaten'.

[182] Mamiani 1860, p. 190. A similar point is made in Kent and Abdy 1866, p. 46.

[183] James Reddie, *Inquiries In International Law*, Edinburgh and London: William Blackwood 1842, pp. 192–193: 'So long as the actions of a people mainly concern the internal welfare of the state, other nations, except in the cases just alluded to [referring to cases of rights of intervention granted through treaties], have neither right to interpose their influence, nor occasion to trouble them. But if the arrangements or preparations, of a people, bear immediate reference to the society of nations, of which it is a member, or are of such nature, as to excite anxiety for the general tranquility and security, other states are entitled to be watchful and on their guard, (...). [T]hese other nations, particularly those more interested, are, by the natural and consuetudinary international law of modern Europe, fully entitled to demand an explanation, with regard to the object of such measures, and the removal of any ground for apprehension on account of them'.

[184] See Grewe 2000, p. 494.

interdependencies between certain states, in some cases institutionalised through 'unequal treaties',[185] have been used by writers on international law to draw diverging conclusions for the scope of sovereignty and possible consequences for a 'right' to sovereign equality.[186] State practice, on the other hand, was dominated for most of the nineteenth century by a system of 'legalized hegemony',[187] in which the superior status of a powerful elite of states 'is recognised by minor powers as a political fact giving rise to the existence of certain constitutional privileges, rights and duties and whose relations with each other are defined by adherence to a rough principle of sovereign equality'.[188] Despite this, international law theory well into the twentieth century continued to treat Great Power status as merely political and compatible with a (fictional) legal status of equal sovereignty.[189] But the Great Powers 'not only enforced their will on Europe but regarded themselves as possessing a *right* to do so'.[190] Some writers on international law did recognise some legal differences between states,[191] and, effectively, this system of 'legalised hegemony'. By the end of the nineteenth century, this system could no longer be sustained, and the Great Powers proved themselves incapable of 'acting as a quasi-supranational authority in legal and political matters'.[192] It is precisely this system of 'legalised hegemony', however, that gave birth to the legal instrument of 'humanitarian intervention'.[193] In this system, interventions were an integral and essential part of international law, 'an act of police for enforcing recognized rights, and the only means, apart from war, for enforcing the rules of International Law'.[194] The legality of 'humanitarian intervention' in this system is a result of the legal superiority of some states and their status with respect to 'humanity'.

---

[185] A clear example is the concept, well-established in nineteenth century international law, of the 'half-sovereign' (or 'sub-sovereign') state, e.g. Dickinson 1920, p. 93. See also von Liszt 1913, pp. 54–55; Paul Heilborn, 'Protektorate', in: Karl Strupp (ed.), *Wörterbuch des Völkerrechts*, Vol. II, Berlin: De Gruyter 1925, p. 326.

[186] For an extensive discussion, see: Dickinson 1920.

[187] Simpson 2004; Nico Krisch, 'International Law in Times of Hegemony', *European Journal of International Law* 2005 pp. 397–398.

[188] Simpson 2004, p. 68.

[189] e.g. Wolfgang Abendroth, 'Großmächte', in: Hans Jürgen Schlochauer (ed.), *Wörterbuch des Völkerrechts*, Vol. I, Berlin: De Gruyer 1960, pp. 713–717.

[190] Simpson 2004, p. 105, my emphasis.

[191] Thomas J. Lawrence, *The Principles of International Law*, 2nd ed., Boston: D. C. Heath 1898, p. 19: 'The Sovereign States that are subjects of International Law must be divided by two classes: (a) The Great Powers of Europe and the United States of America. They are rapidly gaining in many important mattes a position of primacy (. . .). (b) Ordinary Independent States. They possess all the ordinary rights given by International Law to Sovereign States, but do not share the authority claimed by the Great Powers in supervising and altering some of the existing international arrangements'.

[192] Simpson 2004, pp. 126–130, quote on p. 128.

[193] E.g. Simpson 2004, pp. 194–242; Anghie 2005, p. 292; See also: Orford 2003.

[194] William E. Lingelbach, 'The Doctrine and Practice of Intervention in Europe', *Annals of the American Academy of Political and Social Science* 1900, p. 32. A similar characterisation is made by Stowell 1921, pp. 51–53. See also: Neff 2005, p. 217.

It is too easy to reduce this development to a mere theory of writers, using questionable examples from state practice to express the emotions of the middle classes in Western countries.[195] Rather, it is one of the clearest expressions of the 'civilisational' power attributed to the development of international law.[196] This law arguably failed the 'practice test', that is, it was a construction 'irreconcilable with historical reality',[197] but in many aspects it followed the same (or comparable) ideas of 'justice' invoked in discussions in and on international law today. The idea that universal values, accepted in all corners of the world, are to be realised through international law, is still the driving force behind contemporary discussions on 'humanitarian intervention', even if research suggests that universality might be better understood as a goal, rather than a justification.[198]

During the course of the nineteenth century, international lawyers quite naturally perceived themselves as one of the 'sources' of international law.[199] They saw themselves as representatives of the 'conscience of the civilized world' and the public opinion of a 'Kulturgemeinschaft'.[200] For these authors, more often than not, it was international law itself that separated 'civilisation' and 'barbarism', a distinction that followed directly from the *existence* of international law, not rules *in* international law. In the first edition, published in the 1920s, of the three-volume *Wörterbuch des Völkerrechts und der Diplomatie*, which has now evolved into the *Encyclopedia of Public International Law*, international law was still presented as the particular law of the 'Völkerrechtsgemeinschaft', a society of *certain* states constituted by their shared values and their common commitment to 'consider themselves as being bound by certain legal institutions or certain rules of law'.[201] The *Wörterbuch's* project was to present an encyclopaedic analysis of the growing body of international law from the German–Austrian perspective, stressing the independence of the continental European tradition of international law from the Anglo-American version of the law.[202] It seems particularly remarkable that the German–Austrian perspective, which in the early twentieth century was a

---

[195] As did Helmut Rumpf, *Der internationale Schutz der Menschenrechte und das Interventionsverbot*, Baden-Baden: Nomos 1981, p. 78.

[196] See Koskenniemi 2002; Orakhelashvili 2006.

[197] Orakhelashvili 2006, pp. 328–330.

[198] See Ulrich Fastenrath, *Lücken im Völkerrecht – Zu Rechtscharakter, Quellen, Systemzusammenhang, Methodenlehre und Funktionen des Völkerrechts*, Berlin: Duncker & Humblot 1990, p. 40.

[199] Terminology following Carol Baron von Kaltenborn von Stachau, *Kritik des Völkerrechts nach dem jetzigen Standpunkt der Wissenschaft*, Leipzig: Gustav Mayer 1847, p. 234; See also: Wheaton 1846, p. 47, § 16; Halleck 1861, p. 58, § 26; Martens 1883, p. 192.

[200] Koskenniemi 2002, pp. 51–52.

[201] Stier-Somlo 1929, pp. 187–188.

[202] Karl Strupp, 'Vorwort', in: Karl Strupp (ed.), *Wörterbuch des Völkerrechts und der Diplomatie*, Vol. I, Berlin: De Gruyter 1924, p. v–vi.

perspective often developed by German and Austrian international lawyers of Jewish origin,[203] does provide a framework that mirrors others perspectives vital to the development of 'humanitarian intervention' as an institute of international law: not a law of equal states or for states with equal rights, but a sophisticated system of unequal privileges based on the responsibility for the accomplishments of an original, 'European' internationalised order, a law that was the expression of 'legal conscience of the civilized world'.[204] The history of 'humanitarian intervention', then, unfolds as an expression of this 'legal conscience' written into action.

1.6 'HUMANITARIAN INTERVENTION' INTO THE TWENTY-FIRST CENTURY

The 'long' nineteenth century ended in the 'war to end all wars', ushering in what would turn out to be the 'short' twentieth century in a firestorm of industrialised violence. Even if this century, which would have ended with the fall of the Soviet Union, brought a 'long peace' during its 'cold war', it was the most violent century in human history. By the 1960s, this short century saw a renewed interest in the topic of 'humanitarian intervention', followed by the rise of the modern human rights system. Yet it was still hampered by the division of the world into opposing ideological blocs. Once this was apparently overcome in the twenty-first century, the world saw an unprecedented rise in international cooperation in the attempt to counter grave human rights violations, with the Security Council of the United Nations widely expanding its notion of what could constitute a threat to international peace and security, and authorising the Security Council to exercise its powers under Chapter VII of the Charter of the United Nations. The conceptual change, however, translated into relatively little action as the experiences of Rwanda in 1994 and Srebrenica in 1995 show. But it renewed the interest in a narrative that, as Tom Farer put it, could have lead a stranger to our planet to have 'fairly concluded that every Western government with the means to project force beyond its frontiers, above all the United States Government, was straining against the leash woven out of normative uncertainties, awaiting only their resolution to hurl itself into the humanitarian fray'.[205]

The obscenity of that impression has documented itself time and again, yet the break-up of Yugoslavia and the associated atrocities did present itself to some

---

[203] The Wörterbuch's original editors were Karl Strupp (1886–1940) and Julius Hatscheck (1872–1926). Other authors notable for their contributions relevant to this book's themes include Leo Strisower (1857–1931), Fritz Stier-Somlo (1873–1932), and Hans Kelsen (1881–1973).

[204] Koskenniemi 2002, p. 11.

[205] Tom Farer, 'Humanitarian Intervention Before and After 9/11: Legality and Legitimacy', in: J. L. Holzgrefe and Robert O. Keohane (eds.), *Humanitarian Intervention*, Cambridge University Press 2003, p. 54.

members of the 'international community' as a choice between two lessons learned in the violent twentieth century: 'Never Again War' and 'Never Again Auschwitz'. But there is no consensus as to whether this, like the eventual NATO action over Kosovo, could legitimise 'humanitarian intervention'. At the beginning of the twenty-first century, the legality of unilateral 'humanitarian intervention' remains a topic of mainly Western academic interest, even if the historical episodes that would have called for the use of military force in line with the doctrine, increasingly take place outside the Western world. This has led to a broader conceptualisation of the phenomenon, not only in terms of what it means for the future development of international law, but also in the approach to the concept of 'intervention' itself. The concept of the 'Responsibility to Protect' seeks to unite the lessons of 'Never Again War' and 'Never Again Auschwitz' by a renewed understanding of sovereignty as responsibility, while other approaches lead to a more 'constructive international law' and attempt to overcome perceived or actual asymmetries between states in the international order by 'constructive consent'.[206] Insofar as these developments seek to justify the use of force for a 'humanitarian' cause, they are clear signs that the battle over the legality of 'humanitarian intervention' is also a battle over the internationality of international law.[207] At the same time, the tales of past 'humanitarian intervention' have held an appeal, and not only for writers from European or Western countries. They have been discussed more or less favourably, if in sometimes rather shallow fashion, also by writers with Arab, African, or Indian backgrounds.[208] It would take a truly comparative approach to international law to uncover the extent of related narratives and counter-narratives offered in the literature on international law. Anthea Roberts has undertaken a first step on this topic beyond the scope of this book and has shown that Chinese, Russian, and American/British approaches to the subject differ widely not only in their legal conclusions, but also on the question of the importance of the matter in the first place.[209]

The case of the NATO action over Kosovo, however, also revealed the wide rift between American and (Continental) European approaches to the question of the

---

[206] The literature on the 'Responsibility to Protect' is expanding almost daily. For an early version of the argument on 'constructive consent' in international law, now more fully developed in: Matthias Herdegen, *The Dynamics of International Law in a Globalised World*, Frankfurt (Main): Vittorio Klostermann 2016, see: Matthias Herdegen, 'Asymmetrien in der Staatenwelt und die Herausforderungen des "konstruktiven Völkerrechts"', *Zeitschrift für ausländisches öffentliches Recht und Völkerrecht* 2004, pp. 571–582.

[207] E.g. Yvonne C. Lodico, 'The Justification for Humanitarian Intervention: Will the Continent Matter?', *International Lawyer* 2001, pp. 1027–1050.

[208] e.g. Manesh Prasad Tandon, *Public International Law*, 11th ed., Allahabad: Allahabad Law Agency Publishers 1966, p. 198; U. D. Umozurike, 'Tanzania's Intervention in Uganda', *Archiv des Völkerrecht* 1982, p. 309; Ahmad M. Ajaj, 'Humanitarian Intervention: Second Reading of the Charter of the United Nations', *Arab Law Quarterly* 1992, 7(4), pp. 215–236.

[209] Roberts 2017, pp. 192–199.

legality of 'humanitarian intervention' at the beginning of the twenty-first century.[210] The intervening states were, like some of those rejecting the legality of the actions, directly or indirectly affected by what was happening in the Former Republic of Yugoslavia, though not necessarily in proportion to the human rights abuses in Kosovo. Like Cuba for the United States in 1898, or the Balkans for the European Powers in the nineteenth century, the theatre of war was at the periphery of the immediate spheres of interests for the intervening powers. They were close enough to experience its consequences at home, for example through the influx of refugees, but far enough away to be able to conduct a risk-free 'spectator-sport war' (Colin McInnes), a 'virtual war' (Michael Ignatieff), fuelled and its outcome decided by images. Like Gladstone's 'Bulgarian Horrors',[211] or the images furnished by William Randolph Heart for Cuba,[212] or, as in the case of Kosovo, the fabricated Operation Horseshoe,[213] the legitimacy of 'humanitarian intervention' does not depend on what has happened, but on what judgement is passed. Only history will determine which narratives will prevail, for the account of the 'almost legal' use of military force to stop the ethnic cleansing of Albanians in Kosovo will forever stand next to the 'almost successful' ethnic cleansing of Serbs.[214]

---

[210] For a survey, see: Christian-Albrecht Masuch, *Die rechtswissenschaftliche Diskussion der Kosovo-Intervention als Beispiel eines unterschiedlichen Völkerrechtsverständnisses der USA und Kontinentaleuropas*, Berlin: Logos Verlag 2006.

[211] See Section 2.6.

[212] See Section 2.8.

[213] Heinz Loquai, *Der Kosovo-Konflikt. Wege in einen vermeidbaren Krieg. Die Zeit von Ende November 1997 bis März 1999*, Baden-Baden: Nomos 2000.

[214] Philipp Ther, *Die dunkle Seite der Nationalstaaten*, Göttingen: Vandenhoeck & Ruprecht 2011, p. 244.

2

A History of 'Humanitarian Intervention' in Nineteenth-Century International Law

2.1 INTRODUCTION

The nineteenth century has been called the 'heyday' of 'humanitarian interven-tion',[1] the time from the early nineteenth century through to the end of World War II an age of 'imperial humanitarianism'.[2] The period is revisited time and again to draw lessons for the present.[3] Given this use of the past, for the purposes of a history of the legal instrument, the nineteenth century might be considered as the canvas of a picture of 'humanitarian intervention' painted in the twentieth century. While the distinct legal concept of 'humanitarian intervention' did evolve late in the nineteenth century, drawing on the evolution of international law from a form of natural law to its own specific legal system, the humanitarian and legal dimensions of the historic events claimed for this development were rather marginal. It is only in writing about the nineteenth century that these events have gained their significance for the history of a legal concept.

The legal doctrine of 'humanitarian intervention' is said to rest on the most basic human drive of self-preservation and a fundamental shared concern for the preser-vation of humanity.[4] The so-called fathers of international law[5] are commonly called upon as evidence to the fact that the idea of 'humanitarian intervention' exists in international law as a matter of principle.[6] Indeed, parallels can be drawn to the

---

[1] Alexis Heraclidis, 'Humanitarian Intervention in the 19th Century: The Heyday of a Contro-versial Concept', *Global Society* 2012, 26, pp. 215–226.

[2] Barnett 2011, p. 29.

[3] Samuel Moyn, *Human Rights and the Uses of History*, London: Verso 2014.

[4] Bazyler 1987, p. 570.

[5] The question of whether one or more authors should be referred to as such is one of the more pointless discussions in the science of international law, see: Hersch Lauterpacht, 'The Grotian Tradition in International Law', *British Yearbook of International Law* 1946, 23, p. 19; Ipsen 1999, p. 25, § 2/28; Hobe and Kimminich 2004, p. 38.

[6] E.g. Wellhausen 2002, p. 49; Heraclidis and Dialla 2015, pp. 16–23.

discussion of the question of the just war in the writings of Alberico Gentili,[7] or even the more general question of justice in the writings of the early scholars of international law.[8] But the one 'father of international law' to whom the doctrine of 'humanitarian intervention' is most directly tied is Hugo Grotius (1583–1645).[9] In 1946, Hersch Lauterpacht (1897–1960), one of the most renowned international lawyers of the twentieth century,[10] published an influential article which not only signified his commitment to natural law as corrective to a strict positive understanding of all forms of law,[11] but also drew a direct line from Grotius to modern concepts of the protection of human rights through international law: 'The Grotian Tradition in International Law'. In this article, Lauterpacht found in Grotius 'the first authoritative statement of the principle of humanitarian intervention – the principle that exclusiveness of domestic jurisdiction stops when outrage upon humanity begins' and considerer it as 'one of the factors which paved the way for the provisions of the Charter of the United Nations relating to fundamental human rights and freedoms'.[12] Indeed, Grotius was used to bolster the evolution of the theory of 'humanitarian intervention' throughout the nineteenth century.[13] His writings address issues related to the doctrine of 'humanitarian intervention' in at least two instances.[14] In one such example, he discusses the question of '[w]hether we have a just Cause for War with another Prince, in order to relieve his Subjects from their Oppression under him'.[15] Grotius answers in the qualified affirmative: we do 'if he [the other Prince] disturbs and molests his own Country'.[16] But this example and other considerations of related issues by Grotius owe more to the tradition of Just War

---

7   Theodor Meron, 'Common Rights of Mankind in Gentili, Grotius and Suarez', *American Journal of International Law* 1991, 85(1), p. 110.

8   Emmanuel Roucounas, 'The Idea of Justice in the Works of Early Scholars of International Law', in: Laurence Boisson de Chazournes and Vera Gowlland-Debbas (eds.), *The International Legal System in Quest of Equity and Universality*, The Hague: Kluwer Law International 2001, p. 85: 'the *sedes materiae* of what would be later called humanitarian intervention'.

9   An early example of the claim that Grotius was a proponent of 'humanitarian intervention' can be found in Richard Wildman, *Institutes of International Law, Vol. I – International Rights in Time of Peace*, London: William Benning & Co. 1849, p. 62: Grotius 'holds that there is a degree of despotism on the part of a sovereign which will justify foreign invasion on behalf of his subjects'.

10   On Lauterpacht, see: Iain Scobbie, 'Hersch Lauterpacht (1897–1960)', in: Bardo Fassbender and Anne Peters (eds.), *The Oxford Handbook of the History of International Law*, Oxford University Press 2012, pp. 1179–1183, as well as Section 3.2.

11   Scobbie 2012, p. 1181, fn 13.

12   Lauterpacht 1946, p. 46.

13   E.g. Rougier 1910, pp. 472, 489, 498.

14   Chesterman 2001, S. 10; identifies two quotes, Sean D. Murphy, *Humanitarian Intervention – The United Nations in an Evolving World Order*, Philadelphia: University of Pennsylvania Press 1996, p. 43 discusses several more.

15   Hugo Grotius, *The Rights of War and Peace*, Book I, edited by Richard Tuck, Indianapolis: Liberty Fund 2005, p. 1159, III/XXV/VIII.

16   Grotius 2005, p. 1162.

theory than they are attempts to identify exceptional cases of a justified use of force. They are attempts to determine when the undisputed right to the use of force might be *wisely* exercised.[17] The idea that the legitimacy of the use of force might be somehow limited by its purpose was foreign to Grotius.[18] Therefore, it might be a stretch to point to Grotius as the first authoritative exponent of 'humanitarian intervention'.[19] It may very well be the case that 'the men who founded what was to become the Law of Nations' all 'had an enduring concern for the problem of how to deal with events that appalled the conscience of mankind'.[20] However, not only is there little reason to believe that these men could reasonably claim to represent the 'conscience of mankind', there is also no indication that the international law that developed in the decades and centuries after was propelled by such concerns.

With the writings of Emer de Vattel (1714–1767), international law begins to develop the framework in which the natural law principle of sovereignty gives way to a claim to freedom and independence; consequently, international law develops the function to protect the ability of states to determine their 'affaires domestiques': 'It is an evident consequence of the liberty and independence of nations, that all have a right to be governed as they think proper, and that no state has the smallest right to interfere in the government of another'.[21] It is at this point that the question of a right to interfere under exceptional ('humanitarian') circumstances becomes relevant.[22] Vattel's views on the legality of 'humanitarian intervention' have been interpreted in different ways,[23] but his opinion that in cases of resistance against 'insupportable' tyranny a call for assistance from other states by 'an oppressed people' may qualify as a legal justification for an outside intervention[24] would quickly

---

[17] Filadelfio Linares, *Einblicke in Hugo Grotius' Werk 'Vom Recht der Krieges und des Friedens'*, Zürich: Olms 1993, p. 57. Also see: Frank Przetacznik, 'The Basic Ideas of the Philosophical Concept of War and Peace', *Revue de Droit International de Sciences Diplomatiques et Politiques* 1990, p. 284.

[18] R. J. Vincent, 'Grotius, Human Rights, and Intervention', in: Hedley Bull, Benedict Kingsbury, and Adam Roberts (eds.), *Hugo Grotius and International Relations*, Oxford: Clarendon Paperbacks 1990, pp. 241–256.

[19] Vincent 1990, p. 248.

[20] D. J. B. Trim, '"If a prince uses tyrannie towards his people": Intervention on Behalf of Foreign Populations in Early Modern Europe', in: Brendan Simms and D. J. B. Trim (eds.), *Humanitarian Intervention – A History*, Cambridge University Press 2011, p. 41.

[21] Emer de Vattel, *The Law of Nations, or, Principles of the Law of Nature, Applied to the Conduct and Affairs of Nations and Sovereigns*, 1758, edited by Bela Kapossy and Richard Whatmore, Indianapolis: Liberty Fund 2008, p. 289, II/IV/54.

[22] See Günther 1787, pp. 280–320, for a discussion of the consequences of this principle, 'that all free people recognise unquestioningly for it is in their own interest' (p. 280: 'Ein Grundsatz, den alle freien Völker, ihres eignen Vorteils wegen, ohne Widerrede anerkennen').

[23] For example, Thomas E. Behuniak, 'The Law of Unilateral Humanitarian Intervention by Armed Force: A Legal Survey', *Military Law Review* 1978, p. 164; Abiew 1999, p. 36; Wellhausen 2002, p. 57, among others, conclude that Vattel was a supporter of a right of 'humanitarian intervention', Wellhausen even considering calling Vattel a 'father of humanitarian intervention'. Others, however, have come to the opposite conclusion, e.g. Pauer 1985, p. 29.

[24] Vattel 2008, p. 290, II/IV/56.

become of practical importance in the first example of an apparent 'humanitarian intervention', the intervention of the European Powers in the Greek War of Independence.

2.2 THE INTERVENTION OF THE EUROPEAN GREAT POWERS IN THE GREEK WAR OF INDEPENDENCE

The intervention of the European Great Powers (Russia, France, and the United Kingdom) in the Greek War of Independence is the model intervention of the classic version of 'humanitarian intervention' as a legal instrument. It is also the doctrine's 'original sin', the moment in which the construction of moral narrative takes precedence over the historical record. The 'humanitarian' intervention narrative centres on motives marginal to the historic event and creates causal connections that most likely did not exist. In the history of international law, the narrative of the European intervention in the Greek War of Independence has taken on a life of its own, a narrative that conforms to the requirements of a certain vision of international law more than it seeks to present a historically accurate account of events.

To give just one example, the Supplementary Volume to the ICISS Report on the 'Responsibility to Protect' specifically mentions this case as contributing to the idea of 'humanitarian intervention' in a legal sense as an intervention 'to stop Turkish massacres and suppression of populations associated with insurgents'.[25] As apparent in this short summary, the events are often portrayed in the legal literature as a precise and limited military intervention in a protracted conflict on the side of the apparent underdog, with an outcome that appears to have produced no (civilian) casualties. The narratives of the Greek War of Independence and the European intervention in the literature on 'humanitarian intervention' are usually brief and without historical substance, based on a selective reading of mostly contemporary authors to justify the qualification as the 'first precedent' of 'humanitarian intervention'.[26] Even longer treatments focus almost exclusively on 'British, Russian, and US responses to atrocities against Greeks in 1812–27' as examples of how nineteenth-century diplomats had 'some impressively successful ways' of 'using a combination of multilateralism, self-restraint, and treaties as tools to reassure other states about the good motivations behind a humanitarian mission'.[27] Thus, the example of European responses to the Greek War of Independence can be used to support the claim that, by the nineteenth century, sovereigns 'did not have an inexhaustible right to commit mass atrocities', and that the European powers were pushed 'towards humanitarian intervention' by the Ottoman failure to recognise the

---

[25] International Commission on Intervention and State Sovereignty 2001, Suppl. Vol., p. 16.
[26] Hillgruber 2001, p. 169.
[27] Bass 2008, pp. 41–42.

limits imposed on 'the legitimate killing of civilians within Europe'.[28] While such interpretations have a long history and have been supported by international lawyers almost since the events themselves,[29] they reduce a complex historical event to a reductionist narrative bordering on fiction.

For a history of 'humanitarian intervention' as a legal instrument, the events are remarkable not only as such but also for the way they have been and continue to be represented in the literature on international law. Nowhere is it more obvious than in this case that the understanding of 'humanitarian intervention' as an instrument of law was shaped by an *interpretation* of a historical narrative dictated by considerations of how the law *should* be, but was not.

2.2.1 *The Intervention and Its History*

At the beginning of the nineteenth century, present-day Greece was still part of the Ottoman Empire. As the power of the Empire was waning, its presence was increasingly seen as that of an anachronistic 'non-European' power, while a mythological Greece underwent a transformation in the imaginary cartography of European thinkers. In the comparatively short space of time between the late eighteenth to the early nineteenth century, Ancient Greece was elevated to the cradle of European civilisation, 'given its alleged democratic institutions and scientific rationality', and Greece was firmly located within Europe,[30] where the Ottoman Empire did not belong. In 1815, it had still been possible to consider the Ottoman Empire the only non-Christian power *in* Europe.[31] While the Law of Nations at the beginning of the nineteenth century was understood to directly bind only the Christian powers,[32] it was still far from unusual to note the Ottoman Empire's close proximity to the European law of nations, as well as the fact that the Porte enjoyed 'nearly the same rights', it being 'without doubt' that it was the Porte's choice to fully enjoy 'equal rights'.[33] However, the Empire lost its status as (almost) 'European' as quickly as the possibility of enjoying 'equal rights' under the law of 'civilised nations' disappeared in the wake of the Greek War of Independence.

For the purpose of international law as it came to be understood later in the nineteenth century, Europe as the sphere of 'civilised nations' constituted itself through the rejection of the presence of the Ottoman Empire. One consequence

[28] Alex J. Bellamy, *Massacres & Morality*, Oxford University Press 2012, p. 55.
[29] Henry Wheaton, *Elements of International Law*, Philadelphia: Carey, Lea & Blanchard 1836, p. 91: 'a further illustration of the principles of international law authorizing ... an interference, not only where the interests and safety of the other powers are immediately affected by the internal transactions of a particular state, but where the general interests of humanity are infringed by the excesses of a barbarous and despotic government'.
[30] Hobson 2004, p. 227.
[31] Schmalz 1817, p. 15.
[32] Schmalz 1817, p. 31.
[33] Schmalz 1817, p. 36.

of the Greek insurgency was the construct of an 'international society' compromised of only Christian nations in Europe's 'Law of Nations'. In this context, the process of the secularisation of international law, usually associated with its liberation from natural law, performs the same 'paradoxical double move' on religion that can be identified in the European religious nation-building wars of the seventeenth and eighteenth centuries: both neutralising (differences of) religion (among Christians) and turning (one) religion (Christianity) into the foundation of the modern nation state,[34] and, thus, the law and bond that governs the relations between states. Secularisation here, as in the colonial context, was less a liberation from religious values than a 'conversion'[35] of religious values into (identical) 'civilisational' or legal values. The concept of legality united the Christian powers under one law and replaced religion as its moral foundation, though it remained defined by the same values. The place of Russia in this construct was secured and cemented by the empire's unwavering support for the status quo,[36] not Russia's civilisational progressiveness. At least on paper, Greece at the end of the War of Independence appeared 'more Western' than any other country of the Western Mediterranean,[37] and certainly 'more civilised' than Russia's discriminatory and at times despotic monarchy.

In preceding centuries, Europe had defined and formed its own Christian 'self' through a rejection of Judaism and Jews, resulting in the large-scale expulsion and conversion of Jews in many parts of Europe.[38] Where Jewish minorities had remained, their legal status would continue to be defined by discrimination until the successful Jewish emancipation in most of these countries by the end of the nineteenth century.[39] With Europe's 'Christian' character firmly in place by the nineteenth century, the Ottoman Empire (and, with it, Islam) replaced Judaism as the anti-thesis to everything 'European' – at least in the writings of those seeking to establish the new science of international law – thus establishing international law as the monocultural society of 'civilised nations'. Well into the twentieth century, Europeans would consider the 'Ottoman Turk' an 'alien substance', 'embedded in the living flesh of Europe' and remaining different from 'the European family' in 'creed, in race, in language, in social customs' and political aptitudes and traditions, despite over 500 years of co-existence in Europe.[40]

[34] Wolfgang Eßbach, *Religionssoziologie 1*, Paderborn: Wilhelm Fink 2014, p. 28.
[35] I borrow the use of the term 'conversion' in this context from Herman 2011, pp. 16–19.
[36] Dominic Lieven, *The Cambridge History of Russia: Volume 2, Imperial Russia, 1689–1917*, Cambridge University Press 2006, p. 555.
[37] Heinrich August Winkler, *Geschichte des Westens – Von den Anfängen in der Antike bis zum 20. Jahrhundert*, 3rd ed., Munich: C. H. Beck 2012, p. 483.
[38] See generally, David Nirenberg, *Anti-Judaism: The Western Tradition*, New York: W. W. Norton 2013.
[39] Simon Dubnow, *Die neueste Geschichte des jüdischen Volkes*, trans. by Alexander Eliasberg, 2 Vols., Berlin: Jüdischer Verlag 1920.
[40] John Arthur R. Marriott, *The Eastern Question – An Historical Study in European Diplomacy*, 4th ed., Oxford: Clarendon Press 1940, p. 3.

For its own part, the Ottoman Porte never exercised such whole-scale measures as the expulsion of full communities of religious minorities in the way the 'more European' powers had forced out their Jewish communities in the preceding centuries. While the Empire arguably later made up for such relative tolerance, Greek society under Ottoman rule in the early nineteenth century was a multicultural society. Even if Islam was the dominant religion in the Empire, the Porte granted religious autonomy to its Jewish and Christian minorities, whereas the 'more European' Western powers were more likely to pass discriminatory laws against their Jewish communities.[41] In the early nineteenth century, Jews were subject to many such laws in Germany, Austria-Hungary, and, especially, Russia.[42] In other parts of Europe, emancipation and a relaxation of discriminatory laws were underway. In the United Kingdom, where all Jews had been expelled in 1290, but had started to resettle after 1655, Jews still faced considerable social discrimination, and it took until 1871 for Jews to become 'altogether free of constraint',[43] at least in legal terms,[44] while in places like the Netherlands, in the aftermath of the French revolution and its general trend towards religious freedom, Jews had become equal and full citizens.[45] Though the legal sub-ordination to Islam was never in question in the Ottoman Empire, Jewish life in Greece had prospered under Ottoman rule, with Salonica (today: Thessaloniki) becoming a 'new Jerusalem' of 'peace and liberty', a 'refuge' for the Jews of Europe, 'persecuted and banished' elsewhere.[46]

The Greek national movement of the nineteenth century, on the other hand, was characterised by religious intolerance from its inception. Fuelled by the ideals of the European Enlightenment, with its emphasis on secularisation, historicism and the use of language as a binding factor, Greek revolutionaries fought for the creation of a Greek state as part of a cultural mission to reclaim Greece for Christianity: According to the Greek revolutionary draft constitutions of 1822 and 1827, 'Greeks' were defined as those who 'believe in Christ' and were either born in the country or came to Greece from Ottoman-held territory.[47] The relevance of religion to this nation-building effort continues to be a source of debate among historians,[48] but the

[41] For a detailed study on the situation in Germany, see: Colin Judd, Contested Rituals: Circumcision, Kosher Butchering, and Jewish Political Life in Germany, 1843–1933. Ithaca: Cornell University Press 2007.
[42] See generally: Dubnow 1920.
[43] Anthony Julius, Trials of the Diaspora, Oxford University Press 2010, p. 260.
[44] Didi Herman, An Unfortunate Coincidence, Oxford University Press 2011.
[45] See: Bart Wallet, 'Dutch National Identity and Jewish International Solidarity: An impossible Combination? Dutch Jewry and the Significance of the Damascus Affair (1840)', in: Yosef Kaplan (ed.), The Dutch Intersection: The Jews and the Netherlands in Modern History, Leiden: Koninklijke Brill 2008, pp. 319–330.
[46] Mark Mazower, Salonica City of Ghosts: Christians, Muslims and Jews 1430–1950, London: HarperCollins Publishers 2004.
[47] Mark Biondich, The Balkans, New York: Oxford University Press 2011, pp. 14–18.
[48] E.g. Ther 2011, p. 61; Biondich 2011, p. 18; Frederick F. Anscombe, State, Faith, and Nation in Ottoman and Post-Ottoman Lands, Cambridge University Press 2014 (iBooks ed.), ch. 3.

numbers at least partially speak for themselves: War remade Greece's population as it would again elsewhere in Europe and, by the end, the number of Muslims and Jews who lived in the Morea in the Greek Kingdom created by war was significantly reduced.[49]

The Greek nation began as a truly 'imagined' community, positing an imagined continuity dating back to the days of Pericles and Socrates, in an attempt to 'debarbarise' the Modern Greeks.[50] Tellingly, the Greek quest for independence relied heavily on Greek expatriates.[51] The uprising against Ottoman rule began in 1821 and quickly won the support of a wider European public, who were fascinated by the Greek cause and the image of Greece as the birthplace of democracy and Western civilisation. Initially, the insurrection was quite successful and, by January 1822, with the majority of the Greek Islands and all Morea under their control, the revolutionaries declared the independence of Greece. By this time, of the roughly 10 per cent Muslim population of the Greek controlled areas, roughly 25 per cent had been brutally killed.[52]

The revolutionaries made repeated appeals to the European Powers to secure their success, but a request for support addressed to the 'Christian powers, assembled at Verona', dated 28 August 1822, was strongly rejected by the Congress in Verona.[53] This did not deter the revolutionaries from pursuing their wider goal – to convince the European public that the Greeks were a 'civilised' people and deserved to be helped by other 'civilised' (that is, Christian) nations against the 'barbaric' Ottomans. And in this respect they succeeded. Their appeals spoke the 'European' language of the Christian nation state and created the image of a 'national' movement aimed at forming a 'rational state', even where there was hardly any 'national unity' to speak of: The fusion of national movement with popular sovereignty resonated with the ideologies of progress and the rational state that were prevalent in nineteenth-century (Western) Europe.[54]

---

[49] Benjamin Lieberman, *Terrible Fate – Ethnic Cleansing in the Making of Modern Europe*, Maryland: Rowman & Littlefield 2013, ch. 1, text accompanying fn 12 (iBooks ed.). Five thousand Jews were killed on the Morea, with a pogrom taking place on 19 June 1821, where Jewish synagogues, houses, and businesses were attacked and many Jews killed, see Dubnow 1920, pp. 297–298. Entire Jewish communities on some of the Greek islands were wiped out, Stanford J. Shaw, *The Jews of the Ottoman Empire and the Turkish Republic*, New York University Press 1991, p. 190.

[50] Benedict Anderson, *Imagined Communities*, revised ed., London: Verso 1991, p. 72.

[51] See Barbara Jelavich, *History of the Balkans*, Vol. I, Cambridge University Press 1983, p. 204.

[52] Michael Schwartz, *Ethnische 'Säuberungen' in der Moderne*, Munich: Oldenbourg 2013, p. 241.

[53] Georg Friedrich von Martens and Frédéric Saalfeld (eds.), *Supplement au Recueil des principaux Traités*, Vol. VI, Part, Göttingen: Dieterich 1827, p. 233.

[54] Barry Buzan and George Lawson, *The Global Transformation*, Cambridge University Press 2015, ch. 4.

As the war quickly turned into a 'reciprocal orgy of violence'[55] – the Ottomans responded in kind to the anti-Muslim terror perpetrated by the insurgents[56] – the eyes of the European public remained focused almost exclusively on the fate of the Greeks: 'Liberating Greece had become the cause of civilized humanity', as a contemporary put it in 1835.[57] Even returning volunteers, who had left home to actively support the Greek cause but returned quickly, appalled by the brutality of the Greek revolutionaries, found little public interest for their stories.[58]

As the insurgency continued, the initial success of the revolution was jeopardised by serious in-fighting that escalated into civil war in the years between 1822 and 1825.[59] From its onset, the fight for independence was interspersed with massacres, claiming thousands of lives on all sides. There are reports that the first months of the uprising cost the lives of almost 20,000 Muslims,[60] while the massacre at Chios in April 1822 is said to have cost the lives of anywhere tens of thousands.[61] News of this massacre shocked the public, particularly in the United Kingdom: the Crown's traditional policy of supporting the Ottoman Empire became harder to justify in the face of a Philhellenic wave of support for the insurgents. As the safety of commerce across the Mediterranean became seriously undermined by the success of Greek pirates, and public sympathy for the Greek cause continued, Foreign Minister Castlereagh's strategy of isolating the conflict from European international politics by welding the non-intervention principle to the anti-revolutionary principles of the Holy Alliance became increasingly impossible for his predecessor Canning.[62]

In Russia, popular opinion had been on the side of the Greek insurgents from the beginning, but Tsar Alexander originally held back to show loyalty to the principles upon which the Holy Alliance had been founded.[63] In March 1823, the British Foreign Minister formally recognised the legitimacy of the Greek belligerents in a move heavily criticised by Austria, warning that 'recognition of the Greeks "as belligerents today might mean recognition of a Greek sovereign state tomorrow"'.[64] This *de facto*, if not also *de jure*, recognition of the insurgents as subjects of international law would later play an important role in the British justification for intervention in the War of Independence. It was also a way of providing a legal basis

---

[55] Misha Glenny, *The Balkans 1804–1999*, London: Granta Books 2000, pp. 28–29.
[56] Rodogno 2012, p. 65; Biondich 2011, p. 16.
[57] See Hillgruber 2001, p. 171, quoting a text from 1835.
[58] Winkler 2012, p. 480; Rodogno 2012, p. 66.
[59] Glenny 2000, pp. 27–28.
[60] Andrew Wheatcroft, *Infidels*, London: Penguin 2004, p. 249.
[61] Rodogno 2012, p 69.
[62] Vincent 1974, p. 87.
[63] Andrei P. Tsygankov, *Russia and the West from Alexander to Putin*, Cambridge University Press 2012, p. 66.
[64] Stivachtis 1998, p. 130.

for better protection of the British merchant ships in the Mediterranean,[65] though it was rejected by both Russia and the Ottoman Empire.[66] By February 1825, the Sultan had decided to seek the support of his nominal vassal, Mehmet Ali, the ruler of Egypt and Mehmet's son Ibrahim Pasha in his attempt to crush the rebellion.[67] Deploying well-trained Egyptian troops that quickly shattered the Greek armies, Ottoman control of the Peloponnese was more or less re-established.[68] The Greek insurgents once more turned to Britain for help, and later in 1825 presented an 'Act of Submission' to the British government, attempting to place the Greek nation's existence under the protection of the United Kingdom.[69] This proposal, however, was rejected, and rejected a second time when the Greeks offered their submission to France following the British refusal.[70]

In response to the Greek attempt to win British support, Russia was determined to press the issue of Greek independence. In October 1825, the Russian ambassador in London presented the British Foreign Minister with documents on an alleged 'barbarization project', claiming that Ibrahim planned to remove the whole Greek population and enslave them in Egypt.[71] This alleged plan of 'labouring to blot out of existence a whole Christian people, and to establish a new Barbary State on the shores of the Mediterranean, in the very midst of Europe' then found its way as fact into the legal literature on intervention in international law,[72] and has remained there, albeit with some reservations, ever since. While the rumours raised serious – and very real – fears in Greece, partly based on the experience of brutal measures of repression as in the case of Salonica, where several thousand Christians had been massacred in May 1821,[73] the alleged plan most certainly never existed. In 1888, it was revealed what the statesmen in their time probably knew already – that the Russians had deliberately 'rumoured' this plan of extermination without any real basis of fact.[74] Yet these 'rumours' conformed to notions of the 'barbarian Turks' widely held in a Europe that constituted itself as Christian and 'civilised' during this time – the fact that the Ottoman Empire strongly rejected all allegations and denied

---

[65] Matthias Schulz, *Normen und Praxis*, Munich: Oldenbourg 2009, p. 91; Harald Müller, *Im Widerstreit von Interventionsstrategie und Anpassungszwang – Die Aussenpolitik Österreichs und Preußens zwischen dem Wiener Kongreß 1814/15 und der Februarrevolution 1848*, Berlin (East): Akademie der Wissenschaften der DDR 1990, p. 183.

[66] Stivachtis 1998, p. 130.

[67] Richard Clogg, *A Concise History of Greece*, Cambridge University Press 1992, p. 42. Other sources use the name Mohamed Ali, see Rodogno 2012, p. 79.

[68] Andrew Wheatcroft, *The Ottomans – Dissolving Images*, London: Penguin 1993, p. 125; Glenny 2000, p. 32.

[69] Rodogno 2012, p. 79.

[70] Stivachtis 1998, p. 137.

[71] Rodogno 2012, p. 79.

[72] The quote is from Stapleton 1866, p. 32.

[73] Mazower 2004, ch. 6.

[74] Rodogno 2012, p. 80.

the existence of any plan for the deportation of the Greek population[75] made no impression on the European public.

Under the pressure of these developments and popular opinion sympathetic to the Greek cause, the Great Powers intensified their efforts, culminating initially in the St Petersburg Protocol of 4 April 1826. The parties to the Protocol agreed to work towards an end to fighting in Greece for an 'arrangement which shall be consistent with the principles of religion, justice and humanity'.[76] The renowned British historian Harold Temperley (1879–1939) later considered this to be a 'diplomatic revolution', for it 'committed England to work with Russia for some kind of intervention in Greece'.[77] The Crown considered it's involvement justified on account of the Greek request, specifically mentioned in the Preamble of the St Petersburg protocol, and interpreted by Foreign Secretary Canning as a direct authorisation to intervene.[78] The Sultan strongly rejected such 'mediation' in – as contemporary international lawyers described it – 'an able state paper', declaring the 'undoubted principle that no state has a right to interfere in the private affairs of another', and other arguments rooted in international law.[79] Austria also strongly objected to any claim of rightful intervention: Canning's claim that the Greek request could serve as an authorisation for intervention was drastically rejected by Count Metternich:

> It is a question neither more nor less of the foundations of the law of nations recognised up to this hour. What would be the fate of Europe – that of civilisation if the doctrine of *dédoublement des États* were ever admitted by the last supporters of the peace of nations? How can a man of sense advance so subversive a contention, or at least permit himself the attempt to advance it? Is England then ready to *regard as a Power equal in rights to that of the [British] King* the first Irish Club which declares itself the *Insurgent Government of Ireland*? To regard as *fondée dans son droit* the French Power which would accept the office of mediator, by reason of the sole fact that the invitation had been addressed to it by the *Irish Government* – to regard finally as conformable to the law of nations, the menace of compulsory measures, or even of those furnished by France, or of those she should find means to combine with other Powers?[80]

---

[75] Stivachtis 1998, p. 143.
[76] Preamble to the 'Protocole relatif aux affaires de la Grèce entre la Russie et la Grande-Bretagne, St Petersburg, April 4, 1826', in: Georg Friedrich von Martens and Frédèric Saalfeld (eds.), *Nouveau Recuiel de Traites*, Vol. VII, Part 1, Göttingen: Dieterich 1829, p. 40, reprinted from *The Times*, 4 February 1828.
[77] Harold Temperley, 'Princess Lieven and the Protocol of 4 April 1826', *English Historical Review* 1924, XXXIX(CLIII), pp. 55–78.
[78] Letter, Canning to Temple, 19 September 1826, reprinted in: Harold Temperley, *The Foreign Policy of Canning 1822–1827*, 2nd ed., Connecticut: Archon Books 1966, p. 360.
[79] Kent and Abdy 1866, p. 55, citing a letter dated 9 June 1827.
[80] Letter by Metternich to Apponyi, 17 October 1826, cited in Temperley 1966, p. 361, italics in original.

But Count Metternich found no support for his position. On the contrary, France now joined the support for the insurgents and proposed a joint treaty between the three powers. With the Treaty of London of 6 July 1827 the Majesties of the United Kingdom, France and Russia once more offered 'their mediation to the Ottoman Porte, with the view of effecting a reconciliation between it and the Greeks'.[81] The further provisions of the treaty called for an immediate armistice and offered to recognise Greece as a tributary state under the suzerainty of the Ottoman Empire. At the same time, it promised 'to effect a complete separation between the individuals of the two nations, and to prevent the collisions which would be the inevitable consequence of so protracted a struggle', by making the Greeks 'possessors of all Turkish Property situated either upon the Continent, or in the Islands of Greece, on condition of indemnifying the former proprietors, either by an annual sum to be added to the tribute which they shall pay to the Porte, or by some other arrangement of the same nature'.[82] The Porte rejected such offers as illegal interventions in its internal affairs.[83] The three Great Powers were prepared for this reaction, as the Treaty already included a secret article in which they agreed to, *inter alia*, enter into commercial relations with Greece in this case, 'exert all their efforts to accomplish' an armistice, 'without, however, tanking any part in the hostilities between the Two Contending Parties' and 'continue to pursue the work of pacification' by future measures that their representatives in London were already authorised 'to discuss and determine'.

There would be little chance to discuss and determine further measures, as the London Treaty, secret article included, was published in *The Times* on 12 July 1827. There was consequently little room for further negotiations with the Porte, which rejected the terms of the Treaty. Tensions did not ease and, on 20 October 1827, the so-called Battle of Navarino took place, sinking the entire Turkish-Egyptian fleet at the hands of the Allied European powers and killing thousands of Ottoman sailors[84] over the course of several days, the sea 'reddened for some distance with blood'.[85] This 'battle' was described as an 'untoward event' by British contemporaries.[86] Its precise cause is hard to determine. Some international lawyers appear to suggest that

---

[81] Art. 1 of the Traité pour la pacification de la Grèce, entre la Grande-Bretagne, la France et la Russie et signé à Londres, 6 July 1827, reprinted in: Temperley 1966, appendix VIII, pp. 599–606, translation courtesy of the author.

[82] Art. 2 of the Traité pour la pacification de la Grèce, entre la Grande-Bretagne, la France et la Russie et signé à Londres, 6 July 1827, reprinted in: Temperley 1966, appendix VIII, pp. 599–606, translation courtesy of the author.

[83] '. . . [L]'affaire grecque est une affaire interne de la Sublime Porte, et que c'est à elle seule s'en occuper'. *British and Foreign State Papers*, Vol. 14, p. 1044 ff, cited according to Manouchehr Ganji, *International Protection of Human Rights*, Geneva: Librairie E. Droz 1962, p. 23.

[84] Brownlie 1963, p. 31, puts the figure at 'some 4,000 men'; Rodogno 2012, p. 83, speaks of 'no less than 6,000' sailors. Bass 2008, p. 148, puts the figure at 'at least 6,000' dead.

[85] Temperley 1966, p. 409.

[86] Brownlie 1963, p. 31; Bass 2008, p. 149.

it was the result of Allied provocation,[87] others consider it an accident.[88] A biography of British Foreign Minister Canning argues that the British ships seized an opportunity according to the 'spirit' of Canning's instructions,[89] though they had arrived in Navarino without authorisation to open fire.[90] On 8 September 1827 Canning had, in a letter 'to the British Consuls and Agents in the Levant', stressed that 'The Commanders of the Squadrons have received orders to exert themselves to the utmost, in order to prevent the measures which they are charged to execute from degenerating into hostilities'.[91] It is no surprise, then, that the British public protested against the destruction of the Ottoman fleet, while the influential philhellenic groups celebrated the 'intervention'.[92] Count Metternich considered the development a catastrophe (and a violation of international law) that would only serve Russian interests.[93] The Porte unsuccessfully requested satisfaction for the alleged 'war crime' of Navarino and then proceeded to nullify all treaties with Russia, the United Kingdom and France, while seeking a declaration of *jihad* against such 'mediators of peace'.[94] In the aftermath, unity among the Allied powers began to crumble, and Austria-Hungary in tandem with France began to try to stop the impending war between Russia and the Ottoman Empire. It was, however, too late. On 16 April 1828, Russia formally declared war on the Porte and justified this step with reference to the Ottoman failure to adhere to treaties between the empires, not by invoking any (legal) rights to protect the Greek Christians.[95] By then, Nicholas I had succeeded Tsar Alexander and he perceived the war to be fought over long-standing conflicts of interests with the Ottoman Empire, rejecting any support for Greek independence or sympathy for the Greek cause.[96]

The ensuing war terminated British involvement in a French expeditionary corps to be sent to the Morea in order to remove the occupying Egyptian troops as authorised by the Protocol of 19 July 1828 and signed by the three European Great Powers. The Protocol proclaimed that 'the disembarkation of an allied force in the Greek peninsula is not undertaken with hostile views' towards the Ottoman Porte,

[87] Brownlie 1963, p. 31.
[88] Arthur Wegner, *Geschichte des Völkerrechts*, Stuttgart: Kohlhammer 1936, p. 206. Biondich 2011, p. 16, calls it 'inadvertent'.
[89] Temperley 1966, p. 409.
[90] Letter, Codrington to Canning, 20 October 1827, reprinted in: Georg Friedrich von Martens and Frédèric Murhard (eds.), *Supplément au Recueil des principaux Traités*, Vol. XVI, Göttingen: Dieterich 1837, p. 136. See also: Brownlie 1963, p. 31.
[91] Letter, Canning to the British Consuls and Agents in the Levant, 8 September 1827, reprinted in: von Martens and Murhard 1837, p. 42.
[92] Bass 2008, p. 149.
[93] Norman Rich, *Great Power Diplomacy 1814–1914*, New York: McGraw Hill 1992, p. 54.
[94] Bonney 2004, p. 146.
[95] F. R. Bridge and Roger Bullen, *The Great Powers and the European States System 1814–1914*, 2nd ed., Harlow: Pearson Longman 2005, p. 77.
[96] Tsygankov 2012, p. 66.

which was to be notified accordingly.[97] The Protocol stipulated that the French troops were to leave the peninsula 'so soon as the army of Ibrahim Pasha shall be reimbarked'. After these troops landed on 28 August 1828, the resulting constellation was described by Metternich:

> Russia at open war with the Porte, with one half of its squadron engaged in a hostile blockade of the Dardanelles and the other half in a 'pacific blockade' of the Greek coast; France engaged in amicable hostilities by land with a nominal vassal of the Sultan, but neutral at the sea; England neutral but ally and accomplice of the other two.[98]

The French oversaw the displacement of around 2,500 Muslim survivors of previous massacres, who were transferred to Smyrna on French vessels on 5 November 1828, and supervised the return of other displaced civilians to their homes.[99]

The Russian–Greek War lasted for more than a year, but the Ottoman Empire had no chance of winning. Consequently, at its close, Article 10 of the Peace Treaty signed at Adrianopolis (Adrianople, currently Edirne) in 1829, required the Porte to accept the terms of the London Treaty and Greek autonomy.[100] With the London Protocols of 1829 and 1830, the Great Powers established Greece as an independent sovereign kingdom. The internal fight among the Greeks was not over and descended into further civil war, leading to the London Conference of 1832, where the three Great Powers established the Bavarian Prince Otto as King of Greece, finally putting an end to the Greek War of Independence. The Great Powers had succeeded in 'liberating' Greece, not least of its Muslim population, and strengthening their own positions of power over the region, setting in motion a process that would drive the Ottoman Empire further to the brink of the European continent in a series of nationalist revolutions over the next decades. It also left the Porte a place as a 'royal empire' in Europe, listed alongside the Kingdom of Greece, though considered to not be accepting the full scale of 'Practical European International Law' (jus gentium europaearum practicum).[101]

---

[97] Protocol of the Conference held at the Foreign Office, 19 July 1828, reprinted in: *Papers Relative to the Affairs of Greece, Protocols of Conferences Held in London*, London: Harrison & Sons 1830, p. 242.

[98] Quoted according to Stivachtis 1998, p. 170.

[99] Rodogno 2012, pp. 85–86.

[100] Traité de paix entre la Russie et Porte Ottomane, dated 14 September 1829, reprinted in: Georg Friedrich von Martens and Frédèric Saalfeld (eds.), *Supplément au Recueil des principaux Traités*, Vol. XII, Göttingen: Dieterich 1831, p. 143.

[101] Johann Ludwig Klüber, *Europäisches Völkerrecht*, 2nd ed. by Carl Eduard Morstadt, Schaffhausen: Hurter 1851, p. 2, note d, and p. 34.

2.2.2 *The Intervention in Context*

The case of Greece was an important test for the political and legal order of
international relations in Europe, as established at the Vienna Congress in 1815.
As Gerry Simpson has shown, Vienna established a system of legalised hegemony
reinstating a European balance of power without giving up on the idea of sovereign
equality: 'a hierarchical structure in which a small number of states regulate,
through law, the affairs of the rest and a system in which sovereign states interact
with each other as free, equal and independent entities'.[102] At Vienna, the political
landscape had been remodelled to reflect the security needs of the Great Powers, a
'European Concert' was established under their direction to maintain the status quo
as it served their interests. The 'Concert' has been described as a forerunner of the
United Nations Security Council,[103] though it was a much less formal institution
and membership would vary depending on the situation. There was also no clear
agreement on the scope of the status quo to be protected. While Count Metternich
represented the Austro-Hungarian position that the Powers were to act like the
police to preserve the existing order among the European nations,[104] Castlereagh,
still the British Foreign Minister at the outset of the Greek War of Independence,
understood the aims of the Concert to be limited to preserving the general peace in
Europe and the Balance of Power.[105] In other words, the 'Austrian doctrine of
prophylactic intervention', shared by the continental Powers, stood against the
British interpretation that only territorial changes could be considered threats to
the peace within Europe and thus justify interventions to uphold the Balance of
Power. Effectively, the United Kingdom rejected any claims that an intervention
could be legally justified by reference to the internal situation in another state, an
option that was always open to the Continental nations.

The different approaches to the scope of the system first came to a head at the
Congress of Troppau in 1820. The assembled representatives of Russia, Austria and
Prussia, the Holy Alliance powers, agreed to quash any constitutional innovations
'dangerous to the tranquillity of neighbours',[106] and considered the revolution in
Naples a case for action. The United Kingdom objected to this approach in
principle, but conceded a right to intervene in this particular case. The situation
was similar in the case of the French intervention in Spain, when Castleraegh's
successor Canning refused to join the intervention at the Verona Congress, but only

---

[102] Simpson 2004, p. 95.
[103] Schulz 2009.
[104] M. S. Anderson, *The Ascendancy of Europe*, 2nd ed., Reprint, Harlow: Pearson Education
2000, p. 3.
[105] Castlereagh's State Paper, 5 May 1820, reprinted in: A. W. Ward and G. P. Gooch, *The
Cambridge History of British Foreign Policy, 1783–1919*, Vol. II, Cambridge University Press
1923, appendix A, p. 622.
[106] Simpson 2004, p. 208.

mildly objected to the French initiative with the consent of the three Eastern powers, leading to the French occupation of Spain that would last almost five years.

The roles were then reversed in the case of the Greek War of Independence, and no agreement, however limited, could be reached.[107] The intervening powers were not successful in convincing the Austro-Hungarian Empire of the legality of their involvement, with Count Metternich allegedly calling the London Treaty a 'collection of lies and uncertainties'.[108] The alliance between the intervening powers eventually failed as Russia attempted to force the Porte to accept the terms of the London Treaty by war.

Legal arguments were always present during the quest for the 'right' reaction to the Greek insurrection. In the early stages of the Greek struggle for independence, Russia had apparently argued that the Ottoman Empire could no longer be considered one of the civilised states of Europe on account of the treatment of the insurgents.[109] Taking into account the further development of international law in the nineteenth century, constructed as a 'law of civilized nations' that most certainly did not include the Ottoman Empire, this argument seems particularly remarkable. It is not the only indication that international law, as it was to evolve in the years to come, was an ideological, and quite possibly artificial construct that did not reflect state practice. Russia's position for most of the war can only be characterised as traditional. Even when fighting the Russo–Turkish War over Greece, the Tsar remained convinced that the Greek insurgents had conducted an illegal uprising against their lawful sovereign.[110] Nicolas I was outspoken in his rejection of Greek independence, which his actions unintentionally assisted: 'I detest, I abhor the Greeks, I consider them as revolted subjects and I do not desire their independence. My grievance is against the Turks' conduct to Russia'.[111]

It is obvious, then, that Greece's entry into international society as a (semi-) sovereign state was considered a *legal* procedure. Relations between the Greeks, the European Powers and the Ottoman Empire were therefore seen as relations governed, at least in some way, by law – most likely international law. In fact, this was the position of most early nineteenth century writers on international law. It was only later in the century that this position would be reversed to become one of the foundations of international law. Foreign policy in the nineteenth century increasingly made reference to 'international law' as a factor guiding decisions. Attempts to rule out slave-trading framed the problem as a 'legal issue', and British foreign policy

---

[107] In fact, Greek insurgency brought the question to the fore whether the Christian principles of the Holy Alliance extended to the sovereignty of the infidel Turkey, see Tsygankov 2012, p. 66.

[108] Müller 1990, p. 197: His advisor Gentz is said to have called the treaty a 'high point of wrongness' ('Gipfel der Verkehrtheit').

[109] This is how Hillgruber 2001, p. 170 summarises the Russian position, based on a text from 1835.

[110] Stivachtis 1998, p. 145.

[111] Tsygankov 2012, p. 66.

in particular made regular reference to the 'law of nations'.[112] In recognising the Greeks as belligerent, Canning had announced that he had taken this step to bring 'within the bounds of a civilized war a contest which had been marked at the outset on both sides by disgusting barbarity'.[113] Only after recognition was Canning prepared to include the Greek request for help as a justification of the British efforts, as reflected in the Preambles of the St Petersburg Protocol and the London Treaty. The latter listed no less than three grounds for justification of the intervention. First, 'the necessity of putting an end to the sanguinary struggle which, while it abandons the Greek Provinces and the Islands of the Archipelago to all the disorders of anarchy, daily causes fresh impediments to the commerce of the States of Europe, and gives opportunity for acts of Piracy which not only expose the subjects of the High Contracting Parties to grievous losses', then, the 'earnest invitation to interpose' mediation from the Greeks received by the United Kingdom and France, and, finally, 'the desire of putting a stop to the effusion of blood, and of preventing the evils of every kind which the continuance of such a state of affairs may produce'.[114] These were the reasons which had led the three Great Powers 'to combine their efforts, and to regulate the operation thereof, by a formal Treaty, for the object of re-establishing peace between the contending parties, by means of an arrangement called for, no less by sentiments of humanity, than by interests for the tranquillity [sic] of Europe'.[115]

None of this amounted to an authorisation of the use of force as in the Battle of Navarino. On the contrary, the Powers had instructed their interpreters for diplomatic communications after the Battle to reiterate that the European fleets had entered Navarino without any intention of hostilities, when an 'aggression' on part of the Ottoman fleet had caused combat to break out.[116] In his exhaustive study of the Greek War of Independence and Great Power intervention, Oliver Schulz details the break-down of communications between the Great Powers and representatives of the Porte over a number of misunderstandings and miscommunications, which eventually limited options for further courses of action.[117] In fact, the Ottoman elites lacked the ability to understand the phenomenon of Greek nationalism altogether, considering 'Greekness' an 'unnatural disease' that clashed with Ottoman traditions

---

[112] See Vincent 1974, p. 70; Alfred P. Rubin, *Ethics and Authority in International Law*, Cambridge University Press 1997, p. 115; Stivachtis 1998, p. 122.

[113] Rich 1992, p. 52.

[114] The Treaty of London for Greek Independence, 6 July 1827, available at https://ecommons .cornell.edu/handle/1813/662, last accessed 3 February 2019.

[115] Preamble of the Treaty of London, see fn. 115.

[116] Instruction Collective aux Interprêtes de la Grande Bretagne, de la France, et de la Russie, dated 2 November 1827, reprinted in: von Martens and Murhard 1837, p. 140.

[117] Oliver Schulz, *Ein Sieg der zivilisierten Welt?*, Münster: LIT Verlag 2011, pp. 235–274.

of defining the identifications of local people according to their place in the various religious communities.[118]

Greece's entry into international society meant the (territorial and numerical) 'enlargement' of the European society of states, the recognised 'family of nations' under international law. Its importance for the history of Europe can also be seen from the prominent place the events hold in current accounts of the 'History of the West'.[119] As contemporary writers recognised, 'the cause was one that excited the enthusiasm of the civilized world and lent a false luster to the doctrine of Intervention', a 'brilliant and romantic chapter in modern history'.[120] The legal relevance of the events is not limited to the doctrines of intervention and recognition; it also has an impact on what today is understood as the right of the self-determination of peoples, as some contemporaries expressly recognised: The Greeks were considered 'a people which has been subjugated, and which, after constantly refusing to constitute and to have one sole country along with its oppressor, at length arises in fierce insurrection and makes a supreme effort to recover its liberty'.[121] Yet historically, the Greek 'people' only constituted themselves through the struggle for an independent state by adopting nineteenth century ideas of nation-building. As J. A. R. Marriott (1859–1945) pointed out in the classical study on the 'Eastern Question' and European diplomacy, the preceding 400 years had not given any indication that any such thing as the consciousness of Greek national identity had been preserved during the years of Ottoman rule.[122] While other writers have also pointed towards the rights of self-determination as a possible legal justification for the intervention,[123] it is not only the peculiarities of the (legal) relations with the Ottoman Empire that have led to the exclusion of this case from most studies on the development of the right to self-determination.[124]

2.2.3 *The Intervention in the History of International Law*

The Greek drama began to unfold at a time when the emerging discipline of international law had only just begun the discussion as to whether the European Great Powers *should* be authorised to intervene in the affairs of the states of Europe. According to C. Ch. A. H. Kamptz (1769–1849), author of the 1821 treatise 'Völkerrechtliche Erörterung des Rechts der Europäischen Mächte in die Verfassung

---

[118] Ebru Boyar, *Ottomans, Turks and the Balkans – Empire Lost, Relations Altered*, London: Tauris Academic Studies 2007, p. 50.

[119] e.g. Winkler 2012, p. 480.

[120] Kent and Abdy 1866, p. 54.

[121] Mamiani 1860, p. 144.

[122] Marriott 1940, p. 9.

[123] e.g. Stowell 1921, p. 126.

[124] According to Roelofsen 1995, p. 118, 'the first serious challenge in the name of national self-determination to the territorial settlement of 1815' came with the Revolutions in Poland and Belgium in 1830.

eines einzelnen Staates sich einzumischen' (Consideration of the right of the European Powers to interfere with the constitution of other European states under international law), there were a number of circumstances under which the European Powers could exercise such a right, from revolution to internal disturbances and infringements of the rights of co-religionists in different countries.[125] Von Kamptz, later described as a 'spokesman' for the Holy Alliance,[126] considered this 'one of the most fundamental and undisputed principles of European international law, observed for centuries'.[127] In the very same year, Johann Ludwig Klüber (1762–1837), one of the most important representatives of German international law in the early nineteenth century, and in that capacity also referenced by von Kamptz,[128] published his treatise on international law and provided a much more narrow definition of a right to interfere with the internal affairs of another state. In his view, it was only justified if based on an 'acquired right' (erworbenes Recht) or in cases of 'emergency'.[129] According to Klüber, this did not cover 'disturbances between a regent and his subjects', nor intervention by invitation.[130]

Both positions merged in the development of the treatment of Great Power interventions in the affairs of the Ottoman Empire in the growing literature on international law in the later nineteenth and early twentieth century. In one trajectory, the tradition of international law as an 'impartial' law for the intercourse between sovereigns and states on the basis of mutual guarantees for territorial sovereignty and independence emerged.[131] But during international law's once so-called golden age, a different type of international law also developed, a law open only to select sovereigns and states, a law that would authorise interventions beyond its territorial sphere. The idea of 'humanitarian intervention' as developed in late nineteenth century international law combined a law guaranteeing sovereign equality with a law of 'civilised' nations limiting sovereignty by exposing the 'uncivilised' to *authorised* intervention of the 'civilised'. In this constructive effort, knowledge easily available to participants was readily abandoned in favour of a more romantic perspective on the conflict, which largely prevails to this day, at least among writers on 'humanitarian intervention'.

There can be no doubt that the contemporary writers of 'classic' international law had a positive view of the Great Power involvement in the Greek struggle for independence, even if this did not necessarily translate into a positive assessment of the legality of the developments: William Vernon Harcourt (1827–1904), a

---

[125] von Kamptz 1821, pp. 20, 53–54.
[126] Franz von Liszt and Max Fleischmann, *Das Völkerrecht*, 12th ed., Berlin: Verlag von O. Häring 1925, p. 120.
[127] von Kamptz 1821, p. XVI. A similar claim was made by Schmelzing 1818, p. 133.
[128] von Kamptz 1821, p. 64.
[129] Johann Ludwig Klüber, *Europäisches Völkerrecht*, Stuttgart: J. G. Cotta 1821, p. 93, § 51.
[130] Klüber 1821, p. 94, § 52.
[131] This description of nineteenth century international law is based on Kimminich and Hobe 2000, p. 42.

respected British politician and statesman of the nineteenth century, in his 'Letters by Historicus on some Questions of International Law', echoed a sentiment shared by other writers – that the 'emancipation of Greece was a high act of policy above and beyond the domain of law. As an act of policy it may have been and was justifiable; but it was no less a hostile act'.[132] Where the legality of the involvement was asserted, the grounds for justification were diverse and ranged from an endorsement of the *goals* of the insurgency (i.e., self-determination)[133] and an acceptance of Canning's position of the legality of the activity of the Great Powers on account of the request of the Greek insurgents[134] to the justification based on the infringement of legitimate interests, here mainly referring to British commercial interests.[135] 'Interests of humanity' alone were regularly not held to be a sufficient justification: 'As an accessory to others, this ground [intervention on behalf of the general interests of humanity] may be defensible, but as a substantive and solitary justification of Intervention into the affairs of another country it can scarcely be admitted into the code of international law'.[136] Only in later years did the justification based on the 'interests of humanity' gain in importance, when a growing number of authors under the explicit premise of the particularity of (European) international law – a view most prominently expressed by Wheaton[137] and Kaltenborn[138] – and its limited

[132] William Vernon Harcourt, *Letters by Historicus on some Questions of International Law: reprinted from 'The Times' with considerable additions*, London: Macmillan and Co. 1863, p. 6. The quote was widely cited with approval, e.g. in Kent and Abdy 1866, p. 50.

[133] Creasy 1874, p. 299; Mamiani 1860, p. 144.

[134] e.g. Bluntschli 1878, p. 269, nr. 475; August Wilhelm Heffter, *Das Europäische Völkerrecht der Gegenwart auf den bisherigen Grundlagen*, 8th ed. by Friedrich Heinrich Geffcken, Berlin: Verlag von F. H. Müller 1888, p. 114; Georges Bry, *Précis Élémentaire de Droit International Public*, Paris: L. Larose et Forcel 1891, pp. 134–136.

[135] Stapleton 1866, p. 14; Emanuel Ullmann, *Völkerrecht*, Tübingen: JCB Mohr (P. Siebeck) 1908, p. 462. Similarly: Frantz Despagnet, *Cours de Droit International*, 3rd ed., Paris: Librairie de la Société du Recueil Général des Lois et des Arrêts 1905, p. 212; Robert Phillimore, *Commentaries upon International Law*, Vol. I, Philadelphia: T & J W Johnson 1854, p. 321, referring to the need of 'affording protection to the subjects of other Powers who navigated the Levant, in which, for many years, atrocious Piracy had been exercised, while neither Turkey nor revolted Greece were de facto either able or willing to prevent the excesses springing out of this state of anarchy', a reason which 'unquestionably' justified the intervention.

[136] Phillimore 1854, p. 320. The argument developed in Kent and Abdy 1866, p. 56, is similar, as is the position held by Henry W. Halleck, *Elements of International Law*, Philadelphia: J. B. Lippincott & Co 1866, p. 340.

[137] Wheaton 1846, p. 40: 'International law is only a particular law, applicable to a distinct set or family of nations, varying at different times with the change in religion, manners, government and other institutions, among every class of nations'. The original text is similar, see: Wheaton 1836, p. 44: 'The ordinary jus gentium is only a particular law, applicable to a distinct set or family of nations, varying at different times with the change in religion, manners, government and other institutions, among every class of nations'.

[138] von Kaltenborn von Stachau 1847, p. 270: 'Das *allgemeine positive* Völkerrecht ist einzig das *christliche*. Die anderen Staaten haben internationale Beziehungen; diese stehen aber nicht auf der Basis des Rechts. Dies lehrt die Geschichte'. Emphasis in original.

applicability in the relations with 'uncivilised' nations began to treat the involvement of the Great Powers as a civilising act to check Ottoman barbarism.[139]

But even among authors who shared the premise of the particularity of European international law and its full applicability only among 'Christian nations', this did not necessarily mean that the Great Power involvement in the Greek War of Independence was classified as a (legal) 'humanitarian intervention'. August Wilhelm Heffter (1796–1880), for example, author of the 'most successful' 'systematic treatise' on international law in the nineteenth century,[140] was of the opinion that international law was to be applied only 'partially' to relations with non-Christian states, 'as far as reciprocity could be expected'.[141] His treatise went through eight German editions, as well as several editions of a French translation. During the course of the years, Heffter saw it fit to clarify his position on intervention with regard to the 'Battle of Navarino': For Heffter, the legality was based on the Greek request for help, whereas religious persecution or the most extreme injustice ('schreiendste Ungerechtigkeit') alone could only be cause for lawful intercession (and a moral duty, leading to, if necessary, termination of all diplomatic relations), but not active intervention.[142]

European international law, according to Heffter, rested on a 'higher level of humanity' than any law previously known; peace and a 'social human conscience' were its guiding factors.[143] His approach to international law has been considered 'pragmatic'[144] and his concept of the 'European Law of Nations',[145] though not just geographical, was more open to expanding its sphere of validity than the later construct of a 'law of civilised nations':[146] Much to the dismay of the editor of later (posthumous) editions of his treatise, Heffter could see the Treaty of Paris (1855) as the source of a *legal* duty to respect international law in future relations with the Ottoman Porte, though with reservations.[147] This option was categorically unavailable to the 'law of civilised nations', as imagined by Fedor (Friedrich von) Martens

---

[139] E.g.: Hartmann 1878, pp. 6, 19; von Wachter 1911, p. 50.

[140] Nussbaum 1950, p. 230.

[141] Heffter 1844, p. 11, § 8, my translation. In later editions Heffter stressed that relations with non-Christian powers were matters of 'politics and morality' ('Politik und Sittlichkeit') only, see August Wilhelm Heffter, *Das Europäische Völkerrecht der Gegenwart*, 3rd ed., Berlin: Verlag von E. H. Schröder, 1855, p. 14.

[142] See Heffter 1844, pp. 88–89, § 46. The sentence on the battle of Navarino was only added with the 3rd edition, published in 1855, see Heffter 1855, p. 92.

[143] Cited here after Heffter 1888, p. 18. This passage was gradually expanded as the book went through its respective editions, the reference to 'social human conscience' ('sociales Menschenbewusstsein') is not found in earlier editions, see, for example, Heffter 1855, p. 13.

[144] Ingo J. Hueck, 'Pragmatism, Positivism and Hegelianism in the Nineteenth Century', in: Michael Stolleis and Masaharu Yanagihara (eds.), *East Asian and European Perspectives on International Law*, Nomos: Baden-Baden 2004, p. 54.

[145] This is Nussbaum's translation of the title of Heffter's work, Nussbaum 1950, p. 230.

[146] But see Orakhelashvili 2006, p. 323.

[147] Heffter 1888, p. 23, § 7, for Geffcken's criticism, see p. 115, note 3.

(1845–1909), the foremost Russian international lawyer of the Czarist period.[148] He shared the premise of the particularity of international law, always considering his 'law of civilised nations' a *legal* justification for intervention in the affairs of states like Turkey, China, Japan and other Asian states, 'whenever the Christian population in such states is barbarously persecuted or slaughtered: In such cases intervention is always justified by the common religious interests and the dictates of humanity, that is the principles of natural law, which rule the relations between cultivated nations and the uncivilised'.[149] Yet Martens, whose name is forever associated with that cornerstone of International Humanitarian Law, the clause that bears his name, did not rest his consideration of the legality of the Great Power intervention in the Greek War of Independence on *this* interpretation of international law, despite being an outspoke advocate of the legality of an 'intervention d'humanité'in a different context later on[150] – instead, Martens based his opinion of the legality of the Great Power involvement in the Greek War of Independence on an alleged, indisputable right to pursue national interests.[151] But this was not the view that was to dominate the reception of Great Power involvement in the Greek War of Independence in the years to come.

2.2.4 *The Intervention and the History of 'Humanitarian Intervention'*

The relevance of the Greek case for the history of a legal instrument of 'humanitarian intervention' is a product of its reception and result – the entry of Greece into international society as an independent state – rather than the events themselves. These have been portrayed and interpreted in the literature on international law in truly creative ways – as part of a project to create a law that conforms to expectations of morality and justice. One of the earliest treatments of the events from the perspective of an international law grounded on 'reason' (Vernunft) saw the intervention of the Great Powers justified because it was undertaken to protect 'evidently violated general human rights' (evident verletzte[r] Menschenrechte): While political discord in a foreign state was not to be judged by other countries, 'general human rights' were considered to be 'easily recognised by all reasonable people' and their evident violation a legal justification for intervention, according to Karl von Rotteck (1775–1840) and his 1834 'Lehrbuch des Vernunftrechts und der

---

[148] Lauri Mälksoo, 'The History of International Legal Theory in Russia: a Civilizational Dialogue with Europe', *European Journal of International Law* 2008, 19(1), p. 214.

[149] Martens 1883, p. 301.

[150] Friedrich Martens, 'Étude historique sur la politique russe dans la question d'Orient', IX *Revue de droit international et de législation comparée (RDI)* 1877, IX, 49, cited after Martti Koskenniemi, 'International Law in Europe: Between Tradition and Renewal', *European Journal of International Law* 2005, 16(1), pp. 113–114.

[151] Martens 1883, p. 282.

Staatswissenschaften'.[152] This principle, von Rotteck was certain, would have justified an intervention in favour of the 'barbarically treated Greek people' at a much
earlier point in time, and certainly did when the intervention eventually came.[153]

Von Rotteck represents the classic German school of liberal idealism and historicism, and was widely read in his time. As a 'political historian' (and politician), he
was intent on shaping public opinion; ultimately, he was relieved of his duties as a
professor for that very reason. Von Rotteck was a strong believer in reason (Vernunft)
as the source of all law and international law in particular.[154] State practice, he
admitted, might often be in violation of the principles of his law based on reason,
but this would only strengthen the legal order that would arise from future practice
abiding by the principles of the law he described.[155] His explicit reference to 'general
human rights' as a justification for intervention at a time when, it is widely held,[156]
international law did not even know the term, is a reflection more of his republican-
ism than it as a statement of the law as applied in this case. His concept of 'human
rights' was not contingent on providing equal rights to all humans, irrespective of
their religious beliefs, as von Rotteck's position on Jewish emancipation shows.[157]
Von Rotteck's opinion on the legality of 'humanitarian intervention' continued to
be cited in the literature on the subject, even by Raphael Lemkin, when he declared
'humanitarian interventions' of the past a link 'in one chain leading to the proclamation of genocide as an international crime by the United Nations', explicitly
naming 'Turkish abuses against the Greeks' as an instance where 'humanitarian
intervention' had been necessary and pointing to Karl von Rotteck as one the
'authorities who recognize the legality of humanitarian intervention'.[158] Yet in the
mainstream literature on 'humanitarian intervention', it is his son, Hermann von
Rotteck (1816–1845), who is (not always accurately) credited as the first author
'to undertake a systematic and comprehensive study of intervention'[159] and develop
'a theory of intervention on the ground of humanity'.[160]

Hermann von Rotteck may have been the first to discuss the question of 'humanitarian intervention' in a monograph on intervention, but he was hardly the first to
publish a systematic treatment of the question of intervention and he denied the

[152] Karl von Rotteck, *Lehrbuch des Vernunftrechts und der Staatswissenschaften*, Stuttgart: Franckh
1834, p. 40
[153] von Rotteck 1834, p. 41.
[154] von Rotteck 1834, p. 14.
[155] von Rotteck 1834, p. 15.
[156] e.g. Tomuschat 2008, p. 16.
[157] Heiko Haumann, '"Wir waren alle ein klein wenig antisemitisch": ein Versuch über historische Maßstäbe zur Beurteilung von Judengegnerschaft an den Beispielen Karl von Rotteck
und Jacob Burckhardt', *Schweizerische Zeitschrift für Geschichte* 2005, 55, 196–214.
[158] John Cooper, *Raphael Lemkin and the Struggle for the Genocide Convention*, Hampshire:
Palgrave Macmillan 2008, p. 237.
[159] Stowell 1921, p. 525.
[160] See: Brownlie 1963, p. 338; Chesterman 2001, pp. 39–40, both using an imprecise summary of
Stowell's characterisation of von Rotteck's work.

legality of 'humanitarian intervention', even where necessary: 'formal law' was to prevail over acting from morality.[161] Yet he was certain that, despite his explicit statement of the illegality of intervention to protect 'recognised human rights' (anerkannte Menschenrechte), the intervention to 'save Greek freedom' had been legal.[162] And the justification was found in Greece's alleged independence on account of its own declaration and the ability to request foreign support,[163] thus echoing a position held by Vattel a century before and far from the 'humanitarian' justification regularly attributed to von Rotteck.

A similar judgement might be passed on what has been considered an 'original specification' of 'humanitarian intervention',[164] Henry Wheaton's characterisation of the intervention in the Greek War of Independence as 'a further illustration of the principles of international law authorizing such an interference, not only where the interests and safety of the other powers are immediately affected by the internal transactions of a particular state, but where the general interests of humanity are infringed by the excesses of a barbarous and despotic government'.[165] Wheaton is frequently cited as an authority for the claim that 'humanitarian interventions' were legal in the nineteenth century:[166] To an English-speaking audience, Wheaton was the definitive commentator on nineteenth century international law,[167] so the conditions for this opinion of the legality of 'humanitarian intervention' require closer inspection.

Henry Wheaton (1758–1848) was one of the first American international lawyers. His 'Elements of International Law', first published in 1836, was – with the help of different editors – reprinted well into the twentieth century. The book's reputation was also recognised in the non-English speaking world,[168] with translations available in French as early as 1848 and later in Japanese as well as in Chinese. His conception of international law was explicitly 'particular', and rested on the assumption that international law as the law of 'civilized nations' could only apply, where the shared Christian religion was available as its foundation. It was decidedly *not* universal: '[T]he international law of the civilized, Christian nations of Europe and America, is one thing; and that which governs the intercourse of the Mohammedan nations of the East with each other, and with Christians, is another and a very different

---

[161] von Rotteck 1845, p. 36.

[162] von Rotteck 1845, p. 40.

[163] von Rotteck 1845, p. 42.

[164] Howard Adelman, 'Humanitarian Intervention: The Case of the Kurds', *International Journal of Refugee Law* 1992, 4(1), p. 18, quoting Richard B. Lillich.

[165] Wheaton 1836, p. 91; Wheaton 1846, p. 112.

[166] e.g. Jean-Pierre L. Fonteyne, 'The Customary International Law Doctrine of Humanitarian Intervention: Its Current Validity under The UN Charter', *California Western International Law Journal* 1974, p. 203.

[167] Janis 2004, p. 128.

[168] See: Ziegler 2007, p. 190.

thing'.[169] Wheaton was a contemporary to the Battle of Navarino, which, in December 1827 he described as 'the opening scene of a great drama, which is to be enacted in the Eastern world'. He criticised the approach of the Western European powers in a private letter to American President Adams soon afterwards (5 January 1828):

> If the Christian powers had acknowledged the independence of the Greeks three years ago, and labored in good faith to consolidate a real Grecian State to take the place of the Ottoman Empire in the balance of power, they would have adopted a much more sensible course than this their tardy interference, which will probably redound to the advantage of Russia only.[170]

What authorised an 'intervention in the interest of humanity' according to Wheaton, then, was not international law as a legal regime covering the relations between the Great Powers and the Ottoman Empire, but the law that set them *apart* – the law of 'superior humanity, justice, and liberality' of the Christian nations of Europe.[171] It justified 'humanity' – as represented by the European powers – to intervene against 'this cruel warfare, prosecuted for six years against a civilized and Christian people', because the 'interference of the Christian powers to put an end to this bloody contest' was called for by 'the rights of human nature, wantonly outraged'.[172] Wheaton saw moral progress far beyond that seen in the rest of the world in the history of Christian Europe (and the United States), and the international law of the 'civilized, Christian nations' was but an expression of this. In this view, it was clearly not a violation of the law that applied to the Ottoman Empire as well as the European powers that served as the justification for the intervention, but of the law that was a result of European superiority. It is obvious that this view of international law was not shared by the diplomats and statesmen involved in the intervention, yet Wheaton's interpretation of the events was later quoted as an authoritative description of the facts and the law by other writers.[173]

According to research into the history of international law carried out in the 1960s, Wheaton was the first writer in English who utilised the phrase 'interference when the general interests of humanity are infringed by the excesses of barbarous and despotic governments'[174] as an expression of a nascent theory of 'humanitarian intervention' in connection with the Greek War of Independence.

---

[169] Wheaton 1846, p. 40. The original text is identical, see: Wheaton 1836, p. 45.

[170] Henry Wheaton, *Elements of International Law*, 6th ed. by William Beach Lawrence, Boston: Little & Brown 1855, p. lxxxiv.

[171] Janis 2004, p. 44; Brett Bowden, 'The Colonial Origins of International Law. European Expansion and the Classical Standard of Civilization', *Journal of the History of International Law* 2005, 7(1), p. 16.

[172] Wheaton 1846, p. 114.

[173] e.g. Sheldon Amos, *Lectures on International Law*, London: Stevens and Sons 1874, pp. 40–41; Woolsey 1864, pp. 73–74.

[174] Lillich, comment, in: Lillich 1973, p. 25.

Despite the apparent creativity of Wheaton's position, John Stuart Mill, the British philosopher more commonly associated with the defence of the principle of non-intervention,[175] was able to state in 1849 that a 'new doctrine' had been acted upon in the 'interference between Greece and Turkey at Navarino' – the doctrine,

> that whenever two countries, or two parts of the same country, are engaged in war, the war either continues long undecided, or threatens to be decided in a way involving consequences repugnant to humanity or to the general interest, other countries have a right to step in; to settle among themselves what they consider reasonable terms of accommodation, and if these are not accepted to interfere by force, and compel the recusant party to submit to the mandate.[176]

Mill is thought to have acquired his copy of Wheaton's *Elements of International Law* shortly after the American Civil War, 'in the shape of its 1866 (8th) edition',[177] yet he seems to have followed the development of the discussion in the field of international law, 'which was, according to Mill, not law properly so called',[178] much earlier. By 1859, he was already confident in stating that 'it seems now to be an admitted doctrine' of 'what is called international law' that in the case of 'a protracted civil war, in which the contending parties are so equally balanced that there is no probability of a speedy issue: or if there is, the victorious side cannot hope to keep down the vanquished but by severities repugnant to humanity', other states might be justified in intervening. Again, he referenced 'the interference of the European Powers between Greece and Turkey' as a case in point.[179] While Mill's arguments for the justification of this intervention can also be read in the context of his commitment to self-determination,[180] and other authors later more poignantly stressed the 'humanitarian' dimension of the events, it is clear that at no point did the Great Powers themselves claim to be *legally justified* to take *forcible* measures and intervene for the sake of a (universal) 'humanity' or 'human rights'.

Current writing on international law and 'humanitarian intervention' continues to claim this historic episode as an early example of an intervention to 'militarily

---

[175] See: Michael Doyle, 'J. S. Mill on Nonintervention and Intervention', in: Stefano Recchia and Jennifer M. Welsh (eds.), *Just and Unjust Military Intervention, European Thinkers from Vitoria to Mill*, Cambridge University Press 2013, pp. 263–287.

[176] John Stuart Mill, Vindication of the French Revolution of February 1848, in Reply to Lord Brougham and Others (1849), in Dissertations and Discussions: Political, Philosophical, and Historical, Vol. III, New York: Henry Holt and Coö 1873, p. 50.

[177] Georgios Varouxakis, *Liberty Abroad, J. S. Mill on International Relations*, Cambridge University Press 2013, p. 27.

[178] Varouxakis 2013, p. 22.

[179] John Stuart Mill, A Few Words on Intervention, *Fraser's Magazine*, December 1859, cited according to John Stuart Mill, *The Collected Works of John Stuart Mill, Volume XXI – Essays on Equality, Law, and Education*, ed. John M. Robson, Introduction by Stefan Collini, University of Toronto Press 1984, p. 121.

[180] Doyle 2013, p. 277.

defend human rights',[181] while even the most ardent critics of such a practice feel the need to accuse the 'interventionist powers' of displaying 'remarkable sanctimony and hypocrisy in presenting a morality play'.[182] However, it seems more appropriate to view this as an early example of international lawyers creating a narrative of historic events to fit an agenda, to create a false distinction between the lawful and the lawless. To support the view that 'human rights' were militarily defended in the course of the War of Independence, Navarino needs to be seen as an execution of the London Treaty, but this is a fiction based on later interpretations of the events. As Mill described it: 'Barbarians have no rights as a nation, except a right to such treatment as may, at the earliest possible period, fit them for becoming one. The only moral laws for the relation between a civilized and a barbarous government are the universal rules of morality between man and man'.[183]

As more and more authors from a growing number of countries entered the debate, this interpretation – so attractive to believers in progress and justice as driving factors in the development of international law – was to be reinforced from (almost) all sides. One example is the position of Friedrich Geffcken (1830–1896), published in the 1889 four-volume 'Handbook on International Law' ('Handbuch des Völkerrechts'), who – according to Koskenniemi – was among a group of early commentators on international law who showed little awareness of the moral ambivalence of the civilising mission of international law, focusing instead on a justification of Germany's claim to the role of a Great Power.[184] Yet Geffcken, who also was the editor of the posthumous editions of Heffter's well-respected treatise, based his whole concept of international law on the 'necessary' distinction between a law for Christian nations and a law for Muslims. The disparity between the religious, moral and legal convictions between 'our' Christian beliefs and those of the Muslims made it 'impossible' to place both under the same law.[185] For Geffcken, the legal justification for the intervention in the Greek War of Independence rested on this distinction.[186] The 'Handbuch des Völkerrechts' aspired to present a realistic overview of existing international law,[187] and it can be hardly surprising that Geffcken's position – though by this time in conflict with the Treaty of Paris – was mirrored in the writings of other German authors.[188]

In the French speaking world, Antoine Rougier (1877–1927) built his influential 'theory of humanitarian intervention' (the title of his often cited article is 'La

---

[181] Wilfried Hinsch and Dieter Janssen, *Menschenrechte militärisch schützen – Ein Plädoyer für humanitäre Interventionen*, Munich: C. H. Beck 2006, p. 18, my translation.

[182] Menon 2016, p. 78.

[183] Mill 1859, cited according to Mill 1984, p. 119.

[184] Koskenniemi 2002, p. 109.

[185] Heffter 1888, p. 115, note 3.

[186] Geffcken 1889, p. 161.

[187] Ulrich Scupin, 'Völkerrechtsgeschichte', in: Hans-Jürgen Schlochauer (ed.), *Wörterbuch des Völkerrechts*, 2nd ed., Vol. II, Berlin: De Gruyter 1962, p. 738.

[188] e.g. Hartmann 1878.

Théorie de l'intervention d'Humanité') around an idealised version of the Greek case. While Rougier admitted that no right to 'humanitarian intervention' was recognised at the time of the intervention, he saw this mainly as an explanation for the additional grounds of justification put forward by the Great Powers and was confident that the humanitarian motive was elemental in the decision to use force.[189] Rougier's starting point was the distinction between 'civilized' states and nations in the 'sphere of "humanité barbare"', as Rougier characterised the 'non-civilized world', with their different approaches to guarantees of individual freedom. It was precisely this distinction that led Rougier to want to define the conditions for the legality of intervention by the 'civilized' states for the sake of 'humanity'. The intervention of the Great Powers in Greece was one of the rare examples of a *forcible* intervention to fit Rougier's design and – according to Rougier – manifested itself in the battle of Navarino.[190] Just like Wheaton and Mill, Rougier ignored the contemporary view on the Greek insurgency as a reciprocal orgy of violence in favour of the romanticised view of the Philhellennes. This view, in which genocidal violence is only a problem of (civilized) law's (uncivilised) 'other', continues to be the prevailing view in all attempts to consider 'humanitarian intervention' and its substitute, the 'responsibility to protect', a legal instrument to prevent or stop such violence. For Rougier, at least, this made sense, as the 'humanity' he spoke of constituted itself under the law. Rougier developed a framework in which guidelines were laid down to ensure that future 'interventions in the name of humanity' would serve not only individual states' interests, but a greater goal of controlling 'barbarous states' for the sake of the rights of all mankind.[191] Though in no small part based on the intervention undertaken by Christian powers at the expense of the Muslim Ottoman Empire in the Greek War of Independence, Rougier insisted that his 'intervention in the name of humanity' was something other than an intervention on religious grounds.[192] It was, Rougier argued, one of the essential functions of any state to apply this 'droit humain', and it required states to fulfil certain functions towards individuals, including the 'functions' of protection, justice and moral and material development. Failure to fulfil these responsibilities was a failure to live up to a state's legal responsibilities, as there is, according to Rougier, no legal obligation without responsibility. The theory of the 'droit humain', then, recognised the existence of a

---

[189] Rougier 1910, p. 473: 'C'était bien la raison d'humanité, dans la plus large acception du mot, le souci tout ensemble de la paix de l'Europe et de sa dignité morale qui dictaient aux puissances cette intervention, expropriant la Turquie de ses prérogatives souveraines, dans l'intérêt de l'Europe et de la civilisation. Mais la raison d'humanité n'était point considérée encore à cette époque comme une juste cause d'intervention, et le traité de Londres la mentionne timidement en dernier lieu après avoir faire ressortir les raisons d'ordre politique et personnel que les gouvernements signataires pouvaient avoir d'agir'.

[190] Rougier 1910, p. 511.

[191] Rougier 1910, p. 524.

[192] Rougier 1910, p. 472: 'L'intervention en matiére de religion est chose nettement différente de l'intervention d'humanité'.

'société humaine' governed by a law eventually identified by Rougier as 'the law of solidarity'.[193] Rougier drew on the writings of the Belgian jurist Egide Arntz (1812–1884) and the concept of a 'droit humain', the 'law of humanity' developed by the French Professor of International Law Antoine Pillet (1857–1926). As so many others, Pillet was convinced that 'the European ideas were a reflection of the advanced degree of European civilization'.[194] International law, as an expression of this advanced degree, was not to be applied to non-European states in the same way, as no interdependence of the kind found among European states existed between them and non-European states with lesser degrees of civilisation.[195] In other words, intervening in the name of a 'droit humain' meant taking 'international law' to a place were it previously did not (fully) apply. In a way, this is the essence of the doctrine of 'intervention d'humanité': it entrusted the 'civilised' nations of Europe with the 'responsibility to protect' 'humanity' from the misrule of 'less civilised' states – and thought them legally entitled to do so by virtue of their own standing.[196] Yet Rougier accepted that the Greek case was not actually an instance where such a right was exercised and the 'humanitarian' justification was relied upon only timidly.[197]

This characterisation of the Greek War of Independence as a clash between (European) civilisation and (Ottoman) barbarians, between law and 'non-law' is the recurring theme of the representation of these events in the legal literature on 'humanitarian intervention'. The narratives presented by international lawyers pay no attention to the fact that perceptions of the struggle between Greeks and Ottomans were fuelled by European perceptions of the Ottomans as 'barbarians', which greatly romanticised the Greeks and overlooked the savage acts committed on their side. The Ottomans were routinely seen as 'bloodthirsty wild beasts', but Andrew Wheatcroft has pointed out that at that time, in the Peloponnese, the Greeks may have fitted this stereotype better than the Ottomans.[198] The

---

[193] Rougier 1910, p. 492: 'On peut dire que l'État a pour fonction essentielle de dégager et d'appliquer le droit humain, et que ce droit humain impose à l'État d'accomplir certaines fonctions vis-à-vis des individus: fonction de protection; fonction de justice, fonction de développement matériel et moral. Le manquement – à ce devoir entrainera pour l'État une responsabilité d'un genre particulier, une responsabilité devant l'humanité, car il ne peut exister d'obligation juridique sans responsabilité. La théorie du droit humain reconnaît l'existence d'une société humaine primordiale et d'une loi qui conditionne son activité, mais sans arriver à préciser quelle est celle loi. ... [C]elle loi est la solidarité'.

[194] Koskenniemi 2002, p. 282, note 67.

[195] Pillet 1894, p. 27. Pillet is adamant that the Treaty of Paris of 1856 changed nothing in this regard for the Ottoman Empire.

[196] This point was already made by me in Mark Swatek-Evenstein, 'Reconstituting Humanity as Responsibility – The "Turn to History" in International Law and the Responsibility to Protect', in: Julia Hoffmann and André Nollkaemper (eds.), Responsibility to Protect – From Principle to Practice, Amsterdam: Pallas Publications 2012, p. 53.

[197] Rougier 1910, pp. 473–474.

[198] Wheatcroft 2004, p. 254.

interpretation of the Greek War of Independence as a fight between 'our' civilisation and the barbaric 'other', not the 'reciprocal orgy of violence' it in fact was, dominated the debate in international law in its formative years in the late nineteenth century. No attention was paid to the fact that the London Treaty confirmed a separation of communities on the basis of nationality, thus legitimising the very concept that had enflamed the conflict. Instead, the conflict was framed in religious terms, thereby emphasising ties between the intervening powers and the local population that were hardly decisive for the events in Greece. The characterisation of the intervention as a legally justified, civilisational act of 'humanity' is, as Ian Brownlie dismissed the characterisation of the action as a 'humanitarian intervention', 'ex post factoism'.[199] But it is also the creative act of the institutionalisation of a legal argument, operating, as Anne Orford has characterised the legal geography of 'humanitarian intervention', 'not only, or even principally, in the field of state systems, rationality and facts, but also in the field of identification, imagination, subjectivity and emotion'.[200]

International lawyers often cited as supporters of the existence of a right of 'humanitarian intervention', however, have not always relied solely on appealing to a sense of connectedness with the Greeks as a source for the justification of the intervention. For example, Augustus Stapleton (1800–1880), sometimes cited as an authority on the question of 'humanitarian intervention',[201] held that

> there are cases in which forcible interference with the internal concerns of an independent State is justifiable; and those cases are when the condition of those internal concerns is the cause of external injury of sufficient gravity to justify war upon the State inflicting it. Such were the grounds of justification of the Greek treaty in 1827, into which the principle of applying force entered.[202]

Only in retrospect and with insufficient attention to detail does this turn into a statement of the legality of 'humanitarian intervention'.

The emphasis on the separation of spheres of 'civilisation' and 'barbarism' continued to dominate the perception of the intervention and its legality well into the twentieth century. As late as 1918, a German university awarded a PhD in law for a dissertation on intervention in international law that categorically stated that every state could treat religious matters within its own border as it saw fit according to the religious beliefs prevailing in that country. Yet the young lawyer, about whom nothing else is known, was just as certain that there could be no doubt about the

---

[199] Ian Brownlie, 'Humanitarian Intervention', in: John Norton Moore (ed.), *Law and Civil War in the Modern World*, Baltimore: The Johns Hopkins University Press 1974, p. 220.

[200] Orford 2003, p. 77.

[201] International Commission on Intervention and State Sovereignty 2001, Suppl. Vol., p. 16 with note 4, p. 24.

[202] Stapleton 1866, p. 14.

legality of an intervention where Christian subjects in non-Christian countries had to suffer barbarous persecution and slaughter.[203]

This long lasting division of separate spheres of different legal regimes is religious in origin and character, and its gradual and celebrated 'secularisation' during the course of the nineteenth century appears less like the loss of the significance of 'Christian values', than a gradual 'conversion' of 'Christian values' into 'universal' values of 'humanity'. With the Greek War of Independence, the image of the 'terrible Turk', dubious as it is,[204] replaced the Ottoman Empire as a power integral to the European state system at the beginning of the nineteenth century.[205] A certain perception of the events of the War of Independence nurtured the belief in the barbarism of the Ottomans and shaped their perception for the century to come. At the same time, the erosion of power following the loss of Greece became a dominating political factor within the Ottoman Empire, leading the way for a radicalisation of policies.[206] Such were the conditions for the development of an (in part) imagined CORPUS IURIS PUBLICI ORIENTALIS, a politico-legal system for controlling the break-up of the Ottoman Empire under the collective authority of the European Great Powers.[207]

Within the discipline of international law, assessments of the legality of the intervention as a 'humanitarian intervention' began over time to lose some of the distinctions that had been essential to the original writers. The influential treatise on international law by Lassa Oppenheim (1858–1919) is sometimes referenced as if Oppenheim himself had been a proponent of the legality of 'humanitarian intervention' at the beginning of the twentieth century and had treated the Greek case accordingly.[208] However, for Oppenheim himself, it was unclear whether such a right actually existed, and he asked 'who can undertake to lay down a hard-and-fast rule with regard to the amount of inhumanity on the part of a government what would justify intervention according to the Law of Nations?'[209] Only in subsequent editions did the line between what was politically possible and established law,

---

[203] Josef Tenbaum, *Die völkerrechtliche Intervention, insbesondere ihre Arten*, Greifswald: Julius Abel 1918, p. 36.

[204] See generally: Said 1978.

[205] See Georg Friedrich von Martens, *A Compendium of the Law of Nations*, English translation by William Cobbett, Pall Mall: Cobbett and Morgan 1802, p. 5 note *.

[206] Bonney 2004, p. 150.

[207] Malcolm D. Evans, *Religious Liberty and International Law in Europe*, Cambridge University Press 1997, p. 64.

[208] Pauer 1985, p. 34, fn. 33 and p. 39; Grewe 2000, p. 493 ('or at least conceded the validity of humanitarian intervention'); Abiew 1999, p. 41. By contrast, Leo Strisower, *Der Krieg und die Völkerrechtsordnung*, Wien: Manz 1919, pp. 121–122, fn 32, and Hermann Mosler, *Die Intervention im Völkerrecht*, Berlin: Trittsch & Huther 1937, p. 61, fn. 83, considered Oppenheim to reject such a right.

[209] Oppenheim 1905. p. 187, § 138; Oppenheim 1912, p. 195, § 138.

drawn so clearly by Oppenheim,[210] become blurred. Under the hands of Hersch Lauterpacht the prognosis for the future eventually turned into a retroactive description of the state of the law.[211] Oppenheim's status as a legal authority was thus transferred to a more recent epoch of international law, without reference to his own sovereignty-based concept of international law.[212] Attributing Lauterpacht's opinion to Oppenheim creates the false impression of a continuity in views on 'humanitarian intervention' – sometimes deliberately, sometimes more likely accidentally.[213]

Yet there remains an appeal to treat an episode that historians are now considering a contender for an early case of 'ethnic cleansing' (the transfer of the Greek Muslim population to other parts of the Ottoman Empire)[214] and brutality of genocidal dimensions on the part of the Greeks[215] as an example of a 'self-less', humanitarian Great Power intervention for the sake of an embattled population. While historians are becoming more and more interested in the subject of 'humanitarian intervention', their explorations into the details of the historic event that is the Greek War of Independence and the Great Power involvement are becoming more nuanced.[216] Yet, in international law, the narrative of a British diplomacy with humanitarian motives, led on by public pressure and a desire to keep Russian ambitions in check, culminating in the Battle of Navarino to free the Greeks from Ottoman cruelty, continues to be a returning point of departure. The resurrection

[210] Mathias Schmoeckel, 'The Story of a Success. Lassa Oppenheim and his "International Law"', in: Michael Stolleis and Masaharu Yanagihara (eds.), *East Asian and European Perspectives on International Law*, Baden-Baden: Nomos 2004, p. 91.

[211] Lassa Oppenheim, *International Law – A Treatise*, 5th ed., edited by Hersch Lauterpacht, London: Longmans, Green and Co 1935, p. 255, § 137; Oppenheim 1955, p. 313, § 137.

[212] See Schmoeckel 2004, p. 111.

[213] In his chapter on European Great Power intervention in the nineteenth century, War Studies scholar John Bew uses an (unpublished) paper by Nicholas Onuf, available on the Internet, for a quote on the intervention in the Greek War of Independence as having 'often been interpreted as the first example of humanitarian intervention' (p. 119 with fn. 9) and attributes this (via Onuf) to 'See, for example, L. Oppenheim in *International Law: A Treatise*, Vol. I: *Peace*, edited by H. Lauterpacht, 8th ed. (London: Longman Green 1995)'. John Bew, '"From an umpire to a competitor": Castlereagh, Canning and the issue of international intervention in the wake of the Napoleonic Wars', in: Brendan Simms and D. J. B. Trim (eds.), Humanitarian Intervention – A History, Cambridge University Press 2011. As most scholars familiar with at least the basic history of international law will know, this footnote makes a mockery of proper research. The fact that a secondary source was used to give reference to another source is of minor importance, in comparison, even though students are advised to avoid such use of sources from the beginning of the first semester and it is remarkable that – on top of everything – the reference given as Onuf's does not even match the cited text: Onuf actually references Oppenheim 1955, p. 312 – so Bew effectively updated his footnote to reflect the British publisher of Lauterpacht's book and made a typo when copying the year of publication. What *really* matters is that Oppenheim had no hand in the 8th edition of – what is here referred to as – 'International Law: A Treatise', having died decades before this edition was ever published. The statement attributed to Oppenheim is, in fact, Lauterpacht's.

[214] Schwartz 2013, p. 241.

[215] Schulz 2011, p. 90.

[216] e.g. Rodogno 2012; Schwartz 2013.

of this one-sided view and claiming the Greek case as an example in a gradual translation of a 'widely held moral principle of civilian immunity' into a 'shared ethical norm'[217] is a clear appeal to the validity and legitimacy of the framework developed by nineteenth century international lawyers as a tool for resolving such and similar conflicts as they continue to trouble the world. This 'will to continuity', instead of uncovering the lack of reciprocity at the heart of basic rules of international law, offers a narrative that supports international law's claim to justice.

This has been the underlying aim of every attempt to identify the development of a right of 'humanitarian intervention' that begins with the Greek War of Independence in 1823–1827. When the subject aroused the renewed (and limited) interest of some international law scholars after World War II, it was in an attempt to define the ground rules for the 'international protection of human rights' which sought to use the Greek case as a starting point for the claim of 'humanitarian intervention' as a customary right to enforce human rights.[218] The Greek War of Independence's 'second life' in the history of 'humanitarian intervention' after World War II was based on a rather incomplete version of the historical events, which soon returned to the very skewed version of nineteenth century narratives. Now using a more modern language, the event is presented as an example of nations acting upon 'humanitarian considerations',[219] because it suggests it was 'widely accepted that atrocities committed during the Greek struggle for independence caused shock and disbelief in many European countries'.[220] Such accounts are almost exclusive to the literature on international law in general, or 'humanitarian intervention' in particular. National histories of the region or histories of the Balkan do mention the 'Battle of Navarino', but regularly make no mention of any alleged motive or justification. The Greek narrative of national liberation centres around the eruption of the insurgency, not its conclusion through outside intervention, making Navarino little more than an accident and a footnote, except for the construction of a law of civilised nations, or a 'just' international law.

In recent years, the image of Navarino as a 'humanitarian intervention' has been reinforced, despite all the evidence of a more complicated history. Treating Navarino and the surrounding developments as acts of humanitarianism legitimises the 'dark side of the nation state' (Philipp Ther) and the treatment of Muslims, which continued into modern times. The Christian intolerance and wanton violence against the civilian population that defined the Greek War of Independence[221] are downplayed in favour of more romantic narratives of a fight between the guilty and

---

[217] Bellamy 2012, p. 42.
[218] Ganji 1962.
[219] Reisman and McDougal, 'Humanitarian Intervention to Protect the Ibos, 1968 Memorandum', reprinted in: Lillich 1973, p. 180.
[220] Tams 2005, p. 92.
[221] Ther 2011, pp. 60–61.

the innocent, even where the 'civilized-barbarians binary' that dominated the discourse on 'humanitarian intervention' in the nineteenth century is correctly identified.[222]

Navarino as a 'humanitarian intervention' is part of the folklore of the teleological narrative of 'progress' in (and of) international law, an appeal to the law's supposedly obvious relationship to justice, which accounts in part for the attractiveness of that narrative of progress towards human rights protection. Inherent in such narratives is the belief that international law contributed to a positive outcome of these events in some meaningful way. This can be seen in the way some of the first Indian authors on international law presented the subject of 'humanitarian intervention' in books published after India's independence. In Manesh Prasad Tandon's 'Public International Law', published in several editions since 1952, for example, the question of 'humanitarian intervention' is treated by introducing a (short) list of allegedly legal interventions on the ground of humanity, starting with the intervention in the Greek War of Independence 'on the ground of abominable atrocities committed in the war which had shocked the conscience of Europe', the interventions of 1860 and 1878 (discussed in Sections 2.4 and 2.6, respectively) to the 'strong protests from several nations' evoked by the 'persecution of the Jewish community during Hitler's regime', which, according to Tandon, 'was referred as a charge against the Nazi war criminals at the Nuremberg Trial'.[223] Similarly, in 'International Law and Organization' by Payappilly Itty Varghese, published in 1952, the narrative on the intervention on grounds of humanity is reduced to a mention of the interventions of the 'Christian nations of Europe' in the 'affairs of Turkey, when the Christian minorities were ill-treated' and a rather obscure reference to what later would be known as the Holocaust.[224] The attraction of creating a narrative of 'humanitarian interventions' that connects the fights against alleged injustice of the past to the fight against the symbol of absolute evil, Auschwitz, continues to hold sway.[225] The following chapters will explore this relationship further.

---

[222] Heraclidis and Dialla 2015, ch. 6.

[223] Tandon 1966, p. 198.

[224] Payappilly Itty Varghese, *International Law and Organization*, Lucknow: Eastern Book Company 1952: 'In the conflict between the rebellious Greeks and Turkey (1827) when the Greeks were treated with cruelty by the Turks, other European nations intervened to protect the Greeks. When the Jewish community was ill-treated and subjected to discrimination by Hitler's Germany there was great resentment and protest from outside nations'.

[225] See Fernandon R. Tesón, *Humanitarian Intervention*, 3rd ed., Ardsley: Transnational Publishers 2005, p. 227, claiming that World War II was the 'paradigm of a just war' and 'best explained as a humanitarian effort, at least in part'.

2.3 THE PRINCIPLE OF NON-INTERVENTION IN MID-NINETEENTH-CENTURY INTERNATIONAL LAW

2.3.1 Introduction

After Napoleon's removal from power, Europe enjoyed a period of more or less peaceful co-existence that was not particularly threatened by the Greek War of Independence. Early twentieth century theorists on international law would mark the year 1830 as the date for a significant turn towards a principle of non-intervention as a cornerstone of the international system.[226] In the United States, the Monroe Doctrine had established a local version of the principle even earlier. This 1823 Doctrine famously declared all interference of European states in the matters of the American continents illegal, just as it prohibited interventions by American states in the internal affairs of European states. The Doctrine did, however, allow for interventions by the United States in 'matters relating to the American continent', that is, into the internal affairs of other states on the continent. Well into the twentieth century, the United States considered the Monroe Doctrine the basis of a legal justification for interventions as an 'international police force' in the affairs of the American continents.[227] American writers on international law championed a corresponding right of the Great Powers to intervene as necessitated by their leading roles in the development of international law and society.[228] Such a right was held to be compatible with a principle of non-intervention, as it was said to rest in the right of self-preservation.[229]

In its other function, the doctrine served as a deterrent for intervention of the former colonial powers from Europe; it gained in importance during the nineteenth century in the recently established states of Latin America.[230] A specific Latin American tradition of the rejection of the legality of any type of intervention rested on the Monroe Doctrine to declare the illegality of any type of use of force to secure payment on foreign debts, the Drago Doctrine of the early twentieth century.[231] The Latin American approach was guided by what Lara Obregón has called a 'will to civilization', a will to be included. The Latin American states considered themselves the legitimate bearers of their own idea of civilisation, resting on both their own

---

[226] Winfield 1922–1923; Mosler 1937, p. 30.

[227] Neff 2005, p. 222.

[228] Wheaton 1846, pp. 102–112.

[229] Kent and Abdy 1866, pp. 46, 90; Halleck 1861, p. 84, IV/§ 7, p. 340, XIV/§ 22.

[230] Peter Malanczuk, 'Monroe Doctrine', in: Rudolf Bernhardt (ed.), *Encyclopedia of Public International Law*, Vol. 7, Amsterdam: North Holland 1984, p. 340.

[231] Hans von Frisch, 'Drago-Doktrin', in: Karl Strupp (Ed.), *Wörterbuch des Völkerrechts und der Diplomatie*, Vol. I, Berlin: De Gruyter 1924, p. 252.

experiences and achievements as well as the adaption of European principles and ideals.[232] Their status as independent states was to be safeguarded by international law, a law that would protect their independence and freedom from intervention by former colonial powers and reign in their power through the application of legal standards. It was an approach that would be repeated in the years after 1945. The willingness, for example, of Indian authors to include narratives of (European) 'humanitarian intervention' in their overviews of the development of international law as examples of the 'moral' character of international law,[233] demonstrates the power of the European narrative of a 'moral' international law that would be applied equally according to objective legal standards even in places which had previously been denied equality. During decolonialisation, the newly independent states attempted to use international law to challenge established relations of power only to find their attempts 'subsumed within a pervasive rationality that successfully made a claim for the universality of a particular of "provincial" set of values originating in and congenial to the North',[234] again showing that the 'will to be included' follows the 'pull of the mainstream' (Koskenniemi) and would not undermine the law's power and claim to legitimacy, even if the results of the application of the law frustrated the motives of invoking the law in the first place.

Within Europe, the independence of new nation states also influenced the development of the system of international law. It began to lose the characteristics of a family law-based system of interdependent states ruled by related members of one family of monarchs. German and Italian writers, in particular, built a system of international law around a principle of non-intervention as the necessary conclusion of international law's function to guarantee state sovereignty, which largely corresponds to today's perceptions that nineteenth century international law was dominated by the dogma of absolute sovereignty. Yet even in the German perspective, this left room for the existence of a 'right of intervention – it all depends on clarifying the cases in which it can be exercised'.[235] By the mid-nineteenth century, seemingly opposing ideas of international law were debated within the discipline: On the one hand, international law was thought to guarantee that 'all those actions of a State which are internal, are free'.[236] On the other hand, all states were thought to be bound by a 'Standard of 'Civilisation', which other states might be entitled to enforce.[237] As early as the end of the first half of the nineteenth century, a vision

---

[232] Liliana Obregón, 'Completing Civilization: Creole Consciousness and International Law in Nineteenth-Century Latin America', in: Anne Orford (ed.), *International Law and its Others*, Cambridge University Press 2006, pp. 247–264.

[233] e.g. Tandon 1966, p. 198.

[234] Sundhya Pahuja, *Decolonising International Law*, Cambridge University Press 2011, quote from p. 2.

[235] Geffcken 1889, p. 134.

[236] Mamiani 1860, p. 190.

[237] Johann C. Bluntschli, *Das moderne Völkerrecht der civilisirten Staten*, Nördlingen: C. H. Beck 1868, p. 268, § 478: 'Werden in Folge der Verfassungskämpfe das allgemein als nothwendig

emerged of how to connect these competing functions of international law. James Reddie (1773–1852), a now largely forgotten Scottish advocate whose 'Inquiries In International Law' was once the prescribed text for students of international law at the University of Toronto,[238] and who was frequently cited by authors like Lauterpacht and Oppenheim, developed the following framework:

> So long as the actions of a people mainly concern the internal welfare of the state, other nations, [reference to exceptional, treaty-based cases omitted] have neither right to interpose their influence, nor occasion to trouble them. But if the arrangements or preparations, of a people, bear immediate reference to the society of nations, of which it is a member, or are of such nature, as to excite anxiety for the general tranquillity and security, other states are entitled to be watchful and on their guard, (. . .). [T]hese other nations, particularly those more interested, are, by the natural and consuetudinary international law of modern Europe, fully entitled to demand an explanation, with regard to the object of such measures, and the removal of any ground for apprehension on account of them.[239]

This understanding already gives an indication of how the growing uneasiness over the relationship between the developing system of international law and 'morality, religion and reason'[240] might be tamed – by defining (international) law as a bond between nations, coming together in a 'society' of shared values ('general tranquility and security'). Here, law is the result of its environment, and its purpose is to guarantee security and the status quo, not to bring about justice.

The transformation of 'sovereignty' from a quality defining the sovereign to one of the characteristics of the state[241] had freed positive international law from the constraints, but also the guarantees of what might be just or unjust according to natural law (was 'nach denen Göttlichen geschriebenen und natürlichen auch menschlichen Rechten recht oder unrecht seyn').[242] International lawyers at this time had become aware of the possibility that law was no longer created by 'naturally just' sovereigns alone, but by nations capable of infringing upon natural law. Defining international law as an expression of a certain 'Standard of 'Civilisation' was a tool to re-connect positive international law with ideas of justice and natural law. But by the middle of the nineteenth century, state practice did not yet present a clear or uniform picture, as the action undertaken by the United Kingdom and

---

anerkannte Menschenrecht oder das Völkerrecht verletzt, dann wird auch eine Intervention zum Schutze desselben aus denselben Gründen gerechtfertigt, wie das Einschreiten der civilisierten Staaten überhaupt bei gemeingefährlichen Rechtsverletzungen'.

[238] Ronald St John Macdonald, 'Teaching of International Law in Canada', *Canadian Yearbook of International Law* 1974, 12, p. 102.

[239] Reddie 1842, pp. 192–193. spelling of tranquillity in original source.

[240] von Kaltenborn von Stachau 1847, p. 228.

[241] David Kennedy, 'International Law in the Nineteenth Century: History of an Illusion', *Nordic Journal of International Law* 1996, 65, p. 406, has shown that at the time, the term 'sovereign' was in more frequent use in the writings on international law than the term 'sovereignty'.

[242] Moser 1750, preface without page number, no. 3.

France in reaction to events in the Kingdom of the Two Sicilies demonstrates. This case is unusual in the history of the evolution of the doctrine of 'humanitarian intervention' for at least two reasons: First, it has received little mention in the literature of 'classic' international law in the nineteenth century, as it was only introduced to the discussion through Antoine Rougier's ground-breaking 'Theory of Humanitarian Intervention' in the early twentieth century.[243] Second, it is one of those rare occasions where nations faced each other in the heart of Europe, their status as Europeans without doubt, unlike those interventions in the European 'borderlands' of the Ottoman Empire.

2.3.2 *The 'Intervention' in the Kingdom of the Two Sicilies, 1856*

On the occasion of French and British attempts to influence government policy of the King of Naples in the Kingdom of the Two Sicilies, the question of the legality of intervention and the scope of duty to let other states handle their 'own affairs' presented itself on the highest diplomatic level. Ferdinand II reigned in the Kingdom of the Two Sicilies like a despot, arresting, torturing and interning political opponents without trial. The United Kingdom and France initially responded with diplomatic representations. At the Paris Congress of 1856, Lord Clarendon, the British Foreign Secretary, declared that while Her Majesty's Government had to recognise that no government has the right to intervene in the internal affairs of another state, there were cases where an exception to the rule turned this principle into a right if not a duty of intervention:

> We do not want the peace to be disturbed, and there is no peace without justice; we are therefore compelled to express to the King of Naples the desire of the Congress for the improvement of his system of government – a desire which should not remain fruitless – and to request an amnesty in favour of such persons who have been sentenced or are detained without judgement for political reasons.[244]

In the spirit of this declaration, France and the United Kingdom mobilised their fleets for a show of force in the Mediterranean and diplomatic relations were momentarily put on hold. Among the few contemporary writers taking note of the event there was no unanimous opinion of the legality of the action undertaken by the United Kingdom and France, though there was a tendency to disapprove of the means and justification.[245] There is little mention of this episode in the later

---

[243] Rougier 1910, p. 475. This point is also made by Georges Scelle, *Precis du droit des gens*, Vol. II, Paris: Recueil Sirey 1934, p. 53.

[244] Cited after Grewe 2000, p. 491.

[245] Thomas Erskine Holland, Thomas Alfred Walker, and Wyndham Leigh Walker, *Lectures on International Law*, London: Sweet & Maxwell 1933, p. 108: 'philantropic excuses for intervention are viewed with suspicion'; Pradier-Fodéré 1885, p. 597: '[L]e despotisme du roi de Naples, tant qu'il n'atteignait pas les droits des autres Puissances et de leurs nationaux, était l'affaire des seuls Napolitains'. Similar statements can be found in Henry Bonfils and Paul Fauchille,

literature on 'humanitarian intervention'.[246] For Antoine Rougier, however, the leading theorist of 'humanitarian intervention' in 'classic' international law, this case was a cornerstone of his theory, stating that diplomats had considered this case an important exception from the principle of non-intervention in the name of the higher ideal of justice.[247] Similarly, the historian of international law, Wilhelm Grewe (1911–2000), following Rougier in his 'Epochs of International Law', considered this episode to be one 'of the most important cases of intervention that were presented or perceived at the time as having been carried out on humanitarian grounds'.[248]

For his part, King Ferdinand II simply rejected the British and French requests as illegal interferences in the internal affairs of his Kingdom. The same position was expressed by Russia in a note of protest: 'To wish to obtain from the King of Naples concessions in respect of the internal regime of his States through threats of threatening demonstrations, is to violently substitute oneself for his authority, to want to govern in his place and to proclaim openly the right of the strong over the weak'.[249] This part of the note was also quoted by Rougier and, subsequently Grewe, but the second part of the note – which both of them omitted – has been cited more frequently in the literature on 'humanitarian intervention' in international law as a declaration of the illegality of such interventions,[250] notable, as William Edward Hall (1835–1894) pointed out, for its source:

> Exhortation in such a case is all that is allowable (. . .). Less than ever can it now be allowed in Europe to forget that Sovereigns are equal among themselves, and that it is not the extent of territory, but the sacred character of the Rights of each, which regulates the relations which exist between them.[251]

In fact, state practice of the relevant 'civilized' nations seems to provide support for both legal positions: the view shared by the United Kingdom and France, according to which extreme violations of principles of justice could give rise to legal justifications for interventions by other states; and the opposite view of Russia, restricting the legal means available even in such cases to verbal protests. Some authors of the early twentieth century have pointed to this episode as an example of a genuine

---

Lehrbuch des Völkerrechts für Studium und Praxis, 3rd ed., trans. by August Grah, Berlin: Carl Heymanns Verlag 1904, pp. 163–164; Despagnet 1905, p. 214. See also: Scelle 1934, p. 53.

[246] Pauer 1985, p. 73, deals with this incident but treats it as an intercession. Harald Endemann, *Kollektive Zwangsmaßnahmen zur Durchsetzung humanitärer Normen*, Frankfurt am Main: Peter Lang 1997, pp. 15–16, prefers to leave open the question of whether the events amounted to an 'intervention'.

[247] Rougier 1910, p. 475.

[248] Grewe 2000, p. 491.

[249] Cited after the English translation provided by Grewe 2000, p. 491.

[250] Robert Redslob, *Les Principes du Droit des Gens Moderne*, Paris: A. Rousseau 1937, p. 138; Strisower 1919, p. 122, fn. 35.

[251] Hall 1880, p. 248 (footnote).

'humanitarian' intervention and based their call for the legality of such interventions on it,[252] but current legal and historical scholarship on the practice of intervention in the nineteenth century has not considered the events to be particularly important.[253] King Ferdinand II's (limited) role in inter-European relations seems to have been unaffected,[254] though Russia's note of support could not detract from the King's declining international standing after the Crimean War, when the Naples government had favoured its traditional links with Russia and refused to cooperate with the Anglo-French alliance.[255]

To speak of an intervention in the legal sense of nineteenth century international law, however, seems unwarranted in this case. Demonstrations of naval force were not seen as actual threats or uses of (military) force, but rather as action undertaken in preparation or as part of a 'pacific blockade'.[256] Even if their presence could have the effect of an intervention, they were not considered forcible measures. In addition, the events show no sign of any diplomat claiming a *right* to forcible intervention. There is, therefore, no indication that states were considering a new approach to the question of (non-) intervention.[257] The British position is still best understood as an expression of the pragmatic doctrine of non-intervention held since the beginning of the nineteenth century, which allowed for interventions as the situation demanded.[258] At the same time, there is no indication that the United Kingdom moved towards some sort of acceptance of a certain standard of civilisation, of civilian immunity to be respected by all governments in dealing with civilian unrest – on the contrary, as evidenced by the brutality used roughly at the same time to crush the Sepoy rebellion in 1857–1858, which Grewe regarded as 'the most significant event in the history of British expansion in India in the 19th century'.[259]

---

[252] E.g. Hannis Taylor, A *Treatise on Public International Law*, Chicago: Callaghan & Co 1901, p. 429, § 429; Stowell 1921, p. 88; Mandelstam 1923, p. 382.

[253] Peter Malanczuk, *Akehurst's International Law*, 7th ed., London: Routledge 1997, p. 19, specifically mentions this case as an example of a historical case where the 'doctrine of humanitarian intervention' 'played a role'. For similar assessments, see: Wellhausen 2002, p. 68; Christoph Henke, *Die humanitäre Intervention – Völker-und verfassungsrechtliche Probleme unter besonderer Berücksichtigung des Kosovo-Konflikts*, Dissertation, Münster 2002, p. 9, talks of an intervention, as the 'objective war aims' are considered to be decisive, even if the Kingdom of Two Sicilies was proven correct in thinking that the 'military threats' were not serious enough. However, the case receives no mention in Murphy 1996, Chesterman 2001, or Heraclidis and Dialla 2015.

[254] Schulz 2009, pp 446–449.

[255] Lucy Riall, 'Garibaldi and the South', in John A. Davis (ed.), *Italy in the 19th Century*, Oxford University Press 2000, p. 152.

[256] Hans von Frisch, 'Demonstration, kriegerische zur See', in: Karl Strupp (ed.), *Wörterbuch des Völkerrechts*, Vol. I, Berlin: De Gruyter 1924, p. 227.

[257] For the opposite view, see: Harald Hagedorn, *Wandlungen des Interventionsrechtes in der Geschichte*, Zürich: Gatzer & Hahn 1933, p. 98, considering the British position as the sign of a changed approach, while Russia simply remained in the traditional position.

[258] Vincent 1974, p 100.

[259] Grewe 2000, p. 442.

The British tactics in India bore a close resemblance to those in use in the Ottoman Empire to suppress uprisings,[260] and they ended the rebellion in a 'welter of blood'.[261] Yet international law in the nineteenth century continued to be created as an image of European nations acting in pursuit of a higher, international justice in their dealings with other nations, in particular the Ottoman Empire.

2.3.3 The Paris Treaty of 1856

The Ottoman Empire held a special place in most constructs of international law in the nineteenth century, yet its role was not static. In the early part of the century, the inclusion of the Porte in the system of international law was a clear possibility. By the century's end, international law was constructed by most authors as a system defined by the exclusion of the Ottoman Empire. In the latter half of the century, some authors examined the question of the legality of intervention in the affairs of the Ottoman Empire under the special heading of the 'oriental question'. But with the Paris Treaty of 30 March 1856, between France, the United Kingdom, Russia, Sardinia-Piedmont and the Ottoman Empire, the relationship between the 'European' Powers and the Ottoman Empire was given a formal basis, as the Empire was 'admitted to participate in the advantages of the "droit public et du concert européen"'.[262] Once considered to be one of the most important treaties for the history of international law,[263] its meaning and effect is anything but clear, but it should probably have signalled the end for such special treatment. The treaty can be seen as the recognition of the Ottoman Empire as a (fully) sovereign nation with a guarantee of territorial integrity in a legal sense, the Porte's entry as the first non-Christian nation to the European family of nations under international law, or something purely symbolic. Gerrit Gong has shown that there is no sign in British state practice or published documents on international law that the Treaty had any effect on the British position on the legal status of the Ottoman Empire,[264] and indeed, the Treaty seems to have had little impact on the treatment of the Empire by the European Great Powers.[265] Conceptually at least, the treaty represented a commitment to a principle of non-intervention in the international relations within the system of the European concert, formally extending to the Ottoman Empire. The treaty recognised the Sultan's duty to protect the Christians living under his rule: Article IX of the Treaty took note of the Sultan's decision, 'in his constant

---

[260] Wheatcroft 1993, p. 235.
[261] Eric Hobsbawm, *The Age of Capital*, London: Abacus 2001, p. 152.
[262] Traité générale de Paris, 30 March 1856 between the United Kingdom, Austria, France, Prussia, Russia, Sardinia, and the Ottoman Empire, Art. VII: '... déclarent la Sublime Porte admise à participer aux avantages du droit public et du concert européen'.
[263] von Liszt 1913, p. 22.
[264] Gong 1984, p. 112.
[265] Orakhelashvili 2006, p. 337.

solicitude for the welfare of his subjects', to issue a 'Firman, which, while ameliorating their condition without distinction of Religion or of Race, records his generous intentions towards the Christian population of his Empire, and wishing to give a further proof of his sentiments in that respect, has resolved to communicate to the Contracting Parties the said Firman, emanating spontaneously from his Sovereign will'. The European Powers in turn assured the Sultan to 'recognise the high value of this communication'. The Treaty further stipulated expressly that 'it cannot, in any case, give to the said Powers the right to interfere, either collectively or separately, in the relations of His Majesty the Sultan with his subjects, nor in the Internal Administration of his Empire'.

The Treaty was the result of the Crimean War, a war itself sometimes presented within the framework of 'humanitarian intervention'.[266] Russia had justified the war with the Ottoman Empire with reference to the treaty rights to protect Orthodox Christians, as laid down in the treaty of Küçük Kaynarci (1774). Yet the Crimean War, with France and the United Kingdom ultimately joining on the side of the Ottoman Empire, 'was fought to remake the European system'.[267] The relations between the European Powers and the Ottoman Empire up to this point had already been governed by a system that can only be considered one of 'international law', as the system of the capitulations as well as legal arguments exchanged over the Greek War of Independence clearly indicate. This situation was barely affected by the Paris Treaty. Its relevance therefore comes less from any immediate effects than from its alleged contribution to the secularisation of the European state system.[268] The treaty did not change the legal position of the Ottoman Empire,[269] but – at least on the face of it – the basic system of international law, which from then on extended its reach over the 'borders of Christianity' to demonstrate its 'general humane character', as the Swiss international lawyer Joseph Bluntschli put it in his concept of a 'modern international law of civilized nations'.[270] In other words, with the Paris Treaty of 1856, international law was to potentially cover all of 'Europe', not merely 'Christian Europe'.[271] Whatever the intention of the authors

---

[266] Ingeborg Kreutzmann, *Missbrauch der humanitären Intervention im 19. Jahrhundert*, Glücksburg: Baltica 2005, pp. 65–69. These claims will not be analysed further here, because of the treaty-based nature of the justifications for the Russian war effort, see: Tsygankov 2012, pp. 195–196.

[267] A. J. P. Taylor, as quoted by Tsygankov 2012, p. 200.

[268] Evans 1997, p. 64; Ziegler 2007, p. 176.

[269] As E. Pritsch, 'Türkei', in: Karl Strupp (ed.), *Wörterbuch des Völkerrechts*, Vol. II, Berlin: De Gruyter 1925, p. 737 claimed.

[270] Bluntschli 1868, p. 17.

[271] see: Franz von Holtzendorff, 'Einleitung in das Völkerrecht', in: Franz von Holtzendorff (ed.), *Handbuch des Völkerrechts*, Vol. I, Berlin: Verlag von Carl Habel 1885, p. 13: 'Die Terminologie des Europäischen Völkerrechts deckte sich niemals mit den Gränzen des Europäischen Festlandes und der zu ihm gehörigen Inseln. Vor dem Abschluß des Pariser Friedens im Jahre 1856 war das Europäische Gebiet der Türkei gleicherweise wie ihre außereuropäischen Besitzungen der Herrschaft allgemeiner Europäischer Völkerrechtsordnung entzogen'.

of the treaty, the fact remains that the Ottoman Empire continued to hold the position it had acquired at the beginning of the nineteenth century – the unequal and inferior sovereign at the outskirts of European society, a project for the European Powers. As the Empire became the 'Sick Man of Europe', it gradually developed into the unequal sovereign par excellence.[272] This process was not merely complemented in the literature on international law of the nineteenth century; it became the ideological foundation of the law. Simple facts, like the importance of the Ottoman Empire to the system of the balance of power in Europe in the nineteenth century,[273] were ignored in favour of attempts to write a version of international law without the inclusion of the Empire.

The 'recognition' of the Empire as a 'European state' was considered a 'folly',[274] not only by James Lorimer (1818–1890), whose 'eccentric' conception of international law has begun only recently to draw the attention of scholars of the history of international law.[275] Other authors shared the sentiment, but chose to express it in a slightly more reserved manner[276] or explained it in more detail:

> The international law with which we are concerned having arisen among the former of the two classes of populations here contrasted, it is based on the possession by states of a common and in that sense an equal civilisation. The case of Turkey must in this part of our subject be left out of sight, because of the anomalous position of that empire, included on account of its geographical situation in the political system of Europe, but belonging in other respects rather to the second group of contrasted populations. She may benefit by European international law so far as it can be extended to her without ignoring plain facts, but her admission to that benefit cannot react on the statement of the law, which is what it is because it is the law of the European peoples.[277]

The Ottoman Empire retained the function of providing the 'Other'to a 'community spirit' among European nations in the sense of a Christian-European society of nations,[278] even where state practice showed signs of moving in the opposite

---

[272] Simpson 2004, pp. 244–245.

[273] Josef L. Kunz, 'Konzert, Europäisches', in: Karl Strupp (ed.), Wörterbuch des Völkerrechts, Vol. I, Berlin: De Gruyter 1924, p. 252.

[274] Lorimer 1883, p. 177.

[275] Koskenniemi 2002, p. 33. Nussbaum was also very critical of Lorimer's 'backward' conception of international law. For a positive assessment see: D. H. N. Johnson, 'The English Tradition in International Law', International and Comparative Law Quarterly 1962, 11, p. 419. How central Lorimer was to the development of international law may be doubted, neither Ziegler nor Scupin mention Lorimer in their accounts of the development of international law.

[276] Friedrich Martens, Völkerrecht – Das internationale Recht der civilisierten Nationen, German edition, trans, by Carl Bergbohm, Vol. II, Berlin: Weidmannsche Buchhandlung 1886, p. 128: 'Die bekannte Phrase des Pariser Tractates über die Aufnahme der Türkei...'.

[277] John Westlake, The Collected Papers of John Westlake on Public International Law, edited by Lassa Oppenheim, Cambridge University Press 1914, p. 103.

[278] Phrase borrowed from Pritsch 1925, p. 736 ('Zusammengehörigkeitsgefühl der europäischen Völker im Sinne einer christlich-europäischen Staatengemeinschaft'). For Pritsch, the

direction. This strained context of a state practice, in which relations of Christian states with the Ottoman Empire included treaties and other indicators of legality (e.g. permanent diplomatic relations, trade and law reform negotiations),[279] and a science of international law, which considered the Empire the most prominent representative of those 'uncivilised Asians', probably 'incapable' of acting in accordance with international law,[280] formed the backdrop to the next historical episode still considered relevant to the history of 'humanitarian intervention' – the action undertaken by the European Great Powers in response to incidents on the territory of present-day Syria and Lebanon in 1860.

2.4 LEBANON, 1860

The intervention of the European Powers in present-day Lebanon and Syria, undertaken by France with the backing of the other Great Powers, is the famous exception to the rule, the one intervention even critics of 'humanitarian intervention' in the nineteenth century accept as being guided by genuinely 'humanitarian' motives.[281] The importance of this episode for the evolution of the legal doctrine of 'humanitarian intervention', however, lies not with the alleged purity of the motives of the powers involved, but again with the construction of its narrative and the legal implications drawn in the literature on international law.

2.4.1 *The Intervention and Its History*

In 1860, long ongoing social conflicts between Christian Maronites, Druzes and Muslims erupted in violence in what today is Lebanon and the Syrian capital Damascus, back then part of the Ottoman Empire. The violence took place not only between Maronite and Druze communities but also within these communities in an attempt to define their own respective boundaries in an era of upheaval. This has been described as a 'struggle over communal representation that was reflected in episodes of intracommunal social violence that constituted a fundamental part of broader religious violence across sectarian communities'.[282] The ensuing civil war and its consequences have been summed up dryly by contemporaries: 'A personal quarrel between Maronites and Druses, in 1859, became the occasion of a war of extermination by the Druses upon the Maronites, which led to the outbreaks of 1860 in Syria, and brought an interference and settlement by foreign powers. Since

---

Ottoman Empire was outside of the 'society of nations under internaitonal law' (Völkerrechts-gemeinschaft), though in his view 1856 was a turning point.

[279] Kayaoglu 2010, pp. 104–148.

[280] Lorimer 1883, pp. 102, 123.

[281] Brownlie 1963, p. 340.

[282] Ussama Makdisi, *The Culture of Sectarianism*, Berkeley: University of California Press 2000, p. 3.

that time a special Governor has been provided for the Lebanon district'.[283] In nineteenth century international law, the events were seen as 'one of the most gruesome moments in history', a 'revenge' of the 'Druzes, Kurds and Arabs' on 'defenseless Christians',[284] with the complicity of the Ottoman rulers.[285] Current legal literature portrays the events as the 'persecution and murder of perhaps as many as eleven thousand Christian Maronites by Muslim Druze'[286] or simply speaks of 'Turkish massacres of Christians'.[287]

A more detailed review of the historical narratives, however, reveals a more complicated picture, a national and economic conflict between Christian Maronite peasants and their Druze landlords, which turned into a civil war the Ottoman authorities had some initial difficulty to contain. As historian Davide Rodogno in one of the most recent historical studies of the events asserts, the 'Maronites initiated disturbances, though the Druze, who were far superior in military tactics and discipline, retaliated as ferociously as their opponents'.[288] The results of the conflict, therefore, were particularly devastating for the Maronites: Christian property was destroyed in large quantities[289] and thousands were killed and even more were forced to flee.[290] Many fled to Damascus and, while further strife in the Mount Lebanon area could be avoided with a peace treaty concluded between Christians and Druzes under the supervision of the Ottoman authorities on 12 July 1860,[291] those who fled to Damascus were met with more violence: On 9 July 1860, the Christian quarter of the city was attacked by an angry mob of at least 20,000 Druzes and Muslims, not necessarily all from Damascus. Over a period of eight days and nights, the Christian quarter was then pillaged and plundered and a large number of Christian inhabitants were killed, without any interference from the local authorities. Almost half of the quarter's buildings were looted. European eyewitnesses to the scenes quickly reported home there had been about 6,000 victims, a figure still

---

[283] A. J. Schem, *War in the East*, New York: H. S. Goodspeed & Co 1878, p. 160.

[284] Arthur von Kirchenheim, 'Libanon', in: Karl Strupp (ed.), *Wörterbuch des Völkerrechts und der Diplomatie*, Vol. I, Berlin: De Gruyter 1924, p. 828. The tone is similar in Martens 1886, p. 128.

[285] Rougier 1910, p. 473; Carlos Calvo, *Le droit international théorique et pratique; précédé d'un exposé historique des progrès de la science du droit des gens*, Vol. I, 5th ed., Paris: A. Rousseau 1896, p. 308.

[286] Paul Gordon Lauren, *The Evolution of International Human Rights*, 3rd ed., Philadelphia: University of Pennsylvania Press 2011, p. 73.

[287] Luis Kutner, 'World Habeas Corpus and Humanitarian Intervention', *Valparaiso University Law Review* 1985, 19, p. 602.

[288] Rodogno 2012, p. 98.

[289] Nicolae Jorga, *Geschichte des Osmanischen Reiches*, Vol. V (up to 1912), Gotha: Perthes 1913, p. 522, lists 560 churches, 43 monasteries, 28 schools for 1,830 pupils, and no less than 360 villages.

[290] Jorga 1913, p. 522.

[291] The treaty is reprinted in Leila Tarazi Fawaz, *An Occasion for War – Civil Conflict in Lebanon and Damascus in 1860*, Berkeley: University of California Press 1994, pp. 229–230.

found in the international law literature on the incident.[292] Current historical scholarship puts the number of victims at 2,000 to 3,000 Christians[293] 'and an unknown number of Jews', 'plus a few foreigners and an unknown number of refugees'.[294]

While the dramatic events unfolded in Damascus, news of the civil war in Lebanon reached the European public with some delay. The European Powers took this opportunity to remind the Porte of its duties under Article IX of the Paris Treaty. The offer was made to set up an international commission to investigate the incidents and to send in European troops to calm the situation. At the same time, the European powers sent a joint naval expedition to the coast of Lebanon. On 30 July 1860, the Sultan's ambassador in London signalled the Porte's willingness to cooperate, but warned of the dangers of unilateral action on behalf of the Christian powers.[295] It has been pointed out that the reaction of Ottoman statesmen was largely influenced by the fact that the two decades before the massacres of 1860 had been a period of Ottoman modernisation:

> Aware of the Ottoman Empire's image as the 'sick man of Europe,' the Sultan and his ministers had decreed in 1839 that all subjects were equal before the law regardless of their religion. This move and other reforms in the administration known collectively as the Tanzimat were calculated to satisfy European demands for the protection of the Christian communities and to inculcate a notion of a national and secular subjecthood. The local Christian subjects, in other words, had become yardsticks of the modernization of the Ottoman Empire: their slaughter dealt the imperial reform process a cruel blow.[296]

On 31 July 1860, at the behest of France, a conference met in Paris to debate the situation with the participation of the ambassadors of France, Prussia, Russia, the United Kingdom, Austria and the Ottoman Empire. At its conclusion, the Sultan explicitly gave his authorisation to send a contingent of 12,000 French troops to Lebanon and Syria to 'stop the effusion of blood' and to support the Sultan's efforts to restore order.[297] The French troops arrived on 16 August 1860 and found no signs of continued violence. In the meantime, the Sultan had appointed a Special Ambassador to the region who had restored order with draconian measures to

---

[292] Pauer 1985; Wellhausen 2002, p. 69: 5,500 Christians killed. Nineteenth century international law put the number at 'some six thousand Christian Maronites'; Rougier 1910, p. 473; Stowell 1921, p. 65.

[293] See Fawaz 1994, pp. 259–260, for an overview of different estimates. Some accounts still speak of more than 10,000 Christians killed, see D. K. Fieldhouse, *Western Imperialism in the Middle East 1914–1958*, Oxford University Press 2006, p. 305; Menon 2016, p. 78.

[294] Rodogno 2012, p. 101.

[295] Letter Musurus, reprinted in: Louis Sohn and Thomas Buergenthal, *International Protection of Human Rights*, Indianapolis: Bobbs-Merrill 1973.

[296] Makdisi 2000, p. 3.

[297] Jorga 1913, p. 513. See also Articles I and II of the Convention of 5 September 1860, reprinted in: Sohn and Buergenthal 1973, p. 157.

prevent any further action from the European Powers. In Damascus alone, he had more than a hundred Ottoman officials killed, including the local governor, and in the other areas under his control he proceeded in a similar vein.[298] Nevertheless, the French troops remained on Ottoman soil until June 1861, and only left after a treaty had been entered into between the five European Powers and the Ottoman Empire, institutionalising a 'Règlement Organique' for Lebanon, which required the Empire to install a Christian governor for the region in cooperation with the other Powers. Lebanon thus received the status of an autonomous Ottoman province under the guarantee of the signatory Powers and the seeds were sown for the complicated trio-religious set-up of present day Lebanon, with the formulation of public political identities 'which eventually came to find their fullest expression, as well as their deepest contradiction, in the Lebanese state – a republic born through and renewed by latter-day Règlement Organiques known as the National Pacts of 1943 and 1989'.[299]

2.4.2 *The Intervention in Context*

According to the preamble of the joint Paris Convention of 5 September 1860, the aim of the intervention was the cooperation between the European Powers and 'His Imperial Majesty the Sultan' in 'wishing to stop, by prompt and efficacious measures, the effusion of blood in Syria, and to show his firm resolution to establish Order and Peace amongst the Populations placed under his Sovereignty'.[300] The London Protocol of 3 August 1860 further stressed that all contracting Powers 'desirous of establishing, in conformity with the intentions of their respective Courts, the true character of the assistance afforded to the Sublime Porte by the provisions of the Protocol signed this day, the feelings which have dictated the clauses of this Act, and their perfect disinterestedness' declared 'in the most formal manner' that they did not 'intend to seek for, and will not seek for, in the execution of their engagements, any territorial advantages, any exclusive influence, or any concessions with regard to the commerce of their subjects, such as could not be granted to the subjects of all other nations'.[301] The French Foreign Secretary explained the provisions of the London Protocol in a letter to his ambassador with the Porte: 'The object of the mission (...) is to assist in stopping, by prompt and energetic measures, the effusion of blood, and in putting an end to the outrages committed against the Christians, which cannot remain unpunished'.[302] The British secretary of state for

---

[298] Fawaz 1994, pp. 132–139.
[299] Makdisi 2000, p. 166.
[300] Reprinted in Sohn and Buergenthal 1973, pp. 156–157.
[301] Reprinted in Sohn and Buergenthal 1973, p. 158.
[302] Reprinted in Sohn and Buergenthal 1973, p. 159.

external affairs was quoted as saying: 'It is to be hoped that the measures now taken may vindicate the rights of humanity'.[303]

These official explanations may reflect the real motivation behind the intervention of the Powers involved. In the international legal literature, some doubt has been cast on the British support for the French initiative, as the Crown appeared to be moved more by an interest to keep the initiative in check and limit its effects on the Ottoman Empire.[304] Russia, on the other hand, would have gladly taken this opportunity to create options for more future interventions, but without success: the Czar failed to convince France and the United Kingdom to conclude a secret agreement that would have given each partner the right to intervene in the name of the European Concert in every further crisis in the Ottoman Empire.[305] Yet while it is certainly possible to stress the wider context even of the French motivation and the geo-strategic success it presented, from the point of view a history of 'humanitarian intervention', the question is not whether 'the object of French intervention' was indeed 'wholly humanitarian' or not,[306] but how the different motives and objects of the intervention were turned into a legal justification. While early news of the escalating situation were met, particularly in France, with the patterns of reaction familiar from reports of other real or alleged atrocities on the territory of the Ottoman Empire, in this particular case, they were quickly channelled into diplomatic efforts based at least on an attempt to uphold an appearance of sovereign equality among the States involved.[307] The United Kingdom, in particular, had insisted on obtaining Ottoman consent to the deployment of international troops,[308] and only after an agreement could be reached with the Sultan on board were troops actually dispatched. By this time, the Porte's efforts to reestablish order had already proven so successful that the intervention effectively, as a contemporary historian put it, consisted of a 'vain military excursion with solemn Christian processions'.[309]

2.4.3 The Intervention in the History of International Law

In the year before these events, John Stuart Mill had already been confident enough to state that 'it seems now to be an admitted doctrine' of 'what is called international

---

[303] Lauren 2011, p. 73.

[304] Pauer 1985, p. 56.

[305] Schulz 2009, p. 526.

[306] Istvan Pogany, 'Humanitarian Intervention in International Law: The French Intervention in Syria Re-Examined', *International and Comparative Law Quarterly* 1986, p. 188: 'French interest in Syria cannot be considered in isolation from contemporaneous French encroachments on Ottoman territory elsewhere, particularly in North Africa. In 1848, Algeria was declared an integral part of France, after 18 years of French military occupation. In 1881, France seized Tunisia, establishing a protectorate. In these circumstances, it would be naive to view the object of French intervention as wholly humanitarian'.

[307] Fawaz 1994, pp. 101–131.

[308] Fawaz 1994, p. 112.

[309] Jorga 1913, p. 526, my translation; see also Fawaz 1994, p. 127.

law' that in the case of 'a protracted civil war, in which the contending parties are so equally balanced that there is no probability of a speedy issue: or if there is, the victorious side cannot hope to keep down the vanquished but by severities repugnant to humanity', other states might be justified in intervening.[310] And indeed, it took only a few years for the international legal literature to accept the humanitarian motives of the intervening powers, even if that did not necessarily translate into an acceptance of the doctrine of 'humanitarian intervention'.[311] The events occurred at a time when reference to this doctrine, despite Mill's enthusiasm for it, was still quite limited,[312] but it seems quite likely that in France – the main initiator of the intervention – there was an awareness of the treatment the 'intervention' in the Greek War of Independence had received in the works of Wheaton and Mill. By 1848, Henry Wheaton's *Elements of International Law* had already been published in a French version prepared by the author and a second edition of the French version was published in 1853.[313] Yet there is no indication that the French initiative, despite making passing reference to language used in 1827 to justify the intervention against the Ottoman Empire in its Greek provinces, would have been prepared to use military force without Ottoman consent. French officials in their international correspondence and efforts to internationalise the response to the unfolding events emphasised the need to undertake an action in the interest of humanity rather than uniquely on behalf of Maronites.[314]

In the following decades, most authors included comments on this episode in their works, but either refrained from clear statements on the legality of the intervention[315] or made reference to the Paris Treaty of 1856 as the basis of the legal justification.[316] Some ignored the possibility of a legal justification, focusing instead

[310] Mill 1859, cited according to Mill 1984, p. 121.
[311] Emer de Vattel, *Le Droit des Gens*, Nouvelle Edition by Paul Pradier-Fodéré, Vol. II, Paris: Libraire de Guillaumin & Co. 1863, p. 33, note on § 33: 'C'est au nom de l'humanité que les troupes françaises sont allées en Syrie, en vertu d'une convention européenne, protéger les chrétiens contre un fanatisme aveugle'. Pradier-Fodéré was a strict opponent of any corresponding right, see Pradier-Fodéré 1885, p. 594, § 392: 'Il est impossible d'accepter cette doctrine'.
[312] Heraclidis and Dialla 2015, p. 134, maintain that 'France, the main initiator of the intervention, did not yet have thinkers participating in the debate for or against *intervention d'humanité*'.
[313] Wheaton 1855, p. cxlv.
[314] Rodogno 2012, p. 102.
[315] Martens 1886, p. 128; Geffcken 1889, p. 163; Calvo 1896, p. 308, § 176; Bonfils and Fauchille 1904, p. 167; Charles Dupuis, *Le droit des gens et les rapports des grandes puissances avec les autres états avant le pacte de la Société des nations*, Paris: Plon-Nourrit 1921, p. 118; Geoffrey Butler and Simon Maccoby. *The Development of International Law*. London: Longmans, Green and Co., 1928, p. 454.
[316] Bry 1891, p. 134: 'En 1856, les Puissances signataires du traité de Paris prirent sous leur sauvegarde tous les sujets chrétiens de la Porte, substituant ainsi leur protection collective à celle que la Russie s'était anciennement attribuée. C'est en vertu de ce traité que la France intervint en Syrie comme mandataire des Puissances européennes, lorsqu'en 1860, les chrétiens Maronites du Liban furent massacrés par les Druses, encouragés par la complicité et l'inertie des autorités ottomanes'. Similarly: Despagnet 1905, pp. 230–231: 'Bien que l'Art. 9 du

on the 'commendation' the intervention was worthy of.[317] But in engaging with the historical events, the writers on international law soon created a narrative in which it was the intervention itself which 'stopped' the 'persecution and massacre of Christians in the Mount Lebanon district in 1860'.[318] The statement made by historian Davide Rodogno about the European reception of the massacres at the time can be applied to the representation of the historical facts in international law as well: 'A great deal of distortion, exaggeration, and extravagant claims characterized the description of events made by European men on the spot'.[319] Despite the fact that no force was used by the 'intervening' powers, nineteenth century international lawyers generally agreed that an intervention in the legal sense had taken place and that it was based on 'humanitarian' considerations. This becomes most apparent in the discussion of the case in the 'Theory of Humanitarian Intervention' developed by French jurist Antoine Rougier in the early twentieth century: The action of the European Powers, Rougier insisted, was the clearest application of the idea of the 'intervention d'humanité' he formulated, even if it had to be disguised behind a courteous gesture towards the Sultan.[320] The Sultan's consent to the intervention was but a 'fiction', achieved through, as American international lawyer Ellery C. Stowell put it in 1921, 'constraint and a desire to avoid worse'.[321] A number of

traité de Paris in-terdise aux Puissances de s'immiscer dans les rapport du Sultan et de ses sujets et dans l'administration intérieure de la Turquie, il faut l'entendre en ce sens que, si l'on admis la Turquie dans le concert européen et surtout si l'on a garanti son indépendance et son intégrité, c'est à la condition que la Porte réaliserait les réformes promises pour l'égalité religieuse et civile de ses sujets, l'administration de la justice, la gestion des finances, les mesures contre la partialité et la corruption de ses fonctionnaires. En fait, les interventions dans les affaires intérieures de la Turquie s'expliquent par le non accomplissement de ces réformes toujours promises et toujours éludées. (. . .) Le principe d'intervention posé par le traité de Paris a reçu de nombreuses applications. En 1860, à la suite du massacre des chrétiens Maronites du Li- ban par les Druses avec la complicité tacite des autorités turques, la France envoya un corps expéditionnaire en Syrie. . .'.

[317] Thomas J. Lawrence, *The Principles of International Law*, 4th ed., Boston: D. C. Heath & Co. 1910, p. 129. 'When in 1860 the Great Powers of Europe intervened to put a stop to the persecution and massacre of Christians in the district of Mount Lebanon, their proceedings were worthy of commendation, though they could not be brought within the strict letter of the law'.

[318] Taylor 1901, pp. 429–430, § 430; van Lynden van Sandenberg 1899, pp. 192–193. Other interpretations have considered the French 'occupation' of the district to be an independent example of intervention, see: Stowell 1921 p. 63, which from a legal point of view seems hardly convincing: while occupation may be the result of an intervention, establishing a military presence with the consent of the sovereign as expressed in a treaty would hardly qualify as an occupation or an intervention in the legal sense.

[319] Rodogno 2012, p. 97.

[320] Rougier 1910, p. 473 f.: 'En 1860, à la suite du massacre de quelques six mille Chrétiens maronites par les Druses musulmans avec la complicité des autorités ottomanes, la diplomatie réalise une application très nette de l'idée d'intervention d'humanité, tout en en déguisant encore le véritable mobile sous une fiction par courtoisie envers le Sultan'.

[321] Rougier 1910, p. 474 with fn. (1). Stowell 1921, p. 66.

authors did not even mention this aspect of events.[322] This selective process of picking only some of the (legal) facts relevant to the discussion has turned this diplomatic intervention in appreciation of the sovereignty of the Ottoman Empire to a celebrated exemplary case of forceful 'humanitarian intervention', reversing historical development and legal judgement.[323]

For nineteenth century international law, the 'Lebanese' case first and foremost was an opportunity to reinforce the image of the Ottoman Empire as an 'anomaly', a threat to the peace within the international system.[324] A number of authors considered treaties with the Porte to be without legal relevance, as horrendous persecution of Christians would be repeated within the unstable conditions of the Empire and could only be prevented through European support.[325] At the same time, it was clear that, despite these unstable conditions within the Empire, it was always the Porte that was (legally) responsible for attacks on Christians: Ottoman authorities were considered to have, if not explicitly encouraged, at least implicitly supported the massacres of the Maronites.[326] That view still prevails in some more contemporary comments.[327] Yet historical research has found enough evidence to suggest that the civil war between Maronites and Druzes initially was beyond the control of the Ottoman authorities, not least because reorganisation of the administrative system in the North of the Mount Lebanon district with separate administrative authorities for the Maronites after 1842 had weakened the governmental infrastructure in the area. Ironically, this was the result of administrative reforms urged on by the European Powers.[328] In Damascus, on the other hand, the local governor was indeed responsible for the lack of protection of the Christian Quarter, but the corrupt

---

[322] Henry G. Hodges, *The Doctrine of Intervention*, Princeton: Banner Press 1915, p. 81: 'As regards an intervention undertaken in the cause of humanity there seems to be a divergence of opinion among the most prominent writers ranging from strict prohibition, to the choice of public opinion. Lawrence admits that in a few instances in the past, intervention on this principle has been justified, and cites as an example the intervention of the great Powers of Europe in 1860 to put a stop to the massacre of Christians in the district of Mount Lebanon'. Similarly, Graham 1924, p. 325, neglects to mention the Porte's consent.

[323] Wellhausen 2002, p. 69, with reference to Stowell 1921, p. 63.

[324] See: Simpson 2004, p. 242.

[325] von Wachter 1911, p. 53; Martens 1886, p. 128; Geffcken 1889, p. 163.

[326] Rougier 1910, p. 473. See also: Calvo 1896, p. 308, § 176: '... encouragés par l'indifférence, sinon par la complicité des autorités turques'; Stowell 1921, p. 63. Grewe 2000, p. 491, claimed the massacre of 'some six thousand Christian Maronites by Syrian Druzes [...] had been tolerated by the Turkish authorities'. Heraclides and Dialla 2015, p. 138, conclude that no evidence has surfaced that would allow the claim that the Porte was somehow involved.

[327] Ajaj 1992, p. 219, considers this common knowledge ('It is commonly agreed that the unfortunate events were implicitly encouraged by the Turkish authorities').

[328] Fawaz 1994, pp. 28–30; Pogany 1986, pp. 182–183.

and ineffective official was accordingly held accountable by the Sultan and subsequently sentenced to death.[329]

In the legal literature, two related, but separate events (the situation in Damascus exploded after further news from the civil war areas had reached the city)[330] were merged into a singular anti-Christian escalation of violence, despite two different sets of circumstances and different perpetrators. As in the case of the Greek War of Independence, this again did not occur because more comprehensive information was not available to contemporary authors and their followers,[331] but because the events seemed to present another opportunity to reinforce the portrayal of the Ottoman Empire as international law's uncivilised other, unable to fulfil the conditions under which it had been admitted to participate in the advantages of the system of the European concert.

2.4.4 *The Intervention in the History of 'Humanitarian Intervention'*

The image presented of the 'Lebanese' case in the writings on 'humanitarian intervention' is mostly poor on detail and rich in prejudices. While recent studies – both by historians and political scientists – have shown greater attention to the details of the historical events, the development of the law is still under-represented. From the 1960s onwards, the events are characterised as the most authentic case of a 'humanitarian intervention', justified purely on account of humanitarian concerns.[332] The inclusion of extensive materials on the case in one of the pioneering source books for teaching of human rights law in the United States in the 1970s[333] offered some important background information, but cemented the positive view of the European involvement. The inclusion of the 'Lebanese' case presented 'humanitarian intervention' as the first attempt in modern international law to 'break the defense of absolute state sovereignty' in one of the book's 'most useful chapters'.[334] To this day, the events of 1860 feature in virtually every book claiming the legality of 'humanitarian intervention' in nineteenth century international law without much further explanation, as if the often repeated humanitarian motives of the intervening Powers had somehow to

---

[329] Fawaz 1994, p. 150.

[330] Fawaz 1994, p. 81.

[331] See the reports of the British and French consuls, reproduced by Fawaz 1994, p. 51.

[332] Reisman and McDougal 1968 Memorandum, reprinted in: Lillich 1973, pp. 181–182; Fonteyne 1974, p. 208 f.; Henke 2002, p. 10.

[333] Sohn and Buergenthal 1973.

[334] W. Paul Gormley, 'Book Review: International Protection of Human Rights. By Louis B. Sohn and Thomas Buergenthal. Indianapolis, Indiana. Bobbs-Merrill Co. 1973', *Georgia Journal of International and Comparative Law* 1975, 5, p. 332.

do with the legality of the action undertaken.[335] Even critics of the legal doctrine
have conceded the possibility of a – legally speaking: justified – 'humanitarian
intervention' in this particular case.[336]

Yet doing so requires replacing the historical narrative with an image of the
intervening Europeans as the heroic saviour of persecuted Christians, reinterpreting
a predominantly social conflict in religious (and national) terms. This even applies
to those authors who have discussed the question whether the Sultan's consent to
the French expedition might not render the qualification of the action as an
intervention in the legal sense invalid,[337] as the Sultan is considered incapable of
possessing the (political) quality of making an informed decision – as one writer
noted in 1974:

> Apparently, not too much importance should be given to the fact that formally this
> operation did not amount to an intervention since the Sultan gave his consent to
> the activities of the Concert of Europe by signing the Protocol of Paris. One can
> reasonably question the validity of that consent, for it seems clear that, as Ellery
> Stowell, writing in the 1920s, put it, Turkey assented to the French expedition 'only
> through constraint and a desire to avoid worse'.[338]

Stowell's turn of phrase thus lives on, even if it can only relate to the relative value
of the humanitarian considerations and motives, and not the modality of obtaining
legal justification through consent of the target state: While it is clear that consent
obtained through force or coercion is not consent properly so called, it seems far
from clear that it was absolutely impossible for the Sultan to make the decision to
consent to the European proposals for his own independent motives: The Ottoman
authorities did take decisive action to stop the escalating civil war, not only to
prevent more extensive European intervention, but also to pacify the situation on
the ground,[339] and were then caught by surprise by the sudden outbreak of further
violence in Damascus.[340] Even then, if with delay caused by their own corrupt
officials, the situation was resolved relatively quickly, so there is a case for

---

[335] e.g. Charles G. Fenwick, *International Law*, 4th. ed., New York: Appleton-Century-Crofts
1965, p. 287: 'Numerous interventions took place during the nineteenth century upon what
were called in a broad way "grounds of humanity" (...) In spite of the admission of the
Ottoman Empire to participate in the public law and concert of Europe in 1856, intervention
again took place in 1860 to protect the Christians of Mount Lebanon, (...)'. Similarly: Ann Van
Wynen Thomas and A. J. Thomas Jr., *Non-intervention: The Law and Its Import in the
Americas*, Dallas: Southern Methodist University Press 1956, S. 373. 'The French intervened
and by force checked religious atrocities'; Kutner 1985, p. 602; Malanczuk 1997, p 19.

[336] Brownlie 1963, p. 340, considers this the one possible case of a genuine 'humanitarian
intervention' under 'classic international law', while being a strong opponent of this legal
instrument, see: Brownlie 1974, pp. 217–220.

[337] Stephen Kloepfer, 'The Syrian Crisis, 1860–61: A Case Study in Classic Humanitarian Intervention', *Canadian Yearbook of International Law* 1985, p. 255; Pogany 1986, p. 188.

[338] Fonteyne 1974, p. 208.

[339] Fawaz 1994, p. 102.

[340] Fawaz 1994, p. 83.

considering European intervention irrelevant to the ending of the violence. As things were happening, however, the outbreak of violence in Damascus would not have allowed for the Europeans to weaken their commitment to a joint action: In France, in particular, the commitment to act for the sake of 'civilisation' had become so overwhelming that the question as to whether the circumstances could still demand the deployment of troops as they eventually got underway was not open for discussion. Thus, the European powers mandated the French expeditionary corps to undertake the military operation when – as even the French secretly admitted – the Ottoman army had already obtained very satisfactory results and restored order.[341]

The Sultan had achieved precisely what the international lawyers of the nineteenth century thought the Ottoman government incapable of he had restored order and brought to justice those responsible for the violence *without* European support. Yet this simple fact has not been properly represented in the literature on 'humanitarian intervention'. Nor has the fact that the 'intervention' can hardly be said to based on a right to take forcible action because of 'humanitarian concerns'.[342] Four years after the Paris Conference of 1856 and its corresponding Treaty, the decision to insist on another conference to mandate the military expedition into Syria and Lebanon seems like the logical step to honour the guarantees extended to the Ottoman Empire in Paris. That the Great Powers made decisions for and affecting third states was not uncommon in mid-nineteenth century Europe and beyond, nor was it necessarily a legal anomaly. Of relevance, then, is mainly the clear commitment to 'multilateralize' the action and to impose constraints on the conduct of the intervening forces.[343] This would appear to be a signal of the strengthening of the commitment to respect the Ottoman Empire's sovereignty in state practice, yet it was taken by the architects of 'humanitarian intervention' as an opportunity to build a theory of intervention that would undermine any commitment to sovereign equality in international law for the benefit of the 'civilised' European states. The defining moment of the Syrian intervention was the *inclusion* of the Ottoman Empire, that is, the inclusion of the 'target state' of the intervention in the authorisation of the use of force, whereas the *exclusion* of the target state is the *raison d'être* of the idea of 'humanitarian intervention'.

Gary Bass has recently declared the 1860–1861 events 'a success in the management of the tangled international politics surrounding a humanitarian military intervention',[344] while Rajan Menon's scathing critique of the 'conceit of humanitarian intervention' discusses the French intervention in response to 'massacres' of 'over ten thousand Maronite Christians who had earlier risen in revolt against their

---

[341] Fawaz 1994, pp. 119, 126.
[342] But see: Murphy 1996, p. 54; Chesterman 2001, p. 33.
[343] Murphy 1996, p. 54.
[344] Bass 2008, p. 157.

Druze overlords', 'with the participation of Sunni Muslims and the complicity of Ottoman troops' under the headline 'Nineteenth-Century Saviours: Altruism or Humbug?'.[345] This is impressive proof of the longevity of the narratives constructed by nineteenth century international lawyers. Yet to speak of a 'humanitarian intervention' in the legal sense of the term under these circumstances is only possible by turning the historical development on its head. While nineteenth century international lawyers constructing the events as an 'intervention d'humanité' could rest on the expression of 'humanitarian concerns', as evidenced in both British and French official statements and the clearly articulated wish to act in the interest of humanity rather than uniquely on behalf of one side of the conflict, there is no indication that the use of force was ever thought to be legitimised by these circumstances. Therefore, the events might be considered a consequence of the 'humanitarian impulse' in the second half of the nineteenth century, made more convincing by the desire to officially include the Ottoman Empire in the authorisation of the intervention. But constructed as a 'humanitarian intervention', this narrative requires accepting the construct of an international law of 'civilized nations' of 'humanity', which here was reinforced against the 'barbarism' of the 'uncivilised' in the precise moment when 'civilised Europeans' and 'uncivilised Turks' had concluded a treaty to mandate and limit the military expedition. In other words, it is to deny the sovereignty of the Ottoman Empire at the very moment it was honoured by the European Powers, confirming that the construct giving birth to the legal instrument of 'humanitarian intervention' rests on the inequality of nations taking part in the international system.

2.5 INTERVENTION IN MID-NINETEENTH-CENTURY INTERNATIONAL LAW

2.5.1 Introduction

In the years leading up to the Great Balkan Crisis of 1875–1877, the same developments continue to set the scene for the evolution of the theory of 'humanitarian intervention' and provide its specific context, its *Gestalt*. Despite the early expressions of the principles associated with the legal doctrine in the writings of, among others, Wheaton and von Rotteck, it usually is the German-Belgian jurist Egide Arntz (1812–1884) who is credited with having first proclaimed the existence of this right.[346] Arntz presented his ideas on a right to an 'intervention d'humanité' in a 1876 letter to his friend and colleague Gustave Rolin-Jaequemyns (1835–1902), in reaction to the latter's work on 'International law and the Oriental question', later

---

[345] Menon 2016, p. 78.
[346] Rougier 1910, p. 490 with fn. 3. The same claim is made by Mandelstam 1923, pp. 389–390.

published in the Revue de Droit international et de législation comparée[347] (Revue). This first journal of international law has been famously described by Martti Koskenniemi as a journal intended by its editors to be an organ of the 'conscience juridique' of the 'civilized world'.[348] The term 'conscience juridique du monde civilisé' held a prominent place in the statute of the *Institut de droit international*, formed in 1873, of which both Arntz and Rolin-Jaequemyns were members and which was closely associated with the Revue. It is a reference to the work of another member of the *Institut*, the Swiss international lawyer Johann Caspar Bluntschli (1808–1881). Bluntschli had published his 'Das moderne Völkerrecht der civilisirten Staten als Rechtsbuch dargestellt' in 1868 and it became the 'defining' treatise on international law in the continental Europe of the nineteenth century.[349] Two of the book's defining statements were already apparent from its title: It claimed to be both 'modern' and to refer (only) to 'civilised' states. Like the work of the *Institut de droit international*, the book was very ambitious in scope and aimed to contribute to the 'progress' of international society through law. Both are expressions of the all prevalent belief in 'progress' that permeated the nineteenth century, the idea that society could be systematically 'improved' through reason and the professionalisation of scientific knowledge.[350] Bluntschli's book did not necessarily cover the law as its author saw it, but as he wanted it to be seen: He followed a historic-philosophical approach and in a process of consolidation from the practices of European societies, understood to reflect the increasing 'civilisation' of international contacts, sought to lay down rules of scientific codification.[351] Where traditional methods of interpretation lead to inconclusive answers as to the state of the law, Bluntschli filled such voids on the basis of personal preferences and his understanding of the basic principles of law and morality.[352] His system included not only the possibility of the legality of what would eventually be called 'humanitarian intervention', but in fact, a right of intervention for 'the civilised states':

> If in the course of constitutional disputes the commonly accepted law of nations and of man are infringed upon, then intervention to protect this right and law is justified for the same reasons that intervention by civilised states is always justified in cases of violations of the law endangering society as a whole.[353]

In such cases, he continued, a suppressed party may call for intervention, not in the name of the state, 'but with the authority of international law', and, so he explicitly stated in the later editions of his book, the 'Christians in Turkey' had

---

[347] See Section 2.7.
[348] Koskenniemi 2002, pp. 16–49.
[349] Ziegler 2007, p. 190.
[350] Buzan and Lawson 2015, p. 97.
[351] Koskenniemi 2002, p. 42.
[352] Ziegler 2007, pp. 190–191.
[353] Bluntschli 1868, p. 268, § 478; Bluntschli 1878, p. 270, § 478: see above fn. 273, for the original German text of the quote.

done precisely that in the past.[354] One example Bluntschli referenced more explicitly was Russia's war for 'the protection of the Bulgarians' in 1877–1878.[355] The construct of parties eligible to request international help or even intervention in Bluntschli's system clearly transfers European notions of rational nation states onto the multicultural society of the Ottoman Empire, creating agents mirroring the image of their Western European counterparts by referring to 'Bulgarians' and 'Christians' as identifiable groups. While such groups did exist, language was, at least initially, more important to their identity than religion, the latter only gradually taking centre place in the formation of the national identity of individual Balkan nation states, in Bulgaria, too, as it had before in Serbia and Greece, actively excluding Muslim members of local communities.[356]

In Bluntschli's system, the protection of the 'commonly recognised law of nations and of man' (anerkannten Völker- und Menschenrecht) trumped even the otherwise fundamental principle of non-intervention.[357] This principle obviously served a purpose, for example, to uphold the 'general and humane' character of international law, especially once the principle was extended to the Ottoman Empire with the Paris Treaty of 1856.[358] Bluntschli acknowledged that the European Powers had been entering into treaties according to international law with the Ottoman Empire for centuries, yet in his narrative, it was only with this treaty that the Porte had been admitted to the 'European Community of States (Europäische Staatengenossenschaft)' as a holder of rights ('berechtiges Glied'). The narrative of international law arising from the spheres of Christian states[359] and extending the guarantees of religious freedom to all faiths, left Christians as separate, distinct agents in the field of the law, as the ability of 'Christian communities' (though not necessarily existing as such in reality) in non-Christian countries to request protection from oppression in the form of intervention by civilised states aptly demonstrates. While Bluntschli claimed that the 'public conscience of today's mankind' is not only irritated when one's own religion is harmed, but also where the rights of others are infringed upon in the name of religion, and the protection of 'some human rights' (gewisse Menschenrechte) would in the future, according to Bluntschli in 1878, also allow for the justification of interventions undertaken to stop state oppression,[360] at this stage in the development of international law it was only the respect for the 'commonly recognised law of nations and of man' that could lawfully give rise to the justification of such an intervention.[361] The duty to act in accordance with the

---

[354] Bluntschli 1878, p. 270, § 478.
[355] Bluntschli 1878, p. 270, § 478.
[356] Biondich 2011, p. 10.
[357] Bluntschli 1868, p. 265, § 474, § 473; Bluntschli 1878, p. 267, § 474, p. 20.
[358] Bluntschli 1878, p. 19
[359] Bluntschli 1878, p 19.
[360] Bluntschli 1878, p. 20.
[361] Bluntschli 1878, pp. 23–24.

law would, according to Bluntschli, also expand the sphere of international law and, almost logically, Bluntschli did not consider forcing another state to fulfil its duties under international law ('Nötigung eines anderen Staates, seine völkerrechtlichen Pflichten zu erfüllen'), an intervention in the legal sense, as this required 'authoritative interference in the affairs of a third state'.[362] The conditions under which 'humanitarian intervention' would be legal are met by inference, though not as such, but rather as emergency assistance on the invitation of a suppressed people[363] or a (legal) police measure, 'not in the name of the state, but upon the authority of international law'.[364]

Yet Bluntschli's secularisation of natural law values rested on anti-semitic and racist values: In his 'Staatswörterbuch', Bluntschli stressed the 'racial' differences between 'semitic Jews' and 'European-Aryan peoples', while championing equal rights for assimilated Jews, which had 'taken on the language and customs of the people among which they live'.[365] Equality of rights, thus, appears like a gift extended by the civilised only to those sufficiently assimilated (or civilised). The insistence that the 'Aryan' race is somehow superior to other 'races' is central to Bluntschli's political project – German hegemony in Europe – and also reflected in his legal writing.[366]

Bluntschli's position on the 'modern international law of civilised states' stands in contrast to the often reiterated narrative of (continental European) international law of the nineteenth century as a positive law based on the will of states alone, obsessed with the dogma of sovereignty. His book was a tremendous success and even often consulted by contemporary diplomats,[367] but his attempt to cover international law in all its dynamics[368] consciously went beyond an exploration of the law as it was applied in state practice and international relations. At the heart of Bluntschli's international law was a 'necessary legal conscience' (notwendiges Rechtsbewusstsein), which, according to Bluntschli, had already come into existence in the 'civilised' (Christian) states of Europe and America, and put these nations into the position of the 'agents and guardians of international law' (Träger und Schirmer des Völkerrechts), fulfilling the law's purpose and end, 'a humane law for the world'.[369] 'Humanitarian intervention' as a legal instrument to defend the law, but also to extend its reach, found its almost natural environment in this vision of a law arising

---

[362] Bluntschli 1878, p. 269, § 474, nr. 5 (this point was introduced with the 2nd edition).

[363] Bluntschli 1868, 268, § 478; Bluntschli 1878, S. 270, § 478.

[364] Bluntschli 1878, p. 270, § 478.

[365] Johann C. Bluntschli, 'Juden, Rechtliche Stellung der', in: Johann C. Bluntschli and K. Brater (eds.), *Deutsches Staats-Wörterbuch*, Vol. 5, Stuttgart/Leipzig: Expedition des Staats-Wörterbuchs 1860, p. 444.

[366] Marcel Senn, 'Rassistische und antisemitische Elemente im Rechtsdenken von Johann Caspar Bluntschli', *Zeitschrift der Savigny-Stiftung für Rechtsgeschichte* 1993, pp. 372–405.

[367] Nussbaum 1950, p. 236. See also: Ziegler 2007, p. 190.

[368] Koskenniemi 2002, p. 43.

[369] Bluntschli 1878, p. 55.

from necessity and legal conscience seemingly autonomously.[370] It is no coincidence, then, that when theories of 'humanitarian intervention' were formulated more explicitly later on, they relied on this vision. Mid-nineteenth century state practice, however, moved in a different direction.

2.5.2 Poland, 1863

In 1863, an uprising against the Czar's rule broke out in Poland, then part of Russia. The revolt found no international support and was quickly crushed by Russia with considerable brutality. The Great Powers Austria, France and the United Kingdom, but also smaller states like Portugal, Sweden and Spain protested against the Russian treatment of the uprising more or less resolutely, but these 'moral demonstrations' had no impact on the Czar. The Great Powers could not agree on any further action and the 'diplomatic interventions' have hardly left any impact on the 'classic' literature on 'humanitarian intervention'. Only the United Kingdom was even prepared to fight Russia over Poland, but British pressure was deflected by Gorchakov, Russia's Foreign Minister, who claimed that the Polish issue was 'exclusively the matter of Russia, and not Europe'.[371] The most prominent 'classic' source readily available to discuss this event within the context of 'humanitarian intervention', Ellery C. Stowell, was later relied upon by Wilhelm Grewe in his *Epochs of International Law* to list this as a case of 'humanitarian intervention',[372] as well as – though with reservations – by Manouchehr Ganji in his scene-setting *International Protection of Human Rights*,[373] so that the events continue to feature in the literature on 'humanitarian intervention'.[374] Yet while the inclusion of this 'case' may strengthen the claim that 'the humanitarian idea belonged to the moral and ideological substance of the society of civilised nations' in the nineteenth century,[375] and might add to the legitimacy of the doctrine by added historical precedent, but a simple headcount of the toll of the measures undertaken by 'civilised' Russia under only mild protest from other European Powers might also suggest otherwise: 25,000 insurgents were killed directly, another 2,000 after they had been sentenced to death, 12,000 were forced into labour camps, while the number of deportations to Siberia is not known.[376] Applying the rules laid down by Bluntschli, this would

---

[370] Betsy Baker Röben, 'The Method Behind Bluntschli's "Modern" International Law', *Journal of the History of International Law* 2002, 4(2), pp. 249–292.

[371] Tsygankov 2012, p. 141.

[372] Grewe 2000, p. 492.

[373] Ganji 1962, p. 40, classifying the actions of the great powers as 'humanitarian protests' in the absence of any 'peremptory demands'.

[374] Chesterman 2001, p. 26.

[375] Grewe 2000, p. 490. The case is also discussed with details of discussions in the Dutch parliament, in: van Lynden van Sandenberg 1899, pp. 193–195.

[376] Henke 2002, p. 11.

surely have justified a 'humanitarian intervention'[377] on behalf of the Polish independence fighters, yet hardly anything happened. Writing in 1921, Stowell, who did not want to enter further into 'the interesting details of this important instance of humanitarian intervention, undertaken for the purpose of preventing the oppression of the Poles',[378] went to great lengths to prove that Great Power involvement amounted to intervention 'relying upon the armed force of the cooperating states and not a mere intercession', expanding on three related arguments, only to eventually concede that 'all hope of effective action to prevent the Russian government from denying the Poles a reasonable degree of autonomy' disappeared when Gorchakov deflected British pressure and the other Great Powers could not agree on collective action.[379] The lack of any decisive action in this context therefore suggests that there was nothing universal or humanitarian about the idea of 'humanitarian intervention' as developed in nineteenth century international law, that, instead, it was but a concept to bridge the constructed gap between a sphere of 'humanity' and 'barbarism', operating as an 'intervention by humanity'. Russia, it has been said, emerged from the defeat of the Polish rebellion with increased prestige – 'no more loved than' before, 'but [...] more respected',[380] suggesting that a successful and violent put-down of revolution might just as easily cement the position of a Great Power.

2.5.3 *Crete, 1866*

In 1866, political unrest exploded again on the island of Crete. Ottoman rule over the island had not been successfully challenged during the Greek War of Independence and a number of reforms relating to the status of Christians in the Empire had not been carried out on the island. Ongoing tensions between Christians and Muslims, also the result of the social disparities between Muslim landowners and Christian peasants, led to a revolt against Ottoman rule with the aim of (re)uniting the island with mainland Greece. However, the precise nature of the relations between Christians and Muslims on Crete is difficult to describe, as (self-) identifications changed amid social tensions. According to one (secondary) source, the majority of the island were Muslim by the mid-eighteenth century, though many are said to have later reconverted.[381] Other sources speak of either a third or a fifth of the population identifying as Muslim.[382]

By the end of August 1866, civil war had broken out, with the Cretan insurgents finding support from soldiers and officers from mainland Greece. The Greek press

---

[377] Bluntschli 1878, p. 37.
[378] Stowell 1921, p. 92.
[379] Stowell 1921, pp. 93, 98, 99, 100.
[380] Tsygankov 2012, p. 141.
[381] Wolfgang Gust, *Das Imperium der Sultane*, Munich: Hanser 1995, p. 329.
[382] James J. Reid, *Crisis of the Ottoman Empire*, Stuttgart: Franz Steiner Verlag 2000, p. 212.

was quick to report what it called Muslim massacres of Greeks, whereas the governor of Crete distributed soldiers throughout the island to protect Muslim inhabitants from renewed Greek massacres. The Ottoman Empire formally protested against all Greek acts of support – in addition to 'volunteers', Greece also sent war materials – and turned to the European powers with the request to collectively remind Greece of its international duty to remain neutral. Greece seemed to acquiesce to this pressure, but at the same time appealed to the European powers to help solve 'the Cretan Question'. France and Russia, with the support of smaller European powers, then proceeded to present several joint notes to the Sultan in support of the insurgents, including calls for a ceasefire, free elections, and a plebiscite on the future of the ties between the Empire and the island. The Ottoman Porte briskly rejected all such demands and found support from the British government, leaving no doubt as to the Sultan's right to crush the Cretan rebellion. As elsewhere in the empire, the Porte formed representative administrative councils, each including popularly elected Muslim and non-Muslim representatives, made changes to the tax system and divided the island into two new districts according to population.

Nevertheless, the fighting intensified. The Sultan sent strong contingents of troops, consisting of over 10,000 regular soldiers and several thousand so-called irregulars (bashi-bazouks). The fight against the insurgents left a trail of destruction. Russia, France, Prussia and Italy sent a diplomatic note of protest to the Porte, but promised the United Kingdom to not actively intervene. News of this note intensified the conflict on the island, as the insurgents took this development as an expression of support. The only real support, however, came from Greece and the continued supply of arms and men to the insurgents by the Kingdom led the Sultan to propose an ultimatum in December 1868, threatening to go to war should Greece not comply. This war could only be averted through Great Power pressure on Greece, forcing the kingdom to commit to 'lasting neutrality' and culminating in the Paris conference of 20 January 1869. At the conference, the European Powers effectively sanctioned the reforms put into place by the Porte and ordered Greece to compensate all Ottoman subjects injured during the course of the revolt.

The official justifications for the repeated efforts of the European powers in the years 1866 and 1867 based these initiatives on the 'desire to end the bloodshed' on Crete and the 'wish to improve living conditions for the local Christian population'. The acting Powers found the legal basis for their efforts in Article IX[383] of the 1856 Paris Treaty as well as the London Protocol of 1830 and, specifically, in the provisions that had imposed certain duties on the Porte with regard to the population in Crete.[384]

The lack of any definitive intervention by the European powers makes these events an odd example for a narrative of the evolution of the legal instrument of

---

[383] Pauer 1985, p. 58, and sources quoted therein.
[384] Ganji 1962. p. 27, and sources quoted therein.

'humanitarian intervention'. Few writers in 'classic' international law mentioned this case[385] and those who did focused on criticism of the role of the Great Powers, especially as the results of the conflict seemed to strengthen the position of the Ottoman Empire as a legitimate power in that part of Europe.[386] Some forty years after the events, Antoine Rougier, however, in his 'Theorie de l'intervention d'humanité', in part based his concept of 'humanitarian intervention' on a very condensed version of the events of this case, their description hardly taking up more than the space of a footnote.[387] While Rougier lamented the passivity of 'Europe' in the face of the 'massacres' on Crete in 1866,[388] the inclusion of this 'intervention' in his work has, in turn, led to its inclusion in the narrative of alleged 'humanitarian interventions' in the nineteenth century once the discussion reemerged in the literature on international law in the 1960s and early 1970s. A leading proponent of this renewed discussion, American university Professor Richard B. Lillich (1933–1996), an 'early leader in the movement for the affirmation of human rights in international law',[389] considered the 'peremptory demands' of the Powers an intervention in the legal sense and stressed their 'humanitarian' character.[390]

Lillich's work was instrumental in reigniting the debate on 'humanitarian intervention' in American international law theory in the 1960s in response to the war in Biafra. Lillich referred to the alleged practice of 'humanitarian interventions' in the nineteenth century, including this case, in a number of articles from the 1960s to the 1990s.[391] In their influential paper on 'humanitarian intervention' and the United Nations, the lawyers of the 'New Haven School', W. Michael Reisman and Myres S. McDougal, also in the context of the war in Biafra, considered the case a 'highly instructive' example showing 'that adroit and creative diplomacy may achieve the objectives of forcible humanitarian intervention without necessary resort to armed intervention in the territory in question'.[392] The experience of the war in Biafra as a catalyst for the renewal of the discussion of the legality and necessity of 'humanitarian intervention' has already been mentioned and will be returned to. In this context, it seems sufficient to point out that the apparent desire for inspiring historical examples of interventions in European history again seems to have taken

---

[385] Ullmann 1908, p. 458; von Wachter 1911, p. 54; August Quaritsch, *Völkerrecht und auswärtige Politik*, 9th ed., edited by Carl Goesch, Berlin: W. Weber 1913, p. 77; Tenbaum 1918, p. 51.

[386] e.g. Calvo 1896, p. 309, § 177; Despagnet 1905, p. 231; Dupuis 1921, p. 118.

[387] Rougier 1910, pp. 472, 475.

[388] Antoine Rougier, *Les Guerres Civiles et le Droit des Gens*, Paris: L. Larose 1903, p. 360.

[389] Wolfang Saxon, 'Obituary: Richard B. Lillich', New York Times, 16 August 1996, available at: www.nytimes.com/1996/08/16/us/richard-b-lillich-63-professor-and-expert-on-international-law .html, last accessed 26 February 2019.

[390] Richard B. Lillich, 'Humanitarian Intercession and Humanitarian Intervention', Course of Lectures, July 1977, p. 40, as quoted by Pauer 1985, p. 58.

[391] Richard B. Lillich, 'Forcible Self-help by States to Protect Human Rights', *Iowa Law Review* 1967, pp. 325–351; Richard B. Lillich, 'Intervention to Protect Human Rights', *McGill Law Journal* 1969, 15, pp. 205–219; Lillich 1993, pp. 557–575.

[392] Reisman and McDougal 1968 Memorandum, reprinted in: Lillich 1973, p. 181.

precedence over attention to historical detail, probably the most recurring feature of
the narrative of 'humanitarian intervention': The rather vague protests and demands
of some of the European Powers have also been considered an example of a
'humanitarian intervention' by other writers,[393] and even the official Supplementary
Volume to the report of the International Commission of Intervention and State
Sovereignty offered the 'intervention by Austria, France, Italy, Prussia and Russia in
1866–1968 [sic] to protect the Christian population in Crete' as one of 'five prominent interventions undertaken by European powers against the Ottoman Empire
between 1827 and 1908'.[394] Yet the precise form this protection took is not elaborated
on, and rightly so as no one was protected by the European efforts.

The outcome of the revolt in Crete has been considered 'more victorious' for the
Ottoman Empire than it 'had been or would be in almost any other diplomatic
confrontation during the [nineteenth] century'.[395] Indeed, it is striking how closely
the turn of events of the uprising of the Greeks in Crete mirrors the earlier revolt in
mainland Greece after 1822, with the significant difference that in the earlier case
the Great Powers took an active part to secure Greek independence, whereas in this
case some notes of protest and an international conference that sanctioned the
reforms carried out by the Ottoman Empire was all the Great Power involvement
amounted to. To speak, as some writers do, of an 'intervention of the Western
powers' contributing to a 'peaceful solution of the conflict',[396] or in the aforementioned sense of an 'intervention to protect the Christian population in Crete', is to
create a narrative in line with long-standing expectations of Ottoman patterns of
behaviour, yet it only reproduces inaccurate stereotypes about the legitimacy of
alleged European Great Power involvement in struggles against the Ottoman
Empire without sufficient basis of fact. If there is anything 'unusual' about the case
of Crete between 1866 and 1869, it is that the position of the Ottoman Empire as the
legitimate sovereign of Crete was ultimately strengthened, despite clear and direct
appeals to the perceived anachronism of continued Muslim rule over supposedly
predominantly Christian subjects. The type of 'diplomatic interventions' for
'humanitarian reasons' that took place during the course of the revolt were uni-
formly considered legal in the legal literature in the nineteenth century.[397]

---

[393] Grewe 2000, p. 491; Malanczuk 1997, p. 20; Abiew 1999, p. 51. Similarly, Nathan Feinberg,
'The International Protection of Human Rights and the Jewish Question', Israel Law Review,
Vol. 3, No. 4, 1968, p. 489, considering this case an example of an intervention on behalf of
Christians under Ottoman Rule.

[394] International Commission on Intervention and State Sovereignty 2001, Suppl. Vol., p. 16 with
note 4, p. 16 with p. 24, note 6.

[395] Stanford J. Shaw and Ezel Kural Shaw, History of the Ottoman Empire and Modern Turkey,
Vol. II: Reform, Revolution, and Republic: The Rise of Modern Turkey, 1808–1975, Cambridge
University Press 1977, p. 152.

[396] Henke 2002, p. 13, translation by the author.

[397] Halleck 1861, pp. 84–86, IV/§ 7, pp. 340–342, XIV/§ 22; Kent and Abdy 1866, pp. 46, 90–91;
Stapleton 1866, S. 10 ff.; Strauch 1879, pp. 5–8.

Therefore, incorporating the events around the revolt of Crete into a narrative of gradual 'humanisation' of international relations turns a relatively common example of inaction in the face of a failed revolt into an exceptional show of humanitarian concerns. It would seem to de-legitimise the narrative of 'humanitarian intervention' as an instrument to strengthen the value of human rights, if not understood in the sense recently offered by Heraclidis: There, the case of Crete in 1866–1868 is 'not included', but thus described: The case 'witnessed reports of massacres while in fact the Ottoman authorities tried to be restrained in subduing the Cretan uprising so as not to allow foreign intervention on humanitarian grounds'.[398] No source is given for this claim and this author found no indication that the Ottomans showed any particular restraint. One classic description of the events thus simply reads: 'In 1866, an insurrection broke out in the island of Candia, or Crete, which the Turkish Government suppressed after a long effort, marked by many cruelties, but without interference from any of the powers'.[399]

2.6 THE GREAT BALKAN CRISIS

2.6.1 Introduction

In the years between 1875 and 1878 a number of uprisings, disturbances and wars upset the territory now known as the Balkans and claimed tens of thousands of lives, until the borders of this part of Europe were re-drawn at the Berlin Congress of 1878. The Berlin Congress is considered a major achievement in the history of inter-national minority protection by imposing on the Ottoman Empire and its newly formed successor states important provisions on civil and political rights, including religious freedom and the protection of Christians and Jews, as well as recognising 'the rights and interests' of ethnic minorities, such as the Armenians.[400] At the same time, the Congress 'invented' the Balkans as an area of crisis, creating the conditions under which the term Balkan is still best understood as a metaphor for Western understandings of Eastern Europe.[401] What used to be known as 'Turkey in Europe' became – for political reasons – 'the Balkans',[402] but remained Rumelia in Ottoman parlance. The introduction of the term 'the Balkans' seems directly related to the European belief of the imminent end of the Ottoman Empire in the post-Berlin Congress period,[403] making its introduction a self-fulfilling prophecy. The results of the Congress secured the Balkans' decisive role in Europe's development, even to

[398] Heraclidis and Dialla 2015, p. 101.
[399] Schem 1878, p. 98.
[400] Lauren 2011, pp. 74–75.
[401] See Maria Todorova, Imagining the Balkans, 2nd ed., Oxford University Press 2009; Dusan I. Bjelic and Obrad Savic (eds.), Balkan as Metaphor, Cambridge, MA: The MIT Press 2002.
[402] Marriott 1940, p. 21.
[403] Boyar 2007, p. 33.

this day.[404] The aim of the Congress was to settle the 'Oriental Question' (or 'Eastern Question') and brought a century of interventions in the Ottoman Empire to a dramatic close, in the 'brilliant closing performance of the European Concert'.[405] Those European parts of the Ottoman Empire that – by their association with the Ottoman Empire and Muslim rule – were not covered by the same (international) law as the rest of Europe, according to most of the writers on international law in the nineteenth century, were finally returned to 'Europe'. The Treaty of 1878 also established a potential basis for the justification of future 'humanitarian interventions',[406] even if none ever materialised. Viewed from today, it is hard to resist drawing parallels between this nineteenth century Great Balkan Crisis and the much more recent break-up of the former Yugoslavia at the end of the twentieth century.

2.6.2 The 'Interventions' and Their History

The immediate cause of the events that connect this 'great crisis' to a history of 'humanitarian intervention' was a number of peasant revolts in Bosnia and Herzegovina in 1875, in which (Christian) peasants took to arms against the Ottoman authorities and their (Muslim) land owners, often recent converts to Islam. The ensuing civil war claimed thousands of lives among the predominantly Christian civilian population and forced over 150,000 people to flee to neighbouring countries. The Great Powers expressed their wish for a quick and peaceful resolution of the conflict to the Sultan and the Porte expressly recognised the 'humanitarian' nature of this wish.[407] In May 1876, Austria-Hungary together with Prussia and Russia (Three-Kaiser-Bund) presented the Berlin Memorandum to the Porte with the intention of obtaining a truce in the conflict for the protection of both their own nationals as well as the local population.[408] Another aim of the campaign was to improve the general situation for Christians living in the Ottoman Empire, but the Sultan – still enjoying British support – was not impressed.[409]

[404] Danilo Zolo, *Invoking Humanity*, London/New York: Continuum 2002, pp. 12, 136.

[405] Grewe 2000, p. 438.

[406] See Redslob 1937, p. 138, for the claim that the Treaty of 1878 legalised 'humanitarian intervention', allegedly declared illegal previously with the Paris Treaty of 1856. A similar claim is made by Antoine Rougier 1910, p. 475. Kutner 1985, p. 599, writes about the 1878 Treaty: 'The doctrine of humanitarian intervention that was involved within the context of these treaty provisions and which also encompassed protection of the Jews, became a part of diplomatic practice'.

[407] Calvo 1896, p. 309: '... appréciant les sentiments d'humanité qui ont dicté cette démarche, et désireuse avant tout d'éviter l'effusion du sang et de maintenir la pax accepte la proposition des représentants des grandes puissances; (...)'.

[408] Berlin Memorandum 1876, reprinted in: Georg Friedrich von Martens, Charles Samwer and Jules Hopf (eds.), *Nouveau Recueil Général des Traités*, Deuxième Séries, Vol. II, Göttingen: Dieterich 1878, p. 12.

[409] Bridge and Bullen 2005, p. 201.

The Balkans then also caught fire in another corner: In Bulgaria, discontentment with Greek control of the Bulgarian Orthodox Church since the eighteenth century had gradually grown into a movement for national independence.[410] In May 1876, revolution erupted in the Balkan Mountains. Poorly organised activists faced 'irregular' troops of so-called *bashi-bozuks* and another orgy of violence ensued. As was common in late nineteenth century Europe, these 'Bulgarian Horrors' were not viewed as reciprocal battles of destruction, but organised massacres of Christians: According to the British government's official statistics, the Porte's repression of the insurgency resulted in the destruction of about sixty villages and the killing of 12,000 people.[411] An American journalist reporting for the *Daily News* in London in 1878, spoke of estimates of 25,000–40,000 killed.[412] Other estimates put the number of Christian victims at 4,000, while the number of Muslims killed was thought to have been considerably higher.[413] Despite massive public attention — reportedly, more than 3,000 articles were published in some 200 European newspapers in the months following the massacres[414] – no Great Power reaction was forthcoming. Only the leaders of Serbia and Montenegro, still legally part of the Ottoman Empire, felt encouraged to declare war on the Porte in June and July 1876, respectively. The Serbian declaration of war cited the conditions in Bosnia-Herzegovina as a source for threats to the stability of Serbia and the persecution of Christian brethren as causes for war.[415] Recourse to force was justified as an act of national self-protection as well as by the wish to stop the effusion of more blood.[416]

Meanwhile, in the corridors of power of the European Great Powers different strategies were developed to respond to the unfolding events. Austria and Russia held secret negotiations on splitting up the Balkans between them, should the insurrection be successful and bring down the Ottoman Empire as a result. But the Serbian and Montenegrinian campaigns proved disastrous. Neither Romania nor Greece joined the fight and no Balkan-wide solidarity was forthcoming. As Serbia and Montenegro were beaten by the Ottoman forces, Russia imposed an ultimatum on the Porte that led to a ceasefire in October 1876, clearing the way for a conference in Constantinople in late 1876 to solve the crisis. The aim of the conference, held upon British initiative, was to provide detailed reforms for the Balkans and at the same time contain Russian ambitions to further the Czar's

---

[410] Shaw and Shaw 1977, p. 160.

[411] Rodogno 2012, p. 147, quoting A. & P., *Correspondence Respecting the Affairs of Turkey, and the Insurrection in Bosnia and Herzegovina*. In Continuation of Papers Presented to the Parliament, Turkey, No. 2, 1876 TNA: PRO, FO 881/1916, Confidential Prints, Atrocities in Bulgaria, Memorandum by Lord Tenterden, 9 August 1876.

[412] J. A. MacGahan, *The Turkish Atrocities in Bulgaria*, London: Bradbury, Agnew & Co, 1876, p. 11.

[413] Shaw and Shaw 1977, p. 162.

[414] Glenny 2000, p. 109.

[415] Pauer 1985, p. 62.

[416] Serbian Declaration of War, 30 June 1876, reprinted in: von Martens et al. 1878, p. 17.

influences in the region. The Porte, however, rejected all of the Great Power demands, citing Article IX of the Paris Treaty of 1856 as the source of protection against any such foreign intervention.[417] Anticipating the failure of the conference, Russia had already obtained permission from Austria-Hungary for military actions agains the Porte, and in March 1877 the Czar secured the neutrality of the United Kingdom with the London Protocol, which threatened the proper measures to 'assure the well-being of the Christian population and the interests of peace in general', should the Porte refuse to accept the terms of the conference. Not surprisingly, the Porte refused.

Russia declared war on the Ottoman Empire on 24 April 1877 and justified this step by claiming the Czar's intent to protect the Orthodox Christians of the Balkans and move the Porte to undertake necessary reforms, as requested by the London Protocol.[418] The Czar also declared Russia was acting to protect the 'interests of Europe', and by framing the war effort as a result of the refusal of the Ottoman Empire to undertake the measures requested by the London Protocol, gave his actions the character of a quasi legitimised intervention of the European Concert, unilaterally undertaken.[419] The directives sent out to the Russian ambassadors in European capitals accordingly stressed the Czar's intention to act in accordance with the collective European will and to defend 'the sentiments of humanity, and the conscience of Christian nations'.[420]

The outbreak of the Russo-Turkish War also provided the occasion for Romania to declare independence on 10 May 1877. Opposed by the Great Powers, which refused to guarantee Romania's neutrality, the declaration came with the heavy price of another Russian occupation.[421] The war quickly descended into a brutal orgy of destruction and proved disastrous for the Ottoman Empire. Over 300,000 Muslims were massacred and a million people were uprooted in the Balkans and Caucasus.[422] A ceasefire was eventually agreed on 31 January 1878 and a formal peace treaty ended the war on 3 March 1878. The conditions of the peace treaty were so harsh on the Ottoman Empire that they were renegotiated at British

---

[417] See the Second Protocol of the session dated 28/16 December 1876 of the Constantinople Conference, reprinted in: von Martens et al. 1878, p. 97. Also see Circular note of the Ottoman Porte in reaction to the Czar's declaration of war, 24 April 1877, reprinted in: von Martens et al. 1878, p. 192.

[418] Russian Declaration of War, 24 April 1877, reprinted in: von Martens et al. 1878, pp. 190–191.

[419] Pauer 1985, p. 63; Murphy 1996, p. 55.

[420] Circular of the Russian Government to its representatives at all the European Courts, 19 January 1877, English translation in: George Douglas Campbell, *The Eastern Question from the Treaty of Paris to the Treaty of Berlin 1878 and to the Second Afghan War*, London: Strahan 1879, p. 376.

[421] Carole Fink, *Defending the Rights of Others*, Cambridge University Press 2004, p. 19.

[422] Bonney 2004, p. 148.

insistence during the Berlin Congress.[423] The final act of the Berlin Congress on 13 July 1878 brought the conflict to its – temporary – conclusion. It produced a settlement which finally 'destroyed the illusions that the Ottoman state was an eternal, unchanging, great power. Some two-fifths of the territory of the state and one-fifth of the population were lost'.[424]

2.6.3 *The Interventions in Context*

The events in the Balkans are incorporated into the – at least partially imagined – system of a CORPUS IURIS PUBLICI ORIENTALIS, the politico-legal system for controlling the break-up of the Ottoman Empire under the collective authority of the European Great Powers.[425] In this system, the efforts of Serbia and Montenegro, justified as acts of self-determination, are seen as the revolt of semi-sovereign states against the suzerain Ottoman Empire.[426] The image of the events in historiography and international law, however, is largely dictated by the perception of the 'Bulgarian Horrors', as described in the influential pamphlet 'The Bulgarian Horrors and the Question of the East' by (former and future British prime minister) William Gladstone, published in 1876. The pamphlet spoke of 'the horror and infamy' of victims 'murdered, or worse than murdered, by thousands' and of 'rights and duties', with Gladstone telling his readers that this kind of persecution was no longer acceptable and urging them to consider their larger responsibility to 'protect humanity and defend justice'. 'For the purposes of humanity alone', Gladstone concluded, the fleet should be sent 'in concert with the other Powers, for the defense of innocent lives'.[427] British official policy, however, had traditionally been committed to upholding the status quo in Eastern Europe and the serving prime minister Benjamin Disraeli publicly described Gladstone's conduct as 'worse than any of those Bulgarian atrocities which now occupy attention'.[428]

Gladstone had put the question of morality on the table of British politics and made the moral case for intervention, claiming that Disraeli's course was at odds with British traditional commitment to protect honour and justice. He – who had never set foot in the area – spoke of '[c]rimes and outrages, so vast in scale as to exceed all modern example, and so unutterably vile as well as fierce in character, that it passes the power of heart to conceive them', and created a narrative in which

---

[423] British resistance to the terms of the initial peace treaty is sometimes taken as a sign of British opposition to the idea of humanitarian intervention, see: Sybille Tönnies, 'Soll ich meines Bruders Hüter sein?', *Neue Zürcher Zeitung* 5 May 2008, 103, p. 24.

[424] Bonney 2004, p. 148.

[425] Evans 1997, p. 64.

[426] Paul Heilborn, 'Vasallenstaaten', in: Karl Strupp (ed.), *Wörterbuch des Völkerrechts und der Diplomatie*, Vol. III, Berlin: De Gruyter 1929, p. 2.

[427] Gladstone 1876, pp. 13, 17, 19–20, 43, 53.

[428] C. C. Eldridge, *England's Mission, The Imperial Idea in the Age of Gladstone and Disraeli*, London: Palgrave Macmillan 1973, p. 216.

the Ottoman Empire constituted the clear counterpart to Europe's 'civilised' values and order: The Turks were, Gladstone said, 'upon the whole, from the black day when they first entered Europe, the one great anti-human specimen of humanity'.[429] The phrase would later be used against him, when the (exiled) German journalist and former revolutionary Karl Blind commented in 1896: 'How if he had been reminded by a member of the anti-human race that there are some Irish Home Rulers and Secessionists who, in United Ireland, speak of England, on account of its rule of the sister Isle and its many polyglot dominions, as the "Anglo-Saxon Grand Turk"'.[430] And indeed, the strong effect of Gladstone's words did not go unnoticed in the Ottoman Empire, where this type of propaganda prompted a swift response with counter-propaganda, aimed in particular at the Muslim world, emphasising the similarities between British and Ottoman imperial rule and stressing the differences between the Sultan and the Czar.[431] Soon after the 1876 atrocities, the British ambassador to the Sublime Porte, Sir Henry Layard, became a witness to an emotional outburst by the Sultan: 'We are accused in Europe of being savages and fanatics ... [Yet] unlike the Czar, I have abstained till now from stirring up a crusade and profiting from religious fanaticism, but the day may come when I can no longer curb the rights and indignation of my people at seeing their co-religionists butchered in Bulgaria and Armenia. . .'.[432]

The public effect of the 'Bulgarian atrocities' far outweighed their relevance for the historical development, where their immediate impact only prevented the United Kingdom from intervening on the side of the Ottoman Empire. Yet Disraeli resisted the pressure to join the Russian fight against the Empire and the British government is also quoted in the literature of 'humanitarian intervention' as insisting that 'whatever the repressive nature of Turkish rule over the Bulgarians, Herzegovinians and Bosnians, the Russian intervention, sanctioned by the other powers, "based in theory upon religious sympathy and upon humanity ... was a move, in fact, upon the Straits and Constantinople, in pursuance of Russia's century long program"'.[433] Indeed, Russia's support for the nationalist movements in the Balkans seems more directly related to the pan-Slavic movement and the desire to expand Russian spheres of influence. As historian Mark Biondich has observed,

[429] Gladstone 1876, pp. 15, 17.

[430] Karl Blind, 'Young Turkey', *Forthnighly Review* (London 1896) LXVI p. 840, as quoted in Selim Deringil, *The Well-Protected Domains – Ideology and the Legitimation of Power in the Ottoman Empire 1876–1909*, London: I. B. Tauris Publishers 1999, p. 147.

[431] See generally: Deringil 1999.

[432] Joan Haslip, *The Sultan. The Life of Abdul Hamid*, New York 1958, 11, p. 124, as quoted in Deringil 1999, p. 46.

[433] The quote is attributed by Abiew 1999, p. 52, fn. 101, to 'the British government', by quoting Theodore S. Woolsey, *America's Foreign Policy*, New York: The Century Co. 1898. In fact, this appears to be an expanded version of Woolsey's own statement, see: Woolsey 1898, p. 74. Abiew's source is difficult to establish, as his book's internal cross references lead nowhere.

the violence visited upon the Muslims of Bulgaria was shaped to a considerable degree by the Russian presence. In the previous decade Russia had perpetrated systematic violence against Muslim groups in its conquest of the Caucasus. In Bulgaria, the Russian military adopted a similar approach, encouraging or engaging directly in expulsions of Muslims and Jews. In many instances, Bulgarian detachments had a parallel role, either initiating assaults against Muslims or serving as Russian auxiliaries.[434]

While others insist that the Russian-Turkish war 'was casually unrelated to the struggles of Bulgarian nationalists', it is clear that the war 'weakened the Ottoman empire enough to allow for the establishment of the Bulgarian nation-state'.[435] Bulgarian Jews, however, had declared their neutrality during the Bulgarian uprising in 1876, leading to an anti-Jewish outburst which raised alarm among British Jews and stirred Gladstone to also champion the cause of Jewish rights in the Balkans.[436] In the wake of the war, it also became possible to put the emancipation of other Jewish communities in the regions on the table, developments which led to the minority protection clauses inserted into the Final Act of the Berlin Congress, but no Muslim minority in other European states was awarded similar protection. Russian intervention thus not only turned the pattern of massacre on its head – it was indigenous Muslims who were the targets of Russian and Bulgarian mass reprisals, not the bands of Muslim *bashi-bazouks* who were responsible for the original attacks on Bulgarian Christians.[437] It also gave false credit to the nationalist aspirations of the Bulgarians and others which were at odds with the Russian aims of substituting Ottoman power with the Czar's own reign. As genocide scholar Mark Levene points out: '[T]he very notion thrown up by Bulgarian insurrectionists, and others, that they were speaking on behalf of whole "national" populations could only feed the countervailing imperial retort that if such entire populations were behind the insurrectionists then they should be dealt with accordingly'.[438]

2.6.4 The Interventions in the History of 'Humanitarian Intervention'

As the events in the Balkans unfolded, even before the start of the Russian campaign against the Ottoman Empire, the Belgian-German lawyer Egide (Aegidius Rudolph Nicolaus) Arntz penned his influential thoughts, later referred to as the first theory of 'humanitarian intervention' and published in the *Revue de Droit international et de législation comparée*. The relationship of the Ottoman Empire to its Christian

[434] Biondich 2011, p. 29.
[435] Andreas Wimmer, *Waves of War – Nationalism and State*, Cambridge University Press 2012, p. 100.
[436] Fink 2004, p. 25, n 101.
[437] Mark Levene, *Genocide in the Age of the Nation State*, Vol. II – The Rise of the West and the Coming of Genocide, London: I. B. Tauris 2005, p. 280.
[438] Levene 2005, p. 280.

subjects was a recurring theme for the journal and the events in the Balkans only helped to increase the attention of the progress-oriented lawyers writing for the publication. Arntz laid down the basic principle still guiding the idea of 'humanitarian intervention' as a legal concept:

> When a government, acting fully within the limits of its sovereign rights, violates the laws of humanity, either by measures contrary to the interests of other States, or by excesses of injustice and cruelty which profoundly injure our morals and our civilisation, the right of intervention is legitimate. In effect, although the rights of sovereignty and independence of States are important, there is something which is even more important. It is the law of humanity, or of *human society*, which must not be offended. Just as *in* the State the liberty of the *individual* is restricted and must be restricted by the *law* and by the *morals* of *society*, the individual liberty of *States* must be limited by the laws of human society.[439]

The twentieth century German historian of international law, Wilhelm G. Grewe, has called 'constructions of this kind' 'irrelevant to practical international law', completing only 'the picture of a legal institution, which, even if controversial, was still particularly significant for the intellectual character of the international law of this age'.[440] While it is true that it would take until the end of the nineteenth century for an active 'lawmaker' of international law to adopt a legal construction of this kind to justify an armed intervention, it is obvious that the language used by Arntz and other proponents of 'humanitarian intervention' appealed to the human rights values so familiar to the ongoing discourse on the subject. Arntz adopted the language of civilisation and society, community and justice, but ignored the source of the conflicts in the Balkans, seemingly unconsciously applying the 'nationality principle' to the area which, he probably would have admitted, was inconsistent with the applicable law. He wrote from the liberal background of the Western European nation state[441] and failed to see that it was precisely the idea of the (single) nation state that had set in motion the turn of events that led to the 'Europeanisation' of the territories under Ottoman control. During the nineteenth century, European international politics were shaped to a significant degree by nationalism and for many international lawyers minority protection was a necessity and the consequence of sovereignty trumping the 'nationality principle'.[442] International

---

[439] Rolin-Jaequemyns 1876, p. 675 (emphasis in original), cited according to the English translation in Grewe 2000, p. 495.

[440] Grewe 2000, p. 496.

[441] Born in Prussia, Arntz was first active in German politics and studied in Munich and Bonn, before fleeing to Belgium during the 1830s. He returned to Germany and was a member of the 1848 Prussian National Assembly, but went back to Belgium after the dissolution of the National Assembly, see: Raimund Schramm, 'Arntz, Aegidius Rudolph Niclaus', in: *Allgemeine Deutsche Biographie*, Vol. 46, Leipzig: Duncker & Humblot 1902, pp. 55–58, available online at: www.deutsche-biographie.de/sfz1371.html, last accessed 8 October 2018.

[442] Rudolf Laun, 'Nationalitätenfrage, einschließlich des Minderheitenrechts', in: Karl Strupp (ed.), *Wörterbuch des Völkerrechts und der Diplomatie*, Vol. II, Berlin: De Gruyter 1925, p. 82.

protection arrangements thus shifted from religious to national minorities,[443] while deportations and minority protection emerged together at this point in time.

Campaigns of ethnic cleansing made the Balkans more and more Christian and Anatolia more and more Muslim.[444] Writing about the 'conditions of the existence of the Ottoman Empire and her particular situation vis-à-vis of Europe',[445] Arntz and Rolin-Jaequemyns provided the background for a separation of the 'European' parts of the Ottoman Empire from its 'non-European' mainland. The nationalist ideology of the (often: Western educated) 'native scholars' of their own people created a narrative that changed the population of the Balkans. As Genocide scholar Cathie Carmichael has observed, '[t]hese regions have not only lost "minorities", they have had their overwhelming constituency changed. Although it may be somewhat problematic to equate "tradition" with multiethnicity, polytaxis and diversity, there is barely a single region, which remains multiethnic in the Balkans or that has escaped the ravages of ethnic cleansing'.[446]

The simplistic interpretation of the relations between the Ottoman Empire and its diverse population put forward by Arntz and Rolin-Jaequemyns set the tone for discussion of the events in the subsequent literature on international law: In 1877, Fedor (Friedrich von) Martens (1845–1909), the foremost Russian international lawyer of the Czarist period,[447] justified Russia's declaration of war as a decision worthy of the support of all 'civilised' nations – the Czar had declared war, Martens wrote, in the 'interest of humanity', to fight the 'intolerable conditions' the High Porte had created for its Christian subjects.[448] It is obvious that the image of the Ottoman Empire as an oppressive and 'barbaric' ruler dictated the interpretation of the events, even if it seems clear that the conduct of Russian troops in the ensuing escalations did not differ substantially from those of the Ottoman soldiers and irregular fighters. Reports of mass killings, rape and torture of Ottoman civilians even led the members of the *Institut de droit international* to discuss the possibility of a declaration condemning the Russian conduct, but Martens successfully deflected this.[449] By framing the conflict between the individual nationalist movements of the Balkans not in the terms of self-determination but in terms of a conflict between 'humanity' and 'barbarism', the literature on 'humanitarian intervention' bought into the nationalist narrative of the exclusion of local minorities – who had lived in the area for decades, if not centuries – from the national collective and, thus,

---

[443] Janne E. Nijman, 'Minorities and Majorities', in: Bardo Fassbender and Anne Peters (eds.), *The Oxford Handbook of the History of International Law*, Oxford University Press 2012, p. 109.

[444] Cathie Carmichael, *Ethnic Cleansing in the Balkans*, London: Routledge 2002; Schwartz 2013, p. 21.

[445] Rolin-Jaequemyns 1876, p. 675.

[446] Carmichael 2002, p. 12.

[447] Mälksoo 2008, p. 214.

[448] Martens 1877, pp. 49, 50, cited according to the English translation in: Koskenniemi, 'International Law in Europe' 2005, pp. 113–114.

[449] Koskenniemi, 'International Law in Europe' 2005, p. 124.

contributed to creating the problem it set out to solve. Minority protection only became an issue *after* the multi-national Ottoman Empire with its limited guarantees of religious freedom for 'infidels' (i.e., Christians and Jews) ceased to exist. Czar Alexander II, the leading player in this romanticised scenario of European involvement in the gradual breakup of the Ottoman Empire, is credited with making 'the first great attempt' to humanise 'the law of land war' after the epoch of Grotius,[450] nevertheless conducted – in the view of British prime minister Disraeli – 'a war of "extermination . . . against a religion & a race"'.[451] Only ten years prior, the Czar had been quite successful (and ruthless) in curbing Polish nationalism, and while Alexander II is known for important domestic reforms, in particular the emancipation of Russia's serfs, he continued to uphold the Pale of Settlement and the wide-ranging discrimination of Jews in Russia. Narratives of 'humanitarian intervention' conveniently connect the Russian war of 1877–1878 to the minority protection-provisions of the Berlin Congress of 1878,[452] but it seems obvious that the Czar is, at best, a curious choice for a champion for human rights, 'progress of humanity' and minority protection.

In the further discussion of the events in international law, the apparent violations of 'standards of civilisation' by the Russian troops never became an issue. Russia's war for 'the protection of the Bulgarians' in 1877–1878 was explicitly mentioned in the context of interventions to uphold international law by Swiss lawyer and founding member of the *Institut de droit international*, Johann Caspar Bluntschli.[453] In an article for the German weekly 'Die Gegenwart', the Swiss lawyer presented the British and Russian positions on the legality of (non-) intervention 'in the current struggles over and in Turkey' as equally rooted in international law, but giving preference to the view that 'European' intervention was justified because of the extraordinary character of the 'Turkish' State, stating that both the United Kingdom and Russia had demonstrated that it was 'possible to integrate Mohammedan tribes into the European order and state system', but that the Ottoman Empire had resorted to 'barbarism' in dealing with its Christian population in the current struggles.[454] Presenting the underlying values of international law as values developed by the 'aryan' and Christian European nations, but rooted in 'human nature' and 'serving humanity' ('der Menschheit dienen'), Bluntschli held that the Ottoman Empire had failed to live up to the expectations under which it had been admitted to the European Concert in 1856.[455] In an interesting display of racism and

---

[450] Henry Maine, *International Law: A Series of Lectures Delivered Before the University of Cambridge 1887*, London: John Murray 1888, p. 128.

[451] J. P. Parry, 'Disraeli and England', *The Historical Journal* 2000, 43(3), pp. 699–728.

[452] Lauren 2011, pp. 74–75.

[453] Bluntschli 1878, p. 270, § 478.

[454] Johann Caspar Bluntschli, 'Völkerrechtliche Briefe: I. Das Recht der europäischen Intervention in der Türkei', *Die Gegenwart – Wochenschrift für Literatur, Kunst und öffentliches Leben* 1876, pp. 377–379.

[455] Bluntschli 1876, p. 378.

arrogance, Bluntschli held 'even the more educated Turks' incapable of understanding 'our aryan-European concept of law, which is devoid of any religious connotations and even clearly separable from morality', while bestowing upon Russia the
honor of acting on behalf of 'Europe' to 'enable the natural development' and to
restore those old cultured lands of 'Eastern Romania' (Ostromanien) to European
civilisation, for the benefit of the 'progress of humanity'.[456] In his treatise on
international law, Bluntschli justified the Russian war 'for the protection of Christians in Turkey' and the Bulgarians in particular as a necessary intervention to
uphold 'generally recognised human rights'.[457] Later writers also focused on the
'Bulgarian atrocities' as suitable grounds for justification of the Russian decision to
go to war.[458] However, the legal quality of the Russian conduct as a 'humanitarian
intervention' did not play any important role in the classic literature on international
law,[459] where the focus was more on the effects of the Berlin Congress of 1878.[460]

The Final Act of this conference included in Article 62 the 'expression' of the
'intention' of the Ottoman Porte, 'to maintain the principle of religious liberty, and
give it the widest scope', of which the Contracting Parties took 'note'. This 'spon-
taneous declaration' not only could have been a possible legal basis for future
interventions,[461] but also – in the eyes of authors ranging well into the present
day – an explicit justification for 'interventions of humanity' in the Ottoman
Empire.[462] Considered a deviation from a principle of non-intervention, this development was welcomed by most writers, but declared illegal by others.[463] These
diverging interpretations at the beginning of the twentieth century show the continued development of two competing versions of international law as the nineteenth century drew to its close: one with an uncompromising principle of non-
intervention at its core, which is probably the one that is better remembered as the
prevailing version of 'classic international law' and the other with a basic principle of
non-intervention modified by a corresponding 'right' of 'civilised' states to intervene
in the affairs of 'uncivilised' states.

The Berlin Treaty of 1878 also included explicit provisions for the protection of
religious minorities in the newly established de jure sovereign states of Serbia,

---

[456] Bluntschli 1876, p. 379, my translation.
[457] Bluntschli 1878, p. 270, § 478, my translation.
[458] e.g. Amos Hershey; *The Essentials of International Public Law and Organization*, 2nd revised
ed., New York: Macmillan 1930, p. 239; Stowell 1921, p. 83.
[459] Compare Bonfils and Fauchille 1904, p. 167, no. 317, treating the events of 1877–1878 as an
intervention in religious affairs, and Despagnet 1905, pp. 212–213.
[460] Geffcken 1889, p. 164; Bry 1891, pp. 138–139; Calvo 1896, pp. 309–310, § 178; Despagnet 1905,
pp. 232 ff.; Butler and Maccoby 1928.
[461] Geffcken 1889, p. 165: 'Unstreitig aber begründen alle diese Bestimmungen im Gegensatz zum
Pariser Frieden ein umfassendes collectives Interventionsrecht der Mächte in innere Angelegenheiten der Türkei, weil dieselbe von der ihr 1856 belassenen Freiheit schlechten Gebrauch
gemacht hat; (...)'.
[462] Rougier 1910, p. 475; Kutner 1985, p. 599.
[463] Bonfils and Fauchille 1904, p. 167.

Montenegro and Romania as well as Bulgaria as a de facto independent state. The relevant provisions were identical in each case, whereas the Treaty introduced additional requirements for the Ottoman Empire with regard to national minorities, requiring the Porte to carry out 'the improvements and reforms demanded by local requirements in the provinces inhabited by Armenians, and to guarantee their security against the Circassians and Kurds'. (Art. 61 of the Treaty).[464] The Treaty of Berlin can be described as testifying 'to the growing strength of a distinctly European understanding of international order, one in which strategic intervention – intervention in the name of the European state system and "humanity" whose rights and interests it purportedly safeguarded – came increasingly to be invested with greater value'.[465] Accordingly, the idea that a 'humanitarian intervention' in any meaningful sense somehow took place during the Great Balkan Crisis of the years 1875 to 1877 has been gradually woven into the history of international law to the extent that even opponents of the legal instrument continue to see the need to rebuke the claim that Russia 'intervened after Ottoman troops killed thousands of Bulgarian subjects'.[466] In 1910, Antoine Rougier claimed it had been 'the events in Bosnia-Herzegovina and Bulgaria (1875–1877)' which had led Rolin-Jaequemyns and Arntz to give the doctrine of 'humanitarian intervention' its typical form.[467] The statement stretches the chronological narrative somewhat, as do other versions of the historical narrative put forward to suggest that 'humanitarian' considerations had been paramount to a solution of the 'Eastern Question' in this context.[468] Anglo-American authors in particular have shown themselves willing to contribute to a narrative of 'humanitarian' motivation and justification of the Russian move against the Ottoman Empire.[469]

Such willingness stands in marked contrast to the European Powers' failure to protect non-Christian populations from the effects of the interventionist activities,[470] and 'the patronizing attitude of the "saviour" towards the victims'.[471] Effectively, the

---

[464] Treaty between the United Kingdom, Germany, Austria, France, Italy, Russia, and Turkey for the Settlement of Affairs in the East: Signed at Berlin, 13 July 1878, reprinted in: *American Journal of International Law* 1908, 2(4), pp. 401–424, available at JSTOR, www.jstor.org/stable/2212670.

[465] Umut Özsu, *Formalizing Displacement*, Oxford University Press 2015, p. 29

[466] Menon 2016, p. 78.

[467] Rougier 1910, p. 473.

[468] Geoffrey Robertson, *Crimes against Humanity*, 2nd ed., London: Penguin 2002, p. 14: 'Pressure was put on the Ottoman sultans in the 1880s to promulgate measures to protect Christian minorities from discrimination; when these failed, Gladstone obtained parliamentary approval to allocate ships, men and money to protect Christians from slaughter by Turks in Bulgaria'. It is not easy to determine what historical event this statement actually refers to.

[469] e.g. Fenwick 1965, p. 287; Kutner 1985, p. 602.

[470] Rodogno 2012. p. 167.

[471] Heraclidis and Dialla 2015, p. 190.

efforts of the European Powers helped to drive out the Muslim population from the newly constituted states,[472] and by reimagining religious communities as national (or ethnic) minorities, events were set in motion that eventually led to the gradual disappearance of these communities.[473] If there are meaningful appeals to 'humanity' to be found[474] amidst this carnage, they are probably best forgotten. At the same time, the 1870s – and this crisis in particular – marked the birth of the legal doctrine of 'humanitarian intervention' proper, and someone like Martens, whose name is associated with a clause still meaningful to current international law, was arguably a real believer in the 'humanitarian' cause of the Russian efforts. The last decades of the nineteenth century were the formative years of the international law of the 'civilised' nations, the years where a search for a 'principle of humanity' in modern international law begins.[475] It is the time that the 'standard of civilisation' was constructed as 'an ethnocentric precursor to today's human rights'[476] and the idea of progress dominated the discourse and 'rendered non-Europeans outside the scope of historical development'.[477] It is therefore almost inevitable that the 'humanity' of the construct of 'humanitarian intervention' at this stage was all but inclusive.

2.7 THE PRINCIPLE OF NON-INTERVENTION IN LATE NINETEENTH-CENTURY INTERNATIONAL LAW

2.7.1 *The 'Humanitarian Impulse'*

Part of the 'folklore' of the history of international law is the narrative of an 'humanitarian impulse' taking hold at the end of the nineteenth century, which manifests itself first and foremost in the abolition of the slave trade, but also in the success of attempts to 'humanise' modern warfare and the growing number of authors discussing 'humanitarian intervention' in international law and advocating such interventions.[478] The initiative to abolish the slave trade had originated in a popular movement in the United Kingdom in the first quarter of the nineteenth century and drew to a close toward the end of the nineteenth century with the Berlin Congo Conference of 1885 and the Brussels General Act of 1890. It represents an important precedent for the use of law to further a moral ideal, even if the

---

[472] Ther 2011, p. 41.

[473] Cyrill Stieger, *Wir wissen nicht mehr, wer wir sind*, Vienna: Paul Zsolnay Verlag 2017.

[474] see Bass 2008, p. 291.

[475] Robert Kolb, 'The Main Epochs of Modern International Humanitarian Law Since 1864 and Their Related Dominant Legal Constructions', in: Kjetil Mujezinovic Larsen, Camilla Guldahl Cooper, and Gro Nystuen (eds.), *Searching for a 'Principle of Humanity' in International Law*, Cambridge University Press 2013, pp. 23–71.

[476] Jürgen Osterhammel, *The Transformation of the World*, Princeton University Press 2014, p. 832.

[477] Buzan and Lawson 2015, p. 99.

[478] Robertson 2002, pp. 14–15. See also: Lauren 2011, p. 38.

motivation in British circles may not have been purely disinterested.[479] Beyond this
successful example of early 'organised compassion', the scope of the 'humanitarian
big bang'[480] or its success should not be overstated: After the pioneering humanitarian work of Henri Dunant and the establishment of the International Red Cross, the
first impulses to tame the horrors of war through international treaties came from
Russia, calling, for example, for the abolition of certain weapons and for the first
international Peace Conferences of 1899 and 1907, and were, at least partially,
motivated by the desire to reduce the financial (not so much human) cost of
warfare.[481] These initiatives led to more or less binding, more or less successful
conventions and transformed ethical rules to the legal level through codification,
with all the difficulties entailed in that process.[482] This is not to play down the
importance of the social movements that were driven by this compassion, but it is
also not to overstate their immediate effect. Despite the best intentions, warfare itself
only became more deadly and brutal with the technical innovations of the twentieth
century and 'humanity' in this context remained a codeword for what was preferable
to further the 'civilizing mission' of the European States.[483] The settlement of
1878 remodelled the Balkans in the style of (Western) European nation states and
laid the groundwork for the Balkan Wars of the early twentieth century. It also
provided the legal and geographical space that would later be used – conceptualised
as an 'act of kindness' – to 'De-Balkanize the Balkans' through the transfer of
minority populations.[484] An extended practice of 'humanitarian intervention', routinely included in the narrative of the 'humanitarian impulse', on the other hand,
can hardly be considered more than the interpretative magic of the small group of
progress-hungry international lawyers we have already encountered. While this
group grew in numbers and, arguably, international standing, as the nineteenth
century approached its 'long end', the vision of international law propagated by
these lawyers, which contained the conditions for developing the original theory of
the 'intervention d'humanité' proper was undeniably linked to the conceptualisation
of international law as a 'civilising' mission, capable of and in some cases expressly
created for supporting Europe's imperialism in its mission to 'extend the gifts of
European civilisation' to other parts of the world.[485]

---

[479] Rubin 1997, pp. 97–137; Jenny S. Martinez, *The Slave Trade and the Origins of International
    Human Rights Law*, Oxford University Press 2012; Grewe 2000, pp. 554–569.

[480] Barnett 2011, p. 49.

[481] Jost Dülffer, 'Internationales System, Friedensngefährdung und Kriegsvermeidung: Das Beispiel
    der Haager Friedenskonferenzen 1899 und 1907', in: Reiner Steinweg (ed.), *Lehren aus der
    Geschichte?*, Frankfurt am Main: Suhrkamp 1990, pp. 95–116.

[482] Grewe 2000, pp. 541–542.

[483] Svenja Goltermann, *Opfer – Die Wahrnehmung von Krieg und Gewalt in der Moderne*,
    Frankfurt am Main: S. Fischer 2017, p. 98.

[484] Matthew Frank, *Making Minorities History*, Oxford University Press 2017.

[485] Hobson 2004, pp. 257–258 on the 'implicit racism' of British imperialism.

This ambivalent development on the one hand allowed for a deepening of the aforementioned moralistic vision of international law on the basis of 'conscience juridique' of the civilised world,[486] while on the other it excluded large portions of the world's population from the law's immediate sphere of validity – all in the name of 'humanity'. The belief that European culture was more advanced, more 'civilised' than the cultures of other societies led to visions of international law that were both idealistic and racist,[487] where the law was the tool to elevate the 'uncivilised' up to the 'Standard of "civilization"' (Gong). Contemporary international lawyers well into the twentieth century described European endeavours to decide over the fate of entire populations in Africa without consulting them as led by the 'desire to bring to the darkest parts of the darkest continent the blessings of European culture'.[488] Two different traditions of international law continued to exist alongside one another, one in which 'humanitarian interventions' could not be legal, as they would violate the sovereignty of the target state, sovereignty being a right enjoyed equally by all states within the family of nations. In the other tradition, a 'humanitarian intervention' was the civilising measure which would bring the 'uncivilised' closer to the level of the 'civilised' nations. To combine these diverging traditions in one non-contradictory history of international law as the universal law of all states would require recognising the continued importance of the structures of international law as developed under the conditions of imperialism.[489]

2.7.2 *The Principle of Non-intervention*

Latin American international lawyers began to be recognised as independent voices on international law toward the end of the nineteenth century and spoke out in clear favour of an absolute prohibition of intervention even in the face of 'internal oppression, however odious and violent it may be'.[490] The emphasis of the guarantee of the independence and sovereignty of the young Latin American states was of major importance to the countries of these writers. These states were in a complex position: On the one hand, their educated elites were 'European enough' to be accepted as contributors to the debate in international law, but, on the other, the

---

[486] Koskenniemi 2002, p. 41.

[487] Hobson 2004, p. 238, mentions Lorimer and Westlake in this context. On Westlake, see: Said 1978, p. 206 f.

[488] Arthur von Kirchenheim, 'Kongostaat und franz. Congo', in: Karl Strupp (ed.), *Wörterbuch des Völkerrechts*, Vol. I, Berlin: De Gruyter 1924, p. 658.

[489] Anghie 2005, p. 292.

[490] Calvo 1896, p. 352, § 209; Pereira (1902), Principios de Direito Internacional, 'Internal oppression, however odious and violent it may be, does not effect, either directly or indirectly, external relations and does not endanger the existence of other States. Accordingly, it cannot be used as a legal basis for use of force and violent means', cited according to the quote provided by Abiew 1999, p. 38, fn. 56.

countries had only recently won freedom from colonial rule, and still suffered the consequences.[491] At the end of the nineteenth century, interventions of the European Great Powers for the protection of the financial interests of their own nationals were still rather common and generally considered legal. Only in the early twentieth century did the Latin American states succeed in establishing a prohibition of this practice.[492] The negative experience of European interventions in Latin American countries was one of the arguments later used against claims of the legality of 'humanitarian interventions' by writers from these countries.[493]

In other countries, too, the inter-state character of international law and the resulting principle of sovereign equality among states was the major argument against the legality of 'humanitarian intervention'. Italian authors, shaped no doubt by the experience of the 'Risorgimento', the often violent process of Italian unification between 1815 and 1871, represented both sides of discussion: Terenzio Mamiani (1799–1885), actively committed to the cause of the unification, held that '[A]ll those actions of a State which are internal, are free',[494] and concluded: 'By every consideration ... approaching the question on each side, and in several ways, we arrive at this solemn declaration of the law of nations, that all forcible intervention in the internal affairs of a people is to be deemed unjust and oppressive'.[495] He took this position even further by criticising the idea of introducing 'civilization amongst barbarians, and to take them out of their savagery ... at the point of the spear'.[496] On the other hand, Giuseppe Mazzini, another strong advocate of self-determination and national sovereignty, can be read as allowing for some type of collective 'humanitarian intervention' whenever mass atrocities are committed, 'if, for example, there should be, as there has been in our time, a massacre of Christians within the dominions of the Turks – then other nations are not absolved from all concern in the matter simply because of the large distance between them and the scene of the wrong'.[497] Giuseppe Carnazza Amari (1837–1911), whose textbook on international law, published in Italian in 1867 (Vol. I) and 1875 (Vol. II), was successful enough to be translated into French (published in 1880 and 1882), quoted

---

[491] Buzan and Lawson 2015, p. 98.
[492] von Frisch, 'Drago-Porter-Konvention' 1924, pp. 253–254; Hallier 1960, pp. 399–400. See also: Finnemore 2004, p.24 ff.
[493] See Hildebrando Accioly, *Traité de Droit Internatonal Public*, French trans. by Paul Goulé, Vol. I, Paris: Sirey 1940, p. 283, detailing Brazilian, Portuguese and British state practice, though with any use of force. See also Hernan Vales, 'The Latin American View on the Doctrine of Humanitarian Intervention', *Journal of Humanitarian Assistance* 2001, archived at: https://sites.tufts.edu/jha/archives/1491, last accessed 5 March 2019.
[494] Mamiani 1860, p. 190.
[495] Mamiani 1860, p. 177.
[496] Mamiani 1860, p. 195.
[497] Mazzini, 'On Nonintervention', p. 218, cited according to Stefano Recchia, 'The origins of liberal Wilsonianism', in: Stefano Recchia and Jennifer M. Welsh (eds.), *Just and Unjust Military Intervention*, Cambridge University Press 2013, p. 257.

Mamiani at length,[498] and went on to state: 'No case exists where a foreign sovereignty has the right to substitute national sovereignty; consequently intervention is never possible, neither as a rule nor as an exception'.[499]

In France, international law at the beginning of the second half of the nineteenth century was still a 'rather marginal academic topic'.[500] One of the leading textbooks of this era, successful enough to warrant three revised editions between 1877 and 1900, was written by Théophile Funck-Brentano (1830–1906), a sociologist, and Albert Sorel (1842–1906), a diplomatic historian and literary author, and came without very little reference to other authors working in the field, 'describing international law as the practices of nineteenth-century diplomacy: formal relations between sovereigns, treaties, intervention, recognition, responsibility, war, and neutrality. Theirs was a practitioner's handbook',[501] and differentiated strictly between 'theoretical international law' and 'real international law' ('droit des gens théoretique' and 'droit des gens réel').[502] For the latter, they stated clearly that talk of a 'right of intervention' was to be considered a misuse of the term 'right', as there could be no right against the right of sovereignty. This also precluded the possibility of any exceptional right of intervention in special circumstances: Even if such interventions could on occasion lead to beneficial results, for example where one party in a civil war violated the principles of the shared law of the 'civilised states' and therefore became the target on an intervention – even in those cases where history might honour such interventions, but it remained an act like any intervention, not the exercising of a right.[503] This expressly applied to intervention on behalf of Christians under non-Christian rule – 'Religious wars are but the most passionate form of civil wars, the intervention in such a case remains an act of war'. Despite these authors' insistence on the sanctity of sovereignty against intervention, they did recognise the inequality of states as a matter of both fact and law: 'All the existing states are sovereign, but in their mutual relations, they do not all hold the same rights of sovereignty'.[504] They even went as far as recognising that relations outside the realm of the law of 'civilised' nations were not necessarily of a substantially different nature: 'The nomads and the savages, then, have between each other as

[498] Giuseppe Carnazza-Amari, *Traité de Droit International Public*, Vol. I, trans. from the Italian by C. Montanari-Revest, Paris: L. Larose 1880, p. 557.

[499] Giuseppe Carnazza-Amari. 'Nouvel exposé du principie de non-intervention', 370, as quoted in Heraclidis and Dialla 2015, p. 66.

[500] Koskenniemi 2002, p. 274.

[501] Koskenniemi 2002, p. 275.

[502] Funck-Brentano and Sorel 1887, p. 1.

[503] Funck-Brentano and Sorel 1887, p. 222.

[504] Funck-Brentano and Sorel 1887, p. 46: 'Tous les États constitués sont souverains, mas dans leurs relations mutuelles ils ne disposent pas tous des mèmes droits de souveraineté'.

well as with the civilised nations, a law of nations that is observed in the same way as the law of the civilised nations'.[505]

This approach expressly recognises the 'law of the civilised states' as distinct from a more general international law, yet denies the possibility of a legal justification for any intervention based on this distinction. In this sense, this position is quite similar to the one put forward by the British lawyer and historian Edward S. Creasy (1812–1878) at roughly the same time. Also the author of a leading nineteenth century work on imperial and colonial constitution,[506] Creasy laid down the 'general rule' in his 'First Platform of International Law', dedicated to Her Majesty's principal Secretary of State for the Colonial Department, that all intervention is unjustifiable, except for 'certain exceptional cases'. The only one (of three) example that Creasy gives that could relate to the question of the legality of 'humanitarian intervention' is this:

> Where we intervene on behalf of a grievously oppressed people, which has never amalgamated with its oppressors as one nation, and which its oppressors have systematically treated as an alien race, subject to the same imperial authority, but in other respects distinct, the distinction being the distinction between privileged and burdened, between honoured and degraded, between the fully protected and ill protected by law in primordial rights of security for person and property – and the distinction being hereditary, permanent, and practical.[507]

However, this cannot be read as a justification of 'humanitarian intervention' in the general sense, as Creasy elsewhere points out:

> The armed interposition of England, France, and Russia in 1829 in favour of the Greek insurgents against the Turkish governments (. . .), is commonly justified on the ground that the Intervention was necessary in order 'to stay the effusion of blood' caused by protracted and desolating civil warfare; (. . .) and, generally, that it was an intervention justifiable on behalf of the interests of humanity. (. . .) This last is a justification, which commends itself to our feelings, but (. . .) will not bear the test of reasoning. Chancellor Kent, although he is willing to admit it in this case, accompanies his admission of it by observations which show how dangerous a precedent it may be rendered.[508]

Creasy's thinking was guided by the expressed aim of continually comparing 'the actual law' with 'the standard of Justice', and bringing it 'into connexion with the

---

[505] Funck-Brentano and Sorel 1887, p. 23: 'les nomades et les sauvages ont donc, soit entre eux, soit avec les peuples civilisés, un droit des gens qui est observé aus même titre que le droit des gens des nations civilisées'.

[506] Martti Koskenniemi, 'Colonial Laws: Sources, Strategies and Lessons?', *Journal of the History of International Law* 2016, 18, p. 266.

[507] Creasy 1874.

[508] Creasy 1874, pp. 300–301, §§ 310–311.

advances of humanity and civilization',[509] so his rejection of the *legality* of 'humanitarian intervention' seems particularly poignant. He pointed out that the Ottoman Empire 'now long acted, and has long been treated, as bound and as protected by International Law, such as has grown up in European Christendom', tracing the legal interactions between European states and the Porte back to 1737,[510] so to extend the verdict of legality to the intervention in the Greek War of Independence on humanitarian grounds would have created precisely the precedent Metternich had warned of.[511]

Later writers have found it difficult to identify Creasy's position and cited him as being supportive of 'humanitarian intervention',[512] and, more recently, as recognising 'Armed Humanitarian Intervention' as an 'Exceptional Legal Right',[513] yet it seems closer to that of William Edward Hall (1835–1894), author of one the most influential British textbooks on international law of the nineteenth century, whose position has recently been considered as considering humanitarian intervention as 'morally and/or politically acceptable'.[514] Yet Hall, like any good lawyer, was less concerned about whether intervention in such cases might be morally and/or politically acceptable, but where the law might stand – and he was quite clear about this, even if his views have been mis-represented somewhat in the literature on the legality of 'humanitarian intervention' – for this reason, it is worth quoting his statement in its entirety:

> While however it is settled that as a general rule a state must be allowed to work out its internal changes in its own fashion, so long as its struggles do not actually degenerate into internecine war, and intervention to put down a popular movement or the uprising of a subject race is wholly forbidden, intervention for the purpose of checking gross tyranny or of helping the efforts of a people to free itself is very commonly regarded without disfavour. Again, religious oppression, short of a cruelty which would rank as tyranny, has ceased to be recognised as an independent ground of intervention, but it is still used between Europe and the East as an accessory motive, which seems to be thought by many persons to be sufficiently praiseworthy to excuse the commission of acts in other respects grossly immoral. (...) In giving their sanction to interventions of the kind in question jurists have imparted an aspect of legality to a species of intervention, which makes a deep inroad into one of the cardinal doctrines of international law; of which the principle is not even intended to be equally applied to the cases covered by it; and which by the readiness with which it lends itself to the uses of selfish ambition becomes as dangerous in practice as it is plausible in appearance. It is unfortunate that publicists have not laid down broadly and unanimously that no intervention is

[509] Creasy 1874, preface, p. vii.
[510] Creasy 1874, pp. 130–131 with note *.
[511] On Creasy's position toward the legal status of the intervention, see Section 2.2.3.
[512] Stowell 1921, p. 55, fn. 11. Grewe 2000, p. 493; Abiew 1999, p. 43.
[513] Heraclidis and Dialla 2015, pp. 60, 66.
[514] Heraclidis and Dialla 2015, pp. 60, 67.

legal, except for the purpose of self-preservation, unless a breach of the law as between states has taken place, or unless the whole body of civilised states have concurred in authorising it. . . . The record of the last hundred years might not have been much cleaner that it is; but evil-doing would have been at least sometimes compelled to show itself in its true colours; it would have found more difficulty in clothing itself in a generous disguise; and international law would in any case have been saved from complicity in it.[515]

Complicity in a development portrayed by them as the 'progress' of international law relating to interventions in the 'interests of humanity' was quite clearly what some of the publicists criticised by Hall wanted, though very few of the authors named by Hall actually held positions that warranted such criticism.[516] One of the cornerstones of the theory of the 'intervention d'humanité', to bestow legitimacy upon such interventions through the combination of collective action and 'humanitarian' justification, was, however, implicitly rejected by Hall, arguably because his decidedly *European* system of international law was 'a product of the special civilisation of modern Europe, and forms a highly artificial system of which the principles cannot be supposed to be understood or recognised by countries differently civilised'.[517] Yet, in an act of 'submission' such 'differently civilised' countries could join the law of this 'artificial' system: 'States outside European civilisation must formally enter into the circle of law-governed countries. They must do something with the acquiescence of the latter, or of some of them, which amounts to an acceptance of the law in its entirety beyond all possibility of misconstruction'.[518] Once they did, or so Hall's assumption seems to have been, the law applied equally with no room for a legal right to interfere for what would ultimately be moral, rather than legal reasons.[519]

2.7.3 'Humanitarian Intervention' and the 'International Law of Civilised Nations'

The international law of the late nineteenth century as it is chiefly remembered made what might be considered a 'more organic' (and, arguably, less artificial) use of the law of 'civilised nations' in establishing the narrative of 'one' legal doctrine of 'humanitarian intervention'. This narrative contributes to the forging of the

---

[515] Hall 1890, pp. 287–288.
[516] Hall only identified Phillimore and Halleck as authors 'doubtfully admitting' the cause of the interest of 'humanity', and Calvo and Fiore as thinking 'that states can intervene to put an end to crimes and slaughter', see: Hall 1890, p. 289. All the other authors mentioned by Hall he actually deemed critical of such types of interventions.
[517] Hall 1890, p. 42.
[518] Hall 1890, p. 43.
[519] Hall 1890, p. 292, § 95: 'Still, from the point of view of law, it is always to remembered that states so intervening are going beyond their legal powers. Their excuse or their justification can only be a moral one'.

European identity as we know it today, establishing a secular, yet still Christian identity as 'European'.

Egide Arntz had described a violation of 'our customs' and 'our civilisation' as a precondition for a 'humanitarian intervention'.[520] At roughly the same time, the preconditions for a different, but similar type of intervention were described by another author more tellingly as a 'reversionary right' based on the relationship between the states of 'foreign or less developed culture' only recently admitted to the 'family of nations' under international law and 'us Aryans', retaining the right to interfere in the internal affairs of those nations insofar as necessary to secure the rights of 'our' citizens, compatriots (Schutzgenossen), consuls and ambassadors, residing on the territory of these nations. Such rights obviously extended to the territory of the Ottoman Empire, irrespective of the provisions of the Paris Treaty, as the Ottoman Empire had clearly exhausted the expectation that the Sultan would be able to reorganise the internal affairs of his empire in a way satisfactory to European standards.[521] Hermann Strauch (1838–1904), a long forgotten Professor of Legal Philosophy and International Law at the University of Heidelberg, and a rather open anti-Semite,[522] is usually considered an opponent of a right to 'humanitarian intervention' and his support for interventions in the affairs of the Ottoman Empire was decidedly *not* based on any considerations of 'violations of "human rights"' (Strauch does mention the term).[523] Yet there can be no doubt that he would have supported the legality of all the interventions in the Ottoman Empire discussed in this book, based on the alleged superiority of a civilisation he termed 'aryan'. Using language that sounds less offensive to contemporary ears, other German authors shared this position.[524]

Towards the end of the nineteenth century, the legality of 'humanitarian intervention' is supported by a number of writers constructing international law as the 'law of civilised nations', including the aforementioned Bluntschli, Fedor Martens and Egide Arntz. In their vision, 'humanitarian intervention' takes on the appearance of an 'intervention by humanity', the moment in which the 'civilised' states reaffirm their 'humanity'. Some of these authors, like Martens, held the position that such 'interventions by humanity' were conceptually only possible (and legal) in the affairs of 'uncivilised' nations.[525] In this version of international law, arguments of a

---

[520] Rolin-Jaequemyns 1876, p. 675 (emphasis in original), cited according to the English translation in Grewe 2000, p. 495.

[521] Strauch 1879, pp. 23–24, my translation.

[522] Klaus-Peter Schroeder, *'Eine Universität für Juristen und von Juristen': Die Heidelberger Juristische Fakultät im 19. und 20. Jahrhundert*, Tübingen: Mohr Siebeck 2010, p. 328.

[523] Strauch 1879, p. 13.

[524] e.g. Geffcken 1889, p. 157.

[525] von Martens 1883, pp. 301–302. Also see: Resch 1890, p. 52, § 44; van Lynden van Sandenberg 1899, pp. 180–187, in particular p. 186: 'Wel hebben wij gezien, dat een dergelijk interventie-recht in het allgemeen niet kan worden toegekend, doch (…) moet men tegenover de minder beschaafde landen eene tusschenkomst rechtvaardigen, wanneer zij door niet

religious nature are combined with 'civilisational' ones.[526] The later claim of a specific 'humanitarian' appreciation of human life as an integrative part of international law[527] finds its root in a discriminatory distinction based on religious and even racist convictions:[528] These justifications based on 'considerations of humanity' may employ a different language than those based on the alleged 'superiority' of an 'aryan' or otherwise 'more advanced' civilisation, but have the same *exclusionary* character: 'Humanity' in this context is not the all encompassing 'humanity-sentiment' or 'humanity-mankind', but a variation of the exclusion of the other, the not-humanity, those who, *we* have decided, do not share the same values and do not conform to *our* 'Standard of "Civilization"'.

The 'Standard of "Civilization"', as a figure of speech or indeed a legal argument for a certain standard of human rights as guaranteed or to be guaranteed by international law obviously mirrors current arguments about human rights standards. In both cases, the desire to protect fundamental rights is certainly instrumental, but the question remains: Instrumental to what? In the case of the 'Standard of "Civilization"' the focus originally only was on guarantees for the rights of foreign nationals on the territory of 'uncivilised' nations. Yet the explicit distinction between interventions for the sake of 'civilisation' and the 'interests of humanity' was rarely made.[529] And the 'Standard of "Civilisation"' first and foremost was a way to retain the original Christian missionary perspective in international law by claiming quasi-positivist arguments.[530] The idea was that it was a question for international law to decide whether or not international law was to be applied in the relations to a certain nation or to what extent turned a potentially universal law into the law of an exclusive 'society of states'.[531] This idea became the leading idea for so many

na- koming van gesloten tractaten wetten van humaniteit hebben geschonden. (. . .) Dat hier ver- schillend standpunt kann worden ingenomen tegenover minder beschaafde landen, kann ge- grond worden op de roeping der andere staten om als pioniers der beschafving op te treden (. . .)'; p. 187: 'Staten, die op dezelfde hoogte van beschaving staan, hebben dergelijk interventie-recht niet noodig'.
[526] E.g. Hartmann 1878, pp. 58–59 and pp. 6–7 on the relations to the Ottoman Empire in general. See also: Resch 1890, p. 52, § 44, allowing for only very limited lawful cases of intervention, but expressing no doubt as to the lawfulness (and duty) of an intervention by Christian States in cases where the 'Christian population is barbarously oppressed and mistreated in oriental States'. The same position is expressed in: Bry 1891, p. 140: 'L'intervention dans les affaires intérieures d'un État n'est jamais admise en principe, si ce n'est dans un intérêt général de conservation et de défense. Mais le droit positif international admet l'intervention dans les affaires intérieures de la Turquie, au profit des intérêts religieux, et même en toute matière, à raison de la situation précaire de cet État'.
[527] Grewe 2000, p. 490.
[528] See: Gong 1984; Anghie 2005; Bowden 2005; Orakhelashvili 2006.
[529] It was made explicitly by Mosler 1937. pp. 60–61. See also: Strauch 1879, pp. 13–15; Geffcken 1889, pp. 157–158.
[530] Gong 1984; Bowden 2005, pp. 16–17.
[531] John Westlake, *Chapters on the Principles of International Law*, Cambridge University Press 1894, p. 3: 'When we assert that there is such a thing as international law, we assert that there is

theorists of international law that an epoch of international law, stretching from the time of the French Revolution and the ensuing wars of Napoleon until the end of World War I is being remembered in the history of international law as the 'International Law of Civilised Nations', in distinction to the preceding 'International Law of Christianity'.[532]

Yet the 'Standard of "Civilization"' did not so much as replace the shared 'Christian values' at the core of international law, but these values became the – explicit or unspoken – foundation of the 'standard'. The idea of a this shared standard uniting certain states or nations gave international law its own ethical foundation and cemented the leading role of the European Christian nations (and including the United States of America), in particular in relation to the 'uncivilised' or 'savage' nations. As Koskenniemi put it: '[T]he founding conception of late nineteenth-century international law was not sovereignty but a collective (European) *conscience* – understood always as ambivalently either consciousness or conscience, that is, in alternatively rationalistic or ethical ways'.[533] Even an author like William E. Hall, identified by Koskenniemi as the 'paradigmatic positivist of international law in the late 19th century',[534] had no doubts of this specific European character of international law:

> It is scarcely necessary to point out that as international law is a product of the special civilisation of modern Europe, and forms a highly artificial system of which the principles cannot be supposed to be understood or recognised by countries differently civilised, such states only can be presumed to be subject to it as are inheritors of that civilisation.[535]

This starting point intentionally led to the exclusion of any number of 'non-European' states and nations from equal participation in international relations under the law, as Anthony Anghie has shown.[536] States so de-equalised were on a 'lower' level and enjoyed 'less' law to protect them.[537] Even where authors identified a 'tendency' to conduct relations with 'states, which are outside the sphere of international law, to a certain extent in accordance with its rules',[538] this did not put into question the necessity of constructing a world with different spheres of law. Said Edward Hall on China:

---

a society of states: when we recognize that there is a society of states, we recognize that there is international law'.

[532] Heinhard Steiger, 'From the International Law of Christianity to the International Law of the World Citizen', *Journal of the History of International Law* 2001, 3(2), p. 187.

[533] Koskenniemi 2002, p. 51.

[534] Koskenniemi 2002, p. 82.

[535] Hall 1890, p 42.

[536] Anghie 1999; Anghie 2005, pp. 32–114.

[537] Gong 1984, p. 55.

[538] Hall 1890, p. 43.

Tacitly, and by inference from a series of acts, states in the position of China may in the long run be brought within the realm of law; but it would be unfair and impossible to assume, inferentially, acceptance of law as a whole from isolated acts or even from frequently repeated acts of a certain kind. European states will be obliged, partly by their sense of honour, partly by their interests, to be guided by their own artificial rules in dealing with semi-civilised states, when the latter have learned enough to make the demand, long before a reciprocal obedience to those rules can be reasonably expected. For example, it cannot be hoped that China, for a considerable time to come, would be able, if she tried, to secure obedience by her officers and soldiers even to the elementary European rules of war.[539]

James Lorimer's often quoted division of 'humanity, in its present condition' into 'three concentric zones or spheres – that of civilised humanity, that of barbarous humanity, and that of savage humanity'[540] was the clearest – and most racist[541] – expression of this: Lorimer believed in the 'necessity of ascertaining the relative value of states'[542] and saw only 'aryans' and Christians as being in conformity with 'ethical postulates on whihch jurisprudence rests', whereas other 'religions' were not.[543] The 'Turks' he viewed with such suspicion that he felt it necessary to state that they 'as a race, are probably incapable of the political development which would render their adoption of constitutional government possible'.[544] But other writers, including those associated with more mainstream positions on the foundations of international law, shared the basic assumption behind Lorimer's concept.[545]

Here, the distinction between positive international law and a vision of how international law should be, is intentionally blurred: The fact that 'civilised' nations entered into treaties with the 'uncivilised', which not necessarily followed different conditions than treaties between 'civilised' but which the 'civilised' nations simply violated at no legal cost,[546] could not easily be integrated into this concept of international law. Accordingly, recent commentators have argued that this version of international law did not pass the 'practice' test with contemporary state practice.[547] The ideological underpinnings of the 'civilisational' approach and its limits were recognised and criticised by some contemporary voices, both in principle[548] and, more openly, in relation to the Ottoman Empire in particular[549]

---

[539] Hall 1890, p. 44.

[540] Lorimer 1883, p. 101.

[541] Bowden 2005, pp. 16–17; Orakhelashvili 2006.

[542] Lorimer 1883, p. 168.

[543] Lorimer 1883, p. 116.

[544] Lorimer 1883, p. 123.

[545] Bowden 2005, pp. 16–17; Orakhelashvili 2006, p. 318.

[546] See: Gerd Kaminski, *Chinesische Positionen zum Völkerrecht*, Berlin: Duncker & Humblot 1973, for the Chinese experience, in particular pp. 138 and 199.

[547] Orakhelashvili 2006, p. 328.

[548] Both Grewe 2000, p. 456, and Koskenniemi 2002, p. 129, cite the Swiss author Joseph Hornung.

[549] Cf. Creasy 1874, p. 130 f., nr. 136: 'The Ottoman Porte has now long acted and has long been treated, as bound and as protected by International Law, (...)'.

or the interventions in the affairs of 'barbarous nations' in general.[550] Accordingly, none of the theorising over the rights of 'civilised' nations to intervene for the sake of 'humanity' led to interventions when, arguably, they were needed and would have, according to these theories, been justified.

In the years of 1895 and 1896 increased military operations of Ottoman troops against Armenian demands for reform cost the lives of over 100,000 people.[551] The reaction of the European Great Powers was limited to diplomatic protests and the suggestion of a reform program the Sultan duly accepted, but did not put into practice.[552] This despite the fact that the Porte had previously been subjected to the duty to increase the living conditions of the Armenians, as stipulated in Article 61 of the Berlin Treaty of 1878: 'The Sublime Porte undertakes to carry out, without further delay, the improvements and reforms demanded by local requirements in the provinces inhabited by the Armenians, and to guarantee their security against the Circassians and Kurds. It will periodically make known the steps taken to this effect to the Powers, who will superintend their application'.

Contemporary authors considered this provision a possible legal justification for an intervention to protect the Armenians,[553] but nothing came of it. The reaction of the European powers to these events has – especially considering their consequences – been rightfully considered disappointing,[554] though some authors have managed to find traces of an 'intervention' here, albeit without specifying details of who is supposed to have intervened how.[555]

Similarly, it was precisely the 'law of civilised nations' that gave free reign to the Belgian King Leopold II over Congo, all in the name of bringing the 'blessings of European culture' to 'the darkest part of the dark continent',[556] by granting the King sovereignty over the possessions of the Congo Society through the General Act of the 1885 Berlin Conference, a move cynically sugarcoated with a commitment to work together to end the slave trade, but which cost the lives of millions over the course of twenty years.

The 1885 Treaty is often mentioned as an important international law instrument to end the slave trade,[557] but it was concerned almost entirely with free trade and the more contemporary international law literature only mentioned it in passing,

---

[550] Carnazza-Amari 1880, pp. 561–562.

[551] Donald Bloxham, *The Great Game of Genocide*, Oxford University Press 2005, p. 51.

[552] Bloxham 2005, p. 53.

[553] von Liszt 1913, p. 66; Mandelstam 1925, p. 17; Hettlage 1927, p. 61; Georg Erler, *Das Recht der nationalen Minderheiten*, Münster: Aschendorfsche Verlagsbuchhandlung 1931, p. 95; Hagedorn 1933, p. 20.

[554] Pauer 1985, p. 71.

[555] Bonfils and Fauchille 1904, p. 164; Quaritsch 1913, p. 77; Tenbaum 1918, p. 51.

[556] von Kirchenheim, 'Kongostaat und franz. Congo' 1924, p. 658.

[557] e.g. by Winkler 2012, p. 885.

focusing instead on the Brussels Conference Act of 1890 to end the practice.[558] It took the British House of Commons until 1897 to even raise the question of atrocities in the Congo,[559] and the assessment of Belgian rule over Congo remained very shallow in the literature on international well into the 1960s.[560] This alone shows the limited reach of the 'humanitarian impulse', which only remained compatible with the 'civilising' mission of the Europeans, of which the Congo Free State was one disastrous outcome.[561] It is also clear that the 'humanitarian' language that was more widely used toward the end of the nineteenth century also provided a cover for violence increasingly used in the colonial context, as in Cuba toward the end of the nineteenth century.

2.8 CUBA, 1898

2.8.1 Introduction

State practice at the turn from the nineteenth to the twentieth century had not yet agreed on a full prohibition of intervention under international law. No principle of non-intervention yet existed as the 'Grundnorm' in international relations.[562] It was only with the Drago-Porter-Convention of 1907 that the contracting parties agreed to prohibit the recourse to armed force for the recovery of contract debts claimed from the government of one state by another government on behalf of its nationals. In the early twentieth century this was seen as one more step to 'avoid the often grave repercussions of interventions',[563] which had been particularly frequent in Latin America in the nineteenth century. Unsurprisingly, Latin American countries had been instrumental in negotiating this convention, after they had been the target of a series of prestige-seeking military interventions by Spain in the 1860s.[564]

The United States repeated interventions in Cuba, then still part of the Spanish colonial empire, on the occasion of internal unrest on the island, went ahead irrespective of this development. The ensuing Spanish-American War of 1898 produced a remarkable amount of literature after its conclusion, in particular with

---

[558] Gerhard Leibholz, 'Sklavenhandel', in: Karl Strupp (ed.), Wörterbuch des Völkerrechts, Vol. II, Berlin: Walter deGruyer & Co. 1925, p. 542.

[559] Bellamy 2012, p. 90.

[560] e.g. Thomas Oppermann, 'Kongo-Staat', in: Hans-Jürgen Schlochauer, Wörterbuch des Völkerrechts, Vol. 2, Berlin: De Gruyter 1961, pp. 271–272.

[561] Mark Mazower, 'The End of Civilization and the Rise of Human Rights', in: Stefan-Ludwig Hoffmann (ed.), Human Rights in the Twentieth Century, Cambridge University Press 2011, p. 34.

[562] e.g. Strauch 1879, pp. 5, 29; Geffcken 1889, p. 134.

[563] Hans von Frisch, 'Drago-Porter-Konvention', in: Karl Strupp (Ed.), Wörterbuch des Völkerrechts, Vol. I, Berlin: De Gruyter 1924, p. 254.

[564] Ignacio de la Rasilla del Moral, 'The Study of International Law in the Spanish Short Nineteenth Century (1808–1898)' Chicago-Kent Journal of International and Comparative Law 2014, 13(2), p. 133.

regard to its international law dimension.[565] Yet in the debate on the evolution of
the doctrine of 'humanitarian intervention', these events have been reflected only in
a rather formulaic fashion. They are often routinely presented as a 'classic example'
of 'humanitarian intervention',[566] but hardly with the attention to detail one would
expect, when taking Senator Harding's previously mentioned claim seriously. If the
United States had indeed 'unsheathed the sword (. . .) for the first time in the history
of the world in the name of humanity' during their intervention on Cuba,[567] then
this 'potential first humanitarian intervention', whether the American action was
'sullied with imperialism'[568] or not, should be viewed as the moment where a figure
of speech, prominent in the textbooks of international law in the nineteenth
century, may have been turned into policy, transforming the legal concept discussed
up until then into something applied in practice: A potential watershed moment,
where talk is mirrored by action and the reflections cast need to be analysed for the
light they shine on the law of 'humanitarian intervention'.

2.8.2 *The Intervention in Context*

During the nineteenth century, the grip of the Portuguese and Spanish colonial
empires on the states of Latin America evaporated in a series of revolutionary
uprisings. Between 1810 and 1825, former Spanish and Portuguese colonies like
Venezuela, Paraguay and Mexico achieved independence. The struggle for freedom
from their colonial oppressors also repeatedly ignited the island of Cuba. Between
1868 and 1878, a first war for independence had strengthened Cuban national
aspiration, leading to a period of continuous, if limited unrest. In the years after
1878, the colonial administration discouraged the construction of schools, in the
conviction that educating Cubans would only turn them into rebels, as John
Lawrence Tone has put it: 'as persuasive a condemnation of Spanish rule as one
could ever hope to find'.[569]

By the 1890s, Cuba had become part of the American economic imperium.
However, economic dependence on the United States became especially perilous
when Spain raised duties on most imported goods, including American products.

---

[565] Horace Edgar Flack, *Spanish-American Diplomatic Relations Preceding the War of 1898*,
Baltimore: The Johns Hopkins Press, 1906; Elbert J. Benton, *International Law and Diplomacy
of the Spanish-American War*, Baltimore: The Johns Hopkins Press, 1908; Louis LeFur, *Étude
sur la guerre Hispano-Américain de 1898 envisagée au point de vue du droit international public*,
Paris: A. Pedone, 1899.

[566] e.g. Bonfils and Fauchille 1904, p. 166; Reisman and McDougal 1968 Memorandum, reprinted
in: Lillich 1973, p. 183; Thomas Franck and Nigel Rodley, 'After Bangladesh: The Law of
Humanitarian Intervention by Military Force', *American Journal of International Law* 1973, 67,
p. 285; Pauer 1985, p. 66; Wellhausen 2002, p. 71.

[567] See Chapter 1.

[568] Bass 2008, p. 317.

[569] John Lawrence Tone, *War and Genocide in Cuba*, Chapel Hill: University of North Carolina
Press 2008, p. 26.

This turned into a disaster for Cuba when the United States – at the initiative of future president William McKinley – responded with legislation raising tariffs on Spanish products, including Cuban tobacco and sugar, effectively stripping Cuba of its American customers. The following crisis in Cuba affected the whole island and laid the groundwork for the Cuban uprising of 1895.[570]

Initially, there was only limited Cuban support for the dedicated revolutionaries who fought for Cuban independence. They could count on some support from Cuban nationals in America and, importantly, unofficial support from the United States and individual Americans, happy to work behind the scenes to subvert the Spanish colonial regime in Cuba.[571] In 1895, Cuban revolutionaries fought a bitter fight against Spain and Cuban supporters of the colonial regime. To remain 'neutral' was to be against the revolution and so the insurgents did not refrain from targeting Cuban civilians. This caused thousands of Cubans to relocate to protected towns in the fall and winter of 1895 or, alternatively, to move to territory considered part of Cuba Libre.[572]

Gradually, the rebellion turned into the second war of independence, engulfing the whole of the island, though Cuban insurgency tactics meant that casualty rates on both sides as a result of direct fighting remained relatively low.[573] The toll on the civilian population, however, was immense, not just because of Spanish practices, but also because of the insurgency's use of violence against Cubans deemed to be insufficiently patriotic and the equivalent violence of the pro-Spanish Volunteers.[574]

On 10 February 1896, General Valeriano Weyler arrived in Havana as the new governor of the island to an enthusiastic reception. A few days later, he announced his three-part strategy for the pacification of Cuba:

First, he pledged to eliminate garrisons in hundreds of indefensible plantations and hamlets in order to create large field armies capable of forcing decisive battles on the Cubans. Second, he would focus his energies and resources on one part of Cuba at a time, beginning with an assault on Maceo in Pinar del Río. Then he would move east, always driving the insurgents before him, until he could force them back [. . .] into Oriente. [. . .] Third, Weyler would relocate civilians from the countryside into towns, where they could be prevented from aiding the insurgents. Also, removing them from the countryside would eliminate the need to protect hundreds of small towns and hamlets. He called this part of his plan 'reconcentration'.[575]

It is this part of the strategy that attained Weyler the questionable honour of being recognised as the 'real inventor of the concentration camps'.[576]

[570] Tone 2008, p. 28.
[571] Tone 2008, p. 51.
[572] Tone 2008, p. 66.
[573] Tone 2008, pp. 127–128.
[574] Tone 2008, p. 149.
[575] Tone 2008, p. 160.
[576] Andrzej J. Kaminski, *Konzentrationslager 1896 bis heute, Eine Analyse*, Stuttgart: Verlag W. Kohlhammer 1982, p. 34.

The policy of 'reconcentratión' affected around 500,000 people and many died from exhaustion or the appalling conditions inside the internment camps. It was, as John Lawrence Tone has noted,

> one of the most terrible catastrophes in the history of the Americas [and] turned an already cruel war into what some have termed genocide. Beginning in the spring of 1896, and picking up in 1897, Spanish troops uprooted half a million civilians and herded them into hastily built barracks, sometimes grouped into what were called 'concentration camps.' The army supplied rations, enough to prolong the suffering. Though scholars disagree about the number of civilians who perished due to reconcentratión, over 100,000 reconcentrados certainly died, some from starvation, others in epidemics that peaked in the fall of 1897.[577]

As early as April 1896, the United States had warned Spain that intervention was probable, should the colonial power not take effective measures to stabilise the situation on the island through a programme of far-reaching reforms and concessions.[578] While the Spanish tried to justify their 'reconcentratión'-program by referring to previous American practices during the American Civil War,[579] they had to eventually admit that they had not achieved a solution in the fight against the insurgent Cubans this way. By the end of 1897, Weyler was recalled back to Spain, the policy of 'reconcentratión' was terminated and the camps were closed. Spain undertook a substantial reform programme and granted the island autonomy, effective 1 January 1898. But the situation for the population hardly improved and the reforms could not stop the revolution. The insurgents had become convinced that Spain would not have the power to crush the rebellion and thus rejected the government installed by the colonial powers. By this time, they would settle for nothing short of complete independence.[580]

Meanwhile, the Cuban situation had become part of a competition for market leadership among New York newspapers. William Randolph Hearst, the up and coming newspaper tycoon, used sensationalist reports of the brutal Spanish policies and alleged dangers to American property to increase sales of his papers. Other newspapers followed suit, presenting to the American public a distorted view of the troubles in Cuba and creating mounting pressure on the American government to take action: Between the beginning of the unrest in 1895 and the outbreak of war between the US and Spain in 1898, the New York newspapers on all but twenty days reported more or less graphically about Cuba.[581] The effect this had on President William McKinley's foreign policy has been the subject of relatively little debate,

---

[577] Tone 2008, p. 193.
[578] Rich 1992, p. 353.
[579] Schwartz 2013, p. 211.
[580] Rich 1992, p. 353.
[581] Max Zeuske and Michael Zeuske, *Kuba 1492–1902*, Leipzig: Leipziger Universitätsverlag 1998, p. 414.

with most writers assuming, up to now, that the role of the press was 'pivotal not only for laying the broader attitudinal conditions for war, but also for accelerating the proximate triggering events'.[582] Others have claimed that McKinley took little to no notice of the sensationalist press reports.[583] Indeed, even after the US war ship Maine, sent to the port of Havana to provide protection for American citizens and assets in January 1898, exploded several days later for reasons unknown at the time (some eighty years later a US investigation concluded that the explosion had occurred accidentally inside the ship),[584] McKinley stayed on his course to go to the inevitable war only when the timing was right, and the results would give birth to an empire.[585]

Spain wanted to avoid American intervention, fearing it would inevitably lead to the loss of Cuba, and declared an unconditional ceasefire on 4 April 1898, yet would not accept McKinley's central demand: that Spain allow the United States to mediate the conflict.[586] The European powers, too, feared escalation, and the Austro-Hungarian Empire offered its mediation ('bons offices'), for 'humanitarian reasons' and only 'humanitarian motives'.[587] The Great Powers submitted a collective note to the American President on 8 April 1898, stressing the need for further consultations with Spain.[588] McKinley took note and thanked the Europeans for their efforts. In his reply he described 'the chronic condition of disturbance' on Cuba, 'which so deeply injures the interests and menaces the tranquility of the American nation by the character and consequences of the struggle thus kept up at our doors, besides shocking its sentiments of humanity'.[589] He then turned his attention to Congress, where, in his Special Message of 11 April 1898, he requested authorisation for a military intervention in Cuba, as 'all diplomatic means' had been 'exhausted'.[590] 'The forcible intervention of the United States as a neutral to stop the war, according to the large dictates of humanity and following many historical

---

[582] Jon Western, 'Prudence or outrage? Public opinion and humanitarian intervention in historical and comparative perspective', in: Fabian Klose (ed.), The Emergence of Humanitarian Intervention, Cambridge University Press 2015, p. 179.

[583] Walter LaFeber, The Cambridge History of American Foreign Relations, Vol. II – The American Search for Opportunity, Cambridge University Press 1993, p. 140.

[584] LaFeber 1993, p. 140, fn. 14.

[585] LaFeber 1993, pp. 133–145.

[586] LaFeber 1993, p. 142.

[587] Directive of the Foreign Minister of Austria-Hungary, Goluchowski, to his representative in Washington, dated 3 April 1898, reprinted in Stephan Verosta and Ignaz Seidl-Hohenveldern (eds.), Die völkerrechtliche Praxis der Donaumonarchie von 1859 bis 1918, Vienna: Austrian Academy of Sciences Press 1996, pp. 498–499.

[588] Collective note of the Great Powers of the European Concert, 6 April 1898, reprinted in Verosta and Seidl-Hohenveldern 1996, p. 500.

[589] McKinley's reply to the European Powers, 8 April 1898, reprinted in: Verosta and Seidl-Hohenveldern 1996, p. 500.

[590] William McKinley: 'Message to Congress Requesting a Declaration of War With Spain', 11 April 1898. Online by Gerhard Peters and John T. Woolley, The American Presidency Project. www.presidency.ucsb.edu/ws/?pid=103901.

precedents where neighbouring states have interfered to check the hopeless sacrifices of life by internecine conflicts beyond their borders, is justifiable on rational grounds', McKinley stressed. The 'humanitarian' motivation he gave is worth quoting in full:

> First. In the cause of humanity and to put an end to the barbarities, bloodshed, starvation and horrible miseries now existing there, and which the parties to the conflict are either unable or unwilling to stop or to mitigate. It is no answer to say this is all in another country, belonging to another nation, and is therefore none of our business. It is our special duty, for it is right at our door.
>
> Second. We owe it to our own citizens in Cuba to afford them the protection and indemnity, for life and property which no government there can or will afford, and to that end to terminate the conditions that deprive them of legal protection.
>
> Third. The right to intervene may be justified by the very serious injury to the commerce, trade, and business of our people, and by the wanton destruction of property and devastation of the island.
>
> Fourth, and which is of utmost importance. The present condition of affairs in Cuba is a constant menace to our peace, and entails upon this government an enormous expense. With such a conflict waged for years in an island so near with which our people have such trade and business relations, ... and other questions and entanglements thus arising, are a constant menace to our peace and compel us to keep on a semi-war footing with a nation with which we are at peace.

For these reasons, McKinley asked

> the Congress to authorize and empower the President to take measures to secure a full and final termination of hostilities between the Government of Spain and the people of Cuba, and to secure in the island the establishment of a stable government, capable of maintaining order and observing its international obligations, insuring peace and tranquillity and the security of its citizens as well as our own, and to use the military and naval forces of the United States as may be necessary for these purposes.

Toward the end of his long message, Mc Kinley informed Congress that on the preceding day, after the preparation of his message, he had received

> official word that the latest decree of the Queen Regent of Spain directs General Blanco, in order to prepare and facilitate peace, to proclaim a suspension of hostilities, the duration and details of which have not yet been communicated to me. (...) If this measure attains a successful result, then our aspirations as a Christian, peace-loving people will be realized. If it fails, it will be only another justification for our contemplated action.

McKinley's incomplete assessment of the situation – a 'blatantly false statement', as it has been described[591] – infuriated the European diplomats, the British in

---

[591] Rich 1992, p. 356.

particular, who, on 14 April 1898, summoned the ambassadors of the major
European powers to their embassy to draw up similarly worded telegrams to their
respective governments to urge the United States to agree to a peaceful settlement
but to no avail. The ensuing resolution in Congress of 20 April 1898 neglected to
mention the Spanish armistice declaration. Instead, Congress recognised Cuban
independence and requested the removal of all Spanish troops: 'Whereas the
abhorrent conditions which have existed for more than three years on the island
of Cuba, so near to our borders, have shocked the moral sense of the people of the
United States and have been a disgrace to Christian civilisation ... and can not
longer be endured ...'.[592] The United States then proceeded with a blockade of
Cuba's northern coast and the port of Santiago de Cuba. In reaction, Spain
declared war on the United States on 24 April 1898. The United States followed
suit the next day. Fighting, however, did not begin on Cuba, but on the other side
of the world, when the American Marines attacked the Spanish pacific fleet in
Manila Bay in the Philippines and destroyed it.[593] A full-blown attack on the
crumbling Spanish colonial empire thus came underway in different theatres.
President McKinley also justified the action in the Philippines in 'humanitarian'
and 'civilisational' terms, though the claim that it was America's task 'to take care
of the [Filipinos], and educate them and Christianize them' has more than a
slightly hollow ring to it, considering the fact that they had been Christians for
centuries: 'The United States' humanitarian takeover was unsuccessfully resisted
with arms for two years and, sadly for the Filipinos, the "taking care" lasted for fifty
years'.[594] It has also been pointed out that, in crushing the Filipino independence
movement, the United States employed almost the same methods the Spanish
were accused of.[595]

   On 22 June 1898, a 6,000 soldier-strong contingent of American troops landed on
Cuban soil, quickly defeating the Spanish colonialists with the help of Cuban
insurgents and the American Navy. In August 1898, an armistice could be agreed
upon, eventually culminating in the (Peace) Treaty of Paris of 10 December 1898.
The treaty marked the end of the Spanish colonial empire, freeing its last remaining
colonial assets Cuba, Guam, the Philippines and Puerto Rico. In Spanish historiography, the 'catastrophe' of 1898 became a myth that would define the Spanish view

---

[592] Special Message by US President McKinley, 11 April 1898, in: Moore 1906, pp. 219–220.
[593] For remarkable assessments of the legal dimensions of the development on the Philippines, see:
Karl Haushover, 'Philippinen-Frage', in Karl Strupp (ed.), *Wörterbuch des Völkerrechts*, Vol. II,
Berlin: De Gruyter 1925, pp. 265–268; Johannes Leyser, 'Philippinen', in: Hans-Jürgen Schlochauer (ed.), *Wörterbuch des Völkerrechts*, Vol. 2, Berlin: De Gruyter 1961, p. 765.
[594] Coady 2008, p. 76, fn. 16.
[595] Schwartz 2013, p. 213.

on the fate of the Spanish Empire for years to come.[596] It ended Spain's 'short nineteenth century'.[597]

For Cuba, freedom from the Spanish colonialists, however, did not mean freedom from occupation, as the United States replaced the Europeans as masters of the island. While the United States refrained from annexing the island and were restricted by their promise to grant complete independence to the Cuban people,[598] they nevertheless kept tight control over the future development of Cuba, placing a native Cuban administration under the auspices of an American military government and incorporating the so-called Platt amendment[599] into the island's new constitution, effectively reducing Cuba to the status of an American protectorate: The United States padlocked Cubans into its system politically and economically, while giving them the semblance of self-government.[600]

President William McKinley has been described as 'a follower not a leader of public opinion', shifting from his opposition to war over Cuba to authorising invasion only as public opinion shifted toward war.[601] Yet in the end, his opposition to taking up arms seems to have been tactical, rather than principled, as he did seek war and domination in the Caribbean and the southern Pacific when he felt the time was right and achieved it with an impressive show of force in a remarkably short time. His concern for order, as Walter LaFeber has put it, was strictly secondary, for if he had truly sought order, he had other alternatives, notably allowing Spain to crush the rebellion as it had in the 1870s or recognising the Cuban revolutionary government and allowing it to govern its own homeland.[602] The 'humanitarian'

---

[596] Manuel Tuñón de Lara, Julio Aróstegui, Ángel Viñas, Gabriel Cardona, and Josep M. Bricall, *Der Spanische Bürgerkrieg – Eine Bestandsaufnahme*, Frankfurt: Suhrkamp 1987, p. 120. The prevailing opinion among Hispanists today, however, seems to be that the outcome of the war was not bad for Spain, see: Tone 2008, p. 286.

[597] del Moral 2014, p. 148.

[598] Joint Resolution: 'that the United States hereby disclaim any disposition or intention to exercise sovereignty, jurisdiction or control over said island, except for the pacification thereof, and assert its determination when that is accomplished to leave the government and the control of the island to its people', Special Message by US President McKinley, 11 April 1898, in: Moore 1906, p. 226.

[599] '. . . the government of Cuba shall never enter into any treaty or other compact with any foreign power or powers which will impair or tend to impair the independence of Cuba, . . . assume or contract a public debt of which the ordinary revenues of the island shall be inadequate . . . The government of Cuba consents that the United States may exercise the right to intervene for the preservation of Cuban independence, the maintenance of government adequate for the protection of life, property, and individual liberty and for discharging the obligations with respect to Cuba imposed by the treaty of Paris on the United States, now to be assumed and undertaken by the government of Cuba'; *Platt*-Amendment, in: Moore 1906, p. 237.

[600] LaFeber 1993, p. 152.

[601] Western 2015, p. 179, quoting Warren Zimmerman, *First Great Triumph: How Five Americans Made Their Country a World Power*, New York: Farrar, Straus and Giroux 2002, p. 254.

[602] LaFeber 1993, p. 144.

narrative presented in the official justification may have helped to convince the American public that the country was acting for some greater good, but decisive it was not.

2.8.3 The Intervention in the History of International Law

Even though the intervention of the United States in Cuba quickly turned to a declaration of war and full-blown military engagement, the perspective in international law remains focused on an intervention.[603] The American decision to turn against Spain, a former European power in decline, and the willingness to ignore Great Power efforts at mediation showed the powerlessness of the Europeans in this part of the world – and this probably helps to explain why contemporary European writers on international law were quite skeptical in their judgement of the intervention and its justification. While this case represents the first time that a government explicitly used the 'humanitarian' justification for its actions that had been the subject of discussion in the international law literature for decades at this point, it is quite clearly the obviously affected self-interest of the United States that prompted European authors to quickly refute the claims of 'humanitarianism'.[604] As early as 1899, a Dutch dissertation on intervention in international law concluded that while the United States may have held 'humanitarian' considerations in high regard, this could only be considered a pretext, as the situation on Cuba was nowhere near as extraordinary as the United States pretended it to be.[605] It is remarkable how that same judgement could have been passed on the European intervention in Mount Lebanon in 1860–1861, yet the very same author had less doubts of the 'humanitarian' justification (and effect) in that case.[606] In a book-long treatment of the legal aspects of the Spanish-American War, Louis LeFur (1870–1943), later professor for international law at the University of Paris and described by Martti Koskenniemi as a 'Catholic-conservative international lawyer', concentrating on 'advocating a return to universal tradition, represented by natural law, indissociable from Christian morality',[607] was even more dismissive. He compared the devastation in Cuba to the destruction caused by Union troops on Confederate territory during the American Civil War, asking whether this should therefore not have justified European intervention in favour of the Confederates?[608] Sympathetic to the cause

---

[603] Murphy 1996, p. 56; Chesterman 2001, pp. 33–34; Wellhausen 2002, p. 71.

[604] Quaritsch 1913, p. 77, fn. 3; Bonfils and Fauchille 1904, pp. 164–165. Simlarly: Percy Winfield, 'The Grounds of Intervention in International Law', *British Yearbook of International Law* 1924, 5, p. 154: '. . . the constant menace to American peace from the feebleness of Spanish rule in Cuba (. . .) was regarded as the most weighty ground'.

[605] van Lynden van Sandenberg 1899, pp. 255–258.

[606] van Lynden van Sandenberg 1899, pp. 192–193.

[607] Koskenniemi 2002, pp. 316, 318.

[608] LeFur 1899, p. 44, my translation.

of 'humanitarian intervention' in principle, 'a reproduction of the ideas shared by the proponents of the French revolution',[609] he rejected its application in this instance flat-out.[610]

On the other hand, Anglo-American authors in particular stressed the relevance of the American intervention for the development of a right to 'humanitarian intervention' from the earliest moment.[611] The results of the 'Cuban adventure' were considered to lead to a general recognition of a right to unilateral action. As one author wrote early in the twentieth century:

> When these 'human' rights are habitually violated, one or more states may intervene in the name of the society of nations and may take such measures as to substitute at least temporarily, if not permanently its own sovereignty for that of the state thus controlled.[612]

For Ellery C. Stowell (1878–1958), the American international lawyer who addressed the question of intervention in international law during the era of the League of Nations in two major publications,[613] and one of the few voices in international law to call for a 'humanitarian intervention' on behalf of the Jews of Europe,[614] the American efforts represented one of the most important examples of a 'humanitarian intervention'.[615] Justified through precedents and the theoretical groundwork provided by 'weighty authorities', he specifically considered the intervention justified on 'grounds of humanity', stating that the United States intervened 'to put an end to the shocking treatment which the military authorities were inflicting upon the non-combatant population'.[616] It is obvious that Stowell based this description not on the historical record, but on a fabricated narrative, which may have appealed to America's sense of justice and also have corresponded to the image that presented itself to the American public thanks to the distorted picture presented by American newspapers. Yet at the same time, Stowell's approach mirrors the general American approach to international law, or as Francis Boyle has termed it, 'the legalist approach to international relations', which was born in the aftermath of the Spanish-American War of 1898: A presumption that American foreign policy

---

[609] LeFur 1899, p. 44, my translation.

[610] LeFur 1899, p. 45

[611] e.g. Westlake 1910, p. 320; Dickinson 1920 p. 262; Graham 1924.

[612] Edwin Borchard, *The Diplomatic Protection of Citizens Abroad*, New York: Banks 1915/1925, p. 14. See also: Hodges 1915, p. 87.

[613] Stowell 1921; Ellery C. Stowell, 'La théorie et la pratique de l'intervention', *Recueil des cours*, Collected Courses of the Hague Academy of International Law, Den Haag: The Hague Academy of International Law 1932, p. 138.

[614] Ellery C. Stowell, 'Intercession Against the Persecution of Jews', *American Journal of International Law* 1936, 30, pp. 102–106; Ellery C. Stowell, 'Humanitarian Intervention', *American Journal of International Law* 1939, 33, pp. 733–736.

[615] Stowell 1921, pp. 57, 120–121, 481.

[616] Stowell 1921, p. 120.

by virtue of America's commitment to the rule of law produced legal results.[617] For this approach, the Spanish-American War, the 'intervention' of the United States in Cuba, is a catalyst: According to Boyle, the founding of the American Society of International Law is a result of this experience.[618] If this event is remembered as the exercise of a right to intervene in the name of the society of nations to protect against the violation of 'true "human" rights', it is hardly surprising that by the end of World War II, an American writer would claim that the 'case against Spain' appeared to be so convincing 'that it is difficult to understand the critical attitude of a number of European writers who not only repudiated the right of the United States to intervene but saw in the act the violation of the express pledge of President Monroe not to interfere with the existing colonies or dependencies of any European power'.[619]

Yet the criticism of writers, which includes voices from the United States,[620] was much more nuanced than this summary would suggest. In addition to the opinions already discussed, the intervention was also treated by contemporaries as an example of an intervention to protect shared cultural values, though not necessarily justified as such.[621] The claim of the United States to join the ranks of the Great Powers with these events was noted,[622] and this context was also recognised in the American literature: 'the action taken by the United States in 1898 in relation to Cuba' was offered as an illustration of an 'intervention on behalf of citizens residing in the less advanced countries of the world', 'the consequence of differences in civilization', the intervention an example of 'the natural processes of orderly progress'.[623]

The most fundamental criticism levelled at the United States came less from publicists than it came from states, European states in particular. The Austro-Hungarian ambassador to Washington considered the American intervention an 'attack' on Spain,[624] and the aforementioned Collective Note of 6 April 1898 is a clear rejection of the legal case presented by the United States. The French Ambassador to Washington apparently quoted the British Ambassador in the United States as demanding expressions of protest in the name of the public conscience of Europe to not let the Americans engage in this 'act of brigandage' in the earlier stages of the conflict over Cuba, but the Europeans ultimately were not ready to

---

[617] Francis Boyle, *Foundations of World Order*, Durham: Duke University Press 1999; See also: John Murphy, *The United States and the Rule of Law in International Affairs*, Cambridge University Press 2004.

[618] Boyle 1999, p. 18.

[619] Charles G. Fenwick, 'Intervention: Individual and Collective', *American Journal of International Law* 1945, 39(4), p. 651.

[620] e.g. Flack 1906, p. 68.

[621] von Liszt 1913, p. 66.

[622] von Liszt 1913, p. 62.

[623] Dickinson 1920, p. 262.

[624] Report of Ambassador Hengelmüller, 21 April 1898, reprinted in: Verosta and Ignaz Seidl-Hohenveldern 1996, p. 502.

commit themselves to a stronger condemnation of the American action, after their attempts at halting them had been so useless.[625]

2.8.4 *The Intervention in the History of 'Humanitarian Intervention'*

Recent analysis has held that the 'humanitarian elements were more pronounced and more direct in influencing the decision-making in 1898 than they were in 1827'.[626] But it has already been shown that – even if this were true – this would not necessarily mean much, as the humanitarian elements in 1827 were marginal at best. Yet there is a bigger picture to consider here: Even if humanitarian elements were 'more pronounced and more direct in influencing the decision-making', they can hardly be said to have been decisive. In *The Cambridge History of American Foreign Relations*, Walter LaFeber tells the story of American involvement in Cuba and the Spanish-American War of 1898 without any reference to humanitarian ideals.[627] One may not agree with that narrative, but it is clear that *if* humanitarian concerns had been top priority, earlier action would have been called for. By the time the United States did eventually intervene with force, the worst measures had already been reversed by Spain. Yet as the humanitarian elements were *presented* as decisive, this would seem to constitute the required *opinio juris* of customary international law. As the events played out, their main thrust put the distinctively European construct of international law as the law of 'civilised nations' into question, by pitting the idea of 'humanitarian intervention' against a European, 'civilised' by definition, colonial power. It is this situation that makes the Cuban case unique to the history of 'humanitarian intervention'.

When the debate over 'humanitarian intervention' was renewed in the late 1960s in the United States, the intervention was initially presented by Michael Reisman and Myres S. MacDougal as an example of altruistic motivations,[628] though, even then, other American authors held very different opinions.[629] As the debate continued, the assessments became more critical and more skeptical with regard to the 'humanitarian' character of the intervention.[630] From this perspective, the apparent potential for abuse of the doctrine in cases where 'humanitarian' concerns would have allowed for the justification of an intervention which nevertheless 'escalated'

---

[625] Rich 1992, p. 356. Ambassador Hengelmüller describes the performance of the European Powers as 'rather sad', Report of 21 April 1898, reprinted in: Verosta and Seidl-Hohenveldern 1996, p. 502.

[626] Western 2015, p. 177.

[627] LaFeber 1993.

[628] Reisman and McDougal 1968 Memorandum, reprinted in: Lillich 1973, p. 183; see also Fenwick 1965, p. 288; Behuniak 1978, p. 163; Abiew 1999, p. 54.

[629] David S. Bogen, 'The Law of Humanitarian Intervention: United States Policy in Cuba (1898) and in the Dominican Republic (1965)', *Harvard International Law Club Journal* 1966, p. 314.

[630] Fonteyne 1974.

comes into focus.[631] Michael Walzer's famous characterisation of the events as 'benevolent imperialism' seems to strike the same chord.[632]

The debate about American claims that the intervention served 'the interests of humanity' has been raging ever since that claim was first made, but, from the point of view of international law, the focus should not be on whether the intervention was as 'altruistic' as it was presented. Even if there was an element of hypocrisy in the official American position, this says more about the potential of the doctrine of 'humanitarian intervention' to provide legal cover for actions hardly deserving a 'humanitarian' legitimation, than it does about the doctrine's legal relevance. It has been pointed out that the NATO action over Kosovo bears quite a strong resemblance to the United States' intervention in Cuba, even if NATO's action – unlike that of the United States, presumably – is said to *not* have been undertaken out of an overreaching sense of sovereignty, immediate economic interests or a privileged relationship between the intervening state and the victims.[633] In the case of Kosovo, however, the situation for the Albanians in Kosovo seriously deteriorated with the first NATO bombings,[634] whereas the immediate consequences of the United States intervention on Cuba were nowhere near as negative.

The United States' 'potential first humanitarian intervention', whether 'sullied with imperialism' or not, should be viewed as the moment where a figure of speech, prominent in the textbooks of international law in the nineteenth century, was turned into policy, transforming the legal concept discussed up until then into something applied in practice. McKinley's official justification is the explicit claim of a right, even a duty to intervene even in a foreign country, if 'bloodshed, starvation and horrible miseries' so demand. For the first time, a sitting head of state explicitly made the claim that had previously only been interpreted into official justifications for interventions by writers on international law. This corresponds well with American legalist approaches to foreign policy: The American 'crusade for freedom' was already fought in the nineteenth century through legal means,[635] with a 'peculiarly messianic, and distinctively American' approach to international law, as apparent from many early articles in the American Journal of International Law, first published in 1907.[636]

If the intervention of the Great Powers in the Greek War of Independence was 'humanitarian intervention's' original sin, then the American intervention on Cuba

---

[631] Henke 2002, p. 16.

[632] Michael Walzer, *Just and Unjust Wars*, 4th. ed., New York, Basic Books 2006, p. 132.

[633] Georg Nolte, 'Kosovo und Konstitutionalisierung: Zur Humanitären Intervention der NATO-Staaten', *Zeitschrift für Ausländisches Öffentliches Recht und Völkerrecht* 1999, pp. 941–960.

[634] Glenny 2000, p. 269.

[635] Dan Diner, 'Grenzenloses Recht', *Süddeutsche Zeitung*, 16 June 2003.

[636] David J. Bederman, 'Appraising a Century of Scholarship in the American Journal of International Law', *American Journal of International Law* 2006, 100(1), p. 21.

could have been the doctrine's Pandora's box-moment. Yet, international law kept the lid on the American justification for intervention, which was not used as a precedent for future 'humanitarian interventions'. In fact, it would take another 100 years before the question of 'humanitarian intervention' as a legal justification for the international use of force would become practical again.

2.9 THE LONG END OF THE LONG NINETEENTH CENTURY

The idea of 'humanitarian intervention' as a legal instrument is a result of late nineteenth-century thinking about how to move the law closer to current ideas of justice, in a world that was still very much dictated by European beliefs of bringing 'progress' through colonisation to the 'uncivilised' parts of the world. Intervention was a means by which to transform 'backward' places, as Barry Buzan and George Lawson have observed.[637] 'Humanitarian intervention' gave this practice an additional moral dimension, even if, as the long nineteenth century drew to a close, no further actual or alleged 'humanitarian' interventions were forthcoming.

2.9.1 *Antoine Rougier's 'Théorie de l'Intervention de Humanité'*

Later writings on the history of 'humanitarian intervention' regularly follow the narrative established in an article by the French international lawyer Antoine Rougier, 'La Théorie de l'Intervention de Humanité', published in 1910 in the *Revue générale de droit international public*. The journal was established in 1894 and has been described as 'avowedly nationalist' in its outlook: 'that international law was a beneficial part of the conventions of diplomacy was as much a forgone conclusion as the fact that among European States only France was sincerely committed to the advancement of an international rule of law'.[638]

Rougier's 'theory' was based on the idea of the existence of a 'droit humain' rooted in the solidarity between peoples living together in a 'société humaine' and which was transformed into a 'sociéte internationale' among nations.[639] He took the distinction between 'civilised humanity' and 'barbarous humanity' known from Lorimer[640] and other authors a step further, by distinguishing between civilisations,[641] situating the 'intervention d'humanité' in a system of international law under the guidance of Europe. It would operate as a system of solidarity between civilisations, but remained under the control of the 'most civilised' nations.[642] Taking the state practice discussed in this book as his basis, he developed his 'théorie

---

[637] Buzan and Lawson 2015, p. 180.
[638] Koskenniemi 2002, pp. 278–279.
[639] Rougier 1910, p. 491.
[640] Lorimer 1883, p. 101.
[641] Rougier 1910, pp. 505–506.
[642] Rougier 1910, p. 509.

de l'Intervention d'Humanité' to ensure that future interventions in the name of 'humanity' would serve the goals of the 'droit humain'. According to the guidelines contained in this 'theory', interventions should be undertaken by a collective of like-minded powers and only in cases where a government could be held *responsible* for gross violations of not only national or international law, but the overarching system of the 'droit humain'.[643] The element of responsibility was introduced by Rougier to distinguish between violations caused by private individuals and government officials, though for cases in the Ottoman Empire which, according to Rougier, were 'probably not systematically organised' by government officials ('like the massacres of Crete, Syria and Armenia'), he identified a duty to intervene with which the Porte had failed to comply.[644]

In retrospect, it seems clear that Rougier constructed a narrative with the clear aim of establishing a framework for *future* interventions, yet later authors seem to frequently have read his statements about the basis for a 'theory of an intervention in the name of humanity' as commentary on the legality of 'humanitarian intervention' at the time. Grewe's *Epochs of International Law*, for example, treats the cases mentioned by Rougier as examples of 'humanitarian intervention'.[645] Some of the interventions used by Rougier to illustrate the basis of his theory, however, hardly matched his preconditions, but of the cases he did discuss, two not yet mentioned are particularly illustrating in highlighting the thinking behind his theory.

2.9.2 China, 1900

Without much hesitation, Rougier included the 'intervention' of a multinational force in response to the 1900 'Boxer Rebellion' in China in his narrative of the 'intervention d'humanité'. For Rougier, these events represented an example of a justified reaction of a collective of 'civilised' nations against 'barbarous anarchism'.[646] Some other contemporary accounts also considered these events in the context of 'humanitarian intervention' broadly conceived.[647] In the more recent literature, the case is hardly mentioned at all as an example of a 'humanitarian intervention',[648] it is now more commonly viewed as an example of brutal

---

[643] Rougier 1910, p. 512, my translation, emphasis added.

[644] Rougier 1910, p. 513, my translation.

[645] Grewe 2000, pp. 489–493; see also Malanczuk 1997, p. 20.

[646] Rougier 1910, p. 470, my translation.

[647] Bonfils and Fauchille 1904, p. 160, nr. 302, characterise this episode as a military expedition to avenge the murdered diplomats and civilians. Von Liszt 1913, p. 33, just speaks of an 'armed intervention' and mentions that China had to compensate for the murder of the German diplomat by erecting a memorial to Ketteler, executing leading Boxer rebels, and sending a Special Ambassador to Germany to apologise, p. 183. The characterisation in Ernest Nys, *Le Droit International*, Vol. II, 2nd ed., Brussels: M. Weissenbruch 1912, p. 234 is similar.

[648] Gerhard von Glahn, *Law among Nations*, 7th ed., Boston: Ally and Bacon 1996, p. 582, still refers to this case, but it is more common to mention that Rougier cited it, see: Chesterman 2001, p. 27 with n. 149.

colonialism, a 'punitive expedition'[649] of 'interventionary imperialism'.[650] Yet the picture looked quite different to contemporary observers. Seen through their eyes, the conflict over the 'Boxer Rebellion' looked like the archetypal confrontation between 'civilisation' and 'barbarism' from both sides. The Chinese had little doubt that their civilisation was far more advanced than the European version, that was trying to impose itself on China; whereas the European belief in the superiority of its societies (and values) no doubt influenced Rougier and other contemporaries when framing the expedition of the international troops as a justified measure to force China to join ranks with the 'international community of civilized states' under international law.[651] Similarly, the collaboration of the European powers with Japan and the United States in 'a combined military and policing enterprise, which went well beyond the immediate purpose of rescuing their diplomats besieged in Peking' is still considered a 'necessary' intervention 'in the internal affairs of China on behalf of the international community', which may be 'compared with similar interventions under United Nations sponsorship'.[652]

At a time when China had sent some of its most promising minds to Europe to study the European way of thinking and attend universities, and those students produced doctoral dissertations on China's successful entry into the society of states under international law,[653] the European attempts to use the Boxer Rebellion to expand their influence in China were a clear rejection of Chinese claims to equality under the law. Two German dissertations from 1912–1913, which at least partially recognised the work of the Chinese doctoral students in Berlin,[654] discussed the question of whether or not international powers needed to observed international law in their dealings with China and answered in the affirmative.[655] However, the actions of the international powers showed very little signs of acknowledging this perspective.

The uprising of the 'Boxers' began as a movement against the exploitation of China's resources by foreign powers. At the end of the nineteenth century, Russia, France and the United Kingdom in particular, but also Japan, Italy and Germany, occupied significant parts of Chinese territory, controlled commerce and considered

---

[649] Grewe 2000, p. 481; Ziegler 2007, p. 184.

[650] Comment by Rogers, in: Lillich 1973, p. 10.

[651] Thoralf Klein: 'Straffeldzug im Namen der Zivilisation: Der Boxerkrieg in China', in: Thoralf Klein and Frank Schumacher (eds.), *Kolonialkriege*, Hamburg: Hamburger Edition 2006, pp. 146, 165, citing a legal study published 1901 in fn. 56.

[652] Adam Watson, *The Evolution of International Society*, London: Routledge 1992, pp. 272–273.

[653] Ma-Do-Yun, *Der Eintritt des chinesischen Reiches in den völkerrechtlichen Verband*, Inaugural-Dissertation, Berlin: Ebering 1907.

[654] Friedrich Kleine, *Unterdrückung der Boxerunruhen China 1900 nach ihrer völkerrechtlichen Bedeutung*, Berlin: R. Trenkel 1913; Dietrich von Klitzing, *Die Unterdrückung der Boxerunruhen in China 1900 in völkerrechtlicher Beleuchtung*, Breslau: Breslauer Genossenschafts-Buchdruckerei 1912.

[655] Kleine 1913, p. 46; von Klitzing 1912, p. 8. This was, as both authors point out, not necessarily a view shared by all the authorities writing on international law and China at the time.

China part of their respective spheres of influence. Christian missionaries held special powers, Chinese Christians enjoyed special privileges. By the autumn of 1899, the mood among the less privileged population turned violent. The insurgents, referred to as 'Boxers' given their background in martial arts, plundered and massacred Orthodox, Protestant and Catholic missionaries and their Chinese parishioners throughout northern China. They received at least tacit support from Chinese officials. In June 1900, the German Consul was killed and the international quarter in Beijing came under siege. In response, the German government initiated the dispatch of international troops from the European Great Powers, the United States of America and Japan. The troops eventually took Beijing in August 1900. They liberated the international quarter and also plundered the town, committing random executions and burning villages. Contemporary eyewitness reports describe the actions of the international troops as resembling those of street bandits: 'It is certain that the three shortest of the Ten Commandments were constantly violated on an extensive scale'.[656]

In Manchuria, the continued attacks of the Boxers on railways and Russian troops led to a full-scale Russian invasion of the area in October 1900. Unrest continued in other parts of China until the conflict was formally concluded through the 'Boxer-Protocol' of 7 September 1901. The protocol resembled a peace treaty in everything but name and required China to pay extensive damages as well as the cost of the international troops. Still, Beijing and other cities in northern China remained under the control of the international force for more than a year.

In Rougier's narrative, the joint Japanese-European reaction to the 'murderous sect' of the 'Boxers' resembles the patterns established by similar 'troubles' in the Ottoman Empire.[657] Yet his position clearly shows that for all his restrained criticism of some examples of European state practice, his general appreciation for the alleged superiority of European civilisation was never in question: Rougier knew of no 'fundamental right of equality' between states (or civilisations), instead he considered inequality a question of fact: In a world without a superior power, all states had originally found themselves in the identical position, but that equality had subsequently given way to a 'natural hierarchy of power, moral authority and civilisation now established between nations', which, he argued, the law could not 'desecrate'.[658] The 'right' claimed by European states for the authority to punish China, evident in Kaiser Wilhelm's famous 'Hun Speech',[659] therefore

---

[656] see the source cited in Kaminski 1973, p. 124, fn. 346.

[657] Rougier 1910, p. 470.

[658] Rougier 1910, p. 504, my translation.

[659] Wilhelm II: 'Hun Speech' (1900) German History in Documents and Images (GHDI), English translation available at http://germanhistorydocs.ghi-dc.org/sub_document.cfm?document_id=755: '[The Chinese have overturned the Law of Nations', last accessed 25 February 2019. See also: Circular note of 3 July 1900, to the powers cooperating in China, defining the purposes and policy of the United States by the US Department of State, available at https://history.state.gov/historicaldocuments/frus1901China/d4, last accessed 25 February 2019: '[T]he policy of the

corresponded to Rougier's idea of 'international control' through disinterested intervention 'by humanity'.[660] Similarly, the authority of 'such members of the community of nations as are able to perform it' to undertake international 'police work' to uphold international law was seen by international lawyers to manifest itself in the 'punitive expedition' against the Chinese Government, which 'had connived at attacks on the legations by troops and Boxers'.[661] For Stowell, who considered 'humanitarian intervention' an act of international policing, the military intervention in China was the 'best example' of a collective intervention 'for the purpose of punishing the guilty state' for 'some extraordinary crime' against the law of other nations. He noted that the occupying powers addressed a joint note to the Chinese government, dated 22 December 1900, outlining the conditions 'which must be fulfilled before the occupation of Chinese territory by the cooperating states would be terminated – conditions "which", so the note ran, "they deem indispensable to expiate the crimes committed and to prevent their recurrence"'.[662] Other contemporary writers have also had no doubt that the 'intervention of the powers in China in 1900' afforded an illustration of the principle that 'the so-called interventions in the interests of humanity, wherever they can be justified legally, are really the consequence of differences in civilization, and that wherever this is the situation there exist legal incapacities which can only be removed by the natural processes of orderly progress'.[663] Yet historians have termed the international expedition 'the civilized world's revenge', describing how the civilian population

> suffered terribly as the advancing forces on their way to Beijing and put village after village to the torch and left a great swath of destruction in their wake. Once in the capital, everyone joined in the looting: troops of all nationalities (though the Europeans were the worst, and the Japanese the best-behaved), and missionaries who would later justify their activities in articles with such delightful titles as 'The Ethics of Loot.' Patrols passed through the city, and then into the surrounding countryside to seek out and shoot Boxers, as a result of which (in the words of the

---

Government of the United States is to seek a solution which may bring about permanent safety and peace to China, preserve Chinese territorial and administrative entity, protect all rights guaranteed to friendly powers by treaty and international law, and safeguard for the world the principle of equal and impartial trade with all parts of the Chinese Empire'.

[660] Rougier 1910, p. 502.

[661] William Edward Hall, *A Treatise on International Law*, 7th ed., by Alexander Pearce Higgins, Oxford: Clarendon Press 1917, p. 56. Higgins left the part on 'humanitarian intervention', quoted at length above, unchanged. See also Charles Cheney Hyde, *International Law chiefly as Interpreted and Applied by the United States*, Boston: Little, Brown & Co. 1922, p. 350, describing the international expedition as a 'notable example' of action based on the principle that, where 'the safety of foreigners in their persons and property is jeopardized by the impotence or indisposition of the territorial sovereign to afford adequate protection, the landing or entrance of a foreign public force of the State to which such nationals belong, is to be anticipated' and justified.

[662] Stowell 1921, p. 39.

[663] Dickinson 1920, pp. 262–263.

American commander): 'It is safe to say that where one real Boxer has been killed since the capture of Pekin, fifty harmless coolies or labourer on the farms, including not a few women and children, have been slain'.[664]

Accordingly, the later discussion conveniently glossed over the fact that for Rougier the intervention of the European troops in China was just another example of European superiority which allowed for a *droit public spécial* in the interactions of Europe with the Ottoman Empire or Turkey.[665] The more recent characterisation of the European intervention as 'the most gigantic modern punitive expedition'[666] would clearly stand in the way of considering this episode an intervention 'by humanity'.[667]

2.9.3 *Macedonia, 1903–1908 and 1913*

The other case considered by Rougier as part of the state practice on which his theory rested was obviously fresh in his memory and its eventual conclusion was impossible for him to foresee. Later authors also considered the developments in Macedonia between 1903 and 1908 a suitable example of 'humanitarian intervention', though mostly in connection with the later developments of 1912–1913,[668] which obviously were unknown to Rougier at the time of his writing. Yet the views of the contemporary international lawyer on the events as they were unfolding are instructive as a reflection on how proponents of an original right of 'humanitarian intervention' viewed the world and international law in their time.

In his 'Theorie de l'intervention d'humanité', Rougier limited himself to the observation that 'a new European intervention' had taken place in favour of the Macedonian population ten years after the massacres of the Armenians and other interventions for the cause of humanity could be mentioned with respect to the 'Oriental question'.[669] In an earlier article he had detailed the historical facts of the 'European intervention in the Macedonian question' as he saw them.[670] According to this narrative, the origins of the 'Macedonian Question' lay 'principally' with the 'deplorable administration of the Ottoman government' and its failure to deal with different 'ethnic groups' which made up the Macedonian population: Bulgarians,

---

[664] Joseph W. Esherick, *The Origins of the Boxer Uprisings*, Los Angeles: University of California Press 1987, p. 310, footnote omitted.

[665] Rougier 1910, p. 506.

[666] Dierk Walter, *Organisierte Gewalt in der europäischen Expansion*, Hamburg: Hamburger Edition 2014, p. 126, my translation.

[667] A remarkable exception is Mohamed Shahid and Mohamed Khalid, *International Law and Politics of Intervention*, Delhi: Raj Publications 2003, p. 35.

[668] e.g. Ganji 1962, pp. 33–37; Reisman and McDougal 1968 Memorandum, reprinted in: Lillich 1973, p. 182; Fonteyne 1974, pp. 212–213; Behuniak 1978, pp. 162–163; Abiew 1999, p. 53.

[669] Rougier 1910, p. 475.

[670] Antoine Rougier, 'L'Intervention de l'Europe dans la Question de Macédoine', *Revue générale de droit international public* 1906, 13, pp. 178–200.

Serbs, Greeks, 'Koutzo-Valaques' (Arumanians or Vlachs), Albanians, Ottomans and Jews.[671] This view is clearly the result of the application of nineteenth century concepts of nationalism, the very same ideas of 'imagined communities' that fuelled the conflict in the region and were, in turn, fuelled by European intervention to the point where collapse into more violence seemed inevitable.[672] Yet as late as the mid-nineteenth-century, the identity of the population residing in the territory known as Macedonia was primarily defined in religious, not national terms, and hardly affiliated with any ethnic group. By the end of the same century different ethnic groups started to compete to attract the Christians of Macedonia and 'this competition embodied "the Macedonian Question"'.[673]

In Rougier's narrative, this question could be 'solved' through European intervention,[674] and indeed, it is far from unthinkable that the Macedonian situation could have been resolved in the way other, similar conflicts in the region had been 'resolved' in a 'humanitarian' way, had it not been for the ensuing Balkan Wars and the descent into World War I that soon engulfed the region. However, Great Power competition and Balkan state rivalry drove the Macedonian Question to new dimensions of violence between 1878 and 1914. As one recent study of the Balkans has pointed out, in the earlier Balkan revolutionary war, Muslims had been the primary victims of nationalist violence, and, for broad segments of the rural population, religion had still remained a far more formative reality than nationality. The 'conflict in Macedonia represented the first instance of modern political violence *between* Orthodox Christians'; the violence 'served to assert the primacy of national loyalties over religious identities'.[675]

The wider historical events were included as 'the intervention of Austria, Russia, the United Kingdom, Italy and France as a result of insurrection and misrule in Macedonia (1903–1908)' in Manouchehr Ganji's 1962 dissertation 'International Protection of Human Rights'.[676] Ganji seems to have expanded on some cases suggested by Rougier as possible cases of 'humanitarian intervention' – Rougier's article on the 'Theorie de l'intervention d'humanité' is his starting point for the discussion of the status of 'humanitarian intervention' under international law[677] – though his inclusion of the 'Macedonian' case, still unresolved at the time of Rougier's writing, is more problematic for the depiction of an 'intervention of Austria, Russia, the United Kingdom, Italy and France' than for considering this case at all.

---

[671] Rougier 1906, p. 180, my translation.
[672] Biondich 2011, p. 72.
[673] Ana S. Trbovich, A *Legal Geography of Yugoslavia's Disintegration*, Oxford University Press 2008, p. 102.
[674] Rougier 1906, pp. 190–200.
[675] Biondich 2011, p. 72.
[676] Ganji 1962, pp. 33–37.
[677] Ganji 1962, p. 9.

Macedonia did not exist as an administrative entity within the Ottoman Balkans, but was organised after 1878 into three provinces with a remarkably heterogeneous population, with no single nationality possessing a majority and, according to Ottoman census data, equally divided between Muslims and Christians.[678] For the European Powers, the area first and foremost was synonymous with banditry, terrorism and misrule. The reorganisation of other parts of the Balkans with the Berlin Congress of 1878 had introduced new states and therefore new players with national interests and their own peculiar interests in Macedonia. Greece, Serbia and Bulgaria all fuelled the social and national conflicts in the Macedonian region by claiming the area or parts of it for their own national territory. The unrest grew into a civil war the Ottoman authorities found hard to suppress. By 1902, the Ottoman Empire reached out to the European Great Powers to use their authority to convince Bulgaria to stop supporting Macedonian insurgents. Russia and Austria-Hungary had, in April 1897, agreed to uphold the status quo in the Balkans and advocate reform to mitigate the risk of further upheaval, even as they agreed that Ottoman rule would eventually have to end.[679] The Sultan's half-hearted reform attempts only strengthened Bulgarian nationalist's in their conviction that they would provoke the Great Powers into actions against the Empire.[680] In August 1902, an organised uprising in Macedonia began. In the single biggest operation of the uprising, the insurgents captured the Ottoman garrison in Kruševo and established the short-lived Kruševo Republic. Ten days later, it was crushed with a brutality foreshadowing worse things to come. The photographs that remain of the Macedonian villages that suffered retribution after the uprising are shocking even by the standards of today, informed by the experiences of Auschwitz and Hiroshima. The Ottoman forces often razed entire villages, leaving not a single house standing. Thousands of civilians were murdered and women raped; 50,000 refugees forced to flee into the mountains.[681]

The violence brought Russia and Austria-Hungary back into action. In October 1903, Tsar Nicholas II and the Emperor Franz Josef agreed on the Mürzsteg Agreement, which forced the Porte to accept deployment of an international police force attempting to reorganise the local administration in Macedonia; revise the administrative boundaries 'with a view to a more regular group of the different nationalities'; and rebuild the Christian communities.[682] The mission, however, was not a success, and only helped to further erode the Sultan's authority. It was officially cancelled in May 1909. The report of the Commission established by the Carnegie Endowment For International Peace, ironically set up shortly before the outbreak of the First World War to reduce the use of force in international relations through

[678] Biondich 2011, p. 66.
[679] Biondich 2011, p. 49.
[680] Glenny 2000, p. 200.
[681] Glenny 2000, p. 205.
[682] Mürzsteg Protocol of 3 October 1903, reprinted in English in: Ganji 1962, p. 35.

fact-finding,[683] concluded that the nations involved had done little to solve the problems on the ground: 'The Great Powers had nothing more to do in Macedonia. They departed amid the joyous cries of the multitude, while the leaders of the different nationalities, only yesterday on terms of irreconcilable hostility, embraced one another'.[684]

The embrace did not last long. The various nationalist aspirations in and to Macedonia were only strengthened by the promise of the Mürzsteg Agreement to revise the administrative boundaries, which resulted in civil war in Macedonia. Groups of irregulars and different nationalist were fighting against each other and the Ottoman authorities. In June 1908, the Young Turk revolution began, aimed both against the despotic regime of the Sultan and the continued erosion of the Empire through European interference. The resulting power vacuum first allowed Bulgaria to declare independence in October 1908, then Austria-Hungary to proceed to annex Bosnia-Herzegovina, and Greece to subsequently declare unification with Crete.

The domestic struggles of the Ottoman Empire made it impossible for the Young Turk revolutionaries to react promptly after gaining power, and further violence was imminent. As Macedonian insurgents increased their activities and declared war on the Ottoman Empire in October 1912, Greece, Bulgaria and Serbia in October expressed their 'regret' at being forced to take up arms to support their 'compatriots' in a note to Her Majesty's Government.[685] This marked the beginning of the First Balkan War, which devastated Macedonia after only a few weeks of fighting. In June 1913, war flared up again briefly in the Second Balkan War between Serbia and Bulgaria. Ten short weeks of fighting left some 200,000 combatants and an unknown number of civilians dead. Further victims were claimed by typhus and cholera. The affected area spanned almost 170,000 square meters, stretching from

---

[683] International Commission to Inquire into the Causes and Conduct of the Balkan Wars. *The Other Balkan Wars: a 1913 Carnegie Endowment Inquiry in Retrospect.* Washington, DC: Carnegie Endowment for International Peace/Brookings Institution Publications [Reprint], 1993, cited hereinafter as Carnegie Report.

[684] Carnegie Report, p. 34.

[685] Note verbalé by the Greek government to the British Government, British and Foreign State Papers Vol. 106 (1913), pp. 1058–1060:

> ... les Gouvernements Royaux de la Bulgarie, de la Grèce et de la Serbie, ne pouvant plus tolérer les souffrances de leurs congénères en Turquie et une situation grosse de dangers pour leur avenir, avaient décidé de demander un contrôle efficace pour l'élaboration et la ré-alisation des seules réformes radicales capables d'améliorer e sort misérable des Chrétiens et la pacification de la péninsule des Balkans.
>
> Cette dernière tentative, dont la modération contraste avec l'attitude provocataire de la Turquie, qui avait mobilisé sans motif sérieux contre les Etats balkaniques, ayant échoué et la rupture des relations diplomatiques ayant été ordonnée par la Sublime Porte, les Gouvernements Royaux de la Bulgarie, de la Grèce et de la Serbie se sont vus à leur grand regret dans l'obligation de recourir à la force des armes...; cited according to Ganji 1962, p. 36.

the Albanian coast in the west, to a mere 32 kilometers from Istanbul in the east; from the most northerly border of Macedonia down to Thessaly in central Greece.[686]

The European public had initially viewed the insurgencies against Ottoman rule with sympathy, which turned to shock over the atrocities committed against not only the Turkish civilian population, but also by Christians against Christians.[687] The Carnegie Commission dispatched its team of experts shortly before the end of the Second Balkan War, so they would have seen little of the actual hostilities but much of their immediate aftermath. They concluded that there was 'no clause in international law applicable to land war and to the treatment of the wounded, which was not violated, to a greater or less extent, by all the belligerents' and that, whatever 'formal right' there may have been was violated by wars of liberation transformed into war of conquest.[688] The Report made no immediate statement on the legality of the resort to force by the different parties to the conflict as such,[689] but concluded that the division of local populations 'into as many fragments as there are nations fighting each other and wanting to substitute for another' led to excessive violence: 'The populations themselves killed each other'.[690] The Commission aimed to turn 'the minds of men for a short time away from passion, from race antagonism and from national aggrandizement to a contemplation of the individual and national losses due to war and to the shocking horrors which modern warfare entails' as a step 'toward the substitution of justice for force in the settlement of international differences'.[691] Committed to paper roughly four months before the assassination of Archduke Franz Ferdinand set in motion the wheels of national aggrandizement that quickly led to World War I, the Commission spectacularly failed to achieve its goal.

André Mandelstam (1869–1949), another early theorist of 'humanitarian intervention' and human rights, and between 1898 and 1914 a diplomat in the service of the Russian Empire in Constantinople, even characterised the various nationalist interventions that preceded the Balkan Wars of 1912–1913 as an attempt by the Balkan nations Serbia, Bulgaria, Greece and Montenegro to take the 'flame of humanitarian intervention' from the 'weak hands' of the Great Powers in the face of an apparent threat of 'systematic extinction of the Christians of Macedonia'.[692]

---

[686] Glenny 2000, p. 229.
[687] Winkler 2012, p. 1142.
[688] Carnegie Report, pp. 208–209.
[689] Carnegie Report, p. 209.
[690] Carnegie Report, p. 13.
[691] Carnegie Report, p. III, preface by Nicholas Murray Butler.
[692] Mandelstam 1925, p. 21: 'Cependant l'extermination systématique des Chrétiens de la Macédoine finit par émouvoir leurs congénères – les nations balkaniques, la Serbie, la Bulgarie, la Grèce, le Monténégro, qui prirent le flambeau de l'intervention d'humanité des mains défaillantes des Grandes Puissances'.

That the various activities by Greeks, Serbs or Bulgarians 'had more to do with traditional power politics than a desire to protect the Macedonian Christians',[693] as Simon Chesterman characterised it, is by itself no compelling reason to deny their actions the status of a 'humanitarian intervention'. Indeed, the official justification set forth by the Greek government for the declarations of war by Bulgaria, Greece and Serbia on Turkey on 17 October 1912, recorded in a 'Note verbale' addressed to the British government, follows the same pattern as other explanations for interventions in the affairs of the Ottoman Empire.[694] It pitted (Christian) humanity and a desire for peace against (Ottoman) provocation, lack of cooperation and intolerable treatment of religious minorities. But the events found no further mention in the contemporary literature.

They would eventually resurface in Ganji's 1962 dissertation, where there is talk of an 'intervention of Austria, Russia, Great Britain, Italy and France in Turkey as a result of insurrections and misrule in Macedonia (1903–1908)', though the author only identifies 'peremptory demands' of 'the European Powers' 'represented by Austria-Hungary',[695] which do fall within that author's definition of 'intervention'[696] but lack the military element that is otherwise crucial to the establishment of a right to use force. Ganji is not entirely clear on whether he considered the 'armed intervention of Bulgaria, Greece and Serbia' a justified humanitarian intervention, though other authors have later explicitly done so.[697] Most, however, simply reproduce Ganji's narrative,[698] either directly or through research following his.[699] Consequently, the analysis of the events has remained rather shallow, which is unfortunate as this was the last possible candidate of a 'humanitarian intervention' in Europe before the NATO action over Kosovo ninety years later. Nobody knows what might have become of Macedonia, had the developments on the ground not led more or less directly to World War I. The violence of the campaigns and the destruction inflicted on Macedonia in particular do make this an unlikely candidate for a 'humanitarian intervention', even if the 'invention' of the Balkans as an area in constant crisis follows the already established pattern of 'inventing' tradition and creating 'nations' and ethnic divisions in the former provinces of the Ottoman Empire, which continued to be considered 'unEuropean'. Yet there can be no

---

[693] Chesterman 2001, p. 27.

[694] Note verbalé of the Greek Government to the British Government, British and Foreign State Papers Vol. 106 (1913), pp. 1058–1060, cited in fn. 687.

[695] Ganji 1962, pp. 33, 36.

[696] Ganji 1962, pp. 14–15.

[697] Murphy 1996, pp. 56–57.

[698] Reisman and McDougal 1968 Memorandum, reprinted in: Lillich 1973, p. 179 with fn. 44; Fonteyne 1974, pp. 207–208, with fn. 12, 15; Behuniak 1978, p. 159; Kutner 1985, p. 603 with fn. 41, 42.

[699] e.g. Barry M. Benjamin, 'Unilateral Humanitarian Intervention: Legalizing the Use of Force to Prevent Human Rights Atrocities', *Fordham International Law Journal* 1992–1993, 16, p. 129, fn. 50–55.

doubt that the NATO action over Kosovo, too, also led to an initial deterioration of the 'humanitarian' situation on the ground.[700]

Elsewhere, European diplomats felt compelled to write a note to the Sultan of Morocco, Mulai Abdelhafid in September 1909. The Sultan, who reigned from 1908 to 1912 over an increasingly disintegrating, formally still sovereign state, had 'revived the ancient Moroccan custom of torturing his enemies'. In response to the note, the Sultan 'undertook' to abolish the practice quickly.[701] The language of the note, which demanded that the Sultan 'in the future observe the laws of humanity' (observer à l'avenir les lois de l'humanité), led Rougier to include this episode in his 'Theory of Humanitarian Intervention'.[702] Grewe later read the note as a 'recognition of the principle of humanitarian intervention' and its expression 'in the clearest of ways'.[703] The events are discussed in some more detail by Ellery C. Stowell in 1921, who noted that Rougier entered 'upon an interesting discussion on the legality of humanitarian intervention, of which he says, this is an instance'.[704] Rougier's interest for the note has also led to its inclusion as an example of 'international humanitarian intervention to protect the rights of the persecuted' in a history of human rights,[705] but the fact that the protesting powers were already halfway towards obliterating Morocco's sovereignty at the time[706] should be a clear enough indicator that this is more likely to be a story told about international law, rather than a story in which international law was applied for the benefit of any 'laws of humanity'. Stowell even recounts how Rougier reported in a different article in the *Revue* that, in response to the European 'intervention' the Sultan expressed his intention to, indeed, observe these laws of humanity in the future, but not before he had his opponent killed and addressed a long memorandum to a paper in Tangiers 'to justify the measures of repression employed against the adherents of Bou-Hamara'.[707]

2.9.4 Armenia, 1915–1916

In the shadow of World War I, the first European modern genocide was committed by Ottoman troops massacring at least hundreds of thousands of Armenian civilians.

---

[700] Glenny 2000, p. 658; Wheeler 2000, p. 269.

[701] See the contemporary newspaper report 'Torture in Morocco' – *Auckland Star*, XL(212), 6 September 1909, available at: http://paperspast.natlib.govt.nz/newspapers/AS19090906.2.47, last accessed 26 February 2019.

[702] Rougier 1910, p. 477.

[703] Grewe 2000, p. 492.

[704] Stowell 1921, p. 147.

[705] Lauren 2011, p. 82. Ganji 1962, p. 40, also mentions the 'representations or protests', citing Stowell.

[706] Edgar Pröbster, 'Scherifisches Reich', in: Karl Strupp (ed.), *Wörterbuch des Völkerrechts und der Diplomatie*, Vol. II, Berlin: De Gruyter 1925, pp. 449–450.

[707] Stowell 1921, p. 147.

International reaction was limited to diplomatic protests, which, in addition to a profound lack of interest for the events, showed a strong commitment to the principle of non-intervention. The contemporary press reported that the United States warned the Turkish Government that it 'will be formally notified that unless the massacre of Armenians ceases, friendly relations between the American people and the people of Turkey will be threatened. (. . .) Officials (. . .) made it plain, however, that the message did not threat a rupture in the diplomatic relations between the two countries'.[708] At the time,

> United States Secretary of State Robert Lansing admitted what he called the 'more or less justifiable' right of the Turkish government to deport the Armenians to the extent that they lived 'within the zone of military operations'. But, he said, '[i]t was not to my mind the deportation which was objectionable but the horrible brutality which attended its execution. It is one of the blackest pages in the history of this war, and I think we were fully justified in intervening as we did on behalf of the wretched people, even though they were Turkish subjects'.[709]

This justification of a 'right to intervene' is clearly in line with the official American position on the intervention in 1898, but in this case the 'intervention' was limited to a few semi-official protests by the Americans[710] and a joint declaration from the governments of France, the United Kingdom and Russia, dated 24 May 1915, asserting that '[i]n the presence of these new crimes of Turkey against humanity and civilization, the allied Governments publicly inform the Sublime Porte that they will hold personally responsible for the said crimes all members of the Ottoman Government as well as those of its agents who are found to be involved in such massacres'.[711]

The massacres mentioned here originated in deportations of Armenians from zones of supposed military operation, which were quickly exposed as being part of a larger undertaking: 'Persecution of Armenians assuming unprecedented proportions. Reports from widely scattered districts indicate systematic attempt to uproot peaceful Armenian populations and through arbitrary arrests, terrible tortures, whole-sale expulsions and deportations from one end of the Empire to the other accompanied by frequent instances of rape, pillage, and murder, turning into massacre, to bring destruction and destitution on them'.[712] Just how many

---

[708] *New York Evening Post*, 5 October 1915, quoted in Stowell 1921, p. 81.

[709] cited according to the quote in Schabas 2009, p. 20.

[710] Chesterman 2001, p. 25 with fn. 134. Samantha Power, *A Problem from Hell*, New York: Basic Books 2002, pp. 5–12 details the fruitless efforts of the American Ambassador to the Ottoman Empire, Henry Morgenthau, to press his government for a stronger response while the atrocities occurred. The United States never declared war on the Ottoman Empire, Bloxham 2005, p. 138.

[711] cited according to the quote in Schabas 2009, p. 20.

[712] US Ambassador Henry Morgenthau, cable to Washington, 10 July 1915, quoted in Power 2002, p. 6.

Armenians lost their lives is still subject to dispute. According to Donald Bloxham, approximately one million Ottoman Armenians died, half of the pre-war population and two-thirds of those deported,[713] though the numbers can only be estimated, for no reliable records exist.[714] The importance of the events for the prohibition on genocide in international law cannot be overstated, but the impact of the reaction of the Great Powers is questionable. Though the declaration of 1915 is seen as the 'explicit' and 'formal' introduction of the concept of 'Crimes Agains Humanity' in international law,[715] it is clear that nothing immediately followed from it.[716] No 'humanitarian intervention' took place.[717] The phrase 'crimes against humanity and civilization' was the result of a compromise between the participating powers to replace the phrase 'crimes against Christianity and civilization' of the original Russian draft,[718] indicating that behind the talk of 'humanity' the bonds of a common religion still dominated over any all-encompassing sentiment of humanitarianism.

2.9.5 'Humanitarian Intervention' in International Law at the Turn of the Century

As the 'Age of Imperialism' (Hobsbawm) drew to a close in the thunder of genocide and World War I, international law remained stuck in nineteenth-century mode. The 'Age of the European Concert' lasted until 1914, when the last remainders of the balance of power and all attempts at an international order were destroyed in the maelstrom of history. International law's aspiration to progress and civilisation was kept alive in further idealistic 'codifications', which aimed to pave the way for a 'culture of human rights'.

One such example is 'Le droit international codifié et sa sanction juridique' by Pasquale Fiore (1837–1914), published in 1890 as a French translation of the Italian original, and published in English in 1918. Similar in his approach to Bluntschli decades earlier, the Italian Professor of International Law oscillated between academic restatement of the law and suggestions DE LEGE FERENDA. His rather abstract approach to international law has not always been met with approval,[719] even if the goal of overcoming dynastic legitimacy through the idea that all peoples

---

[713] Bloxham 2005, p. 1.

[714] Guenter Lewy, *The Armenian Massacres in Ottoman Turkey*, Salt Lake City: The University of Utah Press 2006, pp. 233–250.

[715] Vahakn N. Dadrian, 'The Historical and Legal Interconnections Between the Armenian Genocide and the Jewish Holocaust: From Impunity to Retributive Justice', *Yale Journal of International Law* 1998, 23, p. 554.

[716] M. Cherif Bassiouni, *Crimes against Humanity*, Cambridge University Press 2011, p. 88.

[717] Graham 1924, explicitly acknowledges this on p. 326.

[718] Bloxham 2005, p. 137.

[719] Nussbaum 1950, p. 244.

are autonomous and individuals enjoy human rights sounds admirable enough.[720] Fiore expressly extended international law's protection to every individual, 'even when not a member of a political body organized as a state'.[721] But he was also committed to the idea that civilisation was a European achievement that gradually brought progress to other, less civilised parts of the world, a notion he shared with most writers of his time.[722] In his vision of international law, a right to 'humanitarian intervention' is the consequence of the duty of states to protect individual rights as well as a result of the 'moral law between states' bound 'by a natural and reciprocal obligation to maintain intact the fundamental principles of "common" law. If it could ever be maintained that a state with impunity violate those principles and that the other states would be bound to remain indifferent, it would be impossible for international society to exist'.[723] The principle of non-intervention[724] was compatible with this type of *collective* interference for maintaining the fundamental principles of international society, but as Fiore only allowed for a 'justified remonstrance' in this context,[725] it is unclear how far such a right would have extended.

Fiore represents a vision of international law in which public opinion, the juridical conscience of European peoples ('convictions juridiques populaires') as the ultimate source of the law, guides states enlightened by reason and 'follow[ing] the movement of incessant progress and history' to act in the 'interests of humanity'.[726] It was an almost romantic version of positivism which Fiore shared with the other members of the Institut du droit international, to whom he dedicated his book. This was a type of positivism that allowed for an organic development of the law, which can be contrasted with the 'extreme statistist' position of Lassa Oppenheim (1858–1919).[727] Born to a German Jewish family, Oppenheim is the author of 'probably the most influential English textbook of international law'[728] and sometimes considered the 'definitive commentator on international law' of the twentieth century.[729] Oppenheim's approach to international law was characterised by his

---

[720] See Koskenniemi 2002, pp. 55–56.

[721] Pasquale Fiore, *International Law Codified and its Legal Sanction*, translated from the fifth Italian edition with an introduction by Edwin M. Borchard, New York: Baker, Voorhis and Company, 1918, p. 291, no. 620.

[722] Koskenniemi 2002, p. 56.

[723] Fiore 1918, p. 271, no. 560.

[724] Fiore 1918, p. 265, no. 550.

[725] Fiore 1918, p. 271, no. 560 – by contrast, Fiore explicitly here allows for 'collective intervention' for the 'protection of national interests'.

[726] See the sources cited by Koskenniemi 2002, p. 54.

[727] The description of Oppenheim's position as 'extreme statistist' has been attributed by Mathias Schmoeckel to Anthony Carty, see: Schmoeckel 2004, p. 111, fn. 372.

[728] Mathias Schmoeckel, 'The Internationalist as a Scientist and Herald: Lassa Oppenheim', 11 *European Journal of International Law* 2000, 11(3), pp. 699–712.

[729] Janis 2004, p. 128. According to Ziegler 2007, p. 191, Oppenheim's treatise 'International Law' became the English standard work for two generations.

commitment to a law that would not fail the practice test and a focus on the description of the actual law:[730] 'The task of internationalists was not to create new law. In case of doubt it was "a thousand times better to leave a question open than to answer it incorrectly"'.[731] The distinction, then, between what the law is and what it ought to be was integral to this approach and it was with this in mind that Oppenheim assessed the legal status of 'humanitarian intervention':

> Many jurists maintain that intervention is likewise admissible, or even has a basis of right, when exercised in the interest of humanity for the purpose of stopping religious persecution and endless cruelties in time of peace and war. That the Powers have in the past exercised intervention on these grounds, there is no doubt. Thus Great Britain, France, and Russia intervened in 1827 in the struggle between revolutionary Greece and Turkey, because public opinion was horrified at the cruelties committed during this struggle. And many a time interventions have taken place to stop the persecution of Christians in Turkey. But whether there is really a rule of the Law of Nations which admits such interventions may well be doubted. Yet, on the other hand it cannot be denied that public opinion and the attitude of the Powers are in favour of such interventions, and it may perhaps be said that in time the Law of Nations will recognise the rule that interventions in the interests of humanity are admissible provided they are exercised in the form of a collective intervention of the Powers.[732]

This quote includes a questionable assessment of past interventions, but Oppenheim's position is remarkable for its restrained statement of the law as he found it:

> Careful analysis of the rules of the Law of Nations regarding intervention and the hitherto exercised practice of intervention make it apparent that intervention is de facto a matter of policy just like war. (...) And who can undertake to lay down a hard and fast rule with the regard to the amount of inhumanity on the part of a Government to admit of intervention according to the Law of Nations.[733]

International law for Oppenheim was the law of the 'civilised' nations, applicable to the relations within the 'family of nations' that made up that sphere of international law, but not to the states beyond this family.[734] While he shared the starting point of Rougier's 'Theory of humanitarian intervention' or Fiore's 'droit international codifié' and Bluntschli's 'modernem Völkerrecht der civilisierten Staaten', he did not come to the same conclusion on the question of the legality of 'humanitarian intervention'. This nicely reflects the state of international law at the beginning of the twentieth century – almost a hundred years after Wheaton, it is still a

[730] Schmoeckel 2004, p. 87.
[731] Schmoeckel 2004, p. 87, citing Lassa Oppenheim, 'The Science of International Law', American Journal of International Law 1908, 2, p. 335.
[732] Oppenheim 1905, p. 185, § 137.
[733] Oppenheim 1905, p. 187, § 138.
[734] Simpson 2004, p. 235.

particular law, limited in its sphere of validity and its application. Among 'civilised' nations, a right to 'humanitarian intervention' seemed unthinkable, because 'civilisation' by definition indicated the incapacity to infringe upon the general interests of humanity through barbarism or despotism. Yet few contributors to the debate expressed this belief in such clear terms. In the relations with 'unequal' states, such interventions would have been permissible, but it remains unclear whether this would still have been considered as the application of international law proper or something else, as exercising the extra-legal privilege of the 'civilised' nations, granted by virtue of their 'Standard of "Civilization"'. Even authors committed to the idea of the 'law of civilised nations' continued to look for the solution for the question of 'humanitarian intervention' in realms beyond the reach of this legal order.

According to Thomas J. Lawrence (1849–1920), one of the leading representatives of Anglo-American international law in the early twentieth century, states subject to international law had to be

> divided by two classes: (a) The Great Powers of Europe and the United States of America. They are rapidly gaining in many important mattes a position of primacy (. . .). (b) Ordinary Independent States. They possess all the ordinary rights given by International Law to Sovereign States, but do not share the authority claimed by the Great Powers in supervising and altering some of the existing international arrangements.[735]

In addition, there also existed 'semi-sovereign' states,[736] and international law was 'defined as *The rules which determine the conduct of the general body of civilised States in their dealings with each other*'.[737]Irrespective of whether 'a rule is morally right or morally wrong, it forms part of International Law if it is generally accepted and acted upon'.[738] Lawrence's vision of international law allowed for great artistic freedom, counting among its sources the works of 'great publicists (. . .), beginning with Gentilis and Grotius and ending with the leading publicists of our own day, whose works have influences, and do still influence, the practice of States, (. . .) [and who] apply admitted principles to doubtful points, and thus often evolve rules which are afterward embodied in the practice of States'.[739] Even though this clearly freed writers to 'develop' international law on the basis of an ideological 'progressive Europe', Lawrence refrained from using this freedom to declare the legality of 'humanitarian intervention':

> We cannot venture to bring them within the ordinary rules of International Law, which does not impose on states the obligation of preventing barbarity on the part of

---

[735] Lawrence 1898, p. 19.
[736] Lawrence 1898, p. 20.
[737] Lawrence 1898, p. 3 emphasis in original.
[738] Lawrence1898, p. 4.
[739] Lawrence 1898, p. 29.

their neighbours. At the same time, it will not condemn interventions for such a cause, if they are undertaken with a single eye to the object the view, and without ulterior considerations of self-interest and ambition. (. . .) An intervention to put a stop to barbarous and abominable cruelty is a question rather of policy than of law.[740]

Here, too, international law had hardly evolved since the mid-nineteenth century.[741]

At the other end of the spectrum of opinions on 'humanitarian intervention', the comprehensive German treatise on international law by Franz von Liszt (1851–1919) declared a right of intervention inadmissible even 'where in the justified opinion of one state the general interests of humanity and culture' might make intervention necessary, as this would give way to arbitrariness and misuse.[742] As the rule 'intervention is contrary to current international law' was, according to von Liszt, a recent development of the nineteenth century,[743] he was prepared to make exceptions for collective interventions which, in the case of the Ottoman Empire, could legitimately be based on the Paris Treaty of 1856, or, more specifically, in the Armenian provinces, on Art. 61 of the 1878 Treaty of Berlin.[744] Of these types, no intervention occurred.

2.9.6 International Law at the Turn of the Century in the History of 'Humanitarian Intervention'

The inconsistent reality of international law at the turn of the twentieth century has not been properly reflected in later historiographies of 'humanitarian intervention'. Advocates of this legal instrument consistently claim that *one* doctrine of 'humanitarian intervention' developed,[745] which gradually evolved into an instrument recognised by customary international law in the years leading up to the outbreak of World War I and triumphed over the 'rigid dogma of non-intervention'.[746] As Richard B. Lillich, one of the leading advocates of the legality of 'humanitarian intervention' in the debate since the 1960s, put it: '[T]he doctrine appears to have been so clearly established under customary international law that only its limits and not its existence is subject to debate'.[747] This narrative coincides with the claim that

---

[740] Lawrence 1910, pp. 128–129.

[741] e.g. Harcourt 1863, p. 14: 'Intervention is rather a question of policy than of law. It is above and beyond the domain of law, and when wisely and equitably handled by those who have the power to give effect to it, may be the highest policy of justice and humanity'.

[742] von Liszt 1913, p.66, my translation.

[743] von Liszt 1913, p. 64, my translation.

[744] von Liszt 1913, p. 66.

[745] Lillich 1967, p. 332, prefers to speak of 'amorphous doctrines on "humanitarian intervention"' as the concept covered both the protection of a state's own nationals and of foreign nations. But the use of the singular here refers to the conceptualisation of the doctrine, not its intended application.

[746] Behuniak 1978, pp. 161 and 178.

[747] Lillich 1969, p. 210.

the cases detailed in these pages are examples of the doctrine put into practice, often adding 'numerous' instances of 'humanitarian intervention' in the nineteenth century to protect the Jews of Romania and, more often, Russia. One such example is the article 'The International Protection of Human Rights and the Jewish Question' by Nathan Feinberg (1895–1988), published in 1968.[748] Feinberg, the 'Father of International Law in Israel',[749] attempted to show that in addition to the 'many interventions on behalf of the Christians under Turkish rule', 'the list of interventions on behalf of the Jews is not shorter'.[750] Even if, as Feinberg conceded by quoting Rougier, 'the results of the interventions were negligible',[751] he attempted to connect a practice of 'humanitarian intervention' to the Minorities Treaties of the League of Nations and, most importantly, to the concept of crimes against humanity, as 'the logical outcome of the humanitarian intervention by States against certain odious acts which rouse the conscience of the civilized world'.[752]

This narrative creates the impression of a frequent practice of 'humanitarian intervention' in the nineteenth century,[753] sanctified by the approval in the literature on international law, which gives the impression of an international law committed to 'humanity'. But doing so negates the fact the international law interpreted in this way did not commit all states to 'humanity' or even 'one humanity'. The justification for 'humanitarian intervention's claim to legality did not rest on the assumption that every epoch of world history recognised one 'legal minimum' below which no member of the family of nations should be allowed to sink, as André Mandelstam put it in the years leading up to World War II.[754] On the contrary, it was the assumption that a law 'of humanity' against 'barbarians' existed to protect humanity against *their* barbarism, as an otherwise forgettable contemporary German dissertation spelt out in no uncertain terms:

> Who would deny the legality of an intervention, when Christian subjects in non-Christian countries suffer from barbarous persecution and cruel violence of the most despicable kind! (. . .) Where the most valuable achievements of mankind are under threat, it is permissible to speak of a justified, legal intervention for the protection of these legal values ('Rechtsgüter') (. . .). Such an intervention conforms with the community of the cultured nations, their solidarity and their 'civilising' aims.[755]

[748] Feinberg 1968.
[749] Ruth Lapidoth, 'Nathan Feinberg – In Memoriam', *Israel Law Review* 1988, 22(4), p. 408.
[750] Feinberg 1968, p. 490.
[751] Feinberg 1968, p. 492.
[752] Quote attributed to Henri Rolin, quoted from Jean Grave, 'Les Crimes contre l'Humanité', R. A. D. I. Paris 1951, 487, by Feinberg 1968, p. 500.
[753] Stowell 1921, p. 62: 'frequently'; Séfériadès, RdC 1930, S. 389: 'nombreux'; Fenwick 1965, p. 287: 'numerous'; Fonteyne 1974, p. 206; Bazyler 1987, p. 582: 'frequent'; Hillgruber 2001, pp. 177–178: 'beträchtliche Anzahl'; Henke 2002, p. 19: 'häufig'.
[754] Mandelstam 1931, p. 366.
[755] Tenbaum 1918, p. 38, my translation.

This international law entitled states to act 'on behalf of humanity', but imposed no duty upon these states to guarantee certain legal standards, even if, presumably, any statement of such a duty would have been to state the obvious. For it was precisely the alleged commitment to a 'Standard of "Civilization"' that enabled states like the United Kingdom, France, Russia or Germany to act in the name of 'humanity' against the 'barbarism' of others, but that same standard did not require the United Kingdom to crush the Sepoy rebellion in 1857–1958 in a less violent way[756] or restrain its soldiers in the battle of Omdurman (1898) in which up to 11,000 members of the Mahdi army were killed in less than half a day.[757] Russia's (albeit contested) position as a 'civilised' state[758] did not compel any Czar to become active in the face of pogroms against Russia's Jewish population. On the contrary, when violent anti-Semitic pogroms took place in 1881, the perpetrators went unpunished,[759] and the 'Temporary Rules', which imposed further restrictions on Jews, were introduced in 1882 and remained in force until the Russian revolutions of 1917.[760] The 'diplomatic notes' sent to the Kremlin on these occasions have been regularly cited as proof of a diplomatic practice of 'humanitarian interventions' in the nineteenth century,[761] but they had no effect on the historic events as they occurred. Another reason to pay no further attention to these fruitless efforts of mainly American diplomats is that anti-Jewish violence only increased in the last years of Czarist Russia.[762]

In 1912, Lucien Wolf (1857–1930), a British journalist and activist who would become an advocate for the Jews of Eastern Europe in the League of Nations system,[763] published *The Legal Sufferings of the Jews in Russia*, documenting the various ways in 'some six millions of human beings are unceasingly subjected to a State-directed torture which is both destructive and demoralising, and constitutes at once a crime against humanity and an international perplexity'.[764] The book contained an introduction by 'one of England's foremost jurists', A. V. Dicey (1835–1922), 'advocating the right to intervene on humanitarian ground on behalf of the Jews of Czarist Russia'.[765] While Dicey claimed that the 'persecution of Russia is not a matter which affects Russia alone', because it 'means the compulsory

---

[756] Azar Gat, *War in Human Civilization*, Oxford University Press 2006, p. 629.

[757] Gat 2006, p. 625.

[758] Lauri Mälksoo, 'Russia-Europe', in: Bardo Fassbender and Anne Peters (eds.), *The Oxford Handbook of the History of International Law*, Oxford University Press 2012, pp. 777–781.

[759] Stefan Wiese, *Pogrome im Zarenreich – Dynamiken kollektiver Gewalt*, Hamburg: Hamburger Edition 2016.

[760] Hugh Seton-Watson, *The Decline of Imperial Russia*, New York: Frederick A. Praeger, 1952, p. 159.

[761] e.g. Stowell 1921, pp. 71, 76–77; Feinberg 1968; Kutner 1985, pp. 599–601.

[762] Wiese 2016, pp. 259–277.

[763] Fink 2004, pp. 283–294.

[764] Lucien Wolf (ed.), *The Legal Sufferings of the Jews in Russia*, London: T. Fisher Unwin 1912, prefatory note.

[765] Feinberg 1968, p. 495.

emigration to other lands of thousands of impoverished and uneducated men and women',[766] thus foreshadowing arguments in favour of international involvement in domestic affairs that would eventually take hold in the 1990s, he also invoked that elusive 'standard of civilization', claiming 'it is assuredly the concern of every civilised state that the slow and laborious progress of mankind should suffer no retrogression. (...) Every state of the civilised world has authority to guard by way of denunciation, if not otherwise, against the arrest of civilisation'.[767]

Yet that progress clearly did not benefit all, as France was hardly committed to any legal minimum by virtue of its standing as a 'civilised' nation when it began to conquer Algeria in 1830 'for the benefit of Christianity'[768] in an endeavour that lasted over 40 years and killed approximately 825,000 indigenous Algerians in what the French themselves termed a 'system of extermination'.[769] Recent research suggests that there are 'many good reasons for believing that 19th century Algeria should be added to the canon of cases analyzed in the comparative history of genocide'.[770] Nor was Germany somehow restrained by its 'civilised' status when turning its colonial adventure in 'Deutsch-Südwestafrika' (now Namibia) into the first genocide of the twentieth century, killing most of the Herero and Nama people between 1904 and 1908. The characterisation of this episode as a genocide is now widely accepted,[771] yet neither the 1924 edition nor the 1960 edition of the 'Wörterbuch des Völkerrechts' contain significant traces of the events. The ninth edition of Franz von Liszt's classic treatise 'Das Völkerrecht' (July 1912) contains no reference to the events, but praises the recent peaceful politics of the German government.[772]

The legal instrument of 'humanitarian intervention' as developed by writers in international law of the nineteenth and early twentieth century is better understood as a right to 'intervention by humanity'. It rested either partly or entirely on interventions of European powers in the Ottoman Empire on the basis of the lack of 'humanity' (i.e., respect for 'human rights') demonstrated by the Ottoman Empire alone. Human rights in Islam were only the 'Rights of the Muslim', with some 'large chunks of rights' extended to the non-Muslim population of the Ottoman Empire; 'real human rights' were seen as a product of Christianity.[773] The observance of

---

[766] A. V. Dicey, Introduction, in: Lucien Wolf (Ed.), *The Legal Sufferings of the Jews in Russia*, London: T. Fisher Unwin 1912, p. x, he went on: 'It means, therefore, the imposition upon the most highly civilised countries of a burden of ignorance and poverty which ought not to be imposed upon them'.

[767] A. V. Dicey, Introduction, in: Wolf 1912, p. x.

[768] Wheatcroft 2004, p. 213.

[769] Ben Kiernan, *Blood and Soil: A World History of Genocide and Extermination from Sparta to Darfur*, New Haven: Yale University Press 2007, p. 374.

[770] William Gallois, 'Genocide in Nineteenth-Century Algeria', *Journal of Genocide Studies* 2013, 15(1), p. 84.

[771] e.g. Winkler 2012, p. 1043. For a critique of the categorisation as genocide, see Boris Barth, *Genozid*, München: C. H. Beck 2006, pp. 128–135.

[772] von Liszt 1913, foreword, p. IV.

[773] Mandelstam 1931, p. 340.

these rights led, as André Mandelstam put it, to an instrument of 'true local customary law' for the European Powers.[774] Yet the commitment of 'civilised' states to 'humanity' was a precondition of this law, which imposed no duties upon these states and thus justified the violence they exercised; this is the law that created the foundations of the legal order we live in. It was the actions of these 'civilised' states that would lead to the formation of the League of Nations and the United Nations to reign in their violence.

[774] Mandelstam 1931, p. 344.

3

'Humanitarian Intervention' in the Era of the League of Nations

3.1 INTRODUCTION

The war to end all wars destroyed the European order and its peculiar system of international law in which the theory of 'humanitarian intervention' had found its natural habitat. By the end of the nineteenth century, the expansion of the European empires had subjected the entire globe to one European system of international law, but by the end of World War I the European claim to moral superiority and 'civilisation' had been severely weakened by the horrors of war. The answer was, in the word of one of its architects, 'a great experiment': the League of Nations.[1] The following decade has been variously considered as the hopeful beginning of an attempt to create an 'improved stage in the history of humanity';[2] a political innovation aimed at the creation of peaceful existence under the rule of international law;[3] and the 'pathological inflation of the law'.[4] The League of Nations represented an attempt to institute a new type of international order based on the international rule of law. Yet, rather than abandon the distinction between 'civilised' and 'uncivilised'

---

[1] Lord Robert Cecil (1864–1958), as quoted in Zara Steiner, *The Lights that Failed*, Oxford University Press 2005, p. 349.
[2] Hans Wehberg, 'Hat Japan durch die Besetzung der Mandschurei das Völkerrecht verletzt?', *Die Friedenswarte* 1932, p. 12.
[3] Nussbaum 1950, p. 251.
[4] 'krankhafte Rechtsaufblähung' is the characterisation of international law in the League of Nations era attributed to 'Carl Schmitt and others' in the 1939 report of the Sozialdemokratische Partei Deutschlands (Sopade), *Deutschlandberichte 1934–1940*, edited by Klaus Behnken, reprint, Frankfurt a.M. 1980, p. 1014. Compare: Carl Schmitt, 'Die Auflösung der europäischen Ordnung im "International Law"', *Deutsche Rechtswissenschaft* 1940, 5, pp. 267–278.

nations, as some apparently feared,[5] this 'Move to Institutions'[6] legitimised the European powers' leading role as 'civilisers' through the Mandate System.[7] Moreover, its founding treaty created the state of tension in which the League would have to operate – the commitment to both the principle of self-determination and the leading role of the 'civilised' states for the advancement of the law. In this spirit, the Covenant of the League of Nations and the treaties concluded in its context introduced a number of provisions for a number of states and regions that related to matters traditionally left to the 'domaine reservé' of 'civilised' states, and thus introduced local regimes of minority protection under the auspices of the League. Attempts to institutionalise a full system for the protection of minorities in all member states of the League failed, however, not least because France and the United Kingdom resisted. These powers were 'determined to maintain control of over a minority-protection regime of which they were the principal authors' and they were also 'committed to making this determination known'.[8]

The break-up of the multi-national empires of Russia and Austria-Hungary and the final retreat of the Ottoman Empire from mainland Europe encouraged the aspirations of millions of members of different peoples to strive for self-determination. Several of these movements were successful and, sanctioned by the remaining Great Powers, led to the formation or extension of nation states in Middle and Eastern Europe, but none of them were as ethnically homogenous as the established nation states in Western Europe. They all had sizeable groups of 'persons belonging to linguistic, racial and religious minorities', a phrase that was used in Article 15 of the Polish Minority Treaty 'in order to avoid recognition of them as a separate legal corporation within the state'.[9] The League was entrusted with their protection under treaties forced on these countries by the remaining Great Powers,.

According to contemporary German theorists of international law, the question of minorities and their protection had become a general problem of international law with the end of the war.[10] In the inter-war years of the early twentieth century war, Rudolf Laun (1882–1975)[11] strongly criticised the lack of protection for German

---

[5]   Professor H. A. Smith of London University, as quoted by Mark Mazower, 'An International Civilization? Empire, Internationalism and the Crisis of the Mid-Twentieth Century', *International Affairs* 2006, 82(3), p. 563, though the quoted is attributed to Professor Smith 'writing in The Listener', the corresponding footnote is G. Schwarzenberger, 'The Rule of Law and the Disintegration of International Society', *Transactions of the Grotius Society* 1937, 22, p. 66.

[6]   David Kennedy, 'The Move to Institutions', 8 *Cardozo Law Review* 1987, 841, pp. 841–988.

[7]   Anghie 2005, pp. 123–156.

[8]   Özsu 2015, p. 39.

[9]   Mohammad Shahabuddin, *Ethnicity and International Law: Histories, Politics and Practices*, Cambridge University Press 2016, Kindle edition: ch. 3 with fn. 25.

[10]   Laun 1925, p. 82.

[11]   On Laun and his continued work on these questions after World War II, see: Lora Wildenthal, 'Rudolf Laun and the Human Rights of Germans in Occupied and Early Western Germany', in: Stefan-Ludwig Hofmann (ed.), *Human Rights in the Twentieth Century*, Cambridge University Press 2010, pp. 125–144.

minorities cut off from the Reich as a result of the war and the Treaty of Versailles,[12] stating that minorities were not protected from 'forcible denationalisation' through the majority population.[13] Even so, he conceded that the system could be taken as a sign of progress, insofar as it applied to 'raw or half-civilised relationships'.[14] Indeed, the system sanctioned some population transfers on the territory of the former Ottoman Empire, in an attempt to, as Matthew Frank succinctly put it, 'make minorities history',[15] that were seen by contemporaries as continuations of the spirit, if not practice of 'humanitarian intervention'.[16] German theorists developed a right of ethnic groups (Volksgruppenrecht) in the mirror image of minority protection,[17] which also enabled the claim of ethnic self-determination and the exclusion of 'staatsfremder Staatsangehöriger' (alien citizens, or, more precisely, Jews).[18]

The system of minority protection was also the basis for what the historian Philipp Graf has termed 'Jewish diplomacy'.[19] One such example is the work of the *Comité des Délégations Juives*, which lobbied on behalf of Jewish minorities in Europe and with the League of Nations, in a continuation of the work done by Jewish groups to establish minority protection in Eastern Europe.[20] The system also provided the framework under which individuals could force the 'intervention' of the League through petitions to the organs of the League, opening 'a path through the barrier of sovereignty that the states maintained with such passionate devotion'.[21]

The Covenant did not break with the idea of different levels of development, but cemented it through the Mandate System which authorised the Mandate Powers ('advanced nations who by reason of their resources, their experience or their geographical position can best undertake this responsibility') to administer the affairs of 'peoples not yet able to stand by themselves under the strenuous conditions of the modern world'.[22] In retrospect, it seems more than justified to speak of an 'international law of the transitional period' for the era of the League of Nations, though not necessarily in Korovin's sense.[23] Yet, as the following will show, when it came to

---

[12] Laun 1925, p. 99.

[13] Laun 1925, p. 101: 'gewaltsame Entnationalisierung seitens des Mehrheitsvolkes' my translation.

[14] Laun 1925, p. 101.

[15] Frank 2017.

[16] Özsu 2015, p. 101.

[17] Laun 1925, pp. 102–105.

[18] Karl Gottfried Hugelmann, *Volk und Staat im Wandel deutscher Schicksals*, Essen: Essener Verlagsanstalt 1940, p. 80. See also: Karl Gottfried Hugelmann, 'Der völkische Staat und der Reichsgedanke', *Deutsche Rechtswissenschaft* 1940, V, pp. 179–201.

[19] Philipp Graf, *Die Bernheim-Petition 1933*, Göttingen: Vandenhoek & Ruprecht 2008, p. 13 contra Mark Levene, *War, Jews, and the New Europe*, Liverpool University Press 2009, p. 9.

[20] Some of the work of the *Comité* is detailed in Graf 2008, pp. 69–94. See also: Fink 2004, in particular pp. 237–294.

[21] D. V. Jones, 'The League of Nations Experiment in International Protection', *Ethics & International Affairs* 1994, 8, p. 89.

[22] Art. 22 of the Covenant.

[23] Grewe has called the inter-war years the 'Transition Period of the Anglo-American Condominium', lasting until 1939; Grewe 2000, pp. 575–579.

the question of 'humanitarian intervention', the law as discussed by the writers of the inter-war years was very much rooted in the past that was destroyed by World War I.

The Covenant of the League of Nations contained no provisions on the question of 'humanitarian intervention' as such, but significantly changed the law on intervention in general. As contemporary commentators put it, Art. 10 and 15 VIII of the Covenant recognised 'the well-established principle of non-intervention in the internal affairs of other states',[24] but at the same time turned the question of what belonged 'solely' to the domestic jurisdiction of a party to the Covenant (Art. 15 VIII) into a question of international law. This created the 'paradox' situation wherein it was ultimately for international law to decide what was not for international law to decide, thus removing the question of what belonged 'solely' to the domestic jurisdiction from the realm of domestic jurisdiction.[25] This first explicit postulation of the principle that the scope of the 'domaine reservé' is to be decided by international law led the Court of International Justice, instituted by the League of Nations, to proclaim in an Advisory Opinion of 1923 that 'whether a certain matter is or is not solely within the jurisdiction of a State is an essentially relative question; it depends upon the development of international relations'.[26] Taken together, these developments may have given the League the authority to 'intervene' in matters that previously would have been considered subject 'solely to the domestic jurisdiction' of the member state, like minority protection and human rights.

In October 1933, the month that Germany left the League of Nations, the League did appoint the American diplomat James G. McDonald (1886–1964) to be the 'High Commissioner for Refugees (Jewish and Other) Coming from Germany'. While his mandate was to address only the consequences of the German treatment of minorities, McDonald resigned in December 1935, having concluded that the 'conditions in Germany which create refugees have developed so catastrophically that a reconsideration by the League of Nations of the entire situation is essential'.[27]

Together with the 1928 Pact of Paris (officially General Treaty for Renunciation of War as an Instrument of National Policy), the Covenant also introduced significant steps to outlaw the use of force in international relations. With its focus on 'war' as a formal state of relations between states under international law, the exact scope of these provisions remained contested in the inter-war years.[28] Neither the

---

[24] Walter Schücking and Hans Wehberg, *Die Satzung des Völkerbunds*, Kommentar, Berlin: Vahlen 1921, p. 275; Axel Freiherr von Freytagh-Loringhoven, *Die Satzung des Völkerbundes*, Berlin: Verlag von Georg Stilke 1926, p. 172.

[25] Kelsen 1952, pp. 190–196.

[26] Advisory Opinion No. 4, Nationality Decrees Issued in Tunis and Morocco, 4, Permanent Court of International Justice, 7 February 1923, available at: www.refworld.org/cases,PCI J,44e5c9fc4.html, last accessed 23 February 2019.

[27] Letter of Resignation of James G. McDonald, High Commissioner for Refugees (Jewish and Other) Coming from Germany, 27 December 1935, available at www.wdl.org/en/item/11604/, last accessed 30 April 018).

[28] See Brownlie 1963, pp. 66–91.

Covenant nor the Paris Pact explicitly touched upon the right of intervention taking the form of a recourse to armed force short of war, 'for the express prohibitions of both instruments applied in terms only to "resort to war"'.[29] Yet later authors have concluded that if a customary right to collective 'humanitarian intervention' had previously existed, it could not have survived the Pact of Paris.[30] In the careful words of a contemporary expert: 'it is in the highest degree doubtful whether reprisals and intervention involving armed force were any longer admissible during the League period, except as sanctions for the violation of the Covenant and the Pact'.[31] The point is purely academic, as it was never tested in practice: No credible 'humanitarian intervention' occurred during the time the League existed.

3.2 INTERNATIONAL LAW THEORY AND 'HUMANITARIAN INTERVENTION' IN THE AGE OF THE LEAGUE OF NATIONS

Contemporary international law theory concerned with the question of 'humanitarian intervention' only sporadically responded to the changed environment brought on by the Covenant of the League of Nations and the Pact of Paris. For the most part, the discussion simply continued on with the same examples of state practice of the nineteenth century and corresponding arguments, without any indication that a new era in international law may have begun. Later claims of the alleged legality of 'humanitarian intervention' under 'classic' customary international law also do not differentiate between the nineteenth century or the time of the League of Nations and routinely include authors from the early twentieth century as proof.[32] The most important of these authors was the American Professor of International Law, Ellery C. Stowell (1875–1958), who would call for an 'intercession' on behalf of the Jews of Germany as early as 1936,[33] and by 1939 considered a 'humanitarian intervention' justified:

> The recent barbarities perpetrated against the Jews in several European states is a case in point. It may not be practicable at this time to secure a sufficient combination of force to bring the principal transgressors to book, but it is important that this temporary miscarriage of international justice should be understood and the right proclaimed even though it cannot be vindicated at present.[34]

[29] J. L. Brierly, *The Law of Nations*, 6th ed., edited by Humphrey Waldock, Oxford: Clarendon Press 1963, p. 412.

[30] Wellhausen 2002, p. 77.

[31] Brierly 1963, pp. 411–412. For Brierly's views at the time, see: J. L. Brierly, 'International Law and Resort to Armed Force', *Cambridge Law Journal* 1932, 4(3), pp. 308–319.

[32] E.g. Behuniak 1978, p. 157.

[33] Stowell 1936.

[34] Stowell, 'Humanitarian Intervention' 1939.

Stowell provided the most comprehensive treatment of the question of 'humanitarian intervention' in English at the time,[35] and his book would remain the exhaustive study on intervention in international law for 35 years, when it was followed up by a study entitled, remarkably, 'Non-intervention: The Law and Its Import in the Americas',[36] That title suggests a conceptual shift from intervention as a possibility to a norm of non-intervention, but whether or when that shift occurred is far from clear. In his 1921 book *Intervention in International Law*, Stowell situated 'humanitarian intervention' in an 'international community',[37] or at least an 'international society',[38] as an instrument of 'international police':[39] 'Humanitarian intervention may be defined as the reliance upon force for the justifiable purpose of protecting the inhabitants of another state from treatment which is so arbitrary and persistently abusive as to exceed the limits of that authority which the sovereign is presumed to act with reason and justice'.[40]

Defending the legality of 'humanitarian intervention', Stowell relied on a 'conditional' definition of sovereignty, considering sovereignty 'the system which reduces outside interference to a minimum'.[41] Yet, he insisted that 'sovereignty is not, as some believe, a right to act with absolute independence. It is no more than a presumption that any action which a state may take within its own territory in the furtherance of international law is correctly taken'.[42] States not only enjoyed rights under international law, but also corresponding obligations: 'When a state ignores its obligations, be it in even an isolated instance, it is liable to encounter the interposition of the state it has wronged, or the intervention of other states who perceive that such conduct constitutes an assault upon the principles sacred to them all, and necessary to the preservation of international society'.[43] Intervention, in particular intervention on humanitarian grounds, was the means to uphold a 'rule of reason' in the name of public opinion, even where states had not yet consented to a proper rule of law.[44] While his position claimed the support of the 'weighty authorities'[45] like Grotius, Wheaton and Bluntschli,[46] Stowell admitted in 1939 that humanitarian intervention was 'of recent, but very vigorous, growth and tends to bind the whole

[35] Mohr 2002, p. 94.
[36] C. Phillips, 'Book Review: Non-intervention: The Law and Its Import in the Americas. By Ann Van Wynen Thomas and A. J. Thomas Jr.', *American Political Science Review* 1954, 51(1), p. 263.
[37] Stowell 1921, p. 45.
[38] Stowell 1921, p. 456.
[39] Stowell 1921, p. 51: 'Intervention for humanity, [. . .] is also an instance of intervention for the purpose of vindicating the law of nations against outrage'.
[40] Stowell 1921, p. 54.
[41] Stowell 1921, p. 2.
[42] Stowell 1921, pp. 2–3.
[43] Stowell 1921, pp. 315–316.
[44] Stowell 1921, pp. 455–460.
[45] Stowell 1921, p. 62.
[46] Stowell 1921, p. 55.

world closer together in defense of elementary principles of justice. It is as yet a toddling infant that becomes stronger every day with the spread of communications'.[47]

Stowell's position stressed the role of the state within a world shared with other states, referred to as an 'international community' and bound by a 'minimum of security and justice to which every individual in a civilized community is entitled', which could even trigger a 'duty of other states to intervene' where the conduct of a state constitutes a deliberate violation of that minimum.[48] Like Rougier's conception of a solidarist 'sociéte internationale', Stowell foreshadowed the idea that the 'society of states bears a "responsibility to protect" populations when host states fail to provide such protection', arguably the 'most innovative aspect of the "responsibility to protect" concept'.[49] Stowell nevertheless barely addressed the contemporary attempts to formalise an international community in the League of Nations, mentioning the organisation only in passing.[50]

André Mandelstam (1869–1949) had been a diplomat for the Russian Empire in the Ottoman Empire, but was driven into exile by the Russian October Revolution. Turning to academic activism, he became 'a pioneer of the idea of the international protection of human rights'.[51] His experience in the Ottoman Empire as well as his Jewish background made him a strong advocate of minority rights protection.[52] He championed the legality of the European Powers' intervention in the Ottoman Empire as genuinely 'humanitarian',[53] and envisaged a more active role for the League of Nations in the field of minority rights protection, after the conditions for a collective Great Power intervention for the sake of humanity seemed less favourable with the reorganisation of international society after World War I, noting that 'it was no longer possible to justify a 'humanitarian intervention on the distinction between civilised and uncivilised nations'.[54] In the 1920s, he became very active in the *Institut*

---

[47] Stowell, 'Humanitarian Intervention' 1939, p. 736.

[48] Stowell, 'Humanitarian Intervention' 1939, p. 734.

[49] Luke Glanville, 'Ellery Stowell and the Enduring Dilemmas of Humanitarian Intervention', *International Studies Review* 2011, 13(2), p. 249.

[50] The new League of Nations hardly features at all in Stowell's 1921 work on intervention and is only mentioned in passing in his 1932 lecture, see: Stowell 1932. In his textbook on international law, Stowell gave some weight to the minority protection regime established after the war in relation to 'humanitarian intervention', see Ellery C. Stowell, *International Law: A Restatement of Principles in Conformity with Actual Practice*, New York: Henry Holt and Company 1931, p. 354.

[51] Helmut Philipp Aust, 'From Diplomat to Academic Activist: André Mandelstam and the History of Human Rights', *European Journal of International Law* 2015, 25(4), p. 1107.

[52] Dzovinar Kévonian, 'André Mandelstam and the internationalization of human rights (1869–1949)', in: Pamela Slotte and Miia Halme-Tuomisaar (eds.), *Revisiting the Origins of Human Rights*, Cambridge University Press 2015, pp. 239–266.

[53] Mandelstam 1923, pp. 362, 388.

[54] Mandelstam 1931, pp. 367–368: 'Heutzutage aber erscheint es unmöglich, eine permanente Humanitätsintervention auf einer Einteilung der Nationen in zivilisierte und nichtzivilisierte zu begründen, und diese Einteilung der einen oder anderen Gruppe zu überlassen. Nach der

de droit international and in this capacity drafted the eventual New York Declaration of the International Rights of Man, adopted by the *Institut* in 1929. Mandelstam worked tirelessly to promote the declaration in the following years, publishing several articles as well as a book on the subject and campaigning at the League of Nations for a declaration that would require 'humanitarian intervention' to be 'directed to all states where necessary, and through the League of Nations as far as League members were concerned'.[55] He had, as Dzovinar Kévonian has put it, 'clearly intended the declaration to be a reference text upon which to hang the controversial notion of humanitarian intervention that had at last been recognised by the various states: 'The Third International that has put down root in unhappy Russia is practising un-humanitarian intervention on a vast scale. It seems that the time has come to oppose it with a covenant of civilized peoples that bans the violation of the rights of man and creates favourable conditions for humanitarian intervention'.[56] Contemporaries, however, noted that the New York Declaration did not claim such a right itself.[57] It is now well known that nothing came of this proposal, but Mandelstam's work has found its place in the historiography of human rights.

A prominent French jurist, Georges Scelle (1878–1961), devoted four pages of his *Précis de Droit des Gens* to a historical exposition of the law on 'l'intervention d'humanité', claiming that 'traditional international law' with its focus on sovereignty had been incapable of 'adapting the practice of humanitarian intervention'.[58] Arguably, the 'new' international law Scelle was describing would be in a better position to fulfill this task, as he placed the protection of human life at its center.[59] Scelle's work has been called 'the best complete treatment of international law in French' of the interwar period,[60] but his treatment of 'humanitarian intervention' romanticises the state practice of the nineteenth century, when he concludes that this practice led to 'the incorporation or subjection of Ottoman constitutional law to international law in the inter-state European society. The Porte resisted this fatal dynamic of the hierarchy of norms as best it could'.[61] And even so, Scelle admitted that this process had been inefficient.[62]

Gründung des Völkerbundes, der eine natürliche Tendenz zur Universalität hat, kann die Menschheit nicht mehr allgemeiner Rechtsregeln entbehren, die mit der erforderlichen Genauigkeit die unantastbare Sphäre der Menschenrechte für die ganze Welt umschreiben'.

55 Jan Herman Burgers, 'The Road to San Francisco: The Revival of the Human Rights Idea in the Twentieth Century', *Human Rights Quarterly* 1992, 14, p. 454.
56 Kévonian 2015, p. 261, citing André Mandelstam, 'La protection international des minorités. Rapport', *Annuaire de l'Institut de Droit International* 1925, 32, pp. 170, 229.
57 Alfred Verdross, *Völkerrecht*, Vienna: Julius Springer 1937, p. 237, § 67.
58 Scelle 1934, p. 50.
59 Scelle 1934, p. 42: 'la protection de la vie humaine devrait constituer la norme juridique essentielle'.
60 Ziegler 2007, p. 208.
61 Scelle 1934, p. 53, my translation.
62 Scelle 1934, p. 53.

The mainstream German-language position on 'humanitarian intervention' was presented in the *Wörterbuch des Völkerrechts* by Leo Strisower (1857–1931), Professor of International Law at the University of Vienna and himself a proponent of the *just war*-theory.[63] Detailing the various arguments put forward to justify different types of intervention, Strisower concluded that none of the alleged statements of law put forward in the literature could be proven to exist in practice: 'There may be instances where the high moral justification of an intervention, in particular into its domaine reservé shine favourably, especially in light of the material inadequacy or failure of the state's rule of law. But norms of customary law in favour of intervention cannot be said to have constituted'.[64] His co-chair for international law at the University of Vienna, Alexander Hold-Ferneck took on the more traditional position that whether or not a state could claim sovereignty as a shield against intervention rested upon the question whether or not the state fulfilled its duties that had gained him recognition as a state in the first place.[65] Hold-Ferneck had been appointed co-chair at the same time as Strisower at the initiative of the University's dean, Hans Kelsen, to secure the confirmation of his former teacher's appointment in the antisemitic climate of early 1920s Vienna,[66] While Hold-Ferneck would later claim to not have published a single line during Hitler's reign over Austria, he was remarkably outspoken in his enthusiasm in 1952, when he claimed that the NSDAP had used his legal arguments against the Treaty of Versailles in a petition to the German Reichstag in 1930.[67] It is perhaps no coincidence, then, that German chancellor Adolf Hitler went on to use a similar, ethnically slanted, justification for the destruction of Czechoslovakia, claiming that Czechoslovakia had not fulfilled its duties to protect the German minorities within its borders.[68]

A perhaps surprising addition to the theory of 'humanitarian intervention' during the era of the League of Nations came from a rather unlikely source, a place otherwise mostly associated with a strong commitment to the principle of non-intervention: the Soviet Union. Of course, the Soviet Union initially rejected traditional international law as 'the totality of forms which the capitalist, bourgeois states apply in their relations with each other. (...) With the emergence of Soviet states in the historical arena, international law assumes a different significance. It

---

[63] Strisower 1919.

[64] Strisower 1924, p. 588, my translation. A less strict position, especially with regard to the legality of 'humanitarian intervention', can be found in: Hettlage 1927, pp. 66–67.

[65] Alexander Hold-Ferneck, *Lehrbuch des Völkerrechts, Zweiter Teil*, Leipzig: Felix Meiner 1932, p. 217.

[66] Thomas Olechowski, Tamara Ehs, and Kamila Staudigl-Ciechowicz, *Die Wiener Rechts- und Staatswissenschaftliche Fakultät 1918–1938*, Göttingen: V & R unipress 2014, pp. 525–526.

[67] Olechowski et al. 2014, pp. 530, 533.

[68] See Section 3.3.1.

becomes the form of a temporary compromise between two antagonistic class systems'.[69] Soviet authors were quick to point out international law's double standard, which offered states and peoples 'outside the international community' no legal protection, enabling 'the French in Madagascar and the Germans in Southwest Africa' to liquidate 'the local population without regard for age and sex' during 'the time of the colonial wars'.[70]

However, by the 1930s, it had become clear that international law could also be used to protect the interests of the USSR and provide an arena to further the state's ideology. In 1934, the Soviet Union joined the League of Nations and in 1935, Professor Aron Naumovic Trainin (1883–1957) of the Moscow State University published a book on intervention in international law which, largely based on the work of the renowned Romanian legal expert and representative of Romania at the League of Nations, Vespasian Pella (1897–1960), developed a theory of 'abuse of sovereignty as an international crime'.[71] Of Jewish origin, Trainin focused on questions of international criminal responsibility for war crimes and 'crimes against peace' in a later publication,[72] but in Уголовная и нтервенция (Criminal Intervention), turned his attention to alleged attempts of the 'capitalist' world to intervene in the Soviet Union's internal matters, not by force but by the movement for harmonisation of criminal legislation.[73] Quoting Pella and foreshadowing developments that still have not quite come to fruition, Trainin considered the maxim that the state was 'sovereign, but not endlessly so', and showed that 'actions undermining the social system' and, particularly terrorism, could be considered 'crimes against peace' that would therefore give rise to a justifiable intervention. Trainin would later become an advisor to the Soviet delegation to Nuremberg, after he had already represented the Soviet Union in the London negotiations to create what would become the International Military Tribunal there.[74] The Soviet Union would continue to utilise the concept of 'crimes against peace', though would not undertake any intervention that claimed to be based on it.

During its existence, relatively few authors engaged with the question of whether the Covenant of the League of Nations could have entitled the League to take action against gross violations of human rights. In the solidarist vision of Georges

[69] Evgeni Pashukanis, *Selected Writings on Marxism & Law*, trans. by Peter B. Maggs, London: Academic Press 1980, p. 172 (from Международное право, Entsiklopediia gosudarstva i prava, Izd. Kommunisticheskoi akademii, Moscow, 1925).

[70] Pashukanis 1980.

[71] Aron N. Trainin, *Уголовная и нтервенция*, Moscow: Sovetskoe zakonodatel'stvo 1935.

[72] Aron N. Trainin, *Hitlerite Responsibility under Criminal Law*, trans. by Andrew Rothstein, London: Hutchinson & Co 1945.

[73] Gennady Esakov, 'International Criminal Law and Russia: From "Nuremberg" Passion to "The Hague" Prejudice', *Europe-Asia Studies* 2017, 69(8), pp. 1184–1200.

[74] On Trainin, see: Michelle Jean Penn, *The Extermination of Peaceful Soviet Citizens: Aron Trainin and International Law*, History Graduate Theses & Dissertations 2017, 39, available at: http://scholar.colorado.edu/hist_gradetds/39, last accessed 27 February 2018.

Scelle's international law, the League (and other states) had 'a duty to intervene and safeguard the law' when individual and collective human rights are 'brutally violated by governments', though Scelle immediately – in 1934 – conceded that they did 'not appear willing to make the necessary effort to fulfil this legal duty. Their excuse can perhaps be found in their impotence'.[75] Others also placed great hopes in the League as an agent of 'humanitarian intervention', as stated in a popular British textbook on international law: 'The League of Nations [was] specifically designed to meet the excuses which history has shown to be most commonly invoked to justify interference, accepted by almost all the States against which intervention might need to be directed, and demonstrably fairer and more effective in practice than the system of the concert of Powers'.[76] The Covenant, however, was considered vague enough to leave room for competing interpretations,[77] and, in the end, the League never had the means to even consider an intervention that went beyond discussing a member state's affairs in its fora.

3.3 STATE PRACTICE

3.3.1 *Introduction*

The time leading up to the advent of the United Nations offers some cases of states claiming 'humanitarian' motives, if not justifications for interventions in other countries. One such example is Japan's 1931 expansion of territory, occupied in China since 1905. Japan initially presented its actions first and foremost as 'justified measures of self-protection',[78] but as time passed also put forward 'humanitarian' arguments:

---

[75] Scelle 1934, p. 15, cited according to the English translation in: Hubert Thierry, 'The Thought of Georges Scelle', *European Journal of International Law* 1990, 1, p. 196. Scelle is considered a supporter of a right of 'humanitarian intervention' by Heraclidis 2014, p. 48, though only based on Thierry's claim in the article cited before that Scelle established 'a sort of duty of interference' in the passage quoted above. Given that Scelle went on to state that he was writing in a 'period of regression' for international law and as led to 'construct a system of legal thought opposed to "the dogmas and mystical beliefs of collective personality", to "state tyrannies", to "medieval anarchy"' (as Thierry 1990 describes it), it seems clear that his statement is not of international law as observed at the time: 'Nothing could be more pernicious than to imagine that the violation of positive law can be confused with its evolution' (Scelle 1934). But see: Scelle 1934, pp. 51–54.

[76] Earl of Birkenhead, *International Law*, 6th ed., by Ronw Moelwyn Hughes. London: J. M. Dent & Sons, Ltd. 1927, p. 89. Similiar statements can be found in: Graham 1924; Mandelstam 1931, p. 348, among others.

[77] Strisower 1924, p. 590.

[78] Statement of the Japanese Government concerning Manchuria, presented to the Council of the League of Nations on 21 November 1931: 'The special position of Japan in Manchuria (...) is a very simple matter. It is nothing but the aggregate of Japan's exceptional treaty rights (...) and vital and justified measures of self-protection, ...', as quoted in: Philip Marshall Brown,

It was Japan's clear duty to render her steps of self-defense as little disturbing as possible to the peaceable inhabitants of the region. It would have been a breach of that duty to have left the population a prey to anarchy – deprived of all the apparatus of civilized life. Therefore, the Japanese military have, at considerable sacrifice, expended much time and energy in securing the safety of persons and property in the districts where the native authorities had become ineffective.[79]

The statements had little effect on public opinion at the time, for as Hersch Lauterpacht put it at the time, 'the *communis consensus* of the civilized world' had answered all the relevant questions already, while lawyers were still debating whether or not Japan had violated the Covenant of the League of Nations and were found unwilling 'to commit themselves to a statement that existing law has been broken'.[80] Given the fact that the Assembly of the League of Nations and also the United States government would eventually unambiguously condemn the illegality of the Japanese action in the clearest manner,[81] there seems to be no reason for concern that this was a revelation of 'how a doctrine of humanitarian intervention may be severely abused'.[82]

Another possible example of an abuse of the doctrine is Italy's brutal annexation and colonisation of Ethiopia, then called the Abyssinian Empire, in 1935–1936.[83] In this case, Italy claimed to have given 'to 16,000 slaves that liberty from which they would have awaited in vain from the Government of Addis Ababa, despite the clauses of the Covenant and the undertakings assumed at the moment of its admission as a member of the League of Nations'. In so doing, Italy cast itself as 'the power which has the right and the capacity of extending that high protection which the very Covenant of the League of Nations, in its Article 22, recognizes as the civilizing mission incumbent upon the more advanced nations'.[84] The story of the Italian war for the conquest of Abyssinia is generally told as revealing 'the true weakness of League system',[85] because this was the only time the League resorted to

---

'Japanese Interpretation of the Kellogg Pact', *American Journal of International Law* 1933, 27, p. 100.

[79] Statement by the Japanese Government, 27 December 1931, cited according to Murphy 1996, pp. 60–61.

[80] Hersch Lauterpacht, 'Japan and the Covenant', originally published in *Political Quarterly* 1932, 3, 174–194, cited here according to Elihu Lauterpacht (ed.), *International Law, being the Collected Papers of Hersch Lauterpacht*, Vol. 5, Cambridge University Press 2004, p. 409.

[81] Brownlie 1963, p. 294.

[82] Murphy 1996, p. 60; Bazyler 1987, pp. 583–584 argues that cases like 'these bogus "humanitarian interventions" illustrate the danger of an unbridled international law doctrine of humanitarian intervention'.

[83] See: Murphy 1996, p. 61.

[84] Note from the Italian Government addressed to all governments which vted for sanctions against Italy, 11 November 1935, as quoted by Murphy 1996, p. 61. The quote in the previous sentence is from the same source.

[85] Grewe 2000, p. 577.

sanctions against a member state (against Italy), and they proved to be a failure.[86] The argument for an abuse of a doctrine of 'humanitarian intervention' might be considered more relevant in this case because of the recognition of the annexation of the Empire by Italy by most States (excluding, among others, both the United States and the Soviet Union) after the League had lifted the sanctions against Italy by July 1936.[87] But the Council of the League did find Italy in violation of its international obligations and rejected the Italian claims that Ethiopia had shown 'that she does not possess the qualifications necessary to enable her to obtain, through participation in the League, the impulse required to raise herself by voluntary efforts to the level of the other civilised nations'.[88] Therefore, it seems somewhat far-fetched to claim that the annexation resulted 'from actions that were *in accordance with*, rather than in violation of, interwar international legal norms regarding sovereignty and the use of force'.[89] The discourse on the 'standard of "Civilization"' underlying the question of the status of Ethiopia at the League of Nations does show that Ethiopia, admitted to the League only with reservations, was not an equal at the table,[90] but because the war for the conquest of the country turned into a racist war of destruction, bordering on genocide,[91] there is little reason to take the triumph expressed by the likes of Carl Schmitt over the collapse of a more formal legal order seriously,[92] even if contemporaries found all the necessary ingredients in the conflict to juxtapose the 'health of Western civilization' with the 'juridical organization of humanity' in an attempt to justify the Italian aggression.[93] Even (Nazi) German lawyers sympathetic to the Italian cause conceded that the Italian 'achievements' would only become permanent once a lasting settlement had been reached,[94] a moment that never came.

The most notorious case of an alleged misuse of the doctrine of 'humanitarian intervention', however, is the German occupation and eventual break-up of Czechoslovakia in 1938–1939. In appearance, the German actions resemble the

[86] Antonio Cassese, *International Law*, 2nd ed., Oxford University Press 2005, p. 37.

[87] Heinrich August Winkler, *Geschichte des Westens – Die Zeit der Weltkriege 1914–1945*, Munich: C. H. Beck 2011, p. 713.

[88] League of Nations, 'Situation in Ethiopia. Memorandum by the Italian Government dated 4 September 1935, and Documents relating Thereto', 4 September 1935, LoN Doc. C.340. M.171.1935.VI, as found in League of Nations, Official Journal, 88th and 89th Council Sessions, Annex 1571, November 1935, p. 1416.

[89] Rose Parfitt, 'Empire des Nègres Blancs: The Hybridity of International Personality and the Abyssinia Crisis of 1935–36', *Leiden Journal of International Law* 2011, 24, pp. 849–872.

[90] Jean Allain, 'Slavery and the League of Nations: Ethiopia as a "Civilised Nation"', *Journal of the History of International Law* 2006, 8, pp. 213–244.

[91] Winkler 2011, p. 711.

[92] Schmitt 1997, p. 216.

[93] Nathaniel Berman, *Passion and Ambivalence: Colonialism, Nationalism, and International Law*, Leiden: Martinus Nijoff Publishers 2012, p. 352, quoting a 1935 article by Joseph Barthélemy, a French jurist and later a minister at Vichy.

[94] Oswalt von Nostitz-Wallwitz, 'Die Annexion Abessiniens und die Liquidation des abessinischen Konflikts', *Zeitschrift für ausländisches öffentliches Recht* 1937, pp. 38–66.

ideal of 'humanitarian intervention' almost perfectly, even if it is hardly the weight of the legal arguments that have made this case so notorious.

In his letter to the British Premier of 23 September 1938, the German chancellor Adolf Hitler noted that 'ethnic Germans and various nationalities in Czechoslovakia have been maltreated in the unworthiest manner, tortured, economically destroyed and, above all, prevented from realizing for themselves also the right of nations to self-determination'. They were subject to the 'brutal will to destruction of the Czechs' whose behavior was "madness" and had led to over 120,000 refugees being forced to flee the country in recent days while the "security of more than 3,000,000 human beings" was at stake'.[95] The letter was published in the still-renowned German *Zeitschrift für ausländisches öffentliches Recht und Völkerrecht*,[96] indicating that it was seen as a legal justification at least by German international lawyers. Even if the justification focused on the treatment of 'ethnic Germans', it was not limited to this group only and rested on the alleged 'brutal will to destruction of the Czechs'.[97] In the German narrative of the time, this was but the culmination of a right of 'co-national' intervention first claimed by Hitler in a speech to the German Reichstag on 20 February 1938.[98]

European statesmen tried to defuse the situation by agreeing to the Munich Agreement of 29 September 1938, permitting the annexation of portions of Czechoslovakia along the country's borders that were mainly inhabited by German speakers. It was the first step towards the destruction of the young republic. In March 1939, German troops invaded further parts of the country's territory and established the 'Protectorate of Bohemia and Moravia', which by decree of the *Führer* was to be 'under the protection of the Reich', while the remaining First Slovak Republic was forced to enter into a 'protection treaty'. Hitler had stepped up the 'humanitarian' rhetoric in the Preamble to the March decree, proclaiming that the Reich had been forced to take action to prevent 'a new monstrous danger to European peace' building in the Czechoslovakian 'space' and to 'serve the true interests of the nationalities ("Völker") of this *Lebensraum*', as well as 'peace and the social welfare of all'.[99] The reality, of course, was quite different.

---

[95]   quoted in the translation provided by Franck and Rodley 1973, p. 284.

[96]   'Völkerrechtliche Urkunden – Dokumente zur Lösung der Sudetendeutschen Frage', *Zeitschrift für ausländisches öffentliches Recht* 1938, p. 772.

[97]   Henke 2002, p. 19, argues that the focus on ethnic Germans as the victims of the 'brutal will to destruction' disqualifies the claim as 'humanitarian', but the justification does rest on the alleged 'brutal will to destruction', not the nationality of the victims. That the 'humanitarian concern for the welfare of the inhabitants of these regions does not bear up under scrutiny', as Murphy 1996, p. 62, put it, is, however, obviously true.

[98]   See Section 3.4.2. for details.

[99]   Preamble of the 'Erlaß des Führers und Reichskanzlers über das Protektorat Böhmen und Mähren', 16 March 1939, *Zeitschrift für ausländisches öffentliches Recht und Völkerrecht* 1939, p. 506, my translation.

Nazi international law theory praised this 'solution of the Sudetenfrage' as the recognition of a right to 'ethnic' (völkisch) intervention.[100] It is often cited as a dangerous precedent for the misuse of the doctrine of 'humanitarian intervention',[101] but outside of the Nazis' own echo chamber, there is no indication that the German claims of legality left much impression.[102] The politics of 'appeasement' that allowed the German 'rape of Czechoslovakia' were not a result of the weight of the German arguments, but of the fear of another war in Europe.[103]

In the case of Japan's invasion into Manchuria, contemporary writers initially seemed to have some difficulty declaring the illegality of Japan's actions, despite a clear moral position against them. But this was quickly resolved and today there is no doubt that Japan was the illegal aggressor, just like there is no doubt that Italy acted against its obligations under international law and that Germany was employing a rhetoric without basis of facts to achieve illegal means, so these examples hardly serve as convincing examples that acceptance of 'humanitarian' justifications would lead to an increase in the use of force in international relations: In both of these cases, it was not the obviously unjustified use of a 'humanitarian' rhetoric that led to the other powers' passive complicity in the unfolding of events.

3.3.2 *The International Response to Nazi Germany's Persecution of Jews*

For contemporaries, the extent of Nazi Germany's persecution of Jews and other minorities may not have been immediately clear from the outset. News of anti-Semitic official policies and violence, however, reached the world public soon after Hitler's rise to power. According to French international lawyer Georges Scelle, writing in 1934, this led to 'some impulses for intervention' in America and the United Kingdom in April 1934 'during the Nazi excesses in Germany'. Scelle does not provide any specifics, but notes that these impulses, though with foundation in the law, led nowhere.[104] One such impulse could have come from Hersch Lauterpacht (1897–1960), the international lawyer 'unsurpassed by any other international lawyer' of the twentieth century.[105] In an unpublished memorandum, most likely written in the short space of time between Hitler's appointment as chancellor on

---

[100] see Section 3.4.2.

[101] e.g. Brownlie 1963, p. 340; Franck and Rodley 1973, p. 304.

[102] Jost Dülffer, 'Humanitarian Intervention as Legitimation of Violence – the German Case 1937–1939', in: Fabian Klose (ed.), *The Emergence of Humanitarian Intervention*, Cambridge University Press 2016, pp. 208–228, claims that 'Human rights violations and humanitarian reasons were the arguments used to spin a tight web of justification' by Nazi Germany, but concedes that '[t]his kind of argument and reasoning was not immediately accepted elsewhere in Europe at face value', p. 214.

[103] Richard J. Evans, *The Third Reich in Power*, London: Allen Lane 2005, pp. 612–688.

[104] Scelle 1934, p. 54.

[105] Stephen M. Schwebel, *International Arbitration: Three Salient Problems*, Cambridge: Grotius Publications 1987, p. xiii.

30 January 1933 and Germany's withdrawal from the League of Nations on 19 October 1933, he pointed out:

> No specific rule of international law binds Germany not to persecute her Jewish minority, but the prohibition of discrimination against minorities because of their race or religion has become part of what has been called the public law of Europe. The character of the present persecution of Jews in Germany is such that opposition to it can be based on legal principles commanding even today general recognition. (. . .) [T]he principle that in the modern State individuals must not be persecuted or discriminated against because of their race or religion does enjoy general recognition as part of the public law of the world. It has been laid down in general terms in the treaties of 1878 as a condition of the recognition of a number of new States. In a number of treaties connected with the peace settlement of 1919 it has been regulated in detail and considerably expanded. But both groups of treaties are merely declarator of a fundamental principle which, apart from present day Germany, no State would deny.[106]

Lauterpacht drafted a resolution for the Council of the League of Nations to re-affirm the 'principle of non-discrimination on account of race or religion' as 'part of the public law of Europe' in light of the 'recent legislation converting the treatment in Germany of persons of Jewish race and religion' and 'considering that it is the function of the League to use its authority in defence of the rights of human personality whose protection is the ultimate object of international', to appeal 'to all Members of the League to observe scrupulously those principles in their treatment of the racial and religious minorities subjected to their sovereignty'.[107]

According to Lauterpacht's son and the editor of his papers, Elihu Lauterpacht (1928–2017), who published this memorandum in 2004, it is not known who Lauterpacht prepared this memorandum for.[108] Around the time of its writing, Lauterpacht had been working with another authority on international law, Norman Bentwich (1883–1971). Bentwich presented, and later published, his unsurprisingly similar legal assessment of the situation in a speech before the Grotius Society on 17 April 1933.[109] While he made it clear that the action he envisaged in response to the persecution of Jews in Germany would not amount to 'intervention' in the legal sense,[110] Bentwich explicitly placed his arguments within a history of international law recognising a right of 'humanitarian intervention':[111]

[106] Hersch Lauterpacht, 'The Persecution of Jews in Germany', unpublished memorandum from 1933, in: Lauterpacht 2004, p. 732.
[107] Hersch Lauterpacht, 'The Persecution of Jews in Germany', unpublished memorandum from 1933, in: Lauterpacht 2004, pp. 735, 736.
[108] Lauterpacht 2004, p. 728.
[109] Norman Bentwich, 'The League of Nations and Racial Persecution in Germany', *Transactions of the Grotius Society* 1933, 19, pp. 75–88. Note the identical beginning to Lauterpacht's quote, cited above.
[110] Bentwich 1933, p. 87.
[111] Bentwich 1933, p. 76.

No specific rule of conventional international law binds Germany not to persecute her Jewish minority – outside Upper Silesia; but the present persecution violates legal principles commanding general recognition which were laid down as long ago as the Treaty of 1831 recognising the independence of Greece [. . .]. There has been a growing tendency to regard the individual as a subject of international law in many respects; and protection of certain fundamental rights of human personality has long been recognised as one of the objects of that law, witness the prohibition of slavery, which, in addition to conventional agreements, may now be regarded as part of customary international law'.

At the time, Bentwich held the chair for International Relations at the Hebrew University in Jerusalem, in which capacity he was still able to publish in the renowned German *Zeitschrift für ausländisches öffentliches Recht und Völkerrecht* in 1934. Yet his appeal to the British government to take initiative at the Council of the League of Nations, which he based on the notion, thoroughly deconstructed in this book, 'that prior to the establishment of the League [of Nations]', 'the practice of armed international intervention and diplomatic representation made to a foreign State on the grounds of humanity were common',[112] also fell on deaf ears. Both lawyers had made it clear in identical terms that taking the persecution of Jews in Germany to the Council would come with 'all the advantages attaching to a public debate of the matter' and would, at worst, be cut short by a 'peremptory declaration by Germany that she would regard a consideration of this matter by the League as a reason for withdrawing from the League', which 'would morally be as damaging to Germany' as an adoption of a resolution by the Council.[113] Though, in Bentwich's view, the British government was in the position to 'raise the question most appropriately, because Great Britain cannot be suspected of ill-will towards Germany and nobody could throw at her the stone of inconsistency', as 'it would be in accordance with the long tradition of Great Britain to take action on behalf of a persecuted people',[114] and despite repeated requests in the House of Commons, her Majesty's governement chose not to concern the League of Nations with the situation of the Jews in Germany.[115]

Instead, it took a private 'intervention' to bring the early stages of the destruction of the Jews of Europe to the League of Nations. A petition, signed by Franz Bernheim, a Jew from Upper Silesia, who had moved to Prague after he lost his job once the Nazis had come to power, was put forward on the initiative of Emil Margulies (1877–1943), a lawyer and Zionist activist in Czechoslovakia. Submitted to the League of Nations on 17 May 1933, by representatives of the *Comité des Délégations Juives* (Leo Motzkin, Emil Margulies and Nathan Feinberg), the so-called Bernheim Petition used Article 147 of the German-Polish Agreement on

---

[112] Bentwich 1933, p. 75.
[113] Bentwich 1933, p. 88.
[114] Bentwich 1933, p. 87.
[115] Mohr 2002.

Upper Silesia of 15 May 1922, valid until 15 July 1937 (henceforth 'the Agreement'), which enabled every inhabitant of Upper Silesia belonging to a minority to submit to the League of Nations complaints about alleged violations of rights guaranteed by the Convention.[116] The Agreement required German authorities to accord inhabitants belonging to a 'racial, religious, or language minority' the same rights as the rest of the population and the Petition detailed the many laws and provisions adopted by Nazi Germany which violated this guarantee through the introduction of the concept of 'non-Aryan descent'. The discriminatory measures of the Third Reich against Jews were all listed and their violation of the Agreement was spelled out. In a separate section, the Petition also described the anti-Jewish boycott, which unlike the other measures did not rest on a publicly available legal basis, although its consequences were apparent even in Upper Silesia and had directly affected the petitioner. The Petition then called upon the League of Nations to declare null and void all the anti-Jewish measures applied in Upper Silesia, as they infringed upon guarantees committed to by Germany under the Agreement; and to reinstate the rights of Upper Silesian Jews reinstated and request that they receive compensation for damages.

The lawyers in the *Comité* had intensely debated the legal fine points of the Petition and, as the *New York Times* noted at the time, it was clear 'that an expert legal hand drafted it'.[117] It was also successful. Despite intense German efforts to block it, the Petition was debated at the League, first in the Council and then in two public sessions, attracting considerable public attention. While it was also the direct cause of the German decision to leave the League, it was clearly a success in practical terms, as the Third Reich agreed to suspend all discriminatory measures against the Jews in Upper Silesia, where subsequently Jews in some cases were called to jury service for the first time after 1933.[118] All this changed after 15 July 1937, when the Treaty ran out and the anti-Jewish measures were automatically enforced again. From then on, the local Jewish population shared the fate of the Jews of the rest of the Reich.

During 1935 and 1936, Bentwich and Lauterpacht had also been involved in the preparation of a petition to be submitted to the League of Nations in support of the letter of resignation of James G. McDonald, High Commissioner for Refugees (Jewish and Other) Coming from Germany, and eventually submitted to the League in September 1936 by a group of American, French and Dutch non-Government organisations.[119] But despite sometimes spectacular events – such as Stefan Lux's

---

[116] The original text of the Bernheim-Petition is reprinted in: Graf 2008, pp. 303–313.

[117] 'Treaty Rights Invoked', *New York Times*, 21 May 1933, cited according to: Graf 2008, p. 142.

[118] J. W. Brugel, 'The Bernheim petition: A challenge to Nazi Germany in 1933', *Patterns of Prejudice* 1983, 17(3), pp. 17–25.

[119] Monty Noam Penkower, 'Honorable Failures against Nazi Germany: McDonald's Letter of Resignation and the Petition in Its Support', *Modern Judaism – A Journal of Jewish Ideas and Experience*, 2010, 30(3), pp. 247–298.

suicide at the General Assembly of the League of Nations during its session on 3 July 1936 to alert the assembled leaders to the rising dangers of German antisemitism – the League would remain incapable of taking action against the now former member state. Accordingly, by 1936, Lauterpacht had come to the rather fatalistic conclusion that 'the conception of "intervention for the sake of humanity" is less acceptable to civilized Governments than it was thirty or forty years ago'.[120]

In 1937, Oscar I. Janowsky (1900–1993) and Melvin M. Fagen (1912–1996) published the book *International Aspects of German Racial Policies*, the 'substance' of which had been submitted in support of the aforementioned September 1936 petition.[121] Anchored to a preface by James Brown Scott (1866–1943), one of the most renowned American international lawyers of the first half of the twentieth century,[122] who recounted the 1929 New York Declaration of the International Rights of Man,[123] the book told of a history of 'humanitarian intercessions' as 'precedents for international action to safeguard human rights', and found that 'States have interceded to uphold human rights for more than three hundred years and the results of such efforts are embodied in important treaties'.[124] The authors apparently chose the term 'intercession' over 'intervention' to tone down their argument,[125] but despite being rooted in rather non-controversial narratives of international law, the petition and the book only reflected 'honorable failure'.[126] In the words of British parliamentarian Josiah C. Wedgwood's (1873–1943) postscript, 'a tragic acknowledgment of moral bankruptcy by what we are pleased to call the civilized world' ensued.[127]

Illustrative of the lack of 'humanitarian' convictions in the years leading up to World War II is the Evian conference held in July 1938, convened by the US American President Franklin D. Roosevelt under pressure from "certain Congressmen with metropolitan constituencies' after the 'Anschluss' hastened Jewish emigration from the expanded Third Reich. The conference had 'a humanitarian face but somewhat darker origins', as the United States attempted to 'get out in front and attempt to guide' any pressure to liberalise immigration policies for the Jews from Germany: 'By making everyone in the world responsible for the fate of the refugees,

---

[120] Hersch Lauterpacht, 'International Law after the Covenant', originally published in *Problems of Peace*, 10th series (1936), pp. 37–56, cited here according to the reprint, in: Elihu Lauterpacht (ed.), *International Law, being the Collected Papers of Hersch Lauterpacht*, Vol. 2, Cambridge University Press 1975, p. 148.

[121] Oscar I. Janowsky and Melvin M. Fagen, *International Aspects of German Racial Policies*, New York: Oxford University Press 1937.

[122] G. A. Finch, 'James Brown Scott, 1866–1943', *The American Journal of International Law* 1944, 38(2), p. 183.

[123] James Brown Scott, 'Preface', in: Janowsky and Fagen 1937, p. VIII.

[124] Janowsky and Fagen 1937, p. 6.

[125] see Penkower 2010.

[126] Penkower 2010, p. 298.

[127] Josiah C. Wedgwood, 'Postscript', in: Janowsky and Fagen 1937, p. 259.

essentially no one would be, including the United States'.[128] And with no one responsible, no one took any meaningful action. All but one (Italy) of thirty-two invited countries attended the conference at Evian-les-Bains, but the Dominican Republic was the only one to agree to increase its quota for Jewish immigration. Even this offer was later reduced in scale. Most countries openly rejected even the possibility of taking in Jewish refugees. The responsible governments could rest assured in the knowledge that their public shared the lack of willingness to offer refuge to the Jews of Europe. German officials had attended the conference as observers, as did representatives of the Jews of Germany and Austria, with Gestapo approval.[129] At the close of the conference, a spokesman for the German foreign ministry "exultingly announced that Western countries wanted the Jews no more than did the Germans themselves'.[130]

3.3.3 World War II and the Shoah

The German attack on Poland was justified by the Third Reich first and foremost by pointing to the alleged attack of Polish forces on German territory on the night of 31 August to 1 September 1939. It is now well known that this was a false flag operation carried out by German forces at the order of the government. In the months leading up to the German attack, Hitler had repeatedly mentioned the alleged mistreatment of the German minority in Poland at the hands of the Polish government as a probable cause for intervention. A note to the British government dated 3 September 1939, then read:

> The German Government, though moved by the sufferings of the German population which was being tortured and treated in an inhuman manner, nevertheless remained a patient onlooker for five months, without undertaking even on one single occasion any similar aggressive action against Poland. They only warned Poland that these happenings would in the long run be unbearable, and that they were determined, in the event of no other kind of assistance being given to this population, to help them themselves. All these happenings were known in every detail to the British Government. It would have been easy for them to use their great influence in Warsaw in order to exhort those in power there to exercise justice and humaneness and to keep to the existing obligations. The British Government did not do this.[131]

---

[128] Manus I. Midlarsky, The Killing Trap – Genocide in the 20th Century, Cambridge University Press 2005, p. 243. See also: Leni Yahil, The Holocaust, Oxford University Press 1990, p. 95.
[129] Yahil 1990, p. 94.
[130] Cited according to Midlarsky 2005, p. 244.
[131] Communication from the German Government to the British Government, Handed to Joachim von Ribbentrop, Minister for Foreign Affairs, to the British Ambassador (Sir Neville Henderson) at 11:20 A.M., 3 September 1939, available at https://fcit.usf.edu/holocaust/resource/document/BRIT.htm, last accessed 23 February 2019.

Similarly, on 1 September 1939, the German Foreign Minister told the French Ambassador to Berlin that no German aggression was taking place, but that Poland's mistreatment of the German minority and border violations were the cause of the war.[132] This 'humanitarian' justification, though clearly fabricated, was invoked by contemporary German international lawyers blaming France and the United Kingdom for the outbreak of the war,[133] though there can be very little doubt that such arguments only resonated within the community of like-minded Nazis. Holding such positions, however, did not necessarily disqualify anyone from continuing their academic careers after the liberation of Germany.[134]

The war forced upon the world by Germany and its allies marks the final break between 'classic' and contemporary international law. The atrocities committed and the responses set in motion for after the war ushered in a new era for international law. The war efforts of the victorious Allied Powers have later been hailed as 'the most important pre-Charter precedent for humanitarian intervention',[135] but it is clear enough that the Third Reich's genocidal policies were not the cause of the Allies' decision to enter the war. The United Kingdom and France had declared war on Germany on 3 September 1939 because they considered themselves bound by treaty obligations to Poland. The Soviet Union was attacked by Hitler's armies on 22 June 1941 in breach of previous agreements and without a declaration of war. The United States only joined the war late in 1941, after first Germany and then Italy had declared war on the United States following the Japanese attack on Pearl Harbor.

The collective memory likes to construct causal connections that never existed. World War II may look like 'the paradigm of a just war' and it may be considered a 'humanitarian intervention' by objective measures, but to say that 'the Allies did not fight fascism just because Hitler and Mussolini engaged in military conquest', and that 'the thrust of that fight was dignity, reason, human rights and decency'[136] conveniently overlooks the low regard held for the dignity, decency, reason, human rights and even lives of the many victims during the war. To claim that, 'retrospectively, the atrocities committed by Germany add to the justification of the war' is to state the obvious,[137] but to pretend that these atrocities were somehow instrumental

---

[132] Ferdinand Schlüter, 'Der Ausbruch des Krieges', *Zeitschrift für öffentliches ausländisches Recht und Völkerrecht* 1940, 10, pp. 244–269.

[133] Hans K. E. L. Keller, *Das Recht der Völker*, Vol. II – *Das Reich der Völker*, Berlin: Standard Verlag Müller-Rath 1941, p. 238, with fn. 54. See also Carl Bilfinger, 'Die Kriegserklärungen der Westmächte und der Kelloggpakt', *Zeitschrift für ausländisches öffentliches Recht und Völkerrecht* 1940, p. 2.

[134] While Hans Keller did not hold any academic positions during the Third Reich, he continued as an activist and politician until his death in 1970. For details on other careers of Nazi international lawyers after World War II, see Section 3.4.

[135] Tesón 2005, p. 227.

[136] Tesón 2005.

[137] Tesón 2005, p. 227, fn. 22.

in any nation's decision to enter the war is to rewrite history – and rewrite it badly. The knowledge of the destruction of the Jews of Europe did not intensify the war efforts of any of the fighting Powers.

Illustrative of the lack of 'humanitarian' convictions during World War II is the fate of the MV Struma, a ship carrying nearly 800 Jewish refugees from Romania. Attempting to bring the refugees to the safety of Palestine, the ship was met with refusals to help by Turkish and British officials. The United Kingdom was determined to minimise Jewish immigration to Palestine and urged Turkey, where the ship was temporarily anchored because of engine problems, to prevent a continuation of the voyage. On 23 February 1942, with the ship's engine inoperable and its refugee passengers aboard, Turkish authorities towed the Struma along the Bosporus and, in a decision eerily foreshadowing current treatment of refugees in the Mediterranean, abandoned it in the Black Sea. There, it was torpedoed and sunk the next day.

The exact moment at which the German discriminatory measures and atrocities became a matter of international law again after the fruitless attempts by the likes of Lauterpacht, Bentwich and Stowell is probably impossible to determine. The original consensus was that Germany was within its rights to exercise discriminatory measures against some of its citizens.[138] Discriminatory, even murderous policies against its own citizens, thought to be the justification for interventions in the Ottoman Empire, were not enough to warrant any serious response in the case of the Third Reich. During the early years of the Third Reich, there was hardly any doubt in the United States and in the United Kingdom, that Germany's actions, while unspeakable, would have been sanctioned by international law. Up until about 1940, it was maintained that these actions *should* be covered by international law, for example by Green Hackworth (1883–1973), then Legal Adviser to the U.S. Department of State who would later become a judge at the International Court of Justice in 1946: for the other Powers to claim otherwise would create a precedent that might rebound on their own nations.[139] As the Nazis expanded their territory, the governments-in-exile of the conquered countries demanded recognition of the crimes committed by the Germans on their former territories, which was granted only gradually. The declarations referring to these, made between 1942 and 1945, may have been legion,[140] their immediate effect was miniscule.

The United Nations Declaration of 1 January 1942 declared the conviction of the undersigned nations that 'complete victory over their enemies is essential to defend life, liberty, independence and religious freedom, and to preserve human rights and justice in their own lands as well as in other lands', but the denial of these rights

---

[138] Fritz Kieffer, *Judenverfolgung in Deutschland – eine innere Angelegenheit?*, Stuttgart: Franz Steiner Verlag 2002.
[139] Simpson 1995, p. 46.
[140] Schwelb 1947, p. 183.

hardly played into the decison to go to war or informed the tactics of the war.[141] The St James' Palace Declaration of 13 January 1942 was issued after the Soviets had already reported about the massacres of Babi Yar, in which SS troops had killed more than 33,000 Jews in the span of two days in September 1941 and spoke of the 'spirit of international solidarity' upheld by the signatory governments-in-exile and placed 'among their principal war aims the punishment, through the channel of *organised justice*, of those *guilty* and responsible' for the German acts of violence against the civilian populations under their control. Yet it received only very limited support from the Great Powers.[142] While the establishment of the United Nations War Crimes Commission in October 1943 clearly signalled a change of course, even at a time when the knowledge of the Shoah was hardly a secret, the Allies refused to even contemplate bombing Auschwitz or the train tracks leading there, despite Jewish pressure to do so and despite the capability of the British and American forces to bomb the I. G. Farben plant and the Buna Works in Monovitz, just outside Auschwitz, to disrupt the production of synthetic oil and rubber. It is by now widely acknowledged that the refusal to bomb Auschwitz in order to disrupt the killing machine stemmed from a general disinclination to be involved with rescue actions. As early as February 1944, the U.S. War Department had determined that it would not contemplate using units of the armed forces for the purpose of rescuing victims of 'enemy oppression unless such rescues are the direct result of military operations conducted with the objective of defeating the armed forces of the enemy'.[143]

And thus, 'classic' international law went up in the smoke that blew over the fields at Auschwitz without any measures undertaken by any nation to halt this ultimate attack on humanity. Death, this master from Germany (Paul Celan) was given free reign over the Jews and Sinti and Roma of Europe and no military force stood in its way. Consequently, World War II is relevant to a history of 'humanitarian intervention' only insofar as it destroyed the foundations on which the legal instrument rested.

3.4 NAZI INTERNATIONAL LAW THEORY AND 'HUMANITARIAN INTERVENTION'

After World War II, Wilhelm Sauer (1879–1962), then Professor of Criminal Law at the University in Münster, sought to offer a conception for a 'true and just'

---

[141] Declaration by the United Nations, 1 January 1942, available at http://avalon.law.yale.edu/20th_century/decade03.asp, last accessed 24 February 2019.

[142] Kochavi 1998, pp. 14–20. Text of the St. James' Palace Declaration cited according to Sheldon Glueck, 'The Nuremberg Trial and Aggressive War', originally published in 1946 in the *Harvard Law Review*, reprinted in: Mettraux 2008, p. 90, with fn. 75.

[143] Quoted here as cited in Yahil 1990, p. 639. See generally: Martin Gilbert, *Auschwitz and the Allies*, London: Pimlico 2001; Shlomo Aronson, *Hitler, the Allies, and the Jews*, Cambridge University Press 2004.

international law in his treatise *Völkerrecht und Weltfrieden* (*International Law and World Peace*).[144] Sauer was one of the relatively few professors whose career teaching law in Germany spanned the Weimar Republic through the Third Reich and into the Federal Republic of Germany. As he saw it, 'positivism' as the leading tradition in international (and national) law, was to blame for not preventing the catastrophes of the two preceding World Wars.[145] This view was quite fashionable in the early years of the Federal Republic,[146] but has since been identified as somewhat simplistic.[147]

Though Sauer's work was of marginal importance in the development of the science of international law in West Germany after the War,[148] it is mentioned here as an example of continuity in international law thinking. Drawing on material completed before the end of the war,[149] Sauer's work includes several, surprisingly uncritical references to arguments on intervention tainted with National Socialist ideology. The most glaring example is the mention of 'Lebensraum' ('living space') as an 'object of international law': 'The people constituting the nation do so for the purposes of international law in their own living space. The living space of the national people is not only their domicile, but also their homeland and their own domain'.[150] The translation cannot quite convey the full weight of these words, as the term 'Lebensraum' (living space) has strong connotations from its use in German colonialism and, in particular, National Socialist ideology, where it referred to the 'natural right' of the German people to expand into and exploit or occupy the territories of Eastern Europe. Even in a later book, published in 1952, Sauer retained the idea that 'Völker' (peoples) are distinct subjects of international law, different from states and nations, understanding the 'Volk' (people) as the 'natural organism, like the body of the human being'.[151] In this context, a people is defined as 'racially separate', yet sharing a 'living space' ('Lebensraum') with shared customs.[152] Sauer's ongoing references to National Socialist scholars like

---

[144] Wilhelm Sauer, *Völkerrecht und Weltfrieden*, Kohlhammer: Stuttgart 1948. A short review can be found in *The Cambridge Law Journal* 1951, 11(1), p. 168.

[145] Wilhelm Sauer, *System des Völkerrechts*, Bonn: Ludwig Röhrscheid Verlag 1952, preface, p. V.

[146] Gustav Radbruch, 'Zur Diskussion über die Verbrechen gegen die Menschlichkeit', *Süddeutsche Juristen-Zeitung* 1946, p. 131.

[147] On Radbruch and positivism, see: Hans Vest, *Gerechtigkeit für Humanitätsverbrechen?*, Tübingen: Mohr Siebeck 2006; David Dyzenhaus, *Hard Cases in Wicked Legal Systems*, 2nd ed., Oxford University Press 2010. For studies of the relationship between positivism and National Socialism, see: Bernd Rüthers, *Entartetes Recht*, Munich: C. H. Beck 1988.

[148] Michael Stolleis, *Geschichte des öffentlichen Rechts in Deutschland Bd. 4: Staats- und Verwaltungsrechtswissenschaft in West und Ost 1945–1990*, Munich: C. H. Beck 2012, p. 204.

[149] Sauer 1948, p. 7.

[150] Sauer 1952, p 123: 'Die Staatsvölker entfalten ihr völkerrechtlich erhebliches Leben und Wirken in dem ihnen eigenen Lebensraum (…) Der Lebensraum der Staatsvölker ist das Staatsgebiet; es ist ihnen also nicht nur Wohnsitz, sondern auch Heimat und Wirkungsstätte'.

[151] Sauer 1952, p. 65.

[152] Sauer 1952, p. 67.

Norbert Gürke (1904–1941)[153] makes the author's attempt to outline a 'true and just' international law read more like a continuation of German 'völkisch' (ethnic) ideology, that centres around the German people and their 'population problem', resulting from a people without adequate 'living space' ('Bevölkerungsproblem "Volk ohne Raum"').[154]

Sauer may have only been a marginal figure among German international law scholars, but continuity in positions on international law after the war was not as uncommon as one might have expected. For example, Carl Bilfinger (1879–1958), referenced in the previous section was a Professor for International Law at the Universities in Halle, Heidelberg and Berlin during the war, and was relieved of his duties in 1945. By 1949, he was reinstated in his position at the University of Heidelberg, despite his membership in the Nazi party and clear support for the regime, which he managed to portray as merely tactical.[155] Georg Erler (1905–1981), a member of the National Socialist Party from May 1933, became a Professor of International Law in 1938. He was formally appointed to the chair in absentia in 1943, while he was interned in Australia as an enemy alien after the outbreak of World War II had caught him by surprise on a research trip. After the war, still in absentia, he was stripped of his position by the British military administration. In 1954, he was reinstated and became a contributor to the *Wörterbuch des Völkerrechts* for its second edition, published in the 1960s.[156] Friedrich Berber (1898–1984), Professor of International Law at the University of Berlin from 1940 and advisor to the Third Reich's foreign minister Joachim von Ribbentrop, was stripped of his position at the end of the war. He was again appointed Professor of International Law in 1954, this time at the University of Munich.[157]

'Humanitarian intervention' was not a subject featured prominently in German textbooks on international law after World War II. In what would become one of the leading works, published in 1960, Berber remarked that the Christian Powers had on a number of occasions during the nineteenth century intervened against the persecution of Christians in the Ottoman Empire, but that the use of force on most occasions

[153] Norbert Gürke, born 1904 in Graz, was an active National Socialist, having become a member of the NSDAP in 1930. His writings were openly anti-semitic, a speech he gave in 1936 was published as *Der Einfluß jüdischer Theoretiker auf die deutsche Völkerrechtslehre*, Berlin: Deutscher Rechts-Verlag 1938. When Germany began the war against Poland, he reported for active duty and was seriously wounded in the war against France on 7 June 1940. He died as a result in Vienna on 29 June 1941. On Gürke, see: Alexander Pinwinkler, 'Norbert Gürke', in: Michael Fahlbusch, Ingo Haar, and Alexander Pinwinkler (eds.), *Handbuch der völkischen Wissenschaften*, Vol. I, 2nd ed., Berlin: De Gruyter 2017, pp. 254–257.

[154] Sauer 1952, p. 69.

[155] Felix Lange: 'Carl Bilfingers Entnazifizierung und die Entscheidung für Heidelberg – Die Gründungsgeschichte des völkerrechtlichen Max-Planck-Instituts nach dem Zweiten Weltkrieg', *Zeitschrift für ausländisches öffentliches Recht und Völkerrecht* 2014, 74, pp. 697–732.

[156] See: Ernst Klee, *Das Personenlexikon zum Dritten Reich*, Frankfurt am Main: S. Fischer 2003, p. 139.

[157] See: Klee 2003, p. 39.

would have been fuelled by other political interests, whereas nothing was known about interventions to stop the pogroms against Jews in Czarist Russia or during the early stages of National Socialist race policies, when an intervention would have been possible without starting a war.[158] It seems quite remarkable then, that Wilhelm Sauer in his book would cite a work from before the end of the war on the subject of questions relating to the field of 'humanitarian intervention'.[159] The arguments of that book, *Die konnationale Intervention* by Helmuth Krasberg, are in line with German National Socialist ideology and understandings of international law, featuring numerous references to Hitler's speeches, as was common among National Socialist writers.[160] Sauer's reference to this book, which presumably was never widely circulated,[161] may be taken as an oversight, an accidental omission during the clean-up of material completed before the end of the war. Nazi theories on international law did, however, generate the vision of a right of intervention that is not as far removed from the ideas of the 'humanitarian intervention' as modern human rights discourse would suggest, given claims that the theory of 'humanitarian intervention' is an advancement in the 'progress' of human rights protection. The term 'konnationale Intervention' (Intervention on behalf of 'co-nationals' living in a different country), with its peculiar spelling, stayed in use in German international law discourse well into the 1960s.[162]

3.4.1 *Intervention in Nazi International Law Theory*

The question of the legality of intervention for very specific purposes interested Nazi lawyers for obvious reasons. It was not only that the German persecution of its Jewish population could spark calls for 'humanitarian intervention' to protect them, however isolated and fruitless they would prove to be. In aiming to realise, or, more precisely, re-establish the (original) 'national unity of a people' – as opposed to the political unity of the state – as its cornerstone, Nazi ideology also called for interventionary rights to reach its goals.

International law doctrine gained remarkably in popularity after the rise of the National Socialists to power, yet no coherent 'National Socialist theory of

---

[158] Friedrich Berber, *Lehrbuch des Völkerrechts*, Vol. I, Munich: C. H. Beck 1960, p. 190, my translation.

[159] Sauer 1948, p. 185.

[160] Helmuth Krasberg, *Die konnationale Intervention*, Dissertation, Manuscript, Münster 1944. This author found no further information about Helmuth Krasberg. The dissertation, overseen by Sauer himself, is not usually cited in German works on intervention in international law.

[161] Arguably little chance existed any of his readers would turn to the referenced work, as it was not actually published according to German rules for dissertations and the only copy still in existence may very well be the only copy which ever existed, the 120 typewritten pages of Krasberg's manuscript that are still on file with University of Münster.

[162] The 'normal' way to spell the term would be 'ko-national', but the spelling 'konnationale intervention' can be found in: Heinz Haedrich, 'Intervention', in: Hans-Jürgen Schlochauer (ed.), *Wörterbuch des Völkerrechts*, Vol. II, 2nd ed., Berlin: de Gruyter 1961, p. 146. See also: Sauer 1952, p. 464 with fn. 8.

international law' developed.[163] The most influential work of Third Reich international law theory, Carl Schmitt's 'Völkerrechtliche Großraumordnung mit Interventionsverbot für raumfremde Mächte' was published only in 1939, shortly before Germany invaded Poland and thus initiated World War II.[164] Until then, and possibly even afterwards, it was certainly not always easy for lawyers to figure out what type of international law National Socialism required, though its most fervent supporters quickly infused their language with the appropriate Nazi vocabulary, the LINGUA TERTII IMPERI,[165] and included some almost random anti-Semitic remarks that seem to serve very little other purpose than to show the author's racist position in their arguments.[166]

Right from the beginning, however, National Socialist theories of international law identified positivism as their enemy. They sought to overcome the apparent incompatibility of law and justice positivism was considered to have brought about, and yearned to return to a law consistent with what was seen as international law's roots, rational natural law and what is 'at the core of a human being' ('in dem Inneren der Menschen'). Nazi constructs centred around an 'ethnic' ('völkisch') idea of international law, in which ideas of race, nation and ethnicity formed a specific territorial order (Raumordnung, Völkerordnung). The point of international law, then, in this vision, was to enable the realisation of a 'natural' order among peoples. Law was to be the 'expression' of this 'natural' order and justice its consequence, not the result of a law-making process.[167]

As Detlef Vagts put it in his still seminal study of 'International Law in the Third Reich', National Socialist thinking on international law reversed the priorities of the relations between the law and the state, putting not the state, but the ethnically defined 'Volk' at the centre. At the core of National Socialist theories of law therefore were values and ideas of a 'natural' order, mythical constructs of 'people' and (their) 'territory'. With ideological connotations that cannot be adequately conveyed in translation, the terms 'Volk' and 'Lebensraum' draw on other racial constructs of the international legal order. Their use in Nazi international law was firmly rooted in nineteenth century concepts of international law, but also in the

---

[163] Peter K. Steck, *Zwischen Volk und Staat*, Baden-Baden: Nomos 2003, p. 1.

[164] William Hooker translates this 'somewhat clunky title' as 'International Law of Large Spaces with a Prohibition on Intervention by External Powers', see: William Hooker, *Carl Schmitt's International Thought*, Cambridge University Press 2009, p. 127, fn 4. Detlef Vagts translates this 'Grossraum' as 'Grand Space', see Detlef F. Vagts, 'International Law in the Third Reich', *American Journal of International Law* 1990, 84, p. 689.

[165] Vagts 1990, p. 686.

[166] e.g. Carl Schmitt, *Völkerrechtliche Großraumordnung mit Interventionsverbot für raumfremde Mächte*, Berlin: Duncker & Humblot 1991, reprint of the 4th ed., originally published in 1941, pp. 78–79. On Carl Schmitt and his anti-semitism, see: Raphael Gross, *Carl Schmitt und die Juden*, Frankfurt am Main: Suhrkamp 2005.

[167] All quotes in this passage from: Reinhard Höhn, 'Volk, Staat und Recht', text from 1938, cited here according to the reprint in: Herlinde Pauer-Studer and Julian Fink (eds.), *Rechtfertigungen des Unrechts*, Berlin: Suhrkamp Verlag 2014, p. 161. Translation by the author.

timeless idea of a right to self-determination. As Alfred Verdross (1890–1980), the respected international law professor and later a judge at the European Court for Human Rights, wrote in the first edition of what was already then one of the most respected German language textbooks on international law:

> There are no human beings as such, only human beings of a certain kind. The highest natural human species is the 'Volkstum' (national identity), so that every human being belongs to a certain type of national identity. (. . .) The 'Volkstum' (national identity) is the natural foundation of all culture. The state needs to reflect this state of affairs in its political setup, as the state by its very nature provides a 'civitas perfecta' (Aristotle) for his citizens, but can only perform this function if it allows its citizens to thrive according to their natural capabilities and character. Because of the natural differences between different species of humans, this can only be achieved in the 'Volksgemeinschaft' (in their people). (. . .) In their people, humans are naturally connected to other humans of the same species, the state is the political union of human beings under distinctive laws.[168]

In Verdross' words, the goal of National Socialism was a 'reform' of the legal regime of Europe of the day, as it was perceived to be in conflict with US President Wilson's famous 'Fourteen Points', in particular on self-determination. It was thus necessary to restructure Europe in accordance with the requirements of the cultural differences between peoples and the right to life of all peoples.[169] Anthony Carty has suggested that Verdross' association with National Socialism was not 'a short-lived, purely opportunistic or otherwise "weak" bowing or bending to circumstances'. The 'apparently cursory approval of National Socialism in the 1937 textbook' is, according to Carty, 'rooted in a deep commitment to German nationalism'.[170] Verdross portrayed National Socialism as 'respecting international law as a prevailing order of the world' with the 'multiplicity of peoples'.[171] Like Sauer, Verdross stressed the importance of peoples and their rights, and attached to this framework the pre-1914 doctrine of the fundamental rights of States, thereby 'radically subjectivizing international law and destabilizing it by relying on a doctrine of absolute State sovereignty'.[172] According to Verdross' early critic Ernst Engelbert (1909–2010), who had to flee Nazi Germany because he was a communist, this combination gave rein to a free and arbitrary and expansive National Socialist foreign policy.[173] Yet compared to more openly National Socialist authors, Verdross stops short of

---

[168] Verdross 1937, pp. 39–41. Translation by the author.

[169] Verdross 1937, p. 29.

[170] Anthony Carty, 'Alfred Verdross and Othmar Spann: German Romantic Nationalism, National Socialism and International Law', European Journal of International Law 1995, 6(1), p. 80.

[171] Verdross, 1937, p. 29: 'Mit der Vielheit der Völker anerkennt der Nationalsozialismus das Völkerrecht als eine dauernde Ordnung der Welt'.

[172] Ernst Engelbert, 'Les bases ideologiques de la nouvelle conception de droit international de M. Alfred von Verdross', Revue générale de droit international public 1939, 46, pp. 39 and 44, as quoted by Carty 1995.

[173] Engelbert 1939, p. 42, as quoted by Carty 1995.

claiming historic precedents for Nazi Germany interventionary rights, only mentioning so-called human rights in passing. His main argument in this context was to claim that state practice in the nineteenth century had repeatedly allowed for European Great Power intervention in the affairs of Turkey for the protection of Turkish Christian citizens and this practice had in turn led to a doctrine that allowed for intervention on grounds of humanity in exceptional cases (which Verdross calls 'intervention d'humanité').[174]

The central legal concept of genuinely National Socialist visions of international law was (non-)intervention, not sovereignty, as it strove to achieve an international order more in line with an allegedly existing (natural) order and in line with the alleged demands of the self-determination of peoples. An early work on intervention in international law in the period of National Socialist reign in Germany thus proclaimed a theory of non-intervention based on 'racially healthy nationalism and ethnic self-restraint'.[175] Based substantially only on the works of Carl Schmitt and speeches made by Adolf Hitler, the author, Ernst Bockhoff (1911–1996),[176] created a vision of international law based on a 'principle of peculiarity, racial self-restraint and the self-fulfilment of peoples'; a proper order among the peoples was, in this view, a precondition to international law.[177] Bockhoff's conclusion that only a strict principle of non-intervention was in line with the demands of a National Socialist concept of international law,[178] however, soon proved to be too limiting for the expansionist drive of National Socialist dreams to restructure Europe according to 'ethnic' (völkisch) principles.

The idea of the 'Ethnic German' (Volksdeutsche) was central to the National Socialist project of proclaiming a united (German) people across international borders. It allowed the Third Reich to define who was an 'ethnic German', empowering only the state, not any German-speaking minority.[179] It also empowered lawyers to deny the most fundamental rights to Germany's Jewish population. On the level of international law, the establishment of 'rights of peoples' (Volksgruppenrechte) and the definition of Germany as an 'ethnic' (völkisch) state served as the entry point to 'eliminate foreign elements from the ethnic community

---

[174] Verdross 1937, p. 237.

[175] Ernst Bockhoff, *Die Intervention im Völkerrecht*, Würzburg: Buchdruckerei Richard Mayr 1935, pp. 42–43.

[176] Bockhoff would go on to publish with Hans Frank (1900–1946), who was found guilty of war crimes and crimes against humanity at the Nuremberg trials and sentenced to death. In 1934, he was already a minister without portfolio in Hitler's government and became Governor-General of the General Government of Poland, overseeing the segregation of the Jews into ghettos, especially the enormous Warsaw ghetto, and the use of Polish civilians as forced labour.

[177] Bockhoff 1935, p. 19.

[178] Bockhoff 1935, p. 43.

[179] Andreas Strippel, *NS-Volkstumspolitik und die Neuordnung Europas*, Paderborn: Ferdinand Schöningh 2011, p. 33.

of the state and allocate them to their own life circle"[180] – or to their death. Nazi international lawyers criticised traditional concepts of 'minority protection' for failing to honour the 'cultural existential rights of ethnic groups' and claimed, as Otto Koellreutter (1883–1972) and the aforementioned Gürke did, that the origins of minority protection lay in Jewish demands, which 'necessarily put a burden' on such rights, as the Jews were 'a substantially different group than the nations of Europe'.[181] The alternative concept of 'rights of peoples' was tied to racial concepts of ethnic purity and allowed to 'racially segregate' German Jews from the majority population through legislation but deny them minority rights.[182]

3.4.2 'Völkische' (Ethnic) and 'Konnationale' (Co-National) Intervention

Nazi international law theory attached two differently named, but similar types, of justifications for interventions to familiar narratives of interventions in the Ottoman Empire. As Nazi Professor of International Law, Gustav A. Walz (1897–1948)[183] put it, the theory developed 'not as a simple parallel to the state practice of intervention in the 19th and early 20th century', but as the right of the 'the ethnic state to ethnic intervention on the territory of the state of residence irregularly interfering in the rights of ethnic groups settled on his territory by force or through discriminatory laws'.[184] This right to 'ethnic' (or 'co-national') intervention built upon the gradual development of a right to intervene on behalf of 'co-national' minorities in third states rooted in always contentious efforts to provide a theoretical backbone to Italian unification (the Risorgimiento) in the second half of the nineteenth century,[185] where Nazi theorists also saw the roots of the idea of 'humanitarian intervention'.[186]

In 1937, Hermann Mosler (1912–2001) – who went on to become a distinguished international lawyer and a highly respected judge at the International Court of Justice – published his doctoral dissertation, 'Die Intervention im Völkerrecht',

---

[180] Hugelmann, 'Der völkische Staat und der Reichsgedanke' 1940, p. 182.
[181] Norbert Gürke, Grundzüge des Völkerrechts, 2nd ed. (Otto Koellreutter ed.), Berlin: Industrieverlag Spaeth & Linde 1942, p. 51: 'Die Schwäche der allgemeinen Minderheitenschutzbestimmungen lag vor allem darin, dass sie die kulturellen Lebensrechte völkischer Gruppen mit formaldemokratischen Mitteln lösen wollten. (...) Auch die enge Verknüpfung des Minderheitenschutzes mit den Emanzipationswünschen der Ostjuden – Wilson berichtet in seinen Memoiren, der Minderheitenschutz sei vornehmlich auf Drängen der Juden geschaffen worden – mußte dieses Recht belasten; denn die Juden sind eine wesentlich andersartige Gruppe als die Nationalitäten Europas'.
[182] Friedrich Wilhelm von Rauchhaupt, Völkerrecht, Munich: Verlag Fritz & Joseph Voglrieder 1936, p. 57.
[183] Ziegler 2007, p. 210, calls Walz a 'committed Nazi' ('Überzeugungstäter').
[184] Gustav A. Walz, Völkerrechtsordnung und Nationalsozialismus, Munich: Eher Verlag, München 1942, p. 116.
[185] Hagedorn 1933, p. 102.
[186] Gerhard Ostermeyer, Die Intervention in der Völkerrechtstheorie und -praxis, Würzburg: Konrad Triltsch Verlag 1940, p. 47.

which contained a commitment to the right of the 'ethnic state' to act to protect the minority rights of 'ethnic co-nationals' with the citizenship of third countries, as a statement on policy rather than law.[187] Mathias Schmoeckel has already noted that Mosler took the then still unique position, contrary to all other major writers on international law, of allowing for a right to intervene on behalf of ethnic (völkisch) minorities for the purpose of reorganising Eastern Europe.[188] In 1939, Ellery C. Stowell reviewed Mosler's book for the *American Journal on International Law*, and found it 'interesting' to note the statement 'that intervention on the ground of humanity is today recognized when occurrences within another state are in blatant opposition to the generally recognized principles of humanity'.[189] Decades later, on the occasion of the fiftieth anniversary of Mosler's PhD, the work was praised for clearly stating that only limited legal grounds for intervention existed under international law, and for 'boldly' including the right to intervene in the case of a persecuted religious minority[190] – apparently because this could have made it legal under international law for other states to intervene for the protection of the Jewish population of Germany.[191] While Mosler's text did not belie such a reading it was at best ambivalent in this regard.[192] Mosler repositioned the question of the admissibility of intervention along ethnic lines, finding that 'ethnicity' trumped 'justice'. The 'völkische' (ethnic) ideology is considered to establish the principle of non-intervention into the affairs of other states as the cornerstone of an international law explicitly based on a modern type of natural law, whereas interventions in the name of justice are considered inadmissible.[193] Minority rights are also no basis for any justified intervention, according to Mosler, as no such rights could yet be considered to be established as legal rights,[194] though Mosler saw, quoting Hitler,[195] Nazi Germany as working toward establishing legal rights for minorities under international law.[196] In Mosler's construct, National Socialist ideas of a reorganisation of international law along ethnic lines ('Volk als Ordnungsprinzip')[197] work to strengthen minority rights, though only those based on bloodlines. For the case of 'alien racial minorities' ('rassefremde Volksgruppe'), living scattered among the

---

[187] Mosler 1937, p. 80.
[188] Mathias Schmoeckel, *Die Großraumtheorie*, Berlin: Duncker & Humblot 1994, p. 103, referring to Mosler 1937, p. 80.
[189] Ellery C. Stowell, 'Book Review: Die Intervention im Völkerrecht, by Hermann Mosler', *American Journal of International Law* 1939, 33, p. 241, referring to Mosler, p. 63.
[190] Christian Tomuschat, *Rede zum 50. Doktorjubiläum*, Bonn: Bouvier 1988, p. 10, referring to Mosler 1937, p. 66. See also Vagts 1990, p. 691, note 157.
[191] Tomuschat 1988, p. 10.
[192] Felix Lange, *Praxisorientierung und Gemeinschaftskonzeption: Hermann Mosler als Wegbereiter der westdeutschen Völkerrechtswissenschaft nach 1945*, Springer: Berlin 2017, p. 106.
[193] Mosler 1937, pp. 80, 54.
[194] Mosler 1937, p. 56.
[195] Mosler 1937, p. 78.
[196] Mosler 1937, p. 80.
[197] Mosler 1937, p. 79.

dominant ethnic groups, no case could be made for any corresponding legal right as a minority, and, thus, there were no grounds for intervention.[198] It seems clear that this passage refers to the German racial persecution of its Jewish citizens, especially considering the fact that Mosler separates the case of an intervention into the racial policies of a state from the question of 'humanitarian intervention' proper. Mosler's position on the legality of 'humanitarian intervention' is based on his allegiance to natural law,[199] and clearly allows interventions where a state violates the 'elemental laws of humanity, the violation of which is considered illegal by the unanimous verdict of all civilised nations and which are therefore norms integral to human nature', as the violation of the order itself justifies intervention for its preservation.[200] Mosler admitted that this position would possibly allow intervention in the cases where he otherwise deems it illegal: 'Intervention in the interest of humanity is the elastic principle that upholds the law of the community of peoples against too rigid an insistence on sovereignty. This principle alone would justify intervention in the aforementioned cases whenever they are accompanied by deliberate and brutal violations of the laws of humanity'.[201] Mosler saw another potential basis for guarding the application of the principle of non-intervention in the formation of 'circles of international law' (Völkerrechtskreis), that is, in areas in which a particular form of international law applied. Mosler gave as examples the British Empire and 'the political order of America';[202] referencing the National Socialist international law Professor Norbert Gürke in this context,[203] however, he suggested that Eastern Europe, territorially reorganised in accordance with National Socialism's 'ethnic' (völkisch) ideas of a 'natural' order, could also be a potential candidate for such a 'circle of international law'.

On 20 February 1938, Adolf Hitler referred publicly to the 'ten million' ethnic Germans living in other countries and warned that the Reich would not 'idly watch their persecution'.[204] Nazi international law theorists interpreted this as the proclamation of the right to intervene to protect those ethnic Germans and quickly deluded themselves into considering this right as 'practically recognised' by other countries.[205] Carl Schmitt (1888–1985), the Nazi it is apparently still OK to consider only 'controversial', took Hitler's speech as proof of a 'real principle of international law' that allowed the Third Reich to act for the protection of ethnic Germans with

---

[198] Mosler 1937, p. 58.
[199] Mosler 1937, pp. 42–47.
[200] Mosler 1937, p. 63.
[201] Mosler 1937, p. 64.
[202] Mosler 1937, p. 60.
[203] Mosler 1937, p. 60, note 78, referencing Norbert Gürke, Volk und Völkerrecht, Tübingen: Mohr Siebeck 1936, p. 91.
[204] Mark Mazower, Hitler's Empire, New York: The Penguin Press 2008, p. 54.
[205] Axel Freiherr von Freytagh-Loringhoven, Deutsche Außenpolitik 1933–1939, Berlin: Verlagsanstalt Otto Stolberg 1939, p. 160.

foreign nationality.[206] After the Munich Agreement of 28 September 1938, that conviction became even more pronounced.[207]

At the University of Münster, Karl Gottfried Hugelmann (1879–1959), considered the 'co-national' intervention one of the most significant phenomena of the contemporary international law of nations/nationalities and decided to make it a special research focus.[208] The main fruit of this research project seems to have been Krasberg's aforementioned dissertation, which according to its author was originally started in 1938, but not completed until 1944.[209] Hugelmann himself wrote extensively on the subject and spoke of the replacement of the human rights of the French revolution by the people's right to life as a principle for the territorial order in Europe.[210] In Carl Schmitt's 'Großraumtheorie', considered 'sage, if subject to some clarifications' by Hugelmann,[211] the focus was less on justifying intervention, than on the prohibition of intervention by states external to the 'Großraum' created by Schmitt and modelled to fit with the Third Reich's foreign policy of its time – an interpretation Schmitt later, albeit unconvincingly, denied.[212] Taking the Monroe Doctrine as a starting point, Schmitt used the apparent demise of the traditional 'Eurocentrism' of international law, its 'empty universalism' to create 'spheres of law', which were to be inhabited by homogeneous ethnic peoples and off-limits to foreign powers.[213] In this vision, a predominant power (the Reich) exists within a larger territorial space (the Großraum), in which it essentially acts as hegemon,[214] but the Reich is defined in its exclusively German ethnic dimension with the obvious intent of delegitimising intervention on more universal grounds.[215] Schmitt even refers to a contemporary work on the 'problem of intervention',[216] which concluded that intervention on emergency (moral) grounds was a remnant of the destroyed European international order of the nineteenth century and a necessary instrument to rebuild Europe's 'community of nations'.[217]

One of the main aims of Nazi international law theory was the transformation of international law from a 'law between nations' to a 'law between peoples', from 'Völkerrecht' to a 'Recht der Völker', as the title of Hans K. E. L. Keller's

---

[206] Schmitt 1991, p. 46.
[207] Hugelmann, *Volk und Staat im Wandel deutschen Schicksals* 1940, p. 189.
[208] Hugelmann, *Volk und Staat im Wandel deutschen Schicksals* 1940, p. 183, fn. 1.
[209] Krasberg 1944, preface, without page number.
[210] Hugelmann, *Volk und Staat im Wandel deutschen Schicksals* 1940, p. 189.
[211] Hugelmann, *Volk und Staat im Wandel deutschen Schicksals* 1940, p. 197, my translation.
[212] Carl Schmitt, *Antworten in Nürnberg*, Berlin: Duncker & Humblot 2000, pp. 68–78, with comments by editor Helmut Quaritsch, pp. 78–82 and 115–120.
[213] Schmitt 1991.
[214] Hooker 2009, p. 133. On Schmitt's 'Großraumtheorie' in general, see Schmoeckel 1994.
[215] Schmitt 1991, pp. 49–50.
[216] Schmitt 1991, p. 50, fn. 60.
[217] Ostermeyer 1940, p. 53.

(1908–1970) *Das Recht der Völker*,[218] published between 1938 and 1941, made clear. Schmitt had praised the work of German theorists that established a right of ethnic groups ('Volksgruppenrecht') as distinct from an 'individualist-liberal' concept of minority protection.[219] A corresponding right of intervention was only the logical next step, or, as Nazi Professor Gustav A. Walz put it, 'With the recognition as the original ethnic people (Urvolk) as the original ethnic community in the world of international politics and law, intervention as a legal institution in international law gains new dimensions. National territory and original ethnic people will hardly ever correspond'.[220] The consequences found their clearest expression in the aforementioned dissertation by Krasberg. It is worth reproducing Krasberg's argument in detail here, as it is not easily accessible anywhere[221] and is representative of strains of German legal thinking on intervention even beyond World War II.[222]

'Co-national intervention' is defined by Krasberg as the intervention of a state with a particular relation to a specific ethnic group for the protection of an ethnic group of the same variation, living in a third state under the rule of a different ethnic group. He considered it a legal instrument of particular international law in South-eastern and Central Europe, as recognised through the Munich Agreement of 1938 and the events leading up to Munich.[223] As Krasberg notes in his exposition on the question of the legality of 'co-national' intervention, the interventions of the Balkan States in the affairs of the Christian population of the Ottoman Empire may have rested on the *motive* of protecting 'co-nationals' (though these were, in fact, more likely 'co-religious' citizens, their nations only created through the wars against the Ottoman Empire), yet only the National Socialist conception of citizenship based on ethnicity, not nationality, allowed the 'motive' to be treated as a legal right.[224] The term 'co-national' holds a meaning similar to the more widely used term 'völkisch' (which translates most commonly as ethnic, though the German term places it more accurately in a distinctively German mythology of 'Volk' and 'Lebensraum'), yet it obfuscates the radical consequences of an intervention for the purposes of achieving the 'co-national' goal. Krasberg places the evolution of his doctrine of 'co-national intervention' in the context of the perceived failure of the minority protection system put in place by the League of Nations. Tracing a political history of interventions in the nineteenth century as exceptions to the legal principle of non-intervention, Krasberg seeks to prove the evolution of a certain 'Ordnungsidee' (idea of order) as a limitation on sovereignty for the states forming this 'order',

[218] Hans K. E. L. Keller, *Das Recht der Völker, Vol. I*, Berlin: Standard Verlag P. H. Müller-Rath 1938; Keller 1941.

[219] Schmitt 1991, p. 43.

[220] Walz 1942, p. 115.

[221] Only one copy of the dissertation seems to have survived (if more were ever printed) and is available on Microfiche through the German library system.

[222] See Sauer 1948, p. 185.

[223] Krasberg 1944, p. 106.

[224] Krasberg 1944, p. 25.

insofar as the states participating in this order recognise this role.[225] Part of this evolutionary tale is the development of a 'true law of ethnic groups' ('echtes Volksgruppenrecht') as the fulfilment of minority protection, transforming the state from a means in itself to a 'means with a purpose' – the fulfilment of self-determination through co-national intervention and the (legal) recognition of this development with the 1938 Munich conference.[226] States like Czechoslovakia had failed – or so Krasberg claimed – to fulfil their obligations of minority protection and this failure, constructed as a breach of international law, gave rise to the right of 'co-national intervention'.[227]

The historical example of a forgotten Nazi theorist of international law is not merely anecdotal, as his attempts to unify the concept of a '(regional) community of nations' with the doctrine of sovereign equality through the 'existential rights of peoples' ('Lebensrechte der Völker') show. Seen through the eyes, for example, of an international lawyer working in 1940, when Krasberg had to stop working on his dissertation as he was called to serve in the German army,[228] it may very well have seemed as if the German efforts had ushered in a new era for international law in a different way than it would appear after 1945.[229] As Mark Mazower has characterised these times: 'Munich marked the moment when the Third Reich took over from the British, the French and the League of Nations as regional arbiter of central Europe'.[230]

Historians of international law in Germany do not agree on when or if National Socialist theories on international law broke substantially from other arguments on law. Some claim that a noticeable break from traditional strains of argument occurred by 1938,[231] whereas others consider the shift to be more gradual.[232] Yet the radicalism of some of the 'solutions' offered by Nazi concepts of international law cannot overshadow the fact that a substantial amount of the writings produced during the area of the Third Reich continued to be based on sources and arguments familiar to any international lawyer. This remained so almost to the very end of the regime, as Krasberg's work demonstrates (he defended his thesis in February 1944).[233] The narratives created by Nazi international lawyers to sustain their arguments may have deviated at some point from more acceptable interpretations of history, but this did not make their uses of history categorically different from other

---

[225] Krasberg 1944, pp. 9–12.

[226] Krasberg 1944, pp. 45–48, 54, 84.

[227] Krasberg 1944, p. 37.

[228] Krasberg 1944, p. 113.

[229] E.g. Schmitt 1940, pp. 267–278.

[230] Mazower 2008, p. 56.

[231] Rüdiger Wolfrum, 'Nationalsozialismus und Völkerrecht', in: Franz Jürgen Säcker (ed.), *Recht und Rechtslehre im Nationalsozialismus*, Baden-Baden: Nomos 1992, p. 91.

[232] Norman Paech and Gerhard Stuby, *Völkerrecht und Machtpolitik in den internationalen Beziehungen*, Baden-Baden: Nomos 1994, p. 189.

[233] Krasberg 1944, p. 113.

such arguments. Attempts to construct the declarations of war by France and the United Kingdom in response to the German attack on Poland as breaches of international law and the Statute of the League of Nations in particular[234] are an example of this and, while they may not have been particularly convincing, they certainly do not fall into a different legal category than attempts to justify America's entry into World War II post-facto as a 'humanitarian intervention'.[235]

In Krasberg's narrative, Munich 1938 does not represent the step into the abyss of the Holocaust and World War II, but a political and legal step towards recognising the legitimacy of German claims to a need for protection of its 'co-nationals' in Czechoslovakia: an instrument of 'particular customary law', recognised by 'four Great Powers and three other states',[236] and a commitment to the protection of ethnic groups and self-determination.[237] The 'co-national intervention' in this context is an instrument to restore ('ethnic') order to the 'ethnically linked regions of Europe',[238] and it is considered legal, because it accords with the basic concept of a legal order and the legal conscience ('Rechtsbewusstsein') of at least a regional community of states, where it is particular customary law.[239] At least initially, 'co-national' intervention is (only) an intervention in the diplomatic sense and, while Krasberg does stop short of explicitly considering the German aggression against Poland a case of a legal 'co-national' intervention,[240] it is clear to him and his readers that any such intervention may lead to war.[241]

Krasberg's work, now only accessible as a microfiche copy of the typewritten original, breathes the spirit of a nation at war, but neither its style, nor its tone, register a clear break from less compromised theories of international law. The author probably could have cited Hermann Mosler's *Die Intervention im Völkerrecht* more frequently than he does,[242] as it covers much of the same ground and draws a similar conclusion. But it is an ironic accident of history that Mosler's work was held in such high regard that his alma mater organised a celebration for its fiftieth anniversary when the contents of the work could hardly warrant such accolades in Krasberg's case. The idea of particular spheres of validity of certain norms of international law, central to both works, was not uncommon then, nor is it uncommon now. Nor was the idea that it was somehow a moral, progressive development

---

[234] Bilfinger 1940.

[235] Tesón 2005, p. 227.

[236] Krasberg 1944, p. 89. The same point is made for what he terms 'völkische' (ethnic) intervention by Walz 1942, p. 116.

[237] Krasberg 1944, p. 90.

[238] Krasberg 1944, p. 108: Ein 'Ordnungsgedanke' für die 'völkisch verzahnten europäischen Gebiete'.

[239] Krasberg 1944, p. 91.

[240] Krasberg 1944, p. 100.

[241] Krasberg 1944, p. 109.

[242] The book is cited only five times. The author also cites Leo Strisower and Karl Strupp, as well as Hermann von Rotteck.

to re-organise Eastern Europe along 'ethnically' (völkisch) defined populations particularly novel, as the popularity of the idea of 'population transfers' in the early twentieth century clearly demonstrates.[243] Yet Nazi international lawyers combined these ideas for a justification of Nazi 'population strategies' that were presented as contributions to an 'ethnic international pacification' ('völkische internationale Befriedung').[244] From this perspective, genocide, as Georg Erler wrote after the war (his Nazi credentials not having stood in the way of his career), was indeed but one of three ways that Germany dealt with the 'minority problem' – the other two being the establishment of the law of ethnic groups ('Volksgruppenrecht') and population transfer.[245]

[243] Özsu 2015.

[244] Walz 1942, p. 110. A similar point is made by Krasberg 1944, p. 108.

[245] Georg Erler, 'Minderheitenrecht', in: Hans-Jürgen Schlochauer (ed.), *Wörterbuch des Völkerrecht*, Vol. II, 2nd ed., Berlin: De Gruyter 1961, p. 533.

4

The World after 1945

4.1 INTRODUCTION

On 26 July 1946, in court room 600 of the majestic 'Palace of Justice' (Justizpalast) in Nuremburg, Germany, Sir Hartley Shawcross (1902–2003), the British Chief prosecutor at the International Military Tribunal, presented his closing arguments on the 187th day in the case against the twenty-two high-ranking Nazi defendants, including Hermann Göring and Rudolf Hess. The British team had met with French professor René Cassin (1887–1976) in preparation for the landmark trial,[1] and Shawcross' speech had in large part been drafted by British law professor Hersch Lauterpacht, though he went off-script to include the charge of 'genocide', the term coined by Polish legal activist Raphael Lemkin (1900–1959).[2] As the British case also covered the charges of 'Crimes against Peace', Shawcross' arguments would have also touched upon the work of Soviet international law scholar Aron N. Trainin (1883–1957), author of 'Hitlerite Responsibility under International Law', a small pamphlet that apparently had been read by many in preparation for the trial in Nuremberg[3] and which, uncharacteristically for Soviet discourse by the end of the war and after, was very explicit in its treatment of the Jewish identity of many of the victims of the Holocaust.[4]

Nuremberg represents the commitment to individual responsibility for crimes against international law and is thus generally seen as a symbol of progress in international law. In this spirit, Shawcross' engagement with the works of four leading European international lawyers, who were also Jewish, in the wake of the genocide of the Jews of Europe, led to another 'progressive' statement on the contemporary state of international law. In his opening address, Shawcross had

---

[1] Mark Lewis, *The Birth of the New Justice*, Oxford University Press 2014, p. 167.
[2] Philippe Sands, *East West Street*, London: Weidenfeld & Nicolson 2016, p. 348.
[3] Michael R. Marrus, *The Nuremburg War Crimes Trial 1945–46*, Boston: Bedford 1997, p. 48.
[4] Trainin 1945, pp. 58–59.

already stated that 'the rights of humanitarian intervention on behalf of the rights of man, trampled upon by a state in a manner shocking the sense of mankind, [had] long been considered to form part of the recognized law of nations'.[5] But now the British prosecutor went even further. After an introductory statement proclaiming that 'absolute sovereignty in the old sense is, very fortunately, a thing of the past', he then went on to state:

[T]he nations adhering to the Charter of this Tribunal have felt it proper and necessary in the interest of civilization to say that these things [like murder, extermination, enslavement, persecution on political, racial, or economic grounds] even if done in accordance with the laws of the German State, as created and ruled by these men and their ringleader, were, when committed with the intention of affecting the international community – that is in connection with the other crimes charged – not mere matters of domestic concern but crimes against the law of nations. I do not minimize the significance for the future of the political and jurisprudential doctrine which is here implied. Normally international law concedes that it is for the state to decide how it shall treat its own nationals; it is a matter of domestic jurisdiction. (. . .) Yet international law has in the past made some claim that there is a limit to the omnipotence of the state and that the individual human being, the ultimate unit of all law, is not disentitled to the protection of mankind when the state tramples upon his rights in a manner which outrages the conscience of mankind. Grotius, the founder of international law, had some notion of that principle when – at a time when the distinction between the just and the unjust war was more clearly accepted than was the case in the nineteenth century – he described as just a war undertaken for the purpose of defending the subjects of a foreign state from injuries inflicted by their ruler. He affirmed, with reference to atrocities committed by tyrants against their subjects, that intervention is justified for 'the right of social connection is not cut off in such a case'. The same idea was expressed by John Westlake, the most distinguished of British international lawyers, when he said:

'It is idle to argue in such cases that the duty of neighboring peoples is to look quietly on. Laws are made for men and not creatures of the imagination and they must not create or tolerate for them situations which are beyond endurance.'

The same view was acted upon by the European powers which in time past intervened in order to protect the Christian subjects of Turkey against cruel persecution. The fact is that the right of humanitarian intervention by war is not a novelty in international law – can intervention by judicial process then be illegal? The Charter of this Tribunal embodies a beneficent principle – much more limited than some would like it to be – and it gives warning for the future. I say, and repeat again, gives warning for the future, to dictators and tyrants masquerading as a state that if, in order to strengthen or further their crimes against the community of

---

[5] Sir Hartley Shawcross, Statement on 12th day of the Nuremberg Trial, 4 December 1945, available at: http://avalon.law.yale.edu/imt/12-04-45.asp, last accessed 1 March 2019.

nations, they debase the sanctity of man in their own country they act at their peril, for they affront the international law of mankind.[6]

Shawcross' use of the alleged legality of military 'humanitarian intervention' in the past to proclaim the legality of an 'intervention by law' now and in the future, is exemplary for the approach to 'humanitarian intervention' in the years after World War II, for this backward-looking vision of the future would dictate the representation of the topic in the years to come. It is also a self-serving contribution to the counterfactual narrative of 'humanitarian intervention' as a response to the Shoah, exonerating the Allies from any accusations of indifference to the plight of the victims of Nazis and their collaborators in general, as well as the criminals on trial. The Shoah existed in Nuremberg mainly as an accessory to war crimes, and the trial exhibited only a primitive analysis of the nature of the Holocaust. As Donald Bloxham points out: 'There is no indication that the accumulated evidence about Auschwitz imposed itself on the consciousness of the non-Soviet judges as constituting anything other than a particularly bad example of a "concentration camp", which was exactly how the Americans had portrayed it'.[7]

In general, the prosecution presented its clearly novel case of bringing the leading war criminals to justice as deeply rooted in the customs and practices of 'civilization', which Lawrence Douglas has characterised as an attempt 'to deliver an argument more consonant with the ideals of liberal legality' than the solid positivist argument of the courts' jurisdiction by resting on 'the exercise of the sovereign legislative power by the countries to which the German Reich unconditionally surrendered', as the Tribunal itself noted.[8] In this way, Nuremberg attempted to shield international law from any charges of complicity to the crimes on trial by offering the guard of sovereignty, as previously rested upon by politicians during the War. Yet the compelling contradiction of shielding international law from complicity in crimes that previously had not been considered crimes under international law remains unresolved to this day. This 'immunisation' of international law against charges of complicity in genocide can also be seen in the way genocide as a legal concept was introduced to the field of international law in the 1940s. As is well known, Raphael Lemkin coined the term in his book 'Axis Rule in Occupied Europe', first published in 1944.[9] He used it, as he put it, to describe 'an old practice in its modern development'.[10] Lemkin, who had started exploring the realities of

---

[6]   Sir Hartley Shawcross, Closing Arguments on 187th day of the Nuremberg Trial, Afternoon Session, 26 July 1946, available at: http://avalon.law.yale.edu/imt/07-26-46.asp, last accessed 1 March 2019.
[7]   Donald Bloxham, *Genocide on Trial*, Oxford University Press 2001, p. 107.
[8]   Lawrence Douglas, *The Memory of Judgement*, New Haven: Yale University Press 2001, p. 84.
[9]   Raphael Lemkin, *Axis Rule in Occupied Europe*, 1st ed. published by Carnegie Endowment for International Peace, Washington, 1944, cited hereinafter from the 2nd ed., Clark: The Lawbook Exchange 2008.
[10] Lemkin 2008, p. 79.

such genocidal practices with regard to the treatment of the Armenians under Ottoman rule, recognised that the Holocaust represented a conceptual shift that had to be reflected when thinking about it in legal terms. His reasoning was based on the view that 'never before' had a genocide occurred that was conducted with such 'an elaborate, almost scientific, system'[11] – the often heard 'never again' was therefore preceded by a 'never before'. But when the term 'genocide' entered the world of diplomatic conferences and law making by states, all sense that something momentous was happening, that the crimes of the Holocaust required a conceptual shift from (and for) international law, disappeared. Nowhere is this more obvious than in the preamble and Article 1 of the United Nations Convention for the Prevention and Punishment if the Crime of Genocide of 1948 and its evolution. The General Assembly, in its 1946 resolution that paved the way for the Genocide Convention, not only stated that 'many instances' of 'the crime of genocide' had occurred in the past, but also 'affirmed' that 'genocide is a crime under international law which the civilized world condemns'.[12] From this, it might be inferred that the 'many instances' of the 'crime of genocide' were not committed by the 'civilized world', but that leaves the questions as to which instances the resolution refers to, and what exactly the phrase 'the civilized world' represents.

The 'affirmation' of the criminality of genocide already diminishes the creative power of naming the 'crime without a name'. During the deliberations within the United Nations system, the 'affirmation' was turned into a 'confirmation', interestingly enough by a Belgian diplomat Raphael Lemkin considered hostile to the whole project of the Convention.[13] This led to the rather paradoxical result of the Convention in the final text confirming (not establishing) the criminality of genocide in international law and expressly stating that this applies to times of both peace and war (Article 1 of the Convention), whereas the exact opposite view had been held while the crimes that gave rise to the genocide convention were still being committed, namely that crimes committed by a state against its own nationals in times of peace were not a concern of international law – and should not be.[14]

Lemkin nevertheless believed in the significance of 'his' convention. Writing in December 1946, immediately after the General Assembly of the United Nations

---

[11] Lemkin 2008, p. 90.

[12] United National General Assembly Resolution, 11 December 1946, 96(I)/1946.

[13] See Hirad Abtahi and Philippa Webb, *The Genocide Convention, The Travaux Préparatoires*, Leiden: Brill 2008, p. 1351 for the suggestion by Georges Kaeckenbeck. For Lemkin's views on Kaeckenbeck, see: Cooper 2008, p. 148. The decision to include the phrase 'recognizing that at all periods of history genocide has inflicted great losses on humanity' in the preamble seems to be the result of the opposition to the Soviet Union's proposal to make explicit reference to crimes of 'Fascism-Nazism', but the vague reference to 'all periods of history' leaves the question, what exactly could or should be cases of previous genocides.

[14] See Kevin Jon Heller, *The Nuremberg Military Tribunals and the Origins of International Criminal Law*, Oxford University Press 2011, p. 235.

approved Resolution 96(1) on 11 December 1946, Lemkin made the obvious connections:

> By declaring genocide a crime under international law and by making it a problem of international concern, the right of intervention on behalf of minorities slated for destruction has been established. This principle is already accepted by the UN and does not need any specific confirmation by treaty. Thus the resolution of December, 11, 1946 changes fundamentally the international responsibilities of a government toward its citizens.[15]

Much has been written about Lemkin's and Lauterpacht's contributions to an international law that responded to the challenges brought by the mass murder committed by the Third Reich and its helpers.[16] It can therefore be hardly surprising that both were proponents of a right to 'humanitarian intervention'. What is remarkable is the difference of the thrust of their legal arguments for the legality of 'humanitarian intervention'. While Lemkin believed that international law had been changed significantly and thus could forthwith better protect citizens against their governments, Lauterpacht remained faithful to a version of international law that had always allowed for such protection, though it is difficult to see why. A 1946 minute prepared by the then Legal Adviser of the British Foreign Office dismissed him as 'when all is said and done, a Jew recently come from Vienna',[17] one who lost his parents and most of his family, who had remained in Poland, to the Shoah. Yet that same year, he published a defence of the independence of international law from the new Charter of the United Nations in 1946, claiming that '[i]t was with some difficulty that the authors of the Charter of the United Nations were persuaded to assign to international law a place within the scheme of the United Nations. The view is widely held that, conceived in the spirit of realism, the Charter in many respects preferred order to law'.[18] Already in 1937, he had maintained that, '[i]f the fundamental rights of human personality [are] part of the international system ... then humanitarian intervention is both a legal and a political principle of the international society'.[19] In his classic article 'The Grotian Tradition in International Law', he had attributed to Hugo Grotius 'the first authoritative statement of humanitarian intervention' as 'the principle that the exclusiveness of domestic jurisdiction stops where outrage upon humanity begins'. While admitting that the doctrine of humanitarian intervention had 'never become a fully acknowledged part of positive

---

[15] Raphael Lemkin, 'Genocide as a Crime under International Law', *American Journal of International Law* 1947, 41, p. 150.

[16] Ana Filipa Vrdoljak, 'Human Rights and Genocide: The Work of Lauterpacht and Lemkin in Modern International Law', *European Journal of International Law* 2010, 20, pp. 1163–1194; Sands 2016.

[17] Elihu Lauterpacht, *The Life of Hersch Lauterpacht*, Cambridge University Press 2010, p. 258.

[18] Lauterpacht 1946, p. 1, fn. 2.

[19] Hersch Lauterpacht, 'Règles générales du droit de la paix', 62 Hague Recueil (1937, I) cited according to Vrdoljak 2010, p. 1190.

international law', Lauterpacht stated that it had 'provided a signpost and a warning. It has been occasionally acted upon, and it was one of the factors which paved the way for the provisions of the Charter of the United Nations relating to fundamental human rights and freedoms'.[20]

In the versions of the seminal textbook on international law originally authored by Lassa Oppenheim and produced under his guidance, Lauterpacht eventually found 'a substantial body of opinion and of state practice in support of the view (...) that when a State renders itself guilty of cruelties against and persecution of its nationals in such a way as to deny their fundamental human rights and to shock the conscience of mankind, intervention in the interest of humanity is legally permissible'.[21] Lauterpacht went on to proclaim that the Charter of the United Nations

> in recognising the promotion of respect for fundamental human rights and freedoms as one of the principal objects of the Organisation, marks a further step in the direction of elevating the principle of humanitarian intervention to a basic rule of organised international society. This is so although under the Charter as adopted in 1945 the degree of enforceability of fundamental human rights is still rudimentary and although the Charter itself expressly rules out intervention in matters which are essentially within the domestic jurisdiction of the State'.[22]

The apparent contradiction between the 'basic rule of organised international society' and the formal stipulations of the Charter prohibiting any enforcement unless authorised by the Security Council, however, was left open by Lauterpacht. It is his version of the argument for the legality of 'humanitarian intervention' that dominated the debate in the first decades after World War II.

4.2 THE CHARTER OF THE UNITED NATIONS AND 'HUMANITARIAN INTERVENTION' IN EARLY INTERPRETATIONS

The question of 'humanitarian intervention' had not been debated during the deliberations of the Charter of the United Nations, or, if so, only indirectly, as no exception to the rule of non-intervention was considered, not even in the exceptional cases that interventions for the 'cause of humanity' would arguably have represented. The Travaux Préparatoires of the Charter are so inconclusive or silent on the question of 'humanitarian intervention', that one observer concluded that there is no answer to the question of whether the drafters of the Charter 'intended to maintain the customary exceptions to the use of force, including humanitarian intervention'.[23] At the same time, it seems clear enough that the drafters of the Charter sought to go beyond existing law 'by banning *all* resorts to armed force and

---

[20] Lauterpacht 1946, p. 46.
[21] Oppenheim 1955, p. 312.
[22] Oppenheim 1955, p. 313.
[23] Tesón 2005, p. 197.

thereby effacing the legal distinction between war and measures short of war'.[24] Yet the Charter of the United Nations introduced a new framework for the discussion of the legality of 'humanitarian intervention' in international law. The Charter's outspoken, if superficial focus on sovereign equality (Art. 2 I of the Charter) and the prohibition of the use of force in international affairs (Art. 2 IV) provided new benchmarks to measure the use of military power by one state or a group of states on the territory of another state, while the Charter's commitment to the protection of human rights in the Preamble provided new fuel for claims of the legitimacy of 'humanitarian interventions'. The Preamble's combination of human rights issues with the sovereign equality of States has been termed 'rather peculiar',[25] but the reality is that, for the first decades, the discussion on 'humanitarian intervention' in international law continued without reference to these parameters.

Returning to the textbooks on international law published in the first decades after the end of World War II, it is easy to see how deeply the spirit of nineteenth-century international law on 'humanitarian intervention' is entrenched in international law in general, especially in books published in previous editions before the war. One striking example is the second edition of Alfred Verdross' *Völkerrecht*, published in 1950. Verdross (1890–1980), currently considered a precursor to international constitutionalism, built his universal law primarily on the idea of the original unity of Christian humanity rather than on a modern world community in the making.[26] In keeping with his previous positions on the foundations of international law,[27] Verdross had only mentioned 'so-called "human rights"' in passing in the first edition of his treatise. His conviction that an important basic principle of international law had emerged during the nineteenth century, reflecting the 'grand idea' that the community of states was allowed to intervene in the affairs of a state violating the most elementary human rights of its citizens,[28] was based on an alleged state practice of the nineteenth century that had repeatedly allowed for European Great Power intervention in the affairs of Turkey for the protection of Turkish Christian citizens and, in the familiar narrative of other international lawyers, had in turn led to a doctrine that allowed for intervention on grounds of humanity in

---

[24] Neff 2005, p. 314, emphasis in original.

[25] Rüdiger Wolfrum, 'Preamble', in: Bruno Simma (ed.), *The Charter of the United Nations – A Commentary*, 2nd ed., Munich: C. H. Beck 2002, p. 35.

[26] Thomas Kleinlein, 'Alfred Verdross as a Founding Father of International Constitutionalism?', *Goettingen Journal of International Law* 2012, 4, pp. 385–416, referencing Alfred Verdross, 'Die allgemeinen Rechtsgrundsätze als Völkerrechtsquelle: Zugleich ein Beitrag zum Problem der Grundnorm des positiven Völkerrechts', in Alfred Verdross (ed.), *Gesellschaft, Staat und Recht: Untersuchungen zur reinen Rechtslehre: Festschrift Hans Kelsen zum 50. Geburtstag gewidmet*, Vienna: Julius Springer 1931, pp. 354, 358, and 364, for the idea of the original unity of Christian humanity as the foundation of Verdross' universal law.

[27] see the discussion in Section 3.4.1.

[28] Alfred Verdross, *Völkerrecht*, 2nd ed., Vienna: Springer-Verlag 1950, pp. 71, 446.

exceptional cases (which Verdross termed 'intervention d'humanité').[29] This passage remained essentially unchanged in later editions.[30]

It could hardly have failed to come to Verdross' attention[31] that no such practice had ever been forthcoming, yet by the time the book was thoroughly revised and expanded with the help of the future International Court of Justice judge, Bruno Simma (born 1941), the perspective on the probability of future legal 'humanitarian interventions' had hardened, while the view of the past had become even more idealistic. In the 1976 edition of their textbook, now titled *Universelles Völkerrecht*, the authors concluded that it was clear that collective intervention on grounds of humanity (intervention d'humanité) had been recognised under classic international law and state practice had reflected this basic principle, but, as the UN Charter prohibits *any* forcible intervention, under current international law only a Security Council resolution could legally justify any such intervention.[32]

Such increasingly romantic and fact-free 'visions' – for they can hardly be called memories – of historic international law prevailed not only among German language authors. Two English language examples shall illustrate this, both from introductions to international law with a long history. In his *The Law of Nations*, first published in 1928, renowned international lawyer and Professor of Public International Law at the University of Oxford from 1922 to 1947, James L. Brierly (1881–1955) left the text on the question of 'humanitarian intervention' essentially unchanged during the course of five editions, the second edition published in 1936, the final fifth edition (under Brierly's authorship) in 1955. According to Brierly, while some writers, under the influence of the 'morally commendable' interventions in the affairs of the former Turkish Empire in the nineteenth century, considered 'humanitarian reasons as a legal justification for intervention', such a position – though held, according to Brierly throughout all the editions of the work, by unnamed contemporary international lawyers – involved a radical departure from the 'present basis of international law to maintain that a state's treatment of its own subject is, in the absence of any treaty protection, anything but a domestic matter which it may decide at its own discretion'.[33] One of the lawyers Brierly might have been referring to could have been Charles Fenwick (1880–1973), who first published

[29] Verdross 1937, p. 237.

[30] See: Alfred Verdross, *Völkerrecht*, 5th ed., Vienna: Springer-Verlag 1964, pp. 562–563.

[31] Verdross 1950, pp. 446–448; Alfred Verdross, *Völkerrecht*, 3rd. ed., Vienna: Springer-Verlag 1955, pp. 480–482.

[32] Alfred Verdross and Bruno Simma, *Universelles Völkerrecht*, Berlin: Duncker & Humblot, 1976, p. 584. The position remained unchanged in the final 3rd edition of the book, see: Verdross and Simma 1984, p. 798.

[33] J. L. Brierly, *The Law of Nations*, 5th ed., Oxford: Clarendon Press 1955, p. 310. The passage is identical in: J. L. Brierly, *The Law of Nations*, 2nd ed., Oxford: Clarendon Press, 1936, p. 249. In the first edition (Oxford: Clarendon Press 1928, pp. 156–157) it appears in a slightly different context, that is, its own chapter on 'intervention', rather than a chapter on 'International Law and the Use of Force' with a sub-chapter on 'Intervention', as in all later editions.

his textbook *International Law* in 1924 as a response to an apparent need for a 'fresh examination of the rules of international law'.[34] In his book, Fenwick maintained in a passage that essentially remained unchanged over the course of the four editions published between 1924 and 1965 that 'numerous' interventions justified on 'grounds of humanity' had occurred in the nineteenth century and were considered legal, as 'it would seem, however, quite as reasonable that a state should protect the moral feelings of its people, shocked by the accounts of the massacre of their coreligionists, as that it should protect their material interests'.[35] Fenwick's work was praised for continually being updated in light of the sometimes dramatic developments in international relations,[36] yet the passage on 'humanitarian intervention' appears like a window locked in time, on a time locked in itself.[37]

The reach of this narrative is remarkable, a success story for the inventors of the tradition. In India, the early textbooks published after the country's independence breathe that same spirit of a law following the 'conscience of mankind', as, according to these writers, the 'Society of Nations' had become 'coextensive with civilization by crossing the bounds of Christendom' in the nineteenth century and 'the rules of International Law developed on consent of the nations'.[38] 'Humanitarian Intervention' appears here in the form of a 'justification for intervention' 'based on the ground of humanity', 'legal' in the opinion of many writers, but outside the ordinary rules of international law, 'which does not impose on States the obligation of preventing barbarity on the part of their neighbours'.[39] Citing the classic examples of the Greek War of Independence and the 1860 Mount Lebanon intervention as

---

[34] Charles G. Fenwick, *International Law*, London: George Allen & Unwin Ltd, 1924, preface, p. vi.

[35] Charles G. Fenwick, *International Law*, 2nd. ed., New York: Appleton-Century-Company 1934, p. 168. In the first edition, published in 1924, this author was even more vague: 'The fact that these interventions were supported by public opinion among the leading nations stamped the action of the Great Powers as legally valid, whatever be the general principle of law to which it can be referred', p. 154 of the 1924 edition.

[36] Clarence A. Berdahl, 'Review of "International Law" by Charles G. Fenwick (3rd Ed.)', *American Journal of International Law* 1948, 42, pp. 958–960.

[37] By the 3rd edition, the statement on 'humanitarian intervention' had not become any more precise: 'The international community [of the late nineteenth century] had not as yet developed any machinery for the assertion of its higher right to maintain law and order. But while differing as to the technical grounds of intervention, jurists found no difficulty in responding to the higher appeal of a common humanity, and in conceding to a state the same right to protect the moral feelings of its people, shocked by the accounts of the massacres of their correligionists, that it had to protect their material interests', Charles G. Fenwick, *International Law*, 3rd. ed., New York: Appleton-Century-Croft 1948, p. 242. Despite the clearly limited historical accuracy of such a statement in 1948, it remained unchanged for the 4th edition, see: Fenwick 1965, p. 287.

[38] Tandon 1966, p. 46.

[39] Tandon 1966, p. 197. For an earlier Indian treatment of the same question and with similar results, see: K. R. R. Sastry, *International Law*, Allahabad: Kitabistan 1937, p. 58. The same author repeated this assessment after World War II, see: K. R. R. Sastry, *Studies in International Law*, Calcutta: Eastern Law House Ltd 1952, p. 78.

well as 'strong protests from several nations' against the 'persecution of the Jewish community during Hitler's regime', Lauterpacht (disguised as Oppenheim) is presented as evidence for the legality of 'humanitarian intervention' under the Charter, though the historical examples offered for such interventions in the 1966 edition of the textbook first published in 1952 are limited to non-forcible diplomatic interventions against South Africa's apartheid regime.[40] Remarkably, by the publication of the book's twentieth edition in 1985, India's intervention in East Pakistan/war with Pakistan was still not discussed in this context.[41]

The Charter of the United Nations as a major new development in international law hardly featured in the passages devoted to the question of 'humanitarian intervention' in those early text books, or equally romantic visions for a future international law untainted by the complicity in the barbarism of the 'civilised',[42] with passages on the law of the Charter and 'humanitarian intervention' existing side by side.[43] The books that focused on the Charter and its effect on the use of force under the new international law gave little mention to 'humanitarian intervention' or the potential consequences of the Charter for the doctrine.[44] In his seminal 1963 monograph 'International Law and the Use of Force by States', Ian Brownlie (1932–2010), one of the most respected international lawyers of the late twentieth and early twenty-first centuries,[45] stated that it was 'extremely doubtful if this form of intervention has survived the express condemnation of interventions which have occurred in recent times or the general prohibitions of resort to force to be found in the United Nations Charter'.[46] Brownlie was quite unambiguous in his statement of the scope of the prohibition of the use of force under the Charter as well as customary international law, calling any difference between Art. 2 (4) of the Charter and 'general international law' 'the merest technicality'.[47] Despite Lauterpacht's 'Oppenheim', as the leading British textbook of the time, asserting the legality of 'humanitarian intervention', Brownlie's position is, for all practical purposes, representative of the prevailing view of the state of international law at around 1960.[48]

However, in the late 1950s new trends in the interpretation of the Charter began to emerge. Julius Stone (1907–1985), a British born Australian scholar of international law, advocated a literal reading of the language of Article 2(4) of the

[40] Tandon 1966, pp. 198–200.
[41] Manesh Prasad Tandon and Rajesh Tandon, *Public International Law*, 20th ed., Allahabad: Allahabad Law Agency Publishers 1985.
[42] E.g. Valentin Tomberg, *Grundlagen des Völkerrechts als Menschheitsrecht*, Bonn: Götz Schwippert Verlag 1947.
[43] E.g. Verdross 1955, pp. 77, 481, 526–527.
[44] E.g. Kelsen 1952.
[45] Philippe Sands, Sir Ian Brownlie obituary, *The Guardian*, 11 January 2010, available at: www.theguardian.com/theguardian/2010/jan/11/sir-ian-brownlie-obituary, last accessed 1 March 2019.
[46] Brownlie 1963, p. 342.
[47] Brownlie 1963, p. 113.
[48] See for a similarly unambiguous statement: Berber 1960, p. 191.

UN Charter as opposed to an 'extreme' one, stressing that the provision contained a qualifying clause that could not be read out of the Charter.[49] The use of force in international relations is, according to this reading, *only* prohibited by Article 2(4) *if* it is directed 'against the territorial integrity and political independence of other states or in any manner inconsistent with the purposes of the United Nations'.[50] The conclusion, though not explicitly drawn by Stone,[51] that this could not possibly prohibit the use of force in a 'genuine humanitarian intervention', because such an intervention 'does not result in territorial conquest or political subjugation', remains the cornerstone of all claims that it should be a 'distortion to argue that Art. 2 (4) UN-Charter prohibits humanitarian intervention', as Professors Reisman and McDougal would claim in their influential 1968 paper, 'Humanitarian Intervention to Protect the Igbos'.[52]

4.3 EARLY STATE PRACTICE UNDER THE UN CHARTER

If Nuremberg as an 'intervention by judicial process' confirmed that 'humanitarian intervention' to stop Crimes against Humanity was a legal option, then – or so some claim – the invasion of Arab forces into the newly independent State of Israel on 15 May 1948 was the first time after the establishment of the United Nations that this card was played.[53] After Israel had proclaimed independence on 14 May 1948 in recognition of the 1947 United Nations General Assembly Resolution 181 on the Partition of Palestine and the termination of British Mandate scheduled for 15 May 1948, the Secretary-General of the League of Arab States sent a message to the Secretary-General of the United Nations, claiming that 'the Arab states find themselves compelled to intervene in order to restore law and order and to check further bloodshed'.[54] The Egyptian representative further elaborated before the Security Council on the same day:

---

[49] Julius Stone, *Aggression and World Order*, Berkeley: University of California Press 1958, p. 95.
[50] For a brief contemporary discussion of the limits of this approach, see: Friedrich Berber, *Lehrbuch des Völkerrechts*, Vol. II, Munich/Berlin: C. H. Beck 1962, pp. 43–44.
[51] But see B. V. A. Röling, *On Aggression, on International Criminal Law, on International Criminal Jurisdiction*, Nederlands: Tijdschrift voor Internationaal Recht 1955, pp. 176–177, where this conclusion is explicitly drawn.
[52] Reisman and McDougal 1968 Memorandum, reprinted in: Lillich 1973, p. 177. This position is explicitly also held verbatim by Tesón 2005.
[53] Natalino Ronzitti, *Rescuing Nationals Abroad through Military Coercion and Intervention on Grounds of Humanity*, Dordrecht: Martinus Nijhoff 1985, pp. 93–94; John Quigley, *The Case for Palestine*, 2nd ed., Durham: Duke University Press 2005, pp. 78–79. Jean Allain, *International Law in the Middle East*, Aldershot: Ashgate 2004, p. 98, only refers to the 'intervention of 1948' without qualifying the type of this alleged 'intervention'.
[54] Cablegram dated 15 May 1948 addressed to the Secretary-General by the Secretary-General of the League of Arab States, pdf-copy available at https://undocs.org/S/745, last accessed 10 August 2018.

The Royal Egyptian Government declares, now that the British Mandate in Palestine has ended, that Egyptian armed forces have started to enter Palestine to establish security and order in place of chaos and disorder which prevailed and which rendered the country at the mercy of Zionist terrorist gangs who persisted in attacking peaceful Arab inhabitants, with arms and equipments amassed by them for that purpose. Horrible crimes, revolting to the conscience of humanity, have been perpetrated by these Zionist gangs. Arab women have been assaulted, pregnant women's stomachs ripped open, children killed before the very eyes of their mothers and prisoners tortured and then brutally murdered.[55]

Even though this is clearly an official justification for the use of military force that bears all the hallmarks of a genuine 'humanitarian intervention', this case has received very little attention in the literature on the subject.[56] It is sometimes discussed in the context of a right to protect the lives and property of nationals abroad,[57] because in a questionnaire drafted by the Security Council, the Arab states gave the necessity of protecting the lives and property of Arab nationals as one reason for their military operations outside the territory subject to their jurisdiction.[58] The more probable reason this justification has not received more attention in the evolution of the doctrine of 'humanitarian intervention', however, is that it simply was not an adequate description of the events eventually leading to the 1948 Arab-Israeli War. The civil war that had erupted in Mandatory Palestine in reaction to the United Nations partition plan cannot – even in the selective world of the constructive narrative of 'humanitarian intervention' – convincingly be reduced to a tale of 'Zionist terrorism',[59] so that even Arab perspectives tend to disregard this apparent misuse of humanitarian considerations.[60] The Egyptian claim that its troops were somehow mandated to maintain order and security in what used to be Mandatory Palestine was unconditionally rejected in the Security Council, with the Soviet representative pointing out the seemingly obvious: 'According to the rules of the international community, each government has the right to restore order only in its own country'.[61]

But if the first appearance of the language of 'humanitarian intervention' in state practice after the establishment of the United Nations did little to strengthen the legitimacy of the doctrine, its next appearances fared no better in attempting to shed

[55] Statement by the Egyptian Representative before the Security Council, 15 May 1948, cited according to Ronzitti 1985, p. 93.

[56] Chesterman 2001, p. 64, dismisses the case as one 'in which humanitarian concerns were marginal, if they operated at all'.

[57] D. W. Bowett, *Self-defence in International Law*, Manchester University Press 1958, p. 100.

[58] D. W. Bowett, 'The Use of Force in the Protection of Nationals', *Transactions of the Grotius Society 1957*, 43, p. 122.

[59] Benny Morris, *The Birth of the Palestinian Refugee Problem Revisited*, 2nd ed., Cambridge University Press 2012.

[60] E.g. Ajaj 1992.

[61] Ronzitti 1985, p. 95.

it from its imperialistic undertones. In 1960, shortly after achieving independence from Belgium, the new Republic of the Congo plunged into predictable chaos. The Belgian authorities had done little to nothing to prepare the country for independence and, when the international pressure for decolonisation proved to be too much, the Belgians effectively abandoned their former colony.[62] The military stayed under the control of the Belgians and this colonialist attitude led to mutinies among Congolese officers, which turned to revolts in the whole country. The army disintegrated 'into roving armed bands, attacking, raping and killing Europeans'.[63] The newly established Congolese authorities under the leadership of prime minister Patrice Lumumba and President Joseph Kasavubu lacked the power to effectively put down the mutinies, facing a secessionist opposition in the province of Katanga under the leadership of Moise Tshombe at the same time.

As the security situation quickly deteriorated, Belgium paratroopers were sent to intervene against Congolese soldiers on 10 July 1960, entering the country simultaneously in several locations, among them the secessionist province of Katanga and the economically strategic port of Matadi, where there were hardly any Belgian residents.[64] The next day, Tshombe declared the independence of Katanga, threatening the unity of the young republic. On 12 July 1960, the President and Prime Minister of the Congo jointly addressed a telegram to the United Nations Secretary-General and asked for military assistance to end a 'Belgian ... act of aggression against our country'.[65] This characterisation received some support in the Security Council meeting called by the United Nations Secretary-General on 13 July 1960, where Tunisia and the Soviet Union accused Belgium of having committed 'an unwarranted act of aggression' and of violating 'both territorial integrity and the political independence of the Republic of Congo'.[66] The Soviet Union emphasised that 'talk about the need for protecting "the lives of residents" and restoring "order" in other countries is a well-worn device which was used on more than one occasion during the nineteenth and early twentieth centuries to conceal armed intervention by the colonial Power'.[67]

Western countries, however, sided with the Belgians. The United States declared that no aggression had taken place, while Italy spoke of 'some Belgian troops' who 'intervene in order to prevent a spreading of the incidents and to keep law and order', calling the actions not 'something which pertains to the realm of intervention, but rather a temporary security action'.[68] The United Kingdom spoke of the

---

[62] Heinrich August Winkler, *Geschichte des Westens – vom Kalten Krieg bis zum Mauerfall*, Munich: C. H. Beck 2014, p. 323; Guy Vanthemsche, *Belgium and the Congo 1885–1960*, Cambridge University Press 2012, pp. 201–202.

[63] Trevor Findlay, *The Use of Force in UN Peace Operations*, Oxford University Press 2002, p. 51.

[64] Vanthemsche 2012, p. 210; Chesterman 2001, p. 65.

[65] UN Doc S/4382, 12 July 1960.

[66] S/PV.873 (1960), para 86 (Tunisia) and 103 (USSR).

[67] S/PV.873 (1960), para. 103.

[68] S/PV.873 (1960), para 95 (USA) and 121 (Belgium).

'humanitarian task' which the Belgian troops allegedly had performed, and France stated that the Belgian troops' 'mission of protecting lives and property is the direct result of the failure of the Congolese authorities and is in accord with a recognized principle of international law, namely, intervention on humanitarian grounds'.[69] The Belgian representative at the Security Council explicitly characterised the Belgian action as a 'humanitarian intervention' without 'any political purposes'.[70]

While these statements have led to the inclusion of the Belgian intervention in some accounts of 'humanitarian intervention',[71] it also sparked the largest military operations by the United Nations itself. Rather than pacifying the mutinous troops, Belgian intervention severely exacerbated an already tense situation.[72] On 14 July 1960, the United Nations Security Council adopted Resolution 143 (1960), calling on Belgium to withdraw its troops and authorising the Secretary-General 'to take the necessary steps, in consultation with the Government of the Republic of the Congo, to provide the Government with such military assistance as may be necessary until (...) the national security forces may be able, in the opinion of the Government, to meet fully their tasks'.[73] It marked the point in time when, under the initial leadership of then-Secretary-General Dag Hammarskjöld, the United Nations established itself as a self-declared neutral authority to protect the interests of the people of decolonised states, but betrayed its claim of neutrality through the need to make choices that shaped the political situation. As Anne Orford has shown, Hammarskjöld chose efficiency and order over parliamentary support or self-determination and dismissed the Lumumba government as inefficient. Yet he offered no account of why power should vest with the UN rather than the peoples of the Congo.[74] From 1960 to 1964, the UN Operation in the Congo used increasing amounts of military force, to the point where it became indistinguishable from a standard military campaign.[75] During this time, the United Nations and states belonging to all of the political groupings restated the position that the right to self-determination does not amount to a right of secession, as they would do again in the Biafra situation several years later.[76]

The Belgian troops withdrew by September 1960, after having supported the rebel provinces rather than the Central Government, arguably with the aim to secure

---

[69] S/PV.873 (1960), para 130 (UK) and para 144 (France).

[70] S/PV.873 (1960), para 197.

[71] With some even claiming that the 'intervention in the Congo crisis provides strong precedent for the argument that the principle of humanitarian intervention survives the Charter', M. Sornarajah, 'Internal Colonialism and Humanitarian Intervention', *Georgia Journal for International and Comparative Law* 1981, 11(1), p. 66.

[72] Peter J. Schraeder, *United States Foreign Policy toward Africa*, Cambridge University Press 1994, p. 53.

[73] Resolution 143 (1960), 14.07.1960.

[74] Anne Orford, *International Authority and the Responsibility to Protect*, Cambridge University Press 2011, pp. 86–87.

[75] Findlay 2002, p. 51.

[76] Antonio Cassese, *Self-determination of Peoples*, Cambridge University Press 1995, p. 123.

future access to the copper-rich province of Katanga, ruled by Tshombe, rather than out of any 'humanitarian' concern.[77] The UN troops eventually defeated the rebel forces in Katanga, which had formed an independent state with the support of Belgium.[78] The secession ended in January 1963, and the last UN troops withdrew on 30 June 1964. By that time, another province of the Congo had come under the control of a new group of rebels by the name of Conseil National de Libération (CNL) and led by supporters of the former prime minister Patrice Lumumba, assassinated in January 1961, which had been systematically excluded from all positions of power within the central government since 1962.[79] Against a backdrop of covert United States operations to prop up the Central Government now led by Tshombe and following a Western course, the vaguely Communist ideology of the CNL presented a threat to the Western interests of supporting a government that would resist any overtures from the Soviet Union. By 5 August 1964, their forces seized control of Stanleyville (now Kisangani), the northeastern provincial capital and Lumumba's former stronghold, and thus controlled approximately half of the Congo. Fearing its own collapse imminent, the Central Government, supported by United States-supplied aircraft, brought in mercenaries from Western countries and gradually regained control over key areas. In response, one of the rebel leaders declared early in September 1964 that the rebels were holding as hostages 500 'white men, women and children' and would begin to execute them if the Central Government continued its use of mercenaries and its air attacks on rebel positions. Fearful of the fate awaiting their own citizens being held hostage, the United States developed a covert military operation plan that was then put on hold. Instead, the order was given to ground the United States-supplied aircrafts until an agreement was reached with the Central Government that no further air-attacks would be made against guerrilla-held cities.[80] Only after President Johnson had secured a convincing victory in the November 1964 United States presidential elections, and Belgium had indicated that it would be prepared to again engage militarily in the former colony, was a military intervention undertaken. On 21 November, Prime Minister Tshombe authorised Belgium and the United States to mount a rescue operation. Three days later, 545 Belgian paratroopers were transported by United States military aircraft into Stanleyville to commence rescue operations.[81] Hours after the rescue attempt began, Brussels and Washington sent letters to the president of the Security Council emphasising the request from the Congolese government and claiming to be undertaking a 'legal, moral and humanitarian operation which conforms to the

---

[77] Vanthemsche 2012, p. 202.
[78] Winkler 2014, p. 325.
[79] Schraeder 1994, p. 68.
[80] Schraeder 1994, p. 72.
[81] Schraeder 1994, p. 73.

highest aims of the United Nations: the defence and protection of fundamental human rights in respect for national security'.[82] On 26 November another 255 Belgian paratroopers were dropped by United States aircraft over the airfield in a town northeast of Stanleyville.[83]

The operation was successful in rescuing over 2,000 hostages, but the rebels still killed between 100 and 300 Westerners and thousands of Congolese after the operation began.[84] As the air operations proceeded, ground forces made up of mercenaries and the regular Congolese army under the command of Colonel Frédéric Vandewalle, a former chief of the Belgian Colonial Security Service and military adviser to the Tshombe government, approached Stanleyville. Regarding the decision to drop commandos in the city so shortly before his arrival, Colonel Vandewalle later would remark that 'a different political solution, involving less improvisation, would have had a less bloody outcome'.[85]

The intervention was widely protested in Africa. At the request of 22 African, Asian and European member states, the Security Council met on 9 December 1964 to consider what the requestors called the Belgian and American aggression against the Congo as well as the Congolese counter-claim that 'certain States have assisted rebel groups in the eastern part of the Congo'. In a lengthy session occupying seventeen meetings of the Security Council, in which eleven African countries and Belgium were invited to take part, the Belgian and the American representatives defended the legitimacy and legality of their operation. Some states pointed to the authorisation of the operation through the government of the Congo. Others, African states in particular, argued that the Tshombe government had no legitimacy. While some states pointed to the established right of a state to protect its own nationals, a concept that is 'recognized in international law', others argued that claims from the United States and Belgium were disingenuous. Algeria, for instance, pointedly stated that 'it is only natural that the main motive of those who helped the prime mover of Katanga's secession or who handed over the leadership of the Leopoldville Government to him should have been to retain a monopoly over the exploitation of enormous wealth'.[86]

The Security Council eventually passed Resolution 199 (1964) calling for a cease-fire and requesting all states to refrain from intervening in the domestic politics of the Congo, thus making no distinction between the United States–Belgian operation and alleged support for the rebel forces by 'certain states'. This brought a

---

[82] S/603 (1964). The American letter stated that the 'sole purpose of this humanitarian mission was to liberate hostages whose lives were in danger', S/6062 (1964).

[83] Schraeder 1994, p. 74.

[84] Vanthemsche 2012, p. 216; Schraeder 1994, p. 74.

[85] Vanthemsche 2012, pp. 216–217, citing F. Vandewalle, *L'ommegang. Odyssée et reconquête de Stanleyville 1961*, Brussels 1970.

[86] All quotes from International Commission on Intervention and State Sovereignty 2001, p. 52.

temporary end to direct international involvement in the Congo, though of course Belgium and the United States would continue to pursue their own interests in the region, severely destabilising the politics of the Congo. In July 1967, this resulted in another military intervention by the United States, though this time without any 'humanitarian' cover.[87]

The Democratic Republic of Congo has been called the 'Land of Humanitarian Interventions',[88] and the Stanleyville Operation was once described as 'one of the clearest modern instances of true humanitarian intervention and [one that] should be viewed as lawful in character'.[89] Writing in 1982, Michael Bazyler recounts the events as if only those 2,000 Western hostages had ever been at risk and had been saved successfully in an operation undertaken 'at the invitation of the central Congo government', before he approvingly cites Richard B. Lillich's verdict on the events: 'One reaches the inescapable conclusion that if ever there was a case for the use of forcible self-help to protect lives, the Congo rescue operation was it'.[90] It is in this context (armed protection of nationals abroad) that the episode continues to be mentioned.[91] As Simon Chesterman has pointed out, its 'humanitarian' star has faded somewhat with time,[92] but the new historians of 'humanitarian intervention' have given the episode a surprisingly uncritical new lease on life, recounting contemporary legal assessments without reflection.[93] Such legal arguments were not renewed and the episode was not cited as a precedent by the Kingdom of Belgium in the International Court of Justice proceedings on the legality of the use of force against the former Federal Republic of Yugoslavia. It is mentioned in the Supplementary Volume to the ICISS report only briefly and quite critically: 'the legacy of actions in the early 1960s in Central Africa continues to colour the debate about intervention and state sovereignty'.[94]

---

[87] Schraeder 1994, pp. 77–78.
[88] Claude Kabemba, 'The Democratic Republic of Congo: The Land of Humanitarian Interventions', in: Bronwen Everill and Josiah Kaplan (eds.), *The History and Practice of Humanitarian Intervention and Aid in Africa*, Hampshire: Palgrave Macmmillan 2013, p. 140.
[89] Gerhard von Glahn, *Law among Nations*, 2nd ed., London: Macmillan 1970, p. 168.
[90] Bazyler 1987, pp. 587–588, citing Lillich 1967, p. 340.
[91] E.g. Malanczuk 1997, p. 315; Franck 2002, pp. 77–79.
[92] Chesterman 2001, p. 67. The recent summary by Robert Kolb, 'The Belgian Intervention in the Congo – 1960 and 1964', in: Tom Ruys, Olivier Corten, and Alexandra Hofer (eds.), *The Use of Force in International Law – A Case-Based Approach*, Oxford University Press 2018, only mentions 'humanitarian' aspects in passing. Many of the state practice oriented works on 'humanitarian intervention' do not mention the events at all, e.g. Wellhausen 2002; Wheeler 2000; Tesón 2005.
[93] D. J. B. Trim and Brendan Simms, 'Towards a History of Humanitarian Intervention', in: Brendan Simms and D. J. B. Trim (eds.), *Humanitarian Intervention – A History*, Cambridge University Press 2011, p. 17.
[94] International Commission on Intervention and State Sovereignty 2001, p. 53.

The next appearance of the 'humanitarian intervention' argument has not yet been quite so indiscriminately resurrected from the dusty pages of unread history books.[95] The United States intervention in the Dominican Republic in 1965 is mentioned in some specialist works on the history of 'humanitarian intervention',[96] but neglected by others.[97] This case originated in the overthrow of the democratically elected government of the left-leaning President Juan Bosch by a military coup d'état after only seven months in office in September 1963. Less than two years later, growing dissatisfaction led to another military rebellion on 24 April 1965, with the aim of reinstating Bosch as President. The situation quickly deteriorated into a civil war, and on 28 April 1965 the newly installed military junta informed the American Embassy that it could no longer guarantee the safety of United States nationals. On the same day, the first United States marines landed in Santo Domingo with the stated objective of protecting United States and other nationals. Over the course of the next several days, the United States purposefully 'escalated' the mission, as evidenced by the order that the Joint Chiefs of Staff gave to the commander of the United States intervention force:

> Your announced mission is to save U.S. lives. Your unannounced mission is to prevent the Dominican Republic from going Communist. The President has stated that he will not allow another Cuba – you are to take all necessary measures to accomplish this mission. You will be given sufficient forces to do the job.[98]

The intervention took place accordingly. The American troops on the island eventually numbered over 20,000, before the United States action morphed into an operation under the authority of the Organization of American States by mid-May 1965 and some American forces were withdrawn. This also paved the way for a prolonged visit from the Inter-American Commission on Human Rights in June 1966, which monitored the human rights situation in the Dominican Republic at the request of both sides in the ongoing civil war and remained in the country for a whole year.[99] General elections were held in the Dominican Republic in June 1966 and all foreign forces were withdrawn by September 1966. In international fora, the United States received limited support: The Security Council rejected a

---

[95] But see: Fabian Klose, 'The Emergence of Humanitarian Intervention', in: Fabian Klose (ed.), *The Emergence of Humanitarian Intervention*, Cambridge University Press 2015, p. 7 with fn. 20.

[96] Pauer 1985, p. 15; Murphy 1996, pp. 94–97; Chesterman 2001, pp. 69–70; Abiew 1999, p. 108.

[97] Wheeler 2000; Wellhausen 2002.

[98] Cited according to Russell Crandall, *Gunboat Democracy: U.S. interventions in the Dominican Republic, Grenada, and Panama*, Lanham: Rowman & Littlefield Publishers 2006, p. 70. The expression 'escalate' in relation to the intervention is also Crandall's, attributed to President Johnson himself, p. 66.

[99] Jan Eckel, *Die Ambivalenz des Guten*, Göttingen: Vandenhoeck & Ruprecht 2014, p. 203.

Soviet-sponsored resolution that would have condemned the intervention, and settled on a compromise resolution calling for a ceasefire.[100]

The United States initially claimed that its intervention was to protect United States nationals and to escort them and nationals of other countries to the United States. Subsequently, they claimed that the presence of their forces was requested by the military authorities in the Dominican Republic. Finally, the claim was made that the additional deployment of forces was necessary to preserve the Dominican people's right to a free choice of government and the alleged need to avoid a 'bloodbath' and to create a safe area for 'humanitarian reasons'.[101] Because the 'announced' mission had a vaguely humanitarian character, American international lawyers in particular were quick to claim this an example of a reliance upon 'two traditional doctrines' in international law, namely 'the protection of nationals abroad and humanitarian intervention'. Richard B. Lillich (1933–1996), an 'early leader in the movement for the affirmation of human rights in international law',[102] made this argument as early as 1967,[103] but when the episode was discussed at the conference Lillich organised on 'Humanitarian Intervention and the United Nations' at the University of Charlottesville in March 1972, Professor Wolfgang Friedmann (1907–1972) summed up the general view of the 'humanitarian intervention' argument for the United States intervention in the Dominican Republic as 'a thin legal fig leaf for power intervention for political purposes'.[104] In the current literature on the use of force in international law, the case is still discussed with regard to the question of the legality of the use of force to protect nationals abroad, but not as a possible 'humanitarian intervention'.[105]

Some accounts of 'humanitarian intervention' feature not only the historical episodes recounted above, but also the various Soviet interventions of the early Cold War.[106] Indeed, during the 1972 conference on 'Humanitarian Intervention and the United Nations', it was noted that there were obvious parallels between the American justification in the Dominican case and those used by the Soviets for their interventions.[107] However, these interventions were not justified by invoking universal values like human rights, nor can it be seen that the Soviet literature drew back to Trainin's arguments recounted in Section 3.2. On the contrary, the language of

---

[100] SC Res 203 (1965). A separate resolution called for a transformation of the suspension of hostilities into a permanent ceasefire, SC Res 205 (1965).

[101] Murphy 1996, pp. 95–96 and sources cited therein.

[102] Saxon 1996, available at www.nytimes.com/1996/08/16/us/richard-b-lillich-63-professor-and-expert-on-international-law.html, last accessed 16 August 2018.

[103] Lillich 1967, p. 341.

[104] Friedmann, Comment, in: Lillich 1973, p. 56.

[105] Christian Walter, 'The US Intervention in the Dominican Republic-1965', in: Tom Ruys, Olivier Corten, and Alexandra Hofer (eds.), *The Use of Force in International Law – A Case-based Approach*, Oxford University Press 2018.

[106] Murphy 1996, pp. 86–92.

[107] Friedmann, Comment, in: Lillich 1973, p. 101.

human rights was more commonly applied to state the illegality of the intervention, as in the case of the intervention in Hungary.[108] The Soviet Union later expanded the justifications for these interventions into the claim that the socialist community had a broad duty to intervene whenever a socialist government came under attack in the aligned countries, while maintaining their support for the general prohibition of the use of force in Art. 2(4) of the Charter of the United Nations.[109]

Unlike the Soviet cases, however, the Dominican case and the other cases discussed have been included, albeit with descriptions sometimes even more brief than offered here, in the Supplementary Volume to the International Commission on Intervention and State Sovereignty (ICISS)'s Report on the Responsibility to Protect, the committee established under the authority of the Canadian government in response to the challenge posited after the NATO action over Kosovo and its perceived legitimacy, but apparent illegality. The ICISS report concludes that '[c]-olonial powers misused humanitarian justifications to mask self-interested motives', while the Dominican 'intervention further fueled Latin American scepticism about disinterested motives, including humanitarian ones, invoked by the US or other major powers'.[110] The reliance on state practice in these cases upon 'humanitarian' motives or justifications was limited at best, and thus the continued relevance of these examples in the eyes of the ICISS seems to stem from a pronounced willingness of American scholars to discuss these cases as possible signs of 'a growing international approval of humanitarian intervention',[111] despite some strongly negative reactions to such narratives in the UN system.[112] The ICISS report's conclusion that at the end of the Cold War, 'most commentators argued that no such norm existed or that it was so contentious that it was necessary to justify intervention on other grounds'[113] stands in marked contrast to the growing intensity of the debate over 'humanitarian intervention' in the wake of the Biafran War, reaffirming once more that the narrative of 'humanitarian intervention' is a narrative of imagination as much as one of fact.

---

[108] Eliav Lieblich, 'The Soviet Intervention in Hungary – 1956', in: Tom Ruys, Olivier Corten, and Alexandra Hofer (eds.), *The Use of Force in International Law – A Case-based Approach*, Oxford University Press 2018, pp. 51–58. Murphy 1996, p. 89. See also: General Assembly Resolution 1004, adopted 4 November 1956 by 50-8-15.

[109] For an extensive discussion of Soviet positions, see: Theodor Schweisfurth, *Sozialistisches Völkerrecht?*, Berlin: Springer 1979, pp. 365–429 (on 'socialist internationalism'), 466 (on the prohibition of the use of force).

[110] International Commission on Intervention and State Sovereignty 2001, pp. 53, 54.

[111] Kathryn Rider Schmeltzer, 'Soviet and American Attitudes toward Intervention: The Dominican Republic, Hungary and Czechoslovakia', *Virginia Journal of International Law* 1970–1971, 11, p. 109 on the Dominican case.

[112] see Franck 2002, pp. 78–79 (Congo) and 81–82 (Dominican Republic) for a collection of negative statements from UN Security Council debates.

[113] International Commission on Intervention and State Sovereignty 2001, p. 47.

4.4 THE 'HUMANITARIAN INTERVENTION' DEBATE REIGNITED: BIAFRA, 1968

The 1960s have been called 'almost a forgotten decade in human rights historiography',[114] and while it is beyond the scope of this book to correct this, two diverging trends relevant to the historiography of 'humanitarian intervention' from this decade are worth resurrecting. The first is decolonialisation in which the universal promise of international law worked as a potential shield against possible foreign intervention by retransferring sovereignty in newly independent states to the indigenous population. While anti-colonialism was not necessarily a 'human rights movement',[115] it effectively delegitimised interference and intervention of former colonial powers in their erstwhile colonies, as seen in the case of the Democratic Republic of Congo. The second development is the emergence of the Shoah as a historical event in public discourse in the 1960s, which was also reflected in the debate over 'humanitarian intervention'. Ignited in part by the experience of the 1961 trial of Adolf Eichmann in Israel, but also the German Auschwitz trial of 1963–1965, which brought the crimes committed by Nazi Germany back into public focus, Auschwitz gradually replaced Hiroshima as a shorthand for the unprecedented evil of which mankind had proved itself capable. As Susan Neiman has reminded us, '[f]or a good two decades after World War II, the conviction that limits had been crossed in ways from which we would never recover was captured more by the word Hiroshima than by Auschwitz'.[116] But this changed during the 1960s, when the televised Eichmann trial showed the 'Banality of Evil' (Hannah Arendt), and it would also have implications for the debate on 'humanitarian intervention'.[117]

In 1962, Manouchehr Ganji, an Iranian diplomat and a government official turned human rights activist after the 1979 revolution, published his doctoral

---

[114] Steven L. B. Jensen, *The Making of International Human Rights*, Cambridge University Press 2016, p. 6.

[115] See generally: Samuel Moyn, *The Last Utopia*, Cambridge, MA: Belknap Press 2010, ch. 3, pp. 84–119; A. W. Brian Simpson, *Human Rights and the End of Empire*, Oxford University Press 2000, p. 300.

[116] Susan Neiman, *Evil in Modern Thought*, Princeton University Press 2002, p. 251.

[117] Fabian Klose has recently claimed that 'the passage of two UN human rights pacts in 1966 and the International Year of Human Rights in 1968, which culminated in the first International Conference on Human Rights in Tehran, lent further momentum to the debate, which soon focused on fundamental questions regarding concrete and robust mechanism to safeguard human rights'. Fabian Klose, 'Protecting Universal Rights through Intervention. International Law Debates from the 1930s to the 1980s', in: Norbert Frei, Daniel Stahl, and Annette Weinke (eds.), *Human Rights and Humanitarian Intervention*, Göttingen: Wallstein Verlag 2017, pp. 179–180. However, the UN human rights pacts are usually absent from legal assessments of the status of 'humanitarian intervention', and indeed the ones cited by Klose, while the International Conference on Human Rights committed itself more to disarmament than to 'robust mechanism to safeguard human rights', see Proclamation of Teheran, Final Act of the International Conference on Human Rights, Teheran, 22 April to 13 May 1968, U.N. Doc. A/ CONF. 32/41 at 3 (1968).

dissertation 'International Protection of Human Rights'. While the book does not specifically refer to the Holocaust in name, it concludes its brief introduction on the development of the relevant law applicable to 'humanitarian interventions' with the statement that the 'magnitude and the nature' of the 'extermination of millions of German Jews and the *"useless eaters"*' could not be called 'anything but crimes against humanity', providing not only a basis for the judgement of the Nuremberg tribunal, but also establishing 'a precedent and a due warning against similar future actions'.[118] The book was moderately well received at the time,[119] and recounted the classical positions on 'humanitarian intervention', while also providing an overview of the European state practice of the nineteenth century, based mainly on British official sources. While Ganji concluded that 'the doctrine of humanitarian inter-vention does not seem to claim the authority of a customary rule of international law', he approvingly quoted Thomas Lawrence's 1915 opinion that 'an intervention to put a stop to barbarous and abominable cruelty is a high act of policy above and beyond the domain of law'.[120] However, Ganji qualified this statement by noting that, 'in an organized international community, as we have today under the aegis of the United Nations, the act of intervention must be the result of a decision of the Organization'.[121] Later Anglo-American works on 'humanitarian intervention' in particular followed Ganji's legal assessment and selection of historical 'facts' for the historical cases, most notably W. Michael Reisman's paper on 'Humanitarian Intervention to Protect the Ibos' circulated at the United Nations in 1968.[122]

The Ibos (also, Igbos) are an ethnic group native to present-day south-central and south-eastern Nigeria. The country had gained independence from the United Kingdom in 1960, but soon descended into chaos and violence. Two successive military coups in 1966 and a series of mob riots directed against the Ibos in Northern and Western Nigeria in May 1966 paved the way for the Nigerian Civil War of 1967–1970, in which the Ibo territories seceded as the short-lived 'Republic of Biafra'. The Ministry of Information in Enugu, Eastern Nigeria, published a book, entitled 'Pogrom', which included graphic photographs and first-hand accounts of attacks and killings along with the claim, singular at this time, that genocide had occurred.[123] After Nigerian government troops had captured Port Harcourt in May 1968 and enforced a comprehensive blockade, severe shortages of food, medicine, clothing and housing led to heavy casualties among Biafran civilians. By the

---

[118] Ganji 1962, pp. 7–8.

[119] see the Reviews: Egon Schwelb, 'Book Review: International Protection of Human Rights. By Manouchehr Ganji', *American Journal of International Law* 1963, 57, p. 172; Rosalyn Higgins, 'Review: International Protection of Human Rights', *International Affairs* 1963, 39(1), p. 85.

[120] Ganji 1962, p. 43, quoting Lawrence 1910, p. 129.

[121] Ganji 1962, p. 44.

[122] Reisman and McDougal 1968 Memorandum, reprinted in: Lillich 1973, p. 179, with fn. 44.

[123] Douglas Anthony, 'Irreconcilable Narratives – Biafra, Nigeria and Arguments about Genocide, 1966–1970', in: A. Dirk Moses and Lasse Heerten (eds.), *Postcolonial Conflict and the Question of Genocide*, New York: Routledge 2017, pp. 47–71.

summer of 1968, the civil war that had gone almost unnoticed since its outbreak in May 1967 became the focus of attention in Europe, Israel and the United States. On 12 June 1968, the British newspaper *The Sun* ran a front-page report about Biafra with the headline 'The Land of No Hope', casting Biafra as a place of suffering innocents – and only the first of a massive wave of media reports on the evolving situation that eventually turned the Nigerian Civil War into a 'humanitarian media event'.[124] Subsequently, public protest was growing, with pressure for political action mounting, particularly in the United Kingdom, the Scandinavian countries, West Germany, and France. On 17 and 22 July 1968, the Knesset, the Israeli parliament, conducted lengthy debates on both the government's diplomatic stance and moral responsibility regarding the 'prevention of genocide'.[125] On 5 August 1968, the secessionist leader of the Biafran provinces, Chukwuemeka Odumegwu Ojukwu (1933–2011), accused the Nigerian Federal Military Government of genocide in a speech to the Organisation of African Unity (OAU) in Addis Ababa.[126] He alleged that massacres that had taken place in previous years, killing somewhere around 30,000 Ibos by September 1966, amounted to genocide and accused the President of the Federal Military Government, Yakubu Gowon, of 'aspiring to be the Hitler of Africa'.

Although the situation drew increasingly more public attention, no material support for the 'Republic of Biafra' was forthcoming. Only a handful of African countries recognised the 'Republic', and no government was willing to provide the required humanitarian assistance or military aid. International organisations were unwilling to become involved. As they had in the Congo situation several years earlier, the United Nations and states belonging to all of the political groupings restated the position that the right to self-determination does not amount to a right of secession.[127] In the United States, the 'American Committee to Keep Biafra Alive' lobbied for the recognition of the alleged genocide in Biafra through 'a "humanitarian intervention" of some sort in Biafra in order to save countless lives'.[128] On 25 September 1968, two committee members travelled to Washington to discuss with American officials what the United States could do in Biafra – and presented the administration with the aforementioned paper prepared by Reisman in collaboration with Myres S. McDougal.[129]

---

[124] Lasse Heerten, *The Biafran War and Postcolonial Humanitarianism*, Cambridge University Press 2017, pp. 108–109, 120.

[125] Zach Levey, 'Israel, Nigeria and the Biafra Civil War', in: A. Dirk Moses and Lasse Heerten (eds.), *Postcolonial Conflict and the Question of Genocide*, New York: Routledge 2017, pp. 177–197.

[126] The following is based on Karen E. Smith, *Genocide and the Europeans*, Cambridge University Press, 2010, pp. 66–81.

[127] Cassese 1995, p. 123.

[128] Brian McNeil, 'And Starvation Is the Grim Reaper', in: A. Dirk Moses and Lasse Heerten (eds.), *Postcolonial Conflict and the Question of Genocide*, New York: Routledge 2017, p. 288.

[129] McNeil 2017, p. 288.

W. Michael Reisman (b. 1939), professor of International Law at Yale University and, together with McDougal (1906–1998) and Harold D. Lasswell (1902–1978), founder of the so-called New Haven School, has been one of the most prolific supporters of the 'employment of the exceptional international legal institution of humanitarian intervention'. In 1969, he considered the doctrine 'the authoritative expectation of the peoples of the world',[130] and in the paper prepared as a petition to the United Nations, he took the position that, following the reading of Article 2(4) of the UN Charter championed by Stone, '[f]orceful intervention' in circumstances like the Biafran situation 'in the territory of another State is permissible and for parties to the Charter and the Genocide Convention is mandatory':[131]

> The validity of humanitarian intervention is not based upon the nation-state-oriented theories of international law; these theories are little more than two centuries old. It is based upon an antinomic but equally vigorous principle, deriving from a long tradition of natural law and secular values: the kinship and minimum reciprocal responsibilities of all humanity, the inability of geographical boundaries to stem categorical moral imperatives, and ultimately, the confirmation of the sanctity of human life, without reference to place or transient circumstance.[132]

Accordingly, the paper, having examined the state practice reconstructed in this book with a more positive conclusion, ends with a moral, rather than a legal plea:

> The pattern of intergroup struggle – from distrust, and hostility to bloody violence – will persist as long as world elites are unable to collaborate in a global system providing the minimum of personal and group security. Whether the banners are racial, ethnic, religious, or the heady metaphysics of political creed, the peoples of the world will be unable to sustain a vision of the unity of mankind, and we will continue to witness the bleeding raw material demanding humanitarian intervention. We have waited too long and have already lost our innocence; if we cannot perfect, as a minimum, a system of humanitarian intervention, we have lost our humanity. If we sit passively by while the Ibos suffer genocide, we have forfeited our right to regain it.[133]

The Biafran War represents a pivotal moment in the ascendance of human rights, humanitarianism and the memorialisation of the Shoah.[134] In the United States, the war was portrayed as an opportunity to draw the lessons from the failures of the responses to the Holocaust for the first time.[135] Asked in 2014 whether he remembered the atmosphere that had led to his compassionate plea, Professor Reisman

---

[130] Myres S. McDougal and W. Michael Reisman, 'Respone', *International Lawyer* 1969, 3(2), p. 438.

[131] Reisman and McDougal 1968 Memorandum, reprinted in: Lillich 1973, p. 178.

[132] Reisman and McDougal 1968 Memorandum, reprinted in: Lillich 1973, p. 168.

[133] Reisman and McDougal 1968 Memorandum, reprinted in: Lillich 1973, p. 195.

[134] See generally: Heerten 2017; Elizabeth Bird and Fraser M. Ottanelli, *The Asaba Massacre – Trauma, Memory, and the Nigerian Civil War*, Cambridge University Press 2017.

[135] Peter Novick, *The Holocaust in American Life*, Boston: Houghton Mifflin 1999, p. 247.

replied that he had needed no reminder of the Holocaust to understand the gravity of the situation.[136] The position taken in his paper, however, certainly was not the mainstream position in international law in the late 1960s. One of the longest running treatises on international law in Germany, first published in 1965, consistently mentioned the practice of nineteenth-century 'humanitarian intervention' (called 'intervention d'humanité' in the book) as an early example of international human rights protection in international law,[137] but by the second edition published in 1969 felt the need to categorically state that such intervention on humanitarian grounds would be illegal under current international law.[138]

According to the entry in the *Encyclopedia of Genocide and Crimes against Humanity*, 'about three million Biafrans are believed to have lost their lives' during the war, 'an estimated one million of them as a result of severe malnutrition'.[139] Whether or not this constitutes genocide in the legal sense might be a matter of dispute.[140] Under the pressure of the British government, the Nigerian Federal Military Government accepted an International Observer Team, which issued reports on its activities from September 1968 to January 1970. The first report, of 2 October 1968, 'concluded that "[t]here is no evidence of any intent by the Federal troops to destroy the Ibo people or their property, and the use of the term genocide is in no way justified". Every subsequent report repeated that message'.[141]

If the submission of Reisman's paper, 'as a legal and political act (...) was inconsequential',[142] because the world organisation did not respond to this or other calls for action (of which there were many),[143] it quickly acquired a remarkable afterlife. It was privately circulated among American international lawyers and then discussed at the conference on 'Humanitarian Intervention and the United Nations' organised by Reisman's colleague Lillich in March 1972. This conference produced a 'consensus', provided by Professor Tom Farer (b. 1935), according to which

almost every member of a group representing a considerable portion of the U.S. Foreign policy spectrum *agreed* on the desirability of humanitarian intervention to prevent large-scale abuse, on the appropriateness of exhausting multilateral

[136] Phone conversation with the author, 2014.
[137] Ignaz Seidl-Hohenveldern, *Völkerrecht*, 1st ed., Cologne: Heymanns 1965, p. 244, no. 1168.
[138] Ignaz Seidl-Hohenveldern, *Völkerrecht*, 2nd ed., Cologne: Heymanns 1969, p. 295, no. 1295.
[139] Kolawole Olaniyan, 'Biafra/Nigeria', in: Dinah L. Shelton (ed.), *Encyclopedia of Genocide and Crimes against Humanity*, Farmington Hills: MacMillan Reference USA 2005, p. 122. Other estimates put the figure at one million dead; Smith 2010, p. 67.
[140] See Yves Ternon, *Der verbrecherische Staat*, Hamburg: Hamburger Edition 1996, p. 258.
[141] Smith 2010, p. 77, citing the Report dated 2 October 1968 on International Observer Team's visit to 1st Nigerian Divisiopn (UKNA file FCO 65/178).
[142] Heerten 2017, p. 316.
[143] See Heerten 2017, and, for a description of an 'intervention' undertaken, though in a different sense: Michael Aaronson, 'The Nigerian Civil War and "Humanitarian Intervention"', in: Bronwen Everill and Josiah Kaplan (eds.), *The History and Practice of Humanitarian Intervention and Aid in Africa*, Hampshire: Palgrave Macmillan 2013, pp. 176–196.

remedies whenever time allowed, on the need to calculate the damage to the target society as well as to the imminent victims, and on the inadmissibility of interventions designed to safeguard commercial property or ideologically congenial regimes.[144]

However, a statement on the desirability of an ideal-type 'humanitarian intervention', the like of which had not occurred before, did not address the legal situation. In fact, Reisman had argued that the rejection of the 'humanitarian' justification of the United States intervention in the Dominican Republic 'confirmed the lawfulness of humanitarian intervention in international law by arguing that if indeed the operation had been a genuine humanitarian one, it would have been permissible'.[145] But history has not been kind to Reisman's hypothetical. In the few years that passed between its formulation and the subsequent discussion at the conference in Charlottesville, whatever humanitarian component the Dominican episode may have had all but disappeared under the hypocrisy of superpower foreign policy during the Cold War.[146]

Reisman may have failed to write into existence the type of intervention he considered not only potentially lawful, but also necessary on the basis of justice and humanity. Yet his efforts contributed substantially to the debate about 'humanitarian intervention' in the next decades. While the pioneering research into the revival of the doctrine of 'humanitarian intervention' as a a living component of contemporary international law may have been executed under the auspices of Richard B. Lillich, it was the paper prepared by Reisman with McDougal that set the tone and established the narrative of a number of (potential) 'humanitarian interventions' for the purpose of protecting a contemporary value like 'human rights' during the nineteenth century. In the years following the Charlottesville conference, countless international law scholars have tested (and mostly confirmed) the validity of this narrative.[147]

This remarkable achievement must be seen in light of the New Haven School's particular approach to international law as a 'great creative instrument of social policy for promoting a preferred social order'.[148] The commitment 'to invent and recommend the authority structures and functions (. . .) necessary to a world public order that harmonizes with the growing aspirations of the overwhelming number of the peoples of the globe and is in accord with the proclaimed values of human

---

[144] Tom J. Farer, 'Humanitarian Intervention: The View from Chralottesville', in Lillich 1973, p. 164.

[145] Reisman and McDougal 1968 Memorandum, reprinted in: Lillich 1973, p. 186.

[146] See: Roy Allison, *Russia, The West, and Military Intervention*, Oxford University Press 2013, p. 26.

[147] E.g. Behuniak 1978, p. 161.

[148] Chen, *An Introduction to Contemporary International Law*, p. 15, cited according to Sandra Voos, *Die Schule von New Haven*, Berlin: Duncker & Humblot 2000, p. 83.

dignity enunciated by the moral leaders of mankind'[149] would lead Reisman to proclaim the necessity of legal 'humanitarian interventions' well into the twenty-first century.[150] The attraction of this approach is obvious, though it translated into zero action. In 2014 he had to concede that 'if the 'mainstream view' in international law on 'humanitarian intervention' had changed to accommodate to his position, 'the movement is very small'.[151]

Biafra, however, did trigger more than an extended discussion over the desirability of 'humanitarian' use of military force as a legal instrument. The experience of working as medical doctors with the French Red Cross during the war led Bernard Kouchner (b. 1939) and other volunteers to form Médecins Sans Frontières (MSF – also known in English as Doctors Without Borders) claiming a 'duty to intervene' that would supersede national sovereignty in cases of humanitarian crisis. Originally applied only to the medical interventions of MSF, Kouchner, together with the French professor of international Mario Bettati (1937–2017) developed the 'right of intervention' (droit d'ingerence), which led to a more pro-interventionist narrative in France in the 1970s and 1980s that tied a 'right to humanitarian assistance' as a universal protection to the 1789 French Declaration of the Rights of Man and of the Citizen.[152]

4.5 THE 'HUMANITARIAN INTERVENTION' THAT NEVER WAS: EAST PAKISTAN, 1971

The conference in Charlottesville took place not only after the experience of Biafra, but also after the Indian intervention in the Bangladesh Liberation War in 1971. This historical episode is a staple of the historiography on 'humanitarian intervention', despite the fact that the official position of the Indian government hardly lends itself to such a treatment. To this day, Indian legal scholarship is remarkably subdued on the 'humanitarian' potential of the events.[153] For example, the comprehensive monograph on 'The State Practice of India and the Development of International Law' by Bimal N. Patel, Professor of Public International Law and the Director of India's Gujarat National Law University, devotes just this short paragraph to India's

[149] Myres S. McDougal and Harold D. Lasswell, 'The Identification and Appraisal of Diverse Systems of Public Order', American Journal of International Law, 1959, 53, p. 28.
[150] W. Michael Reisman, The Quest for World Order and Human Dignity in the Twenty-first Century: Constitutive Process and Individual Commitment, The Pocket Books of The Hague Academy of International Law 2010, 351.
[151] E-mail mail to the author, 24 February 2014.
[152] Eleanor Davey, 'The Language of Ingérence', in: Norbert Frei, Daniel Stahl, and Annette Weinke (eds.), Human Rights and Humanitarian Intervention, Göttingen: Wallstein Verlag 2017, p. 63. See also: Heerten 2017, pp. 321–327.
[153] See also: Shahid and Khalid 2003, p. 148. For a different view and a glowing praise of the 'just' war of India's intervention by a participant, see: Jasjit Singh, 'India', in: Watanabe Koji (ed.), Humanitarian Intervention – The Evolving Asian Debate, Tokyo: Japan Center for International Exchange 2003, pp. 98–99.

state practice to demonstrate that the 'holistic aim of the Indian human rights practice' is to 'ensure a dignified place of each and every human being in the society':[154]

> Protection and promotion of human rights is an integral element of India's foreign policy. Intervention and efforts of India in Bangladesh in the early 1970s, Sri Lanka in the late 1980s and Nepal in late 2010, Myanmar, and Pakistan, all can be seen in the larger perspective of India's support for the assertion of people's rights.[155]

This is all the more remarkable as India is a rarity among Asian countries in having widely adopted the Eurocentric narrative of the legality of 'humanitarian intervention' in classic international law,[156] where Lauterpacht (disguised as Oppenheim) is cited with approval in a widely used Indian textbook on international law published in 1966: 'The Charter of the United Nations, in recognising the promotion of respect for fundamental human rights and freedoms as one of the principal objects of the Organisation, marks a further step in the direction of elevating the principle of humanitarian intervention to a basic rule of organised international society'.[157] A later edition of the same textbook, however, makes no mention of the Indian intervention over East Pakistan in the context of a state practice relating to 'humanitarian intervention'.[158]

At the Charlottesville conference in March 1972, the memory of the events of November and December 1971, and the developments leading up to the Indian use of force in neighbouring East Pakistan (later Bangladesh), seemed to be on the minds of all the participants and numerous references were made during the discussions. As Professor Ellen Frey-Wouters (1927–2015), a participant quite critical of earlier claims of 'humanitarian intervention',[159] said during the second part of the proceedings: 'The Indian intervention in East Pakistan last fall has had a deep impact on our thinking. The whole question of humanitarian intervention has become unclear and must be reexamined'.[160]

What had happened? After the 1947 partition of British India into India and Pakistan, Pakistani territory comprised two geographically separate Muslim-majority areas, with East Pakistan sitting some 1,500 kilometres away on the other side of India. Effectively under military rule from West Pakistan since independence, the country was not the place to foster peaceful relations between its many different ethnic groups. In East Pakistan, the smaller but more populous part of the country, a distinct national identity formed over the course of the next twenty years, fuelled by

---

[154] Bimal N. Patel, *The State Practice of India and the Development of International Law*, Leiden: Brill 2016, p. 152.
[155] Patel 2016, pp. 155–156 (footnote omitted).
[156] See: Tandon 1966, pp. 197–198; Varghese 1952, p. 348.
[157] 'Oppenheim: International law, Vol. 1, 8th ed., p. 313', cited according to Tandon 1966, p. 198.
[158] See Tandon and Tandon 1985, pp. 153–154.
[159] Ellen Frey-Wouters, Comment, in: Lillich 1973, p. 23.
[160] Ellen Frey-Wouters, Comment, in: Lillich 1973, p. 46.

the decisions of the officials in West Pakistan to build the institutions of the new country on a bias against Bengali culture, for example, by making Urdu the official language of Pakistan, despite the fact that in 1947 it was spoken by only 3 per cent of the Pakistani population, whereas Bengali was spoken by 56 per cent.[161] The denial of political rights to East Pakistan eventually led to widespread social and political unrest, and on 25 March 1971, the military ruler of Pakistan, General Yahya Khan, ordered military operations in the East, blaming 'anti-Pakistan and secessionist elements' for the 'gravity of the situation'.[162] Local political leaders issued a 'Declaration of Emancipation' and in response, the West Pakistani army began a campaign of brutal repression, deliberately targeting the civilian population and attempting to 'crush the two Bengali organisations in Dhaka that could offer serious armed resistance: the police and the paramilitary East Pakistan Rifles'.[163] Despite the brutality of the army attack, popular resistance all over the Bengal delta continued for months. The military action caused thousands to flee the cities and towns and, by May 1971, the Indian authorities reported that more than 1,500,000 refugees had reached the country and that 60,000 more were coming in every day.[164]

Over the course of the next months, in weather conditions that favoured guerrilla tactics brought on by the monsoon season, some 100,000 Bengali freedom fighters established control of parts of East Pakistan and continued to engage in ambushes and raids with Pakistani troops. Violence was widespread and not restricted to the Pakistani military: Bengalis on both sides of the war also killed other Bengalis who did not agree with their respective political projects, and Hindu Bengalis were killed not only by the army for their suspected support for India, but also by their Bengali Muslim brethren, sometimes for non-political, material reasons.[165] The number of refugees in India only continued to grow, spreading stories of the atrocities they had fled. The international press began to speak of 'genocide' and, in July 1971, former Beatle George Harrison, then at the peak of his popularity as a solo artist, released the song 'Bangladesh' as a standalone single – pop culture's first ever charity single. International exposure reached its peak with the 'Concert for Bangladesh' at New York's Madison Square Garden on 1 August 1971, organised by Harrison and Indian Sitar master Ravi Shankar with an audience of around 40,000 people and broad international coverage. This translated into financial relief efforts that would sometimes take years to reach those in need, and which brought no change on the ground. By October, after the rainy season had ended, it had become clear that neither the Pakistani army nor the freedom fighters could secure a military victory.

[161] The following is based on Willem van Schendel, *A History of Bangladesh*, Cambridge University Press 2009, p. 110.
[162] van Schendel 2009, p. 162.
[163] van Schendel 2009, p. 162.
[164] van Schendel 2009, p. 164.
[165] Sarmila Bose, 'The Question of Genocide and the Quest for Justice in the 1971 War', *Journal of Genocide Research* 2011, 4, p. 398.

India stepped up its international propaganda campaign and, after Pakistani forces carried out air raids into India on 3 December 1971, invaded East Pakistan. This (third) India-Pakistan War had begun and would end roughly two weeks later, when the Pakistani army surrendered on 16 December. The new independent state of Bangladesh was brought into existence.

Estimates of the death toll resulting from this episode vary between one million and three million, about ten million people fled their homes – and while many of the deaths may have been the result of famine, rather than mass killings, it is clear that mass violence was also the cause of the mass impoverishment and famines that may have killed more people than fell victim to murders directly.[166] It therefore seems that here would be a clear-cut case for 'humanitarian intervention'. Yet, despite all the humanitarian activism and coverage of the atrocities, India never made the argument in the international fora that its military actions were legally justified under this doctrine, though it certainly was not unknown in the country. Instead, the Secretariat of the International Commission of Jurists emphasised in a report published in June 1972 that 'India claims to have acted first in self-defence, and secondly in giving support to the new Government of Bangladesh which she recognised when the hostilities began', but concluded that

> India's armed intervention would have been justified if she had acted under the doctrine of humanitarian intervention, and further that India would have been entitled to act unilaterally under this doctrine in view of the growing and intolerable burden which the refugees were casting upon India and in view of the inability of international organisations to take any effective action to bring to an end the massive violations of human rights in East Pakistan which were causing the flow of refugees.[167]

When the situation was discussed at the UN Security Council on 4 December 1971, Pakistan complained of the unjustified aggression of one member state against another and referred to the resulting 'refugee problem' as a 'humanitarian one',[168] while the Indian representative referred to ten million refugees coming into India as a consequence of Pakistan going through a 'great tragedy' as 'some kind of aggression'.[169] He also said that his country had 'nothing but the purest motives and the purest of intentions: to rescue the people of East Bengal from the way they are suffering'.[170] His statement at the Security Council did use the language of the doctrine, as when he claimed that the military repression was so grave as to 'shock

[166] Christian Gerlach, *Extremely Violent Societies*, Cambridge University Press 2010, p. 164.
[167] International Commission of Jurists, *The Events in East Pakistan, 1971: a legal study*, Geneva 1972, p. 96, available at: www.icj.org/wp-content/uploads/1972/06/Bangladesh-events-East-Pakistan-1971-thematic-report-1972-eng.pdf, last accessed 23 September 2018.
[168] S/PV.1606 (1971), paras 70, 117, 148.
[169] S/PV.1606 (1971), paras 160, 161.
[170] S./PV.1606 (1971), para 186.

the conscience of mankind',[171] but rather than portray his country's reaction as justified in violating Pakistan's sovereignty because of the gravity of military repression, the thread that runs through India's statement is the defence of national sovereignty against the consequences of actions in a neighbouring country.[172] As Simon Chesterman clearly puts it: 'Even if one accepts that India's action constitutes state practice for the purposes of establishing customary international law, there is little evidence of *opinio juris*'.[173] This conclusion, though supported by the International Commission of Jurists' statement in 1972, is largely ignored in the narrative of the legality of 'humanitarian intervention', most profoundly by the Belgian statement in the proceedings at the International Court of Justice over the NATO use of force against the Federal Republic of Yugoslavia.[174] By contrast, the ICISS report discusses the case, noting its 'undeniable humanitarian impact', but makes it clear that, at the time, no country was prepared to accept any 'humanitarian' justification.[175]

Indeed, at the United Nations, India failed to garner support for its claims of legality, the conflict being swallowed up by Cold War antagonism. The Soviet Union openly backed India, while the United States claimed neutrality, but effectively backed Pakistan and was fully aware of the atrocities committed, after receiving the 'Blood Telegram' on 6 April 1971, which spoke of a 'selective genocide' by the Pakistani military.[176] Thus, neither the Soviet proposal for a Security Council resolution calling on Pakistan 'to take measures to cease all acts of violence by Pakistani forces in East Pakistan which have led to deterioration of the situation',[177] nor the American proposal calling *inter alia* on the Governments of India and Pakistan 'to take all steps required for an immediate cessation of hostilities'[178] was approved. The matter was referred to the General Assembly, which then passed resolution 2793 (XXVI) (1971), which, 'mindful of the provisions of the Charter, in particular of Article 2, paragraph 4', essentially followed the American lead by calling on the Governments of India and Pakistan 'to take forthwith all measures for an immediate cease-fire and withdrawal of their armed forces on the territory of the other to their own side of the India-Pakistan borders'. This amounted to a condemnation of the Indian efforts to claim legality for its actions and has to be seen in the context of the Cold War politics that led the United States to actively (and aggressively) undermine the Indian position to defend its own standing in the Vietnam

[171] S./PV.1606 (1971), para 159.
[172] e.g. S/PV.1606 (1971), para 175.
[173] Chesterman 2001, p. 75.
[174] Available at: www.icj-cij.org/docket/files/105/4515.pdf
[175] International Commission on Intervention and State Sovereignty 2001, p. 56.
[176] Gary J. Bass, *The Blood Telegram*, New York: A. A. Knopf 2013. The telegram itself is available at: https://nsarchive2.gwu.edu//NSAEBB/NSAEBB79/BEBB1.pdf, last accessed 26 September 2018.
[177] S/PV.1606 (1971), para 358.
[178] S/PV.1606 (1971), para 200.

War, then in its sixth year of ground operations. President Nixon was certain that India was the aggressor in this case and told his National Security Advisor: 'We can't let these goddam sanctimonious Indians get away with this. They've pissed on us on Vietnam for 5 years, Henry'.[179] The irony is almost heart-breaking: While the Indian intervention and the atrocities committed by the Pakistani military led the (mostly) American lawyers gathered in Charlottesville to search for guidelines that would allow future 'humanitarian interventions' to be recognised as legal, the American government was complicit in the very crimes that caused the intervention.

Yet the events inspired other international lawyers to engage with the subject of 'humanitarian intervention' as well. In 1973, Thomas M. Franck (1931–2009), then Professor of International Law at the New York University and a member of the Board of Editors at the *American Journal of International Law*, and Nigel S. Rodley (1941–2017), then a Research Fellow at the Center for International Studies at the New York University, published 'After Bangladesh: The Law of Humanitarian Intervention by Military Force' in the Journal co-edited by Franck. Franck would go on to be the 'leading American scholar of international law',[180] and Rodley devoted his life to human rights like few other international lawyers, leading the path towards the United Nations conventions against torture. Both may have had their own personal reasons for an interest in a version of international law that allowed for unilateral 'humanitarian intervention'[181] and analysed the Indian actions with an emphasis on a claim of 'Indian Assertions of New "Humanitarian" Principles During the Bangladesh Crisis'.[182] The authors stated that any claim to a historic international 'right' of forceful 'humanitarian intervention' would have had to 'come as a surprise to Biafrans', and others who may have recently found themselves in the need of such a right to be exercised on their behalf.[183] They concluded that such a right did not exist, even if there may be circumstances 'in which the unilateral use of force to overthrow injustice begins to seem less wrong than to turn aside', but that 'this sense of superior "necessity" belongs in the realm not of law, but moral choice'.[184]

---

[179] Bass 2013, p. 287.

[180] David Kennedy, as quoted in 'Thomas Franck, Who Advised Countries on Law, Dies at 77', Obituary in *The New York Times*, 29 May 2009.

[181] Thomas Franck was born in Berlin in 1931 to Jewish parents and his family fled Germany just before so-called Kristallnacht; the Nazi pogrom in November 1938. See: 'Thomas Franck, Who Advised Countries on Law, Dies at 77', Obituary in *The New York Times*, 29 May 2009. Nigel S. Rodley was the son of Hans Rosenfeld, who had arrived in the United Kingdom in 1938 as a refugee from Germany, and he, according to his obituary by Geoffrey Robertson, 'had a horror in his bones of abuse of state power, from which his own family had fatally suffered', see 'Sir Nigel Rodley obituary', *The Guardian*, 2 February 2017, available at: www.theguardian.com/law/2017/feb/02/sir-nigel-rodley-obituary, last accessed 15 May 2019.

[182] Franck and Rodley 1973, p. 276.

[183] Franck and Rodley 1973, p. 296.

[184] Franck and Rodley 1973, p. 304.

Toward the end of their careers, both scholars returned to the question of the legality of unilateral 'humanitarian intervention' in two seminal works on the international law on the use of force: Both remained committed to their view that the law allowed no such interventions, even if on occasion they might be desirable.[185] Franck returned to the case of Bangladesh, concerned enough to mention that 'India's motives were not exactly above suspicion'.[186] Rodley was even less forgiving, noting that this 'may well be the only case in which India has embraced an interpretation of the right to self-determination that would apply to a territory that emerged from colonialism. India also invoked the humanitarian situation, albeit not clearly in terms propounding a legal claim. Again, it would be anomalous Indian practice. There has been no sign of a similar interest when serious bloodshed of Tamils in Sri Lanka on various occasions in the past 30 years could have been expected to arouse that interest'.[187] He also pointed out that the reaction of the 'international community' in particular deprived this action 'of any serious precedential value for the notion of humanitarian intervention', 'which was no more moved by the flow of millions of refugees than it was by the carnage of those who remained. (. . .) Far from suggesting a world *opinio juris* in favour of humanitarian intervention, this reaction is more forceful evidence of the opposite'.[188] Franck, on the other hand, was at least willing to concede that the treatment of the situation in the General Assembly 'constituted a recognition of linkage between the Charter's prohibition on unilateral recourse to force (Article 2(4)) and other humanitarian and human rights requisites of the Charter'.[189] It seems clear enough, however, that any later claim of a precedential value of this case would be up against nothing less than the historical record.

4.6 INTO THE TWENTY-FIRST CENTURY: 'HUMANITARIAN INTERVENTION' AND THE USES OF HISTORY

Fernando Tesón has argued that 'the fresh memories of the Holocaust would have led the framers [of the UN Charter] to *allow* for humanitarian intervention, had they thought about it', claiming the 'all-important humanitarian thrust of World War II and its sequel, the Nuremberg trials' as support for this idea.[190] While it is true that the 'memories' of the Holocaust helped to create a rather brief 'human rights moment' in the 1940s, and the San Francisco conference for the United Nations

---

[185] Franck 2002, pp. 171–191; Nigel Rodley, 'Humanitarian Intervention', in: Marc Weller (ed.), *The Oxford Handbook on the Use of Force in International Law*, Oxford University Press 2015, pp. 775–796.
[186] Franck 2002, p. 142.
[187] Rodley 2015, section III.A.1. (iBooks ed.).
[188] Rodley 2015.
[189] Franck 2002, p. 142.
[190] Tesón 2005, p. 199.

Charter took place in the 'overwhelming presence' of photographs from the concentration camps,[191] the major focus of the Charter was to limit the legal use of force by individual states. There is no indication that anyone participating in the conference would have been interested in establishing or preserving a right to unilaterally use military force outside of the institutions created by the Charter and its provisions against the use of force, building on the Pact of Paris (the General Treaty for the Renunciation of War of 27 August 1928). Hersch Lauterpacht called this development a 'fundamental change in the legal structure of international society',[192] and these structures have evolved with regard to the question of using force in situations that might call for 'humanitarian interventions' that the relevant organs of the United Nations have passed several resolutions that eventually established in the 1990s what international lawyers had been arguing all along: Gross human rights violations in one state can be a matter of a international *legal* concern and thus trigger Security Council backed action. In the absence of such backing, the search for an answer continues into the twenty-first century.

The specific values claimed by Tesón have dominated the discussion over the legitimacy of the use of military force to stop the atrocities committed during and after the break-up of the former Socialist Republic of Yugoslavia in the late 1990s. In 1995, American journalist and human rights-activist David Rieff called for United States intervention after the preventable atrocities in Bosnia:

> To utter words like 'Never again' as [US President Bill] Clinton did at the opening of the Holocaust Museum, was to take vacuity over the border into obscenity as long as the genocide in Bosnia was going and Clinton was doing nothing to stop it. His words were literally meaningless. For if there was to be no intervention to stop a genocide that was taking place, then the phrase 'Never again' meant nothing more than: Never again would Germans kill Jews in Europe in the 1940s. Clinton might as well have said, 'Never again the potato famine', or 'Never again the slaughter of the Albigisians'.[193]

This is not the place to determine whether the choice of words in this quote is legally accurate, but the inadequacy of the international reaction to the events in Bosnia did not only trouble this American activist. In Germany, for example, the 1990s saw the first international operations of the German military since the end of World War II. Owing to Germany's changed role in the world and the emergence of a younger generation of politicians, a trend towards more inclusion and a more active role in international organisations became apparent. At the same time, a restraint for any role in military operations was tied to the historic experience of two

---

[191] Mark Philip Bradley, *The World Reimagined*, Cambridge University Press 2016, p. 81.
[192] as quoted in Oona Hathaway and Scott J. Shapiro, *The Internationalists*, New York: Simon & Schuster 2017, p. 302.
[193] David Rieff, *Slaughterhouse: Bosnia and the Failure of the West*, New York: Simon & Schuster 1995, p. 27.

World Wars and the Shoah. This resulted in conflicting conclusions drawn from the same historic experience, sometimes represented in one and the same person.[194]

The case of Joschka Fischer, German foreign minister during the NATO campaign in Kosovo, is a case in point. On 30 June 1995, during the Bosnian War, the German parliament had debated the momentous decision to deploy the German military beyond the borders of the NATO partners to support the ongoing NATO operations in Bosnia. After German reunification, Chancellor Helmut Kohl had established the maxim that German troops should not serve out of area in any territory occupied by the Nazis in World War II.[195] But in the wake of the horrors of Bosnia, this doctrine was put into question. In the Bundestag debate, Joschka Fischer, then an oppositional member of parliament for the Greens, had argued against a military solution to the conflict and any German military involvement. He had reiterated his (and his party's) pacifism and renewed his commitment never to deploy German military forces to areas where 'the Wehrmacht caused havoc in the cruellest way in the Second World War'.[196] By 1999, when his Green Party was in government in a coalition with the Social Democrats, his pacifism had taken second seat to another lesson allegedly learned from history. At a tumultuous congress of his party that year, themed 'Bringing together Human Rights and Peace', Fischer was hit with a paint-filled balloon, which exploded against his head and covered the right side of his face and upper body with red paint, as activists protested his shift to support military operations against the Serbian actions in Kosovo. Later diagnosed with a broken eardrum, Fischer, traces of the paint still visible, proceeded to give a speech that continues to define his legacy. As Paul Hockenos describes the situation in his 'alternative history of post-war Germany', Fischer

> never thought he'd have to choose between the two axioms that had always guided his political activism: 'Never again war' and 'Never again Auschwitz'. But it had come to that. The international community had to use the instruments of war to stop mass murder, to prevent another genocide in Europe. The veins in his neck pulsing wildly as he spoke, Fischer strained his voice to conclude: 'I understand all too well your arguments and reservations. They're mine, too. I wage this debate with myself everyday. But I nevertheless ask you to have the strength to accept responsibility, as difficult as that may be'.[197]

Fischer got the support he sought from his party, and Germany contributed its forces to the NATO campaign against Milosevic's Serbia. The result was a possible 'humanitarian intervention' by NATO states without Security Council authorisation,

---

[194] See generally: Maja Zehfuss, *Wounds of Memory*, Cambridge University Press 2007.

[195] Brendan Simms, 'From the Kohl to the Fischer Doctrine: Germany and the Wars of the Yugoslav Succession, 1991–1999', *German History* 2003, 21, p. 402.

[196] Deutscher Bundestag, Plenarprotokoll, 13/48, 30/06/1995, 3982, cited according to the translation by Zehfuss 2007, p. 70.

[197] Paul Hockenos, *Joschka Fischer and the Making of the Berlin Republic*, Oxford University Press 2007, p. 272.

but one that still causes division, not just across different strands of international law or philosophy, but across continents. A general Western consensus rests on a narrative of 'known and little disputed' 'terrible facts in and relating to Kosovo in 1998–1999',[198] though even here details are in fact sketchy.[199] Russian and Asian narratives differ considerably.[200] The majority view among Western writers on the Kosovo intervention, can, with the hindsight of roughly twenty years, probably be described best in the words of the 2000 Kosovo Report, the report by the Independent International Commission on Kosovo, established to examine key developments prior to, during, and after the Kosovo war, including systematic violations of human rights in the region: It was legitimate, but illegal.[201] In 2001, Michal J. Glennon famously concluded that NATO's actions had clearly breached the Charter of the United Nations, 'but *international law?* Using international law's traditional methods, no one can say'.[202] 'Fifty years after the drafting of the Charter', he went on,

> it is no longer possible to know when use of force by states violates international law. International law comprised [more] than just the Charter; customary norms, its scholastic apologists reminded us, also count in limiting state behavior. But customary international law contained so many gaps and inconsistencies, and international lawyers had so often distorted it to reach preferred outcomes, that no one confidently could say when intervention was permitted or prohibited.[203]

He constituted that, at the end of the twentieth century, 'an odd duality of interventionist regimes' had developed: 'one a *de jure* regime comprised of formal rules that states felt free to ignore, the other a *de facto* regime governed by geopolitical factors that states knew to be controlling'. It was the latter, he opined that effectively determined whether or not states would intervene in situations such as Kosovo, 'not where law tells them they may, but [w]here wisdom tells them they should, where power tells them, they can, and – perhaps – where justice, as they see it, tells them they must'.[204] Similarly, Fernando Tesón has pointed to the 'relative purity of the incident as an instance of humanitarian intervention', claiming that 'Kosovo is the culmination of a series of events that, seen together, configure an unmistakable

---

[198] Louis Henkin, 'Kosovo and the Law of "Humanitarian Intervention"', *American Journal of International Law* 1999, 93, p. 824.

[199] Loquai 2000; Trbovich 2008, pp. 343–361.

[200] For a South Korean perspective, see: Kim Sung-han, 'South Korea', in: Watanabe Koji (ed.), *Humanitarian Intervention – The Evolving Asian Debate*, Tokyo: Japan Center for International Exchange 2003, pp. 66–68. For the summary of a rather skewed Russian narrative, see: Roberts 2017, pp. 198–199.

[201] Independent International Commission on Kosovo, *The Kosovo Report*, Oxford University Press 2000.

[202] Michael J. Glennon, *Limits of Law, Prerogatives of Power*, New York: Palgrave 2001, pp. 180–181.

[203] Glennon 2001, p. 208.

[204] Glennon 2001, p. 209.

trend toward accepting the doctrine of humanitarian intervention' and that NATO's inability to secure Security Council authorisation is not a shortcoming for the claim of legality, because 'NATO had *stronger* claim to legitimacy in authorizing humanitarian intervention in Kosovo than the Security Council', because 'NATO is the entity that comes closest to representing the liberal alliance, the community of nations committed to the values of human rights and democracy'.[205]

Although Operation Allied Force received the most extensive 'humanitarian' justifications from the nations involved and was considered a watershed moment in the development of international law by many Western writers,[206] the responses from other parts of the world were less enthusiastic.[207] One of the more obvious reasons may be that NATO states in claiming legitimacy and legality for their actions overstretched their arguments into the field of post-truth.[208] In May 1999, Belgium – represented by Rusen Ergec, Professor of International Law at the University of Luxembourg – argued in the proceedings before the International Court of Justice over the NATO use of force against the Federal Republic of Yugoslavia that there was 'no shortage of precedents' of 'armed humanitarian interventions', adding 'Tanzania's intervention in Uganda; Vietnam in Cambodia, the West African countries' interventions first in Liberia and then in Sierra Leone' to the aforementioned Indian intervention in East Pakistan, stating: 'While there may have been certain doubts expressed in the doctrine, and among some members of the international community, these interventions have not been expressly condemned by the relevant United Nations bodies'. Even though this enumeration represents the canon of twentieth century interventions discussed in the legal literature on 'humanitarian interventions', the claim that the relevant United Nations bodies had not condemned them, is, at least in the case of the Vietnamese intervention in Cambodia, manifestly untrue and, in the case of the Indian intervention in East Pakistan, as shown above, at least not entirely accurate. The claim is only true with regard to the Tanzanian intervention in Uganda, but misleading in this case, too, because not one of these interventions was justified as an alleged 'humanitarian intervention' by the acting states.[209] Even the Tanzanian intervention was criticised

---

[205] Tesón 2005, pp. 384, 386, 388.

[206] For a comprehensive overview of the different opinions by American and continental European authors: Masuch 2006.

[207] For an overview of opinions from China, Japan, South Korea, India and ASEAN, see: Watanabe Koji (ed.), *Humanitarian Intervention – The Evolving Asian Debate*, Tokyo: Japan Center for International Exchange 2003. For examples from Chinese and Russian scholarship, see: Roberts 2017, pp. 196–199.

[208] It should be noted that accounts of the Kosovo case (and the trial of Slobodan Milosevic at the ICTY) presented in a Russian textbook, as recounted in Roberts 2017, pp. 198–199, also appear to be counterfactual.

[209] In addition, the ECOWAS interventions in Liberia and Sierra Leone have to be seen in the context of regional organisations taking action against their own member states, see generally: Christine Gray, *International Law and the Use of Force*, 3rd ed., Oxford University Press 2008, pp. 44–51.

by some leaders at the 1979 summit of the Organisation of African Unity, and it simply was never debated at the United Nations.[210] In addition, it would seem clear that a lack of condemnation in no way equals the acceptance of a right and it is therefore hardly surprising that Belgium seems to have had little faith in the legal arguments put forward on the Kingdom's behalf, with the Belgian foreign minister stating in the General Assembly in September 1999: 'We hope that resorting to force without the Council's approval will not constitute a precedent'.[211]

It is, perhaps, not surprising that writers supportive of a right of 'humanitarian intervention' without Security Council authorisation have claimed Kosovo as 'the most important precedent supporting the legitimacy of unilateral humanitarian intervention',[212] a potential 'Grotian Moment' in the development of international law.[213] There are even claims that the 14 April 2018 United States/French/United Kingdom airstrikes on Syrian chemical weapons facilities have provided the ingredients necessary for the crystallisation of a customary international law of a limited right of 'humanitarian intervention', toward which international law 'has been moving in fits and starts' since Kosovo.[214] But maybe the idea that strategic airstrikes of questionable effect in a bloody civil war that has continued since could be the culmination of a process of decades, if not centuries, is not very convincing. And maybe the American administration which ordered these strikes is not a very good candidate to represent the idea of 'good international citizenship',[215] that is at the heart of all claims for a right of 'humanitarian intervention'. Incorporating such a right into international law requires changing the rules about the rules of international law[216] and, contrary to expectations nurtured after Operation Allied Force, this still has not happened. It would require 'a very high standard of evidence of changed state beliefs',[217] of which there is no sign.

---

[210] Ronzitti 1985, pp. 104–105.

[211] A/54/PV.14, 25 September 1999, p. 17.

[212] Tesón 2005, p. 374.

[213] Michael P. Scharf, 'Seizing the "Grotian Moment": Accelerated Formation of Customary International Law in Times of Fundamental Change', *Cornell International Law Journal* 2010, 43, pp. 450–451.

[214] Michael P. Scharf, 'Striking a Grotian Moment: How the Syria Airstrikes Changed International Law Relating to Humanitarian Intervention', *Chicago Journal of International Law* 2018, 19, pp. 3–29. In his book *Customary International Law in Times of Fundamental Change – Recognizing Grotian Moments*, Cambridge University Press 2013, p. 181, Scharf concluded that '[w]hatever ultimately happens in Syria, it is clear that the 1999 NATO intervention did not fulfill its potential to represent a Grotian Moment'.

[215] See: Andrew Linklatler and Hidemi Suganami, *The English School of International Relations*, Cambridge University Press 2006, pp. 223–257.

[216] Michael Byers and Simon Chesterman, 'Changing the Rules about Rules? Unilateral Humanitarian Intervention and the Future of International Law', in: J. L. Holzgrefe and Robert O. Keohane (eds.), *Humanitarian Intervention – Ethical, Legal, and Political Dilemmas*, Cambridge University Press 2003, p. 177.

[217] Brian D. Lepard, *Customary International Law*, Cambridge University Press 2010, p. 260.

Samuel Moyn has forcefully demonstrated that claims of past 'humanitarian interventions' are often read the wrong way if understood as the purported studies of history they are presented as and are actually aimed at the present.[218] In international law, this is particularly true. The claim of applying customary international law (a precedent) is the institutionalised version of using history to claim legality for the present. Even more, the claim of a right of humanitarian intervention is tied to a claim of a 'more just' new world order, in which human rights prevail over injustice.[219] Kosovo is in this light seen as an example of 'not always giving the Devil the benefit of the law' and a way to overcome a law that prohibits what it should not.[220] Yet twenty years later, Kosovo remains a singular incident, though not for a lack of atrocities committed. In that sense, NATO's Operation Allied Force proved to be a dead end for 'humanitarian intervention' and the future of the history of 'humanitarian intervention' may very well be in the past. Strangers, after all, are more often than not left to drown in the Mediterranean and other seas than saved.

---

[218] Moyn 2014.

[219] e.g. John Charvet and Elisa Kaczynska-Nay, *The Liberal Project and Human Rights – The Theory and Practice of a New World Order*, Cambridge University Press 2008, pp. 271–281.

[220] Nigel Biggar, *In Defence of War*, Oxford University Press 2013, p. 223.

Bibliography

LITERATURE PRIOR TO 1945

Johann Heinrich Abicht, *Kurze Darstellung des Natur-und Völkerrechts zum Gebrauch bey Vorlesungen*, Bayreuth: Johan Andreas Lubers Erben 1795.

Hildebrando Accioly, *Traité de Droit Internatonal Public*, French trans. by Paul Goulé, Vol. I, Paris: Sirey 1940.

Sheldon Amos, *Lectures on International Law*, London: Stevens and Sons 1874.

Elbert J. Benton, *International Law and Diplomacy of the Spanish-American War*, Baltimore: The Johns Hopkins Press, 1908.

Norman Bentwich, 'The League of Nations and Racial Persecution in Germany', *Transactions of the Grotius Society* 1933, 19, pp. 75–88.

Carl Bilfinger, 'Die Kriegserklärungen der Westmächte und der Kelloggpakt', *Zeitschrift für ausländisches öffentliches Recht und Völkerrecht* 1940, pp. 1–23.

Johann Caspar Bluntschli, 'Juden, Rechtliche Stellung der', in: Johann C. Bluntschli and K. Brater (eds.), *Deutsches Staats-Wörterbuch*, Vol. 5, Stuttgart/Leipzig: Expedition des Staats-Wörterbuchs 1860, pp. 441–447.

Das moderne Völkerrecht der civilisirten Staten, Nördlingen: C. H. Beck 1868

'Völkerrechtliche Briefe: I. Das Recht der europäischen Intervention in der Türkei', *Die Gegenwart – Wochenschrift für Literatur, Kunst und öffentliches Leben* 1876, pp. 377–379.

Das moderne Völkerrecht der civilisirten Staten, 3rd ed., Nördlingen: C. H. Beck 1878.

Ernst Bockhoff, *Die Intervention im Völkerrecht*, Würzburg: Buchdruckerei Richard Mayr 1935.

Henry Bonfils and Paul Fauchille, *Lehrbuch des Völkerrechts für Studium und Praxis*, 3rd ed, trans. by August Grah, Berlin: Carl Heymanns Verlag 1904.

Edwin Borchard, *The Diplomatic Protection of Citizens Abroad*, New York: Banks 1915/1925.

J. L. Brierly, *The Law of Nations*, Oxford: Clarendon Press 1928.

'International Law and Resort to Armed Force', *Cambridge Law Journal* 1932, 4(3), pp. 308–319.

The Law of Nations, 2nd ed., Oxford: Clarendon Press 1936.

Philip Marshall Brown, 'Japanese Interpretation of the Kellogg Pact', *American Journal of International Law* 1933, 27, pp. 100–102.

Georges Bry, *Précis Élémentaire de Droit International Public*, Paris: L. Larose et Forcel 1891.

Geoffrey Butler and Simon Maccoby, *The Development of International Law*, London: Longmans, Green and Co. 1928.

Carlos Calvo, *Le droit international théorique et pratique; précédé d'un exposé historique des progrès de la science du droit des gens*, Vol. I, 5th ed. Paris: A. Rousseau 1896.

George Douglas Campbell, *The Eastern Question from the Treaty of Paris to the Treaty of Berlin 1878 and to the Second Afghan War*, London: Strahan 1879.

Giuseppe Carnazza-Amari, *Traité de Droit International Public*, trans. from Italian by C. Montanari-Revest, Vol. I, Paris: L. Larose 1880.

Edward S. Creasy, *First Platform of International Law*, London: John Van Voorst 1874.

Frantz Despagnet, *Cours de Droit International*, 3rd ed., Paris: Librairie de la Société du Recueil Général des Lois et des Arrêts 1905.

Edwin DeWitt Dickinson, *The Equality of States in International Law*, Cambridge: Harvard University Press 1920.

Simon Dubnow, *Die neueste Geschichte des jüdischen Volkes*, trans. by Alexander Eliasberg, 2 Vols., Berlin: Jüdischer Verlag 1920.

Charles Dupuis, *Le droit des gens et les rapports des grandes puissances avec les autres états avant le pacte de la Société des nations*, Paris: Plon-Nourrit 1921.

Earl of Birkenhead, *International Law*, 6th ed., by Ronw Moelwyn Hughes. London: J. M. Dent & Sons, Ltd. 1927.

Georg Erler, *Das Recht der nationalen Minderheiten*, Münster: Aschendorfsche Verlagsbuchhandlung 1931.

Charles G. Fenwick, *International Law*, London: Goerge Allen & Unwin Ltd 1924.
International Law, 2nd ed., New York: Appleton-Century-Company 1934.

G. A. Finch, 'James Brown Scott, 1866–1943', *The American Journal of International Law* 1944, 38(2), p. 183.

Pasquale Fiore, *International Law Codified and Its Legal Sanction*, trans. from the fifth Italian edition with an introduction by Edwin M. Borchard, New York: Baker, Voorhis and Company 1918.

Horace Edgar Flack, *Spanish-American Diplomatic Relations Preceding the War of 1898*, Baltimore: The Johns Hopkins Press 1906.

Axel Freiherr von Freytagh-Loringhoven, *Die Satzung des Völkerbundes*, Berlin: Verlag von Georg Stilke 1926.
Deutsche Außenpolitik 1933–1939, Berlin: Verlagsanstalt Otto Stolberg 1939.

Theophile Funck-Brentano and Albert Sorel, *Précis du Droit des Gens*, 2nd ed., Paris: Libraire Plon 1887.

Heinrich Geffcken, 'Das Recht der Intervention', in: Franz von Holtzendorff (ed.), *Handbuch des Völkerrechts*, Vol. IV, Berlin: Verlag von Carl Habel 1889.

William Ewart Gladstone, *Bulgarian Horrors and the Question of the East*, London: Murray 1876.

Malbone W. Graham, 'Humanitarian Intervention in International Law as Related to the Practice of the United States', *Michigan Law Review* 1924, 22, pp. 312–328.

Hugo Grotius, *The Rights of War and Peace*, Book I, edited by Richard Tuck, Indianapolis: Liberty Fund 2005.

Karl Gottlob Günther, *Europäisches Völkerrecht in Friedenszeiten nach Vernunft, Verträgen und Herkommen*, Altenburg: Richtersche Buchhandlung 1787.

Norbert Gürke, *Grundzüge des Völkerrechts*, 2nd ed., edited by Otto Koellreutter, Berlin: Industrieverlag Spaeth & Linde 1942.

Harald Hagedorn, *Wandlungen des Interventionsrechtes in der Geschichte*, Zürich: Gatzer & Hahn 1933.

William Edward Hall, *International Law*, Oxford: Clarendon Press 1880.

International Law, 3rd ed., Oxford: Clarendon Press 1890.

A Treatise on International Law, 7th ed., by Alexander Pearce Higgins, Oxford: Clarendon Press 1917.

Henry W. Halleck, *International Law; or: Rules Regulating the Intercourse of States in Peace and War*, New York: Van Nostrand 1861.

Elements of International Law, Philadelphia: J. B. Lippincott & Co. 1866.

William Vernon Harcourt, *Letters by Historicus on Some Questions of International Law: Reprinted from 'The Times' with Considerable Additions*, London: Macmillan and Co. 1863.

Adolph Hartmann, *Institutionen des praktischen Völkerrechts in Friedenszeiten, mit Rücksicht auf die Verfassung, die Verträge und die Gesetzgebung des Deutschen Reichs*, 2nd ed., Hannover: C. Meyer 1878.

Karl Haushover, 'Philippinen-Frage', in Karl Strupp (ed.), *Wörterbuch des Völkerrechts*, Vol. II, Berlin: De Gruyter 1925, pp. 265–268.

August Wilhelm Heffter, *Das Europäische Völkerrecht der Gegenwart*, Berlin: Verlag von E. H. Schröder 1844.

Das Europäische Völkerrecht der Gegenwart, 3rd ed., Berlin: Verlag von E. H. Schröder, 1855.

Das Europäische Völkerrecht der Gegenwart auf den bisherigen Grundlagen, 8th ed., by Friedrich Heinrich Geffcken, Berlin: Verlag von F. H. Müller 1888.

Paul Heilborn, *Das System des Völkerrechts entwickelt aus den völkerrechtlichen Begriffen*, Berlin: J. Springer 1896.

'Protektorate', in: Karl Strupp (ed.), *Wörterbuch des Völkerrechts*, Vol. II, Berlin: De Gruyter 1925, pp. 324–329.

'Subjekte des Völkerrechts', in: Karl Strupp (ed.), *Wörterbuch des Völkerrechts*, Vol. II, Berlin: De Gruyter 1925, pp. 684–686.

'Vasallenstaaten', in: Karl Strupp (ed.), *Wörterbuch des Völkerrechts und der Diplomatie*, Vol. III, Berlin: De Gruyter 1929, pp. 1–3.

Amos Hershey; *The Essentials of International Public Law and Organization*, 2nd revised ed., New York: Macmillan 1930.

Karl Hettlage, 'Die Intervention in der Geschichte der Völkerrechtswissenschaft, und im System der modernen Völkerrechtslehre', *Niemeyers Zeitschrift für Internationales Recht* 1927, pp. 11–88.

Henry G. Hodges, *The Doctrine of Intervention*, Princeton: Banner Press 1915.

Alexander Hold-Ferneck, *Lehrbuch des Völkerrechts, Zweiter Teil*, Leipzig: Felix Meiner 1932.

Thomas Erskine Holland, Thomas Alfred Walker, and Wyndham Leigh Walker, *Lectures on International Law*, London: Sweet & Maxwell 1933.

Franz von Holtzendorff, 'Einleitung in das Völkerrecht', in: Franz von Holtzendorff (ed.), *Handbuch des Völkerrechts*, Vol. I, Berlin: Verlag von Carl Habel 1885.

Karl Gottfried Hugelmann, 'Der völkische Staat und der Reichsgedanke', *Deutsche Rechtswissenschaft* 1940, V, pp. 179–201.

Volk und Staat im Wandel deutschen Schicksals, Essen: Essener Verlagsanstalt 1940.

Charles Cheney Hyde, *International Law Chiefly as Interpreted and Applied by the United States*, Boston: Little, Brown & Co. 1922.

International Commission to Inquire into the Causes and Conduct of the Balkan Wars. *The Other Balkan Wars: A 1913 Carnegie Endowment Inquiry in Retrospect*. Washington,

DC: Carnegie Endowment for International Peace/Brookings Institution Publications [Reprint] 1993.

Oscar I. Janowsky and Melvin M. Fagen, *International Aspects of German Racial Policies*, New York: Oxford University Press 1937.

Nicolae Jorga, *Geschichte des Osmanischen Reiches*, Vol. V (up to 1912), Gotha: Perthes 1913.

Carol Baron von Kaltenborn von Stachau, *Kritik des Völkerrechts nach dem jetzigen Standpunkt der Wissenschaft*, Leipzig: Gustav Mayer 1847.

Carl Christoph A. H. von Kamptz, *Völkerrechtliche Erörterung des Rechts der Europäischen Mächte in die Verfassung eines einzelnen Staates sich einzumischen*, Berlin: Nicolaische Buchhandlung 1821.

Hans K. E. L. Keller, *Das Recht der Völker*, Vol. I, Berlin: Standard Verlag Müller-Rath 1938.

Das Recht der Völker, Vol. II – *Das Reich der Völker*, Berlin: Standard Verlag Müller-Rath 1941.

James Kent and J. T. Abdy, *Kent's Commentary on International Law*, 2nd ed., Cambridge: Deighton, Bell & Co. 1866.

Arthur von Kirchenheim, 'Kongostaat und franz. Congo', in: Karl Strupp (ed.), *Wörterbuch des Völkerrechts*, Vol. I, Berlin: De Gruyter 1924, pp. 656–663.

'Libanon', in: Karl Strupp (ed.), *Wörterbuch des Völkerrechts und der Diplomatie*, Vol. I, Berlin: De Gruyter 1924, pp. 827–828.

Friedrich Kleine, *Unterdrückung des Boxerunruhen China 1900 nach ihrer völkerrechtlichen Bedeutung*, Berlin: R. Trenkel 1913.

Dietrich von Klitzing, *Die Unterdrückung der Boxerunruhen in China 1900 in völkerrechtlicher Beleuchtung*, Breslau: Breslauer Genossenschafts-Buchdruckerei 1912.

Johann Ludwig Klüber, *Europäisches Völkerrecht*, Stuttgart: J. G. Cotta 1821.

Europäisches Völkerrecht, 2nd ed., by Carl Eduard Morstadt, Schaffhausen: Hurter 1851.

Helmuth Krasberg, *Die konnationale Intervention*, Dissertation, Manuscript, Münster 1944.

Josef L. Kunz, 'Konzert, Europäisches', in: Karl Strupp (ed.), *Wörterbuch des Völkerrechts*, Vol. I, Berlin: De Gruyter 1924, pp. 697–701.

'Zum Begriff der "nation civilisée" im modernen Völkerrecht', *Zeitschrift für öffentliches Recht* 1927–1928, pp. 86–99.

Rudolf Laun, 'Nationalitätenfrage, einschließlich des Minderheitenrechts', in: Karl Strupp (ed.), *Wörterbuch des Völkerrechts und der Diplomatie*, Vol. II, Berlin: De Gruyter 1925, pp. 82–108.

Thomas J. Lawrence, *The Principles of International Law*, 2nd ed., Boston: D. C. Heath 1898.

The Principles of International Law, 4th ed., Boston: D. C. Heath & Co. 1910.

Louis LeFur, *Étude sur la guerre Hispano-Américain de 1898 envisagée au point de vue du droit international public*, Paris: A. Pedone 1899.

Gerhard Leibholz, 'Sklavenhandel', in: Karl Strupp (ed.), *Wörterbuch des Völkerrechts*, Vol. II, Berlin: Walter deGruyer & Co. 1925, pp. 542–545.

Raphael Lemkin, *Axis Rule in Occupied Europe*, 1st ed. published by Carnegie Endowment for International Peace, Washington, 1944, 2nd ed., Clark: The Lawbook Exchange, 2008.

William E. Lingelbach, 'The Doctrine and Practice of Intervention in Europe', *Annals of the American Academy of Political and Social Science* 1900, pp. 1–32.

Franz von Liszt, *Das Völkerrecht*, 9th ed., Berlin: Verlag von O. Häring 1913.

Franz von Liszt and Max Fleischmann, *Das Völkerrecht*, 12th ed., Berlin: Verlag von O. Häring 1925.

James Lorimer, *The Institutes of the Law of Nations*, Vol. I, Edinburgh and London: William Blackwood & Sons 1883.

Frederik A. C. van Lynden van Sandenberg, *Eenige Beschouwingen over Interventie in het Internationaal Recht*, Utrecht: P. Den Boer 1899.

J. A. MacGahan, *The Turkish Atrocities in Bulgaria*, London: Bradbury, Agnew & Co. 1876.

Ma-Do-Yun, *Der Eintritt des chinesischen Reiches in den völkerrechtlichen Verband*, Inaugural-Dissertation, Berlin: Ebering 1907.

Henry Maine, *International Law: A Series of Lectures Delivered before the University of Cambridge 1887*, London: John Murray 1888.

Terenzio Count Mamiani, *Rights of Nations, or the New Law of European States*, trans. by Roger Acton, London: W. Jeffs 1860.

André Mandelstam, 'La Protection des Minorités', *Recueil Des Cours*, Collected Courses of the Hague Academy of International Law, The Hague Academy of International Law 1923.

  'La Protection International des Minorités. Rapport', *Annuaire de l'Institut de Droit International* 1925, p. 32.

  La Société des Nations et les puissances devant le problème Arménien, Paris: Pédone 1925.

  'Der Internationale Schutz der Menschenrechte und die New Yorker Erklärung des Instituts für Völkerrecht', *Zeitschrift für ausländisches öffentliches Recht und Völkerrecht* 1931, pp. 335–377.

John Arthur R. Marriott, *The Eastern Question – An Historical Study in European Diplomacy*, 4th ed., Oxford: Clarendon Press 1940.

Friedrich Martens, *Völkerrecht – Das internationale Recht der civilisierten Nationen*, German ed. trans. by Carl Bergbohm, Vol. I, Berlin: Weidmannsche Buchhandlung 1883.

  Völkerrecht – Das internationale Recht der civilisierten Nationen, German ed. trans. by Carl Bergbohm, Vol. II, Berlin: Weidmannsche Buchhandlung 1886.

Georg Friedrich von Martens, *Einleitung in das positive Europäische Völkerrecht auf Verträge und Herkommen gegründet*, Göttingen: Dieterich 1796.

  A Compendium of the Law of Nations, English trans. by William Cobbett, Pall Mall: Cobbett and Morgan 1802.

  The Law of Nations, 4th ed., trans. by D. B. Cobbett, London: Cobbett 1829.

John Stuart Mill, 'A Few Words on Intervention', *Fraser's Magazine*, December 1859, reprinted in John Stuart Mill, *The Collected Works of John Stuart Mill, Volume XXI – Essays on Equality, Law, and Education*, edited by John M. Robson, Introduction by Stefan Collini, University of Toronto Press 1984, pp. 111–124.

  Vindication of the French Revolution of February 1848, in Reply to Lord Brougham and Others (1849), in Dissertations and Discussions: Political, Philosophical, and Historical, Vol. III, New York: Henry Holt and Co. 1873, pp. 5–81.

Johann Jacob Moser, *Grundsätze des jetzt üblichen Europäischen Völcker-Rechts in Friedenszeiten*, Hanau 1750.

  Grundsätze des jetzt üblichen Europäischen Völcker-Rechts in Friedenszeiten, 2nd ed., Frankfurt a.M.: Johann August Raspe 1763.

Hermann Mosler, *Die Intervention im Völkerrecht*, Berlin: Trittsch & Huther 1937.

Oswalt von Nostitz-Wallwitz, 'Die Annexion Abessiniens und die Liquidation des abessinischen Konflikts', *Zeitschrift für ausländisches öffentliches Recht* 1937, pp. 38–66.

Ernest Nys, *Le Droit International*, Vol. II, 2nd ed., Brussels: M. Weissenbruch 1912.

Heinrich Bernhard Oppenheim, *System des Völkerrechts*, 2nd ed., Stuttgart and Leipzig: Kröner 1866.

Lassa Oppenheim, *International Law – A Treatise, Vol. I – Peace*, London: Longmans, Green and Co 1905.

'The Science of international Law', *American Journal of International Law* 1908, 2, p. 335.

International Law – A Treatise, Vol. I – Peace, 2nd ed., London: Longmans, Green and Co 1912.

International Law – A Treatise, 5th ed., edited by Hersch Lauterpacht, London: Longmans, Green and Co. 1935.

Gerhard Ostermeyer, *Die Intervention in der Völkerrechtstheorie und -praxis*, Würzburg: Konrad Triltsch Verlag 1940.

Robert Phillimore, *Commentaries upon International Law*, Vol. I, Philadelphia: T. & J. W. Johnson 1854.

Antoine Pillet, 'Le Droit International Public', *Revue générale de droit international public* 1894, pp. 1–22.

Paul Pradier-Fodéré, *Traité de Droit International Public Européen & Américain*, Vol. I, Paris: A. Pedone 1885.

E. Pritsch, 'Türkei', in: Karl Strupp (ed.), *Wörterbuch des Völkerrechts*, Vol. II, Berlin: De Gruyter 1925.

Edgar Pröbster, 'Scherifisches Reich', in: Karl Strupp (ed.), *Wörterbuch des Völkerrechts und der Diplomatie*, Vol. II, Berlin: De Gruyter 1925, pp. 449–450.

August Quaritsch, *Völkerrecht und auswärtige Politik*, 9th ed., edited by Carl Goesch, Berlin: W. Weber 1913.

Friedrich Wilhelm von Rauchhaupt, *Völkerrecht*, Munich: Verlag Fritz & Joseph Voglrieder 1936.

James Reddie, *Inquiries in International Law*, Edinburgh: William Blackwood 1842.

Robert Redslob, *Les Principes du Droit des Gens Moderne*, Paris: A. Rousseau 1937.

Peter Resch, *Das Völkerrecht der heutigen Staatenwelt europäischer Gesittung*, 2nd ed., Graz and Leipzig: Verlag von Ulr. Mosers Buchhandlung (J. Meyerhoff) 1890.

Gustave Rolin-Jaequemyns, 'Note sur la théorie du droit d'intervention, a propos d'une lettre de M. le Professeur Arntz', *Revue de droit international et de législation comparée* 1876, 8, p. 673–682.

Hermann von Rotteck, *Das Recht der Einmischung in die inneren Angelegenheiten eines fremden Staates*, Freiburg: Adolph Emmerling 1845.

Karl von Rotteck, *Lehrbuch des Vernunftrechts und der Staatswissenschaften*, Stuttgart: Franckh 1834.

Antoine Rougier, *Les Guerres Civiles et le Droit des Gens*, Paris: L. Larose 1903.

'L'Intervention de l'Europe dans la Question de Macédoine', *Revue générale de droit international public* 1906, 13, pp. 178–200.

'La Théorie de l'Intervention de Humanité', *Revue générale de droit international public* 1910, pp. 468–562.

Friedrich Saalfeld, *Handbuch des positiven Völkerrechts*, Tübingen: Verlag von C. F. Osiander 1833.

K. R. R. Sastry, *International Law*, Allahabad: Kitabistan, 1937.

Ernst Sauer, *Der Welthilfsverband und seine Rechtsstellung*, Göttingen: Vandenhoeck & Ruprecht 1932.

Georges Scelle, *Precis du droit des gens*, Vol. II, Paris: Recueil Sirey 1934.

A. J. Schem, *War in the East*, New York: H. S. Goodspeed & Co. 1878.

Ferdinand Schlüter, 'Der Ausbruch des Krieges', *Zeitschrift für öffentliches ausländisches Recht und Völkerrecht* 1940, 10, pp. 244–269.

Theodor Schmalz, *Das europäische Völker-Recht in acht Büchern*, Berlin: Duncker und Humblot 1817.

Julius Schmelzing, *Systematischer Grundriß des praktischen Europäischen Völker-Rechts*, Band I, Rudolfstadt: Verlag der Hof-Buch- und Kunsthandlung 1818.

Carl Schmitt, 'Die Auflösung der europäischen Ordnung im "International Law"', *Deutsche Rechtswissenschaft* 1940, 5, pp. 267–278.

    Völkerrechtliche Großraumordnung mit Interventionsverbot für raumfremde Mächte, Berlin: Duncker & Humblot 1991, reprint of the 4th ed., originally published in 1941.

    Der Begriff des Politischen, Berlin: Duncker & Humblot, text from 1932, reprint of the 3rd ed. 1963, 1991.

Raimund Schramm, 'Arntz, Aegidius Rudolph Niclaus', in: *Allgemeine Deutsche Biographie*, Vol. 46, Leipzig: Duncker & Humblot 1902, pp. 55–58.

Walter Schücking and Hans Wehberg, *Die Satzung des Völkerbunds, Kommentar*, Berlin: Vahlen 1921.

Sozialdemokratische Partei Deutschlands (Sopade), *Deutschlandberichte 1934–1940*, edited by Klaus Behnken, reprint, Frankfurt a.M. 1980.

Augustus Granville Stapleton, *Intervention and Non-intervention, or the Foreign Policy of Great Britain from 1790 to 1865*, London: John Murray 1866.

Fritz Stier-Somlo, 'Völkerrechtsgemeinschaft', in: Karl Strupp (ed.), *Wörterbuch des Völkerrechts und der Diplomatie*, Vol. 3, Berlin: De Gruyter 1929, pp. 187–189.

Ellery C. Stowell, *Intervention in International Law*, Washington: John Byrne & Co 1921.

    International Law: A Restatement of Principles in Conformity with Actual Practice, New York: Henry Holt and Company 1931.

    'La théorie et la pratique de l'intervention', *Recueil des cours*, Collected Courses of the Hague Academy of International Law, The Hague Academy of International Law 1932.

    'Intercession against the Persecution of Jews', *American Journal of International Law* 1936, 30, pp. 102–106.

    'Book Review: Die Intervention im Völkerrecht, by Hermann Mosler', *American Journal of International Law* 1939, 33, p. 241.

    'Humanitarian Intervention', *American Journal of International Law* 1939, 33, pp. 733–736.

Hermann Strauch, *Zur Interventionslehre – Eine völkerrechtliche Studie*, Heidelberg: Carl Winter's Universitätsbuchhandlung 1879.

Leo Strisower, *Der Krieg und die Völkerrechtsordnung*, Wien: Manz 1919.

    'Intervention', in: Karl Strupp (ed.), *Wörterbuch des Völkerrechts und der Diplomatie*, Vol. I, Berlin: De Gruyter 1924, pp. 581–591.

Karl Strupp, 'Vorwort', in: Karl Strupp (ed.), *Wörterbuch des Völkerrechts und der Diplomatie*, Vol. I, Berlin: De Gruyter 1924, pp. V–VI.

Hannis Taylor, *A Treatise on Public International Law*, Chicago: Callaghan & Co 1901.

Harold Temperley, 'Princess Lieven and the Protocol of 4 April 1826', *English Historical Review* 1924, XXXIX(CLIII), pp. 55–78.

Josef Tenbaum, *Die völkerrechtliche Intervention, insbesondere ihre Arten*, Greifswald: Julius Abel 1918.

Aron N. Trainin, *Уголовная и нтервенция*, Moscow: Sovetskoe zakonodatel'stvo 1935.

    Hitlerite Responsibility under Criminal Law, trans. by Andrew Rothstein, London: Hutchinson & Co 1945.

Travers Twiss, *Two Introductory Lectures on the Sciences of International Law*, London: Longman, Brown, Green, and Longmans 1856.

Emanuel Ullmann, *Völkerrecht*, Tübingen: JCB Mohr (P. Siebeck) 1908.

Emer de Vattel, *Le Droit des Gens*, Nouvelle ed. by Paul Pradier-Fodéré, Vol. II, Paris: Libraire de Guillaumin & Co. 1863.
   The Law of Nations, or, Principles of the Law of Nature, Applied to the Conduct and Affairs of Nations and Sovereigns, 1758, edited by Bela Kapossy and Richard Whatmore, Indianapolis: Liberty Fund 2008.
Alfred Verdross, *Völkerrecht*, Vienna: Julius Springer 1937.
Hans von Frisch, 'Demonstration, kriegerische zur See', in: Karl Strupp (ed.), *Wörterbuch des Völkerrechts*, Vol. I, Berlin: De Gruyter 1924.
   'Drago-Doktrin', in: Karl Strupp (ed.), *Wörterbuch des Völkerrechts und der Diplomatie*, Vol. I, Berlin: De Gruyter 1924.
   'Drago-Porter-Konvention', in: Karl Strupp (ed.), *Wörterbuch des Völkerrechts und der Diplomatie*, Vol. I, Berlin: De Gruyter 1924.
Alfred von Wachter, *Die völkerrechtliche Intervention als Mittel der Selbsthilfe*, Munich: Krämer 1911.
Gustav A. Walz, *Völkerrechtsordnung und Nationalsozialismus*, Munich: Eher Verlag, München 1942.
A. W. Ward and G. P. Gooch, *The Cambridge History of British Foreign Policy, 1783–1919*, Vol. II, Cambridge University Press 1923.
Arthur Wegner, *Geschichte des Völkerrechts*, Stuttgart: Kohlhammer 1936.
John Westlake, *Chapters on the Principles of International Law*, Cambridge University Press 1894.
   International Law, Part I – Peace, 2nd ed., Cambridge University Press 1910.
   The Collected Papers of John Westlake on Public International Law, edited by Lassa Oppenheim, Cambridge University Press 1914.
Henry Wheaton, *Elements of International Law*, Philadelphia: Carey, Lea & Blanchard 1836.
   Elements of International Law, 3rd ed., Philadelphia: Lea & Blanchard 1846.
   Elements of International Law, 6th ed., by William Beach Lawrence, Boston: Little & Brown 1855.
Richard Wildman, *Institutes of International Law, Vol. I – International Rights in Time of Peace*, London: William Benning & Co. 1849.
Percy H. Winfield, 'The History of Intervention in International Law', *British Yearbook of International Law* 1922–1923, 3, pp. 130–149.
   'The Grounds of Intervention in International Law', *British Yearbook of International Law* 1924, 5, pp. 149–162.
Lucien Wolf (ed.), *The Legal Sufferings of the Jews in Russia*, London: T. Fisher Unwin 1912.
Theodore S. Woolsey, *Introduction to the Study of International Law*, 2nd ed., New York: Charles Scribner 1864.
   America's Foreign Policy, New York: The Century Co. 1898.

LITERATURE AFTER 1945

Journal Articles

Howard Adelman 'Humanitarian Intervention: The Case of the Kurds', *International Journal of Refugee Law* 1992, 4(1), pp. 4–38.
Ahmad M. Ajaj, 'Humanitarian Intervention: Second Reading of the Charter of the United Nations', *Arab Law Quarterly* 1992, 7(4), pp. 215–236.
Jean Allain, 'Slavery and the League of Nations: Ethiopia as a "Civilised Nation"', *Journal of the History of International Law* 2006, 8, pp. 213–244.

Sheldon Anderson, 'Metternich, Bismarck and the Myth of the "Long Peace," 1815–1914', *Peace & Change* 2007, 32, pp. 301–328.

Antony Anghie, 'Finding the Peripheries: Sovereignty and Colonialism in Nineteenth-Century International Law', *Harvard International Law Journal* 1999, 40, pp. 1–80.

Helmut Philipp Aust, 'From Diplomat to Academic Activist: André Mandelstam and the History of Human Rights', *European Journal of International Law* 2015, 25(4), pp. 1105–1121.

Michael J. Bazyler, 'Reexamining the Doctrine of Humanitarian Intervention in Light of the Atrocities in Kampuchea and Ethiopia', *Stanford Journal of International Law* 1987, pp. 547–619.

David J. Bederman, 'Appraising a Century of Scholarship in the American Journal of International Law', *American Journal of International Law* 2006, 100(1), pp. 20–63.

Thomas E. Behuniak, 'The Law of Unilateral Humanitarian Intervention by Armed Force: A Legal Survey', *Military Law Review* 1978, p. 157.

Barry M. Benjamin, 'Unilateral Humanitarian Intervention: Legalizing the Use of Force to Prevent Human Rights Atrocities', *Fordham International Law Journal* 1992–1993, 16, pp. 120–158.

Clarence A. Berdahl, 'Review of "International Law" by Charles G. Fenwick (3rd Ed.)', *American Journal of International Law* 1948, 42, pp. 958–960.

John Kuhn Bleimaier, 'The Future of Sovereignty in the 21st Century', *Hague Yearbook of International Law* 1993, 6, pp. 17–27.

David S. Bogen, 'The Law of Humanitarian Intervention: United States Policy in Cuba (1898) and in the Dominican Republic (1965)', *Harvard International Law Club Journal* 1966, pp. 296–315.

Sarmila Bose, 'The Question of Genocide and the Quest for Justice in the 1971 War', *Journal of Genocide Research* 2011, 4, pp. 393–419.

Katia Boustany, 'Intervention humanitaire et intervention d'humanité – évolution ou mutation en Droit International?', *Revue québécoise de droit international* 1993–1994, 8, pp. 103–111.

Brett Bowden, 'The Colonial Origins of International Law. European Expansion and the Classical Standard of Civilization', *Journal of the History of International Law* 2005, 7(1), pp. 1–24.

D.W. Bowett, 'The Use of Force in the Protection of Nationals', *Transactions of the Grotius Society* 1957, 43, pp. 111–126.

Ian Brownlie, 'International Law and the Use of Force by States Revisited', *Australian Year Book of International Law* 1993, 21, pp. 21–37.

J.W. Brugel, 'The Bernheim Petition: A Challenge to Nazi Germany in 1933', *Patterns of Prejudice* 1983, 17(3), pp. 17–25.

Jan Herman Burgers, 'The Road to San Francisco: The Revival of the Human Rights Idea in the Twentieth Century', *Human Rights Quarterly* 1992, 14, pp. 447–477.

Anthony Carty, 'Alfred Verdross and Othmar Spann: German Romantic Nationalism, National Socialism and International Law', *European Journal of International Law*, 1995, 6(1), pp. 78–97.

Robin Coupland, 'Humanity: What Is it and How Does it Influence International Law?', *Revue Internationale De La Croix-Rouge/International Review of the Red Cross* 2001, pp. 969–989.

Vahakn N. Dadrian, 'The Historical and Legal Interconnections Between the Armenian Genocide and the Jewish Holocaust: From Impunity to Retributive Justice', *Yale Journal of International Law* 1998, 23, pp. 503–559.

Ignacio de la Rasilla del Moral, 'The Study of International Law in the Spanish Short Nineteenth Century (1808–1898)', *Chicago-Kent Journal of International and Comparative Law* 2014, 13(2), pp. 122–149.

Dan Diner, 'Grenzenloses Recht', *Süddeutsche Zeitung* 16 June 2003.

Gennady Esakov, 'International Criminal Law and Russia: From "Nuremberg" Passion to "The Hague" Prejudice', *Europe-Asia Studies* 2017, 69(8), pp. 1184–1200.

H. Scott Fairley, 'State Actors, Humanitarian Intervention and International Law: Reopening Pandora's Box', *Georgia Journal of International and Comparative Law* 1980, 10(1) pp. 29–63.

Nathan Feinberg, 'The International Protection of Human Rights and the Jewish Question', *Israel Law Review* 1968, 3(4), pp. 487–500.

Charles G. Fenwick, 'Intervention: Individual and Collective', *American Journal of International Law* 1945, 39(4), pp. 645–663.

Jean-Pierre L. Fonteyne, 'The Customary International Law Doctrine of Humanitarian Intervention: Its Current Validity under The UN Charter', *California Western International Law Journal* 1974, 4, pp. 203–270.

Thomas M. Franck and Nigel Rodley, 'After Bangladesh: The Law of Humanitarian Intervention by Military Force', *American Journal of International Law* 1973, 67, pp. 275–305.

Thomas M. Franck, 'Is Justice Relevant to the International Legal System?', *Notre Dame Law Review* 1989, 64, pp. 945–963.

William Gallois, 'Genocide in Nineteenth-Century Algeria', *Journal of Genocide Studies* 2013, 15(1), pp. 69–88.

Luke Glanville, 'Ellery Stowell and the Enduring Dilemmas of Humanitarian Intervention', *International Studies Review* 2011, 13(2), pp. 241–258.

Edward Gordon, 'Article 2(4) in Historical Context', *Yale Journal of International Law* 1985, 10, pp. 271–278.

W. Paul Gormley, 'Book Review: International Protection of Human Rights. By Louis B. Sohn and Thomas Buergenthal. Indianapolis, Indiana. Bobbs-Merrill Co. 1973', *Georgia Journal of International and Comparative Law* 1975, 5, 330–337.

Heiko Haumann, '"Wir waren alle ein klein wenig antisemitisch": ein Versuch über historische Maßstäbe zur Beurteilung von Judengegnerschaft an den Beispielen Karl von Rotteck und Jacob Burckhardt', *Schweizerische Zeitschrift für Geschichte* 2005, 55, pp. 196–214.

Louis Henkin, 'Kosovo and the Law of "Humanitarian Intervention"', *American Journal of International Law*, 1999, 93, pp. 824–828.

Alexis Heraclidis, 'Humanitarian Intervention in the 19th Century: The Heyday of a Controversial Concept', *Global Society* 2012, 26, pp. 215–226.

'Humanitarian Intervention in International Law 1830–1939 – The Debate', *Journal of the History of International Law* 2014, 16, pp. 26–62.

Matthias Herdegen, 'Asymmetrien in der Staatenwelt und die Herausforderungen des "konstruktiven Völkerrechts"', *Zeitschrift für ausländisches öffentliches Recht und Völkerrecht* 2004, pp. 571–582.

Rosalyn Higgins, 'Review: International Protection of Human Rights', *International Affairs* 1963, 39(1), p. 85.

Christian Hillgruber, 'Humanitäre Intervention, Großmachtpolitik und Völkerrecht', *Der Staat* 2001, 40(2), pp. 165–191.

Josef Isensee, 'Die alte Frage nach der Rechtfertigung des Staates', *Juristenzeitung* 1999, pp. 265–278.

D. H. N. Johnson, 'The English Tradition in International Law'. *International and Comparative Law Quarterly* 1962, 11, pp. 416–445.

D. V. Jones, 'The League of Nations Experiment in International Protection', *Ethics & International Affairs* 1994, 8, pp. 77–95.

David Kennedy, 'The Move to Institutions', *Cardozo Law Review* 1987, 8, pp. 841–988.

'International Law in the Nineteenth Century: History of an Illusion', *Nordic Journal of International Law* 1996, 65, pp. 385–420.

Otto Kimminich, 'Der Mythos der Humanitären Intervention', *Archiv des Völkerrechts* 1995, 33(4), pp. 430–458.

Ben Kioko, 'The Right of Intervention under the African Union's Constitutive Act: From Non-interference to Non-intervention', *International Review of the Red Cross* 2003, 85 (852), pp. 807–825.

Thomas Kleinlein, 'Alfred Verdross as a Founding Father of International Constitutionalism?', *Goettingen Journal of International Law* 2012, 4, pp. 385–416.

Stephen Kloepfer, 'The Syrian Crisis, 1860–61: A Case Study in Classic Humanitarian Intervention', *Canadian Yearbook of International Law* 1985, p. 246.

Robert Kolb, 'Note on Humanitarian Intervention', *Revue Internationale De La Croix-Rouge/ International Review of the Red Cross* 2003, pp. 119–134.

Martti Koskenniemi, 'International Law in Europe: Between Tradition and Renewal', *European Journal of International Law* 2005, 16(1), pp. 113–124.

'Colonial Laws: Sources, Strategies and Lessons?', *Journal of the History of International Law* 2016, 18, pp. 248–277.

Nico Krisch, 'International Law in Times of Hegemony', *European Journal of International Law* 2005 p. 369.

Luis Kutner, 'World Habeas Corpus and Humanitarian Intervention', *Valparaiso University Law Review* 1985, 19, pp. 593–631.

Felix Lange: 'Carl Bilfingers Entnazifizierung und die Entscheidung für Heidelberg – Die Gründungsgeschichte des völkerrechtlichen Max-Planck-Instituts nach dem Zweiten Weltkrieg', *Zeitschrift für ausländisches öffentliches Recht und Völkerrecht* 2014, 74, pp. 697–732.

Ruth Lapidoth, 'Nathan Feinberg – In Memoriam', *Israel Law Review* 1988, 22(4), p. 408.

Hersch Lauterpacht, 'The Grotian Tradition in International Law', *British Yearbook of International Law* 1946, 23, pp. 1–54.

Raphael Lemkin, 'Genocide as a Crime under International Law', *American Journal of International Law* 1947, 41, pp. 145–151.

Richard B. Lillich, 'Forcible Self-help by States to Protect Human Rights', *Iowa Law Review* 1967, pp. 325–351.

'Intervention to Protect Human Rights', *McGill Law Journal* 1969, 15, pp. 205–219.

'Humanitarian Intervention through the United Nations: Towards the Development of Criteria', *Zeitschrift für ausländisches öffentliches Recht und Völkerrecht* 1993, pp. 557–575.

Yvonne C. Lodico, 'The Justification for Humanitarian Intervention: Will the Continent Matter?', *International Lawyer* 2001, pp. 1027–1050.

Ronald St John Macdonald, 'Teaching of International Law in Canada', *Canadian Yearbook of International Law* 1974, 12, pp. 67–110.

Lauri Mälksoo, 'The History of International Legal Theory in Russia: A Civilizational Dialogue with Europe', *European Journal of International Law* 2008, 19(1), pp. 211–232.

Mark Mazower, 'An International Civilization? Empire, Internationalism and the Crisis of the Mid-Twentieth Century', *International Affairs* 2006, 82(3), pp. 553–566.

Myres S. McDougal and Harold D. Lasswell, 'The Identification and Appraisal of Diverse Systems of Public Order', *American Journal of International Law*, 1959, 53, pp. 1–29.

Myres S. McDougal and W. Michael Reisman, 'Respone', *International Lawyer* 1969, 3(2), pp. 438–445.

Theodor Meron, 'Common Rights of Mankind in Gentili, Grotius and Suarez', *American Journal of International Law* 1991, 85(1), p. 110.

Djamchid Momtaz, '"L'intervention d'humanité" de l'OTAN au Kosovo et la règle du non-recours à la force'. *Revue Internationale De La Croix-Rouge/International Review of the Red Cross* 2000, pp. 89–102.

Georg Nolte, 'Kosovo und Konstitutionalisierung: Zur Humanitären Intervention der NATO-Staaten', *Zeitschrift für Ausländisches Öffentliches Recht und Völkerrecht* 1999, pp. 941–960.

Nicolas Onuf, 'Henry Wheaton and "The Golden Age of International Law"', *International Legal Theory* 2000, 6, pp. 2–9.

Yasuki Onuma, 'International Law in and with International Politics: The Functions of International Law in International Society', *European Journal of International Law* 2003, 14, pp. 105–139.

Alexander Orakhelashvili, 'The Idea of European International Law', *European Journal of International* 2006, 17(2), pp. 315–347.

Rose Parfitt, 'Empire des Nègres Blancs: The Hybridity of International Personality and the Abyssinia Crisis of 1935–36', *Leiden Journal of International Law* 2011, 24, pp. 849–872.

J. P. Parry, 'Disraeli and England', *The Historical Journal* 2000, 43(3), pp. 699–728.

Monty Noam Penkower, 'Honorable Failures against Nazi Germany: McDonald's Letter of Resignation and the Petition in Its Support', *Modern Judaism – A Journal of Jewish Ideas and Experience* 2010, 30(3), pp. 247–298.

C. Phillips, 'Book Review: Non-intervention: The Law and Its Import in the Americas. By Ann Van Wynen Thomas and A. J. Thomas Jr.', *American Political Science Review* 1954, 51(1), 263–264.

Istvan Pogany, 'Humanitarian Intervention in International Law: The French Intervention in Syria Re-Examined', *International and Comparative Law Quarterly* 1986, p. 182.

Frank Przetacznik, 'The Basic Ideas of the Philosophical Concept of War and Peace', *Revue de Droit International de Sciences Diplomatiques et Politiques* 1990, p. 281.

Gustav Radbruch, 'Zur Diskussion über die Verbrechen gegen die Menschlichkeit', *Süddeutsche Juristen-Zeitung* 1946, pp. 131/132–135/136.

Betsy Baker Röben, 'The Method Behind Bluntschli's "Modern" International Law', *Journal of the History of International Law* 2002, 4(2), pp. 249–292.

B. V. A. Röling, 'On Aggression, on International Criminal Law, on International Criminal Jurisdiction', *Nederlands Tijdschrift voor Internationaal Recht* 1955, pp. 167–196.

Anne Ryniker, 'Position du Comité international de la Croix-Rouge sur l'"intervention humanitaire"', *Revue Internationale De La Croix-Rouge/International Review of the Red Cross* 2001, pp. 521–526.

Wolfang Saxon, 'Obituary: Richard B. Lillich', *New York Times* 16 August 1996.

Michael P. Scharf, 'Seizing the "Grotian Moment": Accelerated Formation of Customary International Law in Times of Fundamental Change', *Cornell International Law Journal* 2010, 43, pp. 439–469.

'Striking a Grotian Moment: How the Syria Airstrikes Changed International Law Relating to Humanitarian Intervention', *Chicago Journal of International Law* 2018, 19, pp. 3–29.

Dietrich Schindler, 'Völkerrecht und Zivilisation', *Schweizerisches Jahrbuch für internationales Recht* 1956, pp. 79–96.

Kathryn Rider Schmeltzer, 'Soviet and American Attitudes toward Intervention: The Dominican Republic, Hungary and Czechoslovakia', *Virginia Journal of International Law* 1970–1971, 11, p. 109.

Mathias Schmoeckel, 'The Internationalist as a Scientist and Herald: Lassa Oppenheim', *European Journal of International Law* 2000, 11(3), pp. 699–712.

Nico Schrijver. 'The Changing Nature of State Sovereignty', *British Yearbook of International Law* 2000, 70, pp. 65–98.

Egon Schwelb, 'Crimes against Humanity', *British Yearbook of International Law* 1947, 23, pp. 178–189.

'Book Review: International Protection of Human Rights. By Manouchehr Ganji', *American Journal of International Law* 1963, 57, p. 172.

Marcel Senn, 'Rassistische und antisemitische Elemente im Rechtsdenken von Johann Caspar Bluntschli', *Zeitschrift der Savigny-Stiftung für Rechtsgeschichte* 1993, pp. 372–405.

Brendan Simms, 'From the Kohl to the Fischer Doctrine: Germany and the Wars of the Yugoslav Succession, 1991–1999', *German History* 2003, 21, pp. 393–414.

M. Sornarajah, 'Internal Colonialism and Humanitarian Intervention', *Georgia Journal for International and Comparative Law* 1981, 11(1), pp. 45–77.

Heinhard Steiger, 'From the International Law of Christianity to the International Law of the World Citizen', *Journal of the History of International Law* 2001, 3(2), pp. 153–260.

Hubert Thierry, 'The Thought of Georges Scelle', *European Journal of International Law* 1990, 1, pp. 193–209.

Sybille Tönnies, 'Soll ich meines Bruders Hüter sein?', *Neue Zürcher Zeitung*, 2008, 103, p. 24.

U. D. Umozurike, 'Tanzania's Intervention in Uganda', *Archiv des Völkerrecht* 1982, pp. 301–313.

Detlef F. Vagts, 'International Law in the Third Reich', *American Journal of International Law* 1990, 84, pp. 661–704.

Hernan Vales, 'The Latin American View on the Doctrine of Humanitarian Intervention', *Journal of Humanitarian Assistance* 2001, archived at: https://sites.tufts.edu/jha/archives/1491, last accessed 5 March 2019.

Ana Filipa Vrdoljak, "Human Rights and Genocide: The Work of Lauterpacht and Lemkin in Modern International Law", *European Journal of International Law* 2010, 20, pp. 1163–1194.

Hans Wehberg, 'Hat Japan durch die Besetzung der Mandschurei das Völkerrecht verletzt?', *Die Friedenswarte* 1932, p. 1.

Lora Wildenthal, 'Human Rights Advocacy and National Identity in West Germany', *Human Rights Quarterly* 2000, 22, pp. 1051–1059.

Books

Michael Aaronson, 'The Nigerian Civil War and "Humanitarian Intervention"', in: Bronwen Everill and Josiah Kaplan (eds.), *The History and Practice of Humanitarian Intervention and Aid in Africa*, Hampshire: Palgrave Macmillan 2013, pp. 176–196.

Wolfgang Abendroth, 'Großmächte', in: Hans Jürgen Schlochauer (ed.), *Wörterbuch des Völkerrechts*, Vol. I, Berlin: De Gruyer 1960, pp. 713–717.

Francis Kofi Abiew, *The Evolution of the Doctrine and Practice of Humanitarian Intervention*, The Hague: Kluwer Law International 1999.

Hirad Abtahi and Philippa Webb, *The Genocide Convention, The Travaux Préparatoires*, Leiden: Brill 2008.

Payam Akhavan, *Reducing Genocide to Law*, Cambridge University Press 2012.

Jean Allain, *International Law in the Middle East*, Aldershot: Ashgate 2004.

Roy Allison, *Russia, The West, and Military Intervention*, Oxford University Press 2013.

Benedict Anderson, *Imagined Communities*, revised ed., London: Verso 1991.

M. S. Anderson, *The Ascendancy of Europe*, 2nd ed., Reprint, Harlow: Pearson Education 2000.

Antony Anghie, *Imperialism, Sovereignty and the Making of International Law*, Cambridge University Press 2005.

Frederick F. Anscombe, *State, Faith, and Nation in Ottoman and Post-Ottoman Lands*, Cambridge University Press 2014.

Douglas Anthony, 'Irreconcilable Narratives – Biafra, Nigeria and Arguments about Genocide, 1966–1970', in: A. Dirk Moses and Lasse Heerten (eds.), *Postcolonial Conflict and the Question of Genocide*, New York: Routledge 2017, pp. 47–71.

Hannah Arendt, *The Origins of Totalitarianism*, New York: Harcourt Brace Jovanovich 1951.

Shlomo Aronson, *Hitler, the Allies, and the Jews*, Cambridge University Press 2004.

Jörg Baberowski, *Räume der Gewalt*, Frankfurt am Main: S. Fischer Verlag 2015.

Michael Barnett, *Empire of Humanity*, Ithaca: Cornell University Press 2011.

Boris Barth, *Genozid*, München: C. H. Beck 2006.

Gary J. Bass, *Freedom's Battle*, New York: Alfred A. Knopf 2008.

   The Blood Telegram, New York: A. A. Knopf 2013.

M. Cherif Bassiouni, *Crimes against Humanity*, Cambridge University Press 2011.

Alex J. Bellamy, *Massacres & Morality*, Oxford University Press 2012.

Friedrich Berber, *Lehrbuch des Völkerrechts*, Vol. I, Munich: C. H. Beck 1960.

   Lehrbuch des Völkerrechts, Vol. II, Munich: C. H. Beck 1962.

Nathaniel Berman, *Passion and Ambivalence: Colonialism, Nationalism, and International Law*, Leiden: Martinus Nijoff Publishers 2012.

John Bew, '"From an umpire to a competitor": Castlereagh, Canning and the issue of international intervention in the wake of the Napoleonic Wars', in: Brendan Simms and D. J. B. Trim (eds.), *Humanitarian Intervention – A History*, Cambridge University Press 2011.

Ulrich Beyerlin, 'Humanitarian Intervention', in: Rudolf Bernhardt (ed.), *Encyclopaedia of Public International Law*, Vol 2, Amsterdam: North-Holland Publishing 1995.

Nigel Biggar, *In Defence of War*, Oxford University Press 2013.

Mark Biondich, *The Balkans*, New York: Oxford University Press 2011.

Elizabeth Bird and Fraser M. Ottanelli, *The Asaba Massacre – Trauma, Memory, and the Nigerian Civil War*, Cambridge University Press 2017.

Dusan I. Bjelic and Obrad Savic (eds.), *Balkan as Metaphor*, Cambridge, MA: The MIT Press 2002.

Albert Bleckmann, *Völkerrecht*, Baden-Baden: Nomos 2001.

Donald Bloxham, *Genocide on Trial*, Oxford University Press 2001.

   The Great Game of Genocide, Oxford University Press 2005.

Richard Bonney, *Jihad: From Qur'an to bin Laden*, Basingstoke, Hampshire: Palgrave Macmillan 2004.

D. W. Bowett, *Self-defence in International Law*, Manchester University Press 1958.

Ebru Boyar, *Ottomans, Turks and the Balkans – Empire Lost, Relations Altered*, London: Tauris Academic Studies 2007.

Francis Boyle, *Foundations of World Order*, Durham: Duke University Press 1999.

Mark Philip Bradley, *The World Reimagined*, Cambridge University Press 2016.

F. R. Bridge and Roger Bullen, *The Great Powers and the European States System 1814–1914*, 2nd ed., Harlow: Pearson Longman 2005.

J. L. Brierly, *The Law of Nations*, 5th ed., Oxford: Clarendon Press, 1955.

  The Law of Nations, 6th ed., edited by Humphrey Waldock, Oxford: Clarendon Press 1963.

Ian Brownlie, *International Law and the Use of Force by States*, Oxford: Clarendon Press 1963.

  'Humanitarian Intervention', in: John Norton Moore (ed.), *Law and Civil War in the Modern World*, Baltimore: The Johns Hopkins University Press 1974.

Brun-Otto Bryde, 'Die Intervention mit wirtschaftlichen Mitteln', in: Ingo von Münch (ed.), *Staatsrecht – Europarecht – Völkerrecht – Festschrift für Hans-Jürgen Schlochauer zum 75. Geburtstag*, Berlin: De Gruyter 1981, pp. 227–247.

Allen Buchanan, *Justice, Legitimacy, and Self-determination*, Oxford University Press 2004.

Hedley Bull, *The Anarchical Society*, 3rd ed., Basingstoke, Hampshire: Palgrave Macmillan 2002.

Barry Buzan and George Lawson, *The Global Transformation*, Cambridge University Press 2015.

Michael Byers and Simon Chesterman, 'Changing the Rules about Rules? Unilateral Humanitarian Intervention and the Future of International Law' in: J. L. Holzgrefe and Robert O. Keohane (eds.), *Humanitarian Intervention – Ethical, Legal, and Political Dilemmas*, Cambridge University Press 2003.

Cathie Carmichael, *Ethnic Cleansing in the Balkans*, London: Routledge 2002.

Antonio Cassese, *Self-determination of Peoples*, Cambridge University Press 1995.

  International Law, 2nd ed., Oxford University Press 2005.

John Charvet and Elisa Kaczynska-Nay, *The Liberal Project and Human Rights – The Theory and Practice of a New World Order*, Cambridge University Press 2008.

Simon Chesterman, *Just War or Just Peace*, Oxford University Press 2001.

Ian Clark, *The Vulnerable in International Society*, Oxford University Press 2013.

Richard Clogg, *A Concise History of Greece*, Cambridge University Press 1992.

C. A. J. Coady, *Morality and Political Violence*, Cambridge University Press 2008.

John Cooper, *Raphael Lemkin and the Struggle for the Genocide Convention*, Basingstoke, Hampshire: Palgrave Macmillan 2008.

Russell Crandall, *Gunboat Democracy: U.S. interventions in the Dominican Republic, Grenada, and Panama*, Lanham: Rowman & Littlefield Publishers 2006.

Eleanor Davey, 'The Language of Ingérence', in: Norbert Frei, Daniel Stahl, and Annette Weinke (eds.), *Human Rights and Humanitarian Intervention*, Göttingen: Wallstein Verlag 2017, pp. 46–63.

Selim Deringil, *The Well-Protected Domains – Ideology and the Legitimation of Power in the Ottoman Empire 1876–1909*, London: I. B. Tauris Publishers 1999.

Alison Des Forges, *Leave None to Tell the Story*, Human Rights Watch Report, New York: Human Rights Watch 1999.

Dan Diner (ed.), *Zivilisationsbruch: Denken nach Auschwitz*, Munich: Fischer Taschenbuch 1988.

Dan Diner *Gegenläufige Gedächtnisse. Über Geltung und Wirkung des Holocaust*, Göttingen: Vandenhoeck & Ruprecht 2007.

Karl Doehring, 'Die Humanitäre Intervention – Überlegungen zu ihrer Rechtfertigung', in: Antonio Augusto Cançado Trindade (ed.), *The Modern World of Human Rights*, Essays in honour of Thomas Buergenthal, San José, Costa Rica: Inter-American Institute of Human Rights 1996.

  Völkerrecht, Heidelberg: C. F. Müller Verlag 2004.

Jack Donnelly, *Universal Human Rights in Theory and Practice*, 2nd ed., Ithaca: Cornell University Press 2003.

Lawrence Douglas, *The Memory of Judgement*, New Haven: Yale University Press 2001.

Michael Doyle, 'J. S. Mill on Nonintervention and Intervention', in: Stefano Recchia and Jennifer M. Welsh (eds.), *Just and Unjust Military Intervention, European Thinkers from Vitoria to Mill*, Cambridge University Press 2013, pp. 263–287.

Jost Dülffer, 'Internationales System, Friedesngefährdung und Kriegsvermeidung: Das Beispiel der Haager Friedenskonferenzen 1899 und 1907', in: Reiner Steinweg (ed.), *Lehren aus der Geschichte?*, Frankfurt am Main: Suhrkamp 1990, pp. 95–116.

'Humanitarian Intervention as Legitimation of Violence – The German Case 1937–1939', in: Fabian Klose (ed.), *The Emergence of Humanitarian Intervention*, Cambridge University Press 2016, pp. 208–228.

David Dyzenhaus, *Hard Cases in Wicked Legal Systems*, 2nd ed., Oxford University Press 2010.

Jan Eckel, *Die Ambivalenz des Guten*, Göttingen: Vandenhoeck & Ruprecht 2014.

C. C. Eldridge, *England's Mission: The Imperial Idea in the Age of Gladstone and Disraeli*, Basingstoke, Hampshire: Palgrave Macmillan 1973.

Harald Endemann, *Kollektive Zwangsmaßnahmen zur Durchsetzung humanitärer Normen*, Frankfurt am Main: Peter Lang 1997.

Georg Erler, 'Minderheitenrecht', in: Hans-Jürgen Schlochauer (ed.), *Wörterbuch des Völkerrecht*, Vol. II, 2nd ed., Berlin: De Gruyter 1961.

Joseph W. Esherick, *The Origins of the Boxer Uprisings*, Los Angeles: University of California Press 1987.

Wolfgang Eßbach, *Religionssoziologie 1*, Paderborn: Wilhelm Fink 2014.

Malcolm D. Evans, *Religious Liberty and International Law in Europe*, Cambridge University Press 1997.

Richard J. Evans, *The Third Reich in Power*, London: Allen Lane 2005.

Tom J. Farer, 'Humanitarian Intervention: The View from Chralottesville', in Richard B. Lillich (ed.), *Humanitarian Intervention and the United Nations*, Charlottesville: University of Virginia Press 1973.

'Humanitarian Intervention Before and After 9/11: Legality and Legitimacy', in: J. L. Holzgrefe and Robert O. Keohane (eds.), *Humanitarian Intervention*, Cambridge University Press 2003.

Ulrich Fastenrath, *Lücken im Völkerrecht – Zu Rechtscharakter, Quellen, Systemzusammenhang, Methodenlehre und Funktionen des Völkerrechts*, Berlin: Duncker & Humblot 1990.

Leila Tarazi Fawaz, *An Occasion for War – Civil Conflict in Lebanon and Damascus in 1860*, Berkeley: University of California Press 1994.

J. E. S. Fawcett, 'Intervention in International Law', *Recueil de Cours*, Collected Courses of the Hague Academy of International Law, The Hague Academy of International Law 1961.

Charles G. Fenwick, *International Law*, 3rd ed., New York: Appleton-Century-Croft 1948.
International Law, 4th ed., New York: Appleton-Century-Crofts 1965.

D. K. Fieldhouse, *Western Imperialism in the Middle East 1914–1958*, Oxford University Press 2006.

Trevor Findlay, *The Use of Force in UN Peace Operations*, Oxford University Press 2002.

Carole Fink, *Defending the Rights of Others*, Cambridge University Press 2004.

Martha Finnemore, *The Purpose of Intervention – Changing Beliefs about the Use of Force*, Ithaca: Cornell University Press 2004.

Jörg Fisch, *Die europäische Expansion und das Völkerrecht*, Stuttgart: Steiner 1984.

David Fisher, 'Humanitarian intervention', in Charles Reed and David Ryall (eds.), *The Price of Peace*, Cambridge University Press 2007.

Carlo Focarelli, *International Law as a Social Construct*, Oxford University Press 2012.

Thomas Franck, *The Power of Legitimacy among Nations*, Oxford University Press 1990.
Recourse to Force, Cambridge University Press 2002.

Matthew Frank, *Making Minorities History*, Oxford University Press 2017.

Manouchehr Ganji, *International Protection of Human Rights*, Geneva: Librairie E. Droz 1962.

Azar Gat, *War in Human Civilization*, Oxford University Press 2006.

Christian Gerlach, *Extremely Violent Societies*, Cambridge University Press 2010.

Martin Gilbert, *Auschwitz and the Allies*, London: Pimlico 2001.

Gerhard von Glahn, *Law among Nations*, 2nd ed., London: Macmillan 1970.
Law among Nations, 7th ed., Boston: Ally and Bacon 1996.

Michael J. Glennon, *Limits of Law, Prerogatives of Power*, New York: Palgrave 2001.

Misha Glenny, *The Balkans 1804–1999*, London: Granta Books 2000.

Jonathan Glover, *Humanity: A Moral History of the Twentieth Century*. London: Jonathan Cape 1999.

Svenja Goltermann, *Opfer – Die Wahrnehmung von Krieg und Gewalt in der Moderne*, Frankfurt am Main: S. Fischer 2017.

Gerrit W. Gong, *The Standard of 'Civilization' in International Society*, Oxford: Clarendon Press 1984.

Stefan Gosepath and Georg Lohmann (eds.), *Philosophie der Menschenrechte*, Frankfurt am Main: Suhrkamp 1998.

Philipp Graf, *Die Bernheim-Petition 1933*, Göttingen: Vandenhoek & Ruprecht 2008.

Christine Gray, *International Law and the Use of Force*, 3rd ed., Oxford University Press 2008.

Wilhelm G. Grewe, *The Epochs of International Law*, trans. by Michael Byers, Berlin: De Gruyter 2000.

Raphael Gross, *Carl Schmitt und die Juden*, Frankfurt am Main: Suhrkamp 2005.

Wolfgang Gust, *Das Imperium der Sultane*, Munich: Hanser 1995.

Heinz Haedrich, 'Intervention', in: Hans-Jürgen Schlochauer (ed.), *Wörterbuch des Völkerrechts*, Vol. II, 2nd ed., Berlin: De Gruyter 1961, pp. 144–147.

Hans-Joachim Hallier, 'Drago-Porter-Konvention von 1907', in: Hans-Jürgen Schlochauer (ed.), *Wörterbuch des Völkerrechts*, Vol. I, Berlin: De Gruyter 1960, pp. 399–400.

Oona Hathaway and Scott J. Shapiro, *The Internationalists*, New York: Simon & Schuster 2017.

Lasse Heerten, *The Biafran War and Postcolonial Humanitarianism*, Cambridge University Press 2017.

Kevin Jon Heller, *The Nuremberg Military Tribunals and the Origins of International Criminal Law*, Oxford University Press 2011.

Christoph Henke, Die humanitäre Intervention – Völker-und verfassungsrechtliche Probleme unter besonderer Berücksichtigung des Kosovo-Konflikts, Dissertation, Münster 2002.

Louis Henkin, 'International Law: Politics, Values and Functions, General Course on Public International Law', *Recueil des Cours*, Collected Courses of the Hague Academy of International Law, The Hague Academy of International Law 1989.

Alexis Heraclidis and Ada Dialla, *Humanitarian Intervention in the Long Nineteenth Century – Setting the Precedent*, Manchester University Press 2015.

Matthias Herdegen, *The Dynamics of International Law in a Globalised World*, Frankfurt (Main): Vittorio Klostermann 2016.

Didi Herman, *An Unfortunate Coincidence*, Oxford University Press 2011.

Friedrich August Freiherr von der Heydte, 'Ein Betrag zum Problem der Macht im "klassischen" und im "neuen" Völkerrecht', in: Walter Schätzel and Hans-Jürgen Schlochauer (eds.), *Rechtsfragen der Internationalen Organisation*, Festschrift für Hans Wehberg, Frankfurt a.M.: Vittorio Klostermann 1956.

Völkerrecht, Vol. I, Cologne: Verlag für Politik und Wirtschaft 1958.

Rosalyn Higgins, *Problems & Process – International Law and How We Use It*, Oxford: Clarendon Press 1994.

Wilfried Hinsch and Dieter Janssen, *Menschenrechte militärisch schützen – Ein Plädoyer für humanitäre Interventionen*, Munich: C. H. Beck 2006.

Wilfried Hinsch, *Die Moral des Krieges*, Munich: Piper 2017.

Stephan Hobe and Otto Kimminich, *Einführung in das Völkerrecht*, 8th ed., Tübingen: A. Francke 2004.

Eric Hobsbawm, *The Age of Capital*, London: Abacus 2001 (reprint of the 1975 ed.).

John M. Hobson, *The Eastern Origins of Western Civilisation*, Cambridge University Press 2004.

Paul Hockenos, *Joschka Fischer and the Making of the Berlin Republic*, Oxford University Press 2007.

J. L. Holzgrefe, 'The Humanitarian Intervention Debate', in: J. L. Holzgrefe and Robert O. Keohane (eds.), *Humanitarian Intervention*, Cambridge University Press 2003.

William Hooker, *Carl Schmitt's International Thought*, Cambridge University Press 2009.

Ingo J. Hueck, 'Pragmatism, Positivism and Hegelianism in the Nineteenth Century', in: Michael Stolleis and Masaharu Yanagihara (eds.), *East Asian and European Perspectives on International Law*, Nomos: Baden-Baden 2004, pp. 41–55.

Independent International Commission on Kosovo, *The Kosovo Report*, Oxford University Press 2000.

International Commission on Intervention and State Sovereignty, *The Responsibility to Protect*, Ottawa: International Development Research Centre 2001.

Knut Ipsen, *Völkerrecht*, 4th ed., Munich: C. H. Beck 1999.

Akira Iriye, Petra Goedde, and William I. Hitchcock (eds.), *The Human Rights Revolution*, Oxford University Press 2012.

Robert Jackson, *The Global Covenant*, Oxford University Press 2000.

Mark Weston Janis, *The American Tradition of International Law*, Cambridge University Press 2004.

Barbara Jelavich, *History of the Balkans*, Vol. I, Cambridge University Press 1983.

Steven L. B. Jensen, *The Making of International Human Rights*, Cambridge University Press 2016.

Fleur Johns, Richard Joyce, and Sundhya Pahuja, *Events: The Force of International Law*, Abingdon: Routledge 2011.

Emanuelle Jouannet, *The Liberal-Welfarist Law of Nations*, Cambridge University Press 2011.

Colin Judd, *Contested Rituals: Circumcision, Kosher Butchering, and Jewish Political Life in Germany, 1843–1933*, Ithaca: Cornell University Press 2007.

Anthony Julius, *Trials of the Diaspora*, Oxford: Oxford University Press 2010.

Claude Kabemba, 'The Democratic Republic of Congo: The Land of Humanitarian Interventions', in: Bronwen Everill and Josiah Kaplan (eds.), *The History and Practice of Humanitarian Intervention and Aid in Africa*, Hampshire: Palgrave Macmillan 2013.

Walter Kälin and Jörg Künzli, *Universeller Menschenrechtsschutz*, Basel: Helbig & Lichtenhan 2005.

Andrzej J. Kaminski, *Konzentrationslager 1896 bis heute, Eine Analyse*, Stuttgart: Verlag W. Kohlhammer 1982.

Gerd Kaminski, *Chinesische Positionen zum Völkerrecht*, Berlin: Duncker & Humblot 1973.

Turan Kayaoglu, *Legal Imperialism*, Cambridge University Press 2010.

Alexis Keller, 'Justice, Peace, and History: A Reappraisal', in: Pierre Allan and Alexis Keller (eds.), *What Is a Just Peace?*, Oxford University Press 2006, pp. 19–51.

Hans Kelsen, *Principles of International Law*, New York: Rinehart & Company 1952.

Alison Kesby, *The Right to Have Rights*, Oxford University Press 2012.

Dzovinar Kévonian, 'André Mandelstam and the Internationalization of Human Rights (1869–1949)', in: Pamela Slotte and Miia Halme-Tuomisaar (eds.), *Revisiting the Origins of Human Rights*, Cambridge University Press 2015, pp. 239–266.

Fritz Kieffer, *Judenverfolgung in Deutschland – eine innere Angelegenheit?*, Stuttgart: Franz Steiner Verlag 2002.

Ben Kiernan, *Blood and Soil: A World History of Genocide and Extermination from Sparta to Darfur*, New Haven: Yale University Press 2007.

Otto Kimminich and Stephan Hobe, *Einführung in das Völkerrecht*, 7th ed., Tübingen: A. Francke 2000.

Henry Kissinger, *Diplomacy*, New York: Simon & Schuster 1994.

Ernst Klee, *Das Personenlexikon zum Dritten Reich*, Frankfurt am Main: S. Fischer 2003.

Thoralf Klein: 'Straffeldzug im Namen der Zivilisation: Der Boxerkrieg in China', in: Thoralf Klein and Frank Schumacher (eds.), *Kolonialkriege*, Hamburg: Hamburger Edition 2006, pp. 145–166.

Fabian Klose, 'The Emergence of Humanitarian Intervention', in: Fabian Klose (ed.), *The Emergence of Humanitarian Intervention*, Cambridge University Press 2015.

'Protecting Universal Rights through Intervention. International Law Debates from the 1930s to the 1980s', in: Norbert Frei, Daniel Stahl, and Annette Weinke (eds.), *Human Rights and Humanitarian Intervention*, Göttingen: Wallstein Verlag 2017.

Rolf Knieper, *Nationale Souveränität – Versuch über Anfang und Ende einer Weltordnung*, Frankfurt: Fischer Taschenbuch 1991.

Arieh J. Kochavi, *Prelude to Nuremberg*, Chapel Hill: University of North Carolina Press 1998.

Watanabe Koji (ed.), *Humanitarian Intervention – The Evolving Asian Debate*, Tokyo: Japan Center for International Exchange 2003.

Robert Kolb, 'The Main Epochs of Modern International Humanitarian Law Since 1864 and Their Related Dominant Legal Constructions', in: Kjetil Mujezinovic Larsen, Camilla Guldahl Cooper, and Gro Nystuen (eds.), *Searching for a 'Principle of Humanity' in International Law*, Cambridge University Press 2013, pp. 23–71.

'The Belgian Intervention in the Congo – 1960 and 1964', in: Tom Ruys, Olivier Corten, and Alexandra Hofer (eds.), *The Use of Force in International Law – A Case-based Approach*, Oxford University Press 2018.

Theo Kordt, 'Völkerrechtsgemeinschaft', in: Hans-Jürgen Schlochauer (ed.), *Wörterbuch des Völkerrechts*, Vol. 3, Berlin: De Gruyter 1962.

Martti Koskenniemi, *The Gentle Civilizer of Nations: The Rise and Fall of International Law 1870–1960*, Cambridge University Press 2002.

From Apology to Utopia, Reissue, Cambridge University Press 2005.

Ingeborg Kreutzmann, *Missbrauch der humanitären Intervention im 19. Jahrhundert*, Glücksburg: Baltica 2005.

Walter LaFeber, *The Cambridge History of American Foreign Relations, Vol. II – The American Search for Opportunity*, Cambridge University Press 1993.

Felix Lange, *Praxisorientierung und Gemeinschaftskonzeption: Hermann Mosler als Wegber-eiter der westdeutschen Völkerrechtswissenschaft nach 1945*, Berlin: Springer 2017.

Paul Gordon Lauren, *The Evolution of International Human Rights*, 3rd ed., Philadelphia: University of Pennsylvania Press 2011.

Elihu Lauterpacht (ed.), *International Law, Being the Collected Papers of Hersch Lauter-pacht*, Vol. 2, Cambridge University Press 1975.

(ed.), *International Law, Being the Collected Papers of Hersch Lauterpacht*, Vol. 5, Cambridge University Press 2004.

Elihu Lauterpacht *The Life of Hersch Lauterpacht*, Cambridge University Press 2010.

Hersch Lauterpacht, *International Law and Human Rights*, 2nd ed., London: Stevens & Sons 1951.

Brian D. Lepard, *Customary International Law*, Cambridge University Press 2010.

Mark Levene, *Genocide in the Age of the Nation State*, Vol. II – The Rise of the West and the Coming of Genocide, London: I. B. Tauris 2005.

War, Jews, and the New Europe, Liverpool University Press 2009.

Zach Levey, 'Israel, Nigeria and the Biafra Civil War', in: A. Dirk Moses and Lasse Heerten (eds.), *Postcolonial Conflict and the Question of Genocide*, New York: Routledge 2017, pp. 177–197.

Mark Lewis, *The Birth of the New Justice*, Oxford University Press 2014.

Guenter Lewy, *The Armenian Massacres in Ottoman Turkey*, Salt Lake City: The University of Utah Press 2006.

Johannes Leyser, 'Philippinen', in: Hans-Jürgen Schlochauer (ed.), *Wörterbuch des Völker-rechts*, Vol. 2, Berlin: De Gruyter 1961.

Benjamin Lieberman, *Terrible Fate – Ethnic Cleansing in the Making of Modern Europe*, Maryland: Rowman & Littlefield 2013.

Eliav Lieblich, 'The Soviet Intervention in Hungary – 1956', in: Tom Ruys, Olivier Corten, and Alexandra Hofer (eds.), *The Use of Force in International Law – A Case-based Approach*, Oxford University Press 2018.

Dominic Lieven, *The Cambridge History of Russia: Volume 2, Imperial Russia, 1689–1917*, Cambridge University Press 2006.

Richard B. Lillich (ed.), *Humanitarian Intervention and the United Nations*, Charlottesville: University of Virginia Press 1973.

Filadelfio Linares, *Einblicke in Hugo Grotius' Werk 'Vom Recht der Krieges und des Friedens'*, Zürich: Olms 1993.

Andrew Linklatler and Hidemi Suganami, *The English School of International Relations*, Cambridge University Press 2006.

Heinz Loquai, *Der Kosovo-Konflikt. Wege in einen vermeidbaren Krieg. Die Zeit von Ende November 1997 bis März 1999*, Baden-Baden: Nomos 2000.

Ussama Makdisi, *The Culture of Sectarianism*, Berkeley: University of California Press 2000.

Peter Malanczuk, 'Monroe Doctrine', in: Rudolf Bernhardt (ed.), *Encyclopedia of Public International Law*, Vol. 7, Amsterdam: North Holland 1984, pp. 339–344.

Akehurst's International Law, 7th ed., London: Routledge 1997.

Lauri Mälksoo, 'Russia-Europe', in: Bardo Fassbender and Anne Peters (eds.), *The Oxford Handbook of the History of International Law*, Oxford University Press 2012, pp. 777–781.

Michael R. Marrus, *The Nuremburg War Crimes Trial 1945–46*, Boston: Bedford 1997.

Jenny S. Martinez, *The Slave Trade and the Origins of International Human Rights Law*, Oxford University Press 2012.

Christian-Albrecht Masuch, *Die rechtswissenschaftliche Diskussion der Kosovo-Intervention als Beispiel eines unterschiedlichen Völkerrechtsverständnisses der USA und Kontinentaleuropas*, Berlin: Logos Verlag 2006.

Larry May, *Crimes against Humanity*, Cambridge University Press 2005.

Mark Mazower, *Salonica City of Ghosts: Christians, Muslims and Jews 1430– 1950*, London: HarperCollins Publishers 2004.

  Hitler's Empire, New York: The Penguin Press 2008.

  'The End of Civilization and the Rise of Human Rights', in: Stefan-Ludwig Hoffmann (ed.), *Human Rights in the Twentieth Century*, Cambridge University Press 2011.

Brian McNeil, 'And Starvation Is the Grim Reaper', in: A. Dirk Moses and Lasse Heerten (eds.), *Postcolonial Conflict and the Question of Genocide*, New York: Routledge 2017, pp. 278–300.

Robert Meister, *After Evil*, New York: Columbia University Press 2011.

Rajan Menon, *The Conceit of Humanitarian Intervention*, Oxford University Press 2016.

Guenual Mettraux (ed.), *Perspectives on the Nuremberg Trial*, Oxford University Press, 2008.

Manus I. Midlarsky, *The Killing Trap – Genocide in the 20th Century*, Cambridge University Press 2005.

Petra Minnerop, *Paria-Staaten im Völkerrecht?*, Berlin: Springer 2004.

Philipp Caspar Mohr, *Kein Recht zur Einmischung?*, Tübingen: Mohr Siebeck 2002.

Benny Morris, *The Birth of the Palestinian Refugee Problem Revisited*, 2nd ed., Cambridge University Press 2012.

Samuel Moyn, *The Last Utopia*, Cambridge, MA: Belknap Press 2010.

  Human Rights and the Uses of History; London: Verso 2014.

Harald Müller, *Im Widerstreit von Interventionsstrategie und Anpassungszwang – Die Aussenpolitik Österreichs und Preußens zwischen dem Wiener Kongreß 1814/15 und der Februarrevolution 1848*, Berlin (East): Akademie der Wissenschaften der DDR 1990.

John Murphy, *The United States and the Rule of Law in International Affairs*, Cambridge University Press 2004.

Sean D. Murphy, *Humanitarian Intervention –The United Nations in an Evolving World Order*, Philadelphia: University of Pennsylvania Press 1996.

Thomas Naff, 'The Ottoman Empire and the European State System', in: Hedley Bull and Adam Watson (eds.), *The Expansion of International Society*, Oxford University Press 1984, pp. 143–170.

Stephen C. Neff, *War and the Law of Nations*, Cambridge University Press 2005.

Susan Neiman, *Evil in Modern Thought*, Princeton University Press 2002.

Janne E. Nijman, 'Minorities and Majorities', in: Bardo Fassbender and Anne Peters (eds.), *The Oxford Handbook of the History of International Law*, Oxford University Press 2012.

David Nirenberg, *Anti-Judaism: The Western Tradition*, New York: W. W. Norton 2013.

Peter Novick, *The Holocaust in American Life*, Boston: Houghton Mifflin 1999.

Arthur Nussbaum, *A Concise History of the Law of Nations*, London: Macmillan 1950.

Liliana Obregón, 'Completing Civilization: Creole Consciousness and International Law in Nineteenth-Century Latin America', in: Anne Orford (ed.), *International Law and Its Others*, Cambridge University Press 2006, pp. 247–264.

Stephan Oeter, 'Humanitäre Intervention und Gewaltverbot: Wie handlungsfähig ist die Staatengemeinschaft?', in Hauke Brunkhorst (ed.), *Einmischung erwünscht?*, Frankfurt am Main: S. Fischer 1998.

Kolawole Olaniyan, 'Biafra/Nigeria', in: Dinah L. Shelton (ed.), *Encyclopedia of Genocide and Crimes against Humanity*, Farmington Hills: MacMillan Reference USA 2005.

Thomas Olechowski, Tamara Ehs, and Kamila Staudigl-Ciechowicz, *Die Wiener Rechts- und Staatswissenschaftliche Fakultät 1918–1938*, Göttingen: V & R unipress 2014.

Lassa Oppenheim, *International Law: A Treatise, Vol. I, Peace*, 8th ed., ed. by H. Lauterpacht, London: Longmans, Green and Co 1955.

Thomas Oppermann, 'Kongo-Staat', in: Hans-Jürgen Schlochauer, *Wörterbuch des Völkerrechts*, Vol. 2, Berlin: De Gruyter 1961.

Anne Orford, *Reading Humanitarian Intervention*, Cambridge University Press 2003.
International Authority and the Responsibility to Protect, Cambridge University Press 2011.

Jürgen Osterhammel, *The Transformation of the World*, Princeton University Press 2014.

Umut Özsu, *Formalizing Displacement*, Oxford University Press 2015.

Norman Paech and Gerhard Stuby, *Völkerrecht und Machtpolitik in den internationalen Beziehungen*, Baden-Baden: Nomos 1994.

Norman Paech, '"Humanitäre Intervention" und Völkerrecht', in: Ulrich Albrecht and Paul Schäfer (eds.), *Der Kosovo-Krieg*, 2nd ed., Cologne: Papyrossa 1999.

Sundhya Pahuja, *Decolonising International Law*, Cambridge University Press 2011.

Evgeni Pashukanis, *Selected Writings on Marxism & Law*, trans. by Peter B. Maggs, London: Academic Press 1980.

Bimal N. Patel, *The State Practice of India and the Development of International Law*, Leiden: Brill 2016.

James Pattison, *Humanitarian Intervention and the Responsibility to Protect – Who Should Intervene*, Oxford University Press 2010.

Alexander Pauer, *Die humanitäre Intervention*, Basel: Helbing & Lichtenhahn 1985.

Herlinde Pauer-Studer and Julian Fink (eds.), *Rechtfertigungen des Unrechts*, Berlin: Suhrkamp Verlag 2014.

Andreas Paulus, *Die internationale Gemeinschaft im Völkerrecht*, Munich: C. H. Beck 2001.

Michelle Jean Penn, *The Extermination of Peaceful Soviet Citizens: Aron Trainin and International Law*. History Graduate Theses & Dissertations, 2017, 39, available at: http://scholar.colorado.edu/hist_gradetds/39, accessed 27 February 2018.

Alexander Pinwinkler, 'Norbert Gürke', in: Michael Fahlbusch, Ingo Haar, and Alexander Pinwinkler (eds.), *Handbuch der völkischen Wissenschaften*, Vol. I, 2nd ed., Berlin: De Gruyter 2017, pp. 254–257.

Samantha Power, *A Problem from Hell*, New York: Basic Books 2002.

René Provost, *International Human Rights and Humanitarian Law*, Cambridge University Press 2002.

John Quigley, *The Case for Palestine*, 2nd ed., Durham: Duke University Press 2005.

Steven R. Ratner, *The Thin Justice of International Law*, Oxford University Press 2015.

Stefano Recchia, 'The Origins of Liberal Wilsonianism', in: Stefano Recchia and Jennifer M. Welsh (eds.), *Just and Unjust Military Intervention*, Cambridge University Press 2013, pp. 237–262.

James J. Reid, *Crisis of the Ottoman Empire*, Stuttgart: Franz Steiner Verlag 2000.

W. Michael Reisman, *The Quest for World Order and Human Dignity in the Twenty-first Century: Constitutive Process and Individual Commitment*, The Pocket Books of The Hague Academy of International Law 2010, p. 351.

W. Michael Reisman and Andrew R. Willard (eds.), *International Incidents*, Princeton University Press 1988.

Lucy Riall, 'Garibaldi and the South', in John A. Davis (ed.), *Italy in the 19th Century*, Oxford University Press 2000.

Norman Rich, *Great Power Diplomacy 1814–1914*, New York: McGraw Hill 1992.

David Rieff, *Slaughterhouse: Bosnia and the Failure of the West*, New York: Simon & Schuster 1995.

Anthea Roberts, *Is International Law International?*, Oxford University Press 2017.

Geoffrey Robertson, *Crimes against Humanity*, 2nd ed., London: Penguin 2002.

Nigel Rodley, 'Humanitarian Intervention', in: Marc Weller (ed.), *The Oxford Handbook on the Use of Force in International Law*, Oxford University Press 2015, section III.A.1. (iBooks ed.).

Davide Rodogno, *Against Massacre: Humanitarian Interventions in the Ottoman Empire, 1815–1914*, Princeton University Press 2012.

C. G. Roelofsen, 'The Right to National Self-determination in the 18th and 19th Century, an emerging Principle of Public International Law?', in: Nerl Sybesma-Knol and Jef van Bellingen (eds.), *Naar een nieuwe interpretatie van het Recht of Zelfbeschikking*, Brussels: VUB Press 1995.

Natalino Ronzitti, *Rescuing Nationals Abroad through Military Coercion and Intervention on Grounds of Humanity*, Dordrecht: Martinus Nijhoff 1985.

Emmanuel Roucounas, 'The Idea of Justice in the Works of Early Scholars of International Law', in: Laurence Boisson de Chazournes and Vera Gowlland-Debbas (eds.), *The International Legal System in Quest of Equity and Universality*, The Hague: Kluwer Law International 2001, pp. 19–99.

Alfred P. Rubin, *Ethics and Authority in International Law*, Cambridge University Press 1997.

Helmut Rumpf, *Der internationale Schutz der Menschenrechte und das Interventionsverbot*, Baden-Baden: Nomos 1981.

Peter H. Russell, *Recognizing Aboriginal Title*, Toronto: University of Toronto Press 2005.

Bernd Rüthers, *Entartetes Recht*, Munich: C. H. Beck 1988.

Edward Said, *Orientalism*, New York: Pantheon Books 1978.

Philippe Sands, *East West Street*, London: Weidenfeld & Nicolson 2016.

R.R. Sastry, *Studies in International Law*, Calcutta: Eastern Law House Ltd 1952.

Wilhelm Sauer, *Völkerrecht und Weltfrieden*, Kohlhammer: Stuttgart 1948.

System des Völkerrechts, Bonn: Ludwig Röhrscheid Verlag 1952.

William A. Schabas, *Genocide in International Law*, 2nd ed., Cambridge University Press 2009.

Michael P. Scharf, *Customary International Law in Times of Fundamental Change – Recognizing Grotian Moments*, Cambridge University Press 2013.

Willem van Schendel, *A History of Bangladesh*, Cambridge University Press 2009.

Hans-Jürgen Schlochauer (ed.), *Wörterbuch des Völkerrechts*, Vol. 2, Berlin: De Gruyter 1961.

Carl Schmitt, *Der Nomos der Erde*, Berlin: Duncker & Humblot, reprint of the 1950 ed., 1997.

Antworten in Nürnberg, Berlin: Duncker & Humblot 2000.

The Nomos of the Earth, trans. by G. L. Ulmen, New York: Telos Press 2004.

Mathias Schmoeckel, *Die Großraumtheorie*, Berlin: Duncker & Humblot 1994.

'The Story of a Success. Lassa Oppenheim and his "International Law"', in: Michael Stolleis and Masaharu Yanagihara (eds.), *East Asian and European Perspectives on International Law*, Baden-Baden: Nomos 2004, pp. 57–138.

Peter J. Schraeder, *United States Foreign Policy toward Africa*, Cambridge University Press 1994.

Klaus-Peter Schroeder, '*Eine Universität für Juristen und von Juristen': Die Heidelberger Juristische Fakultät im 19. und 20. Jahrhundert*, Tübingen: Mohr Siebeck 2010.

Matthias Schulz, *Normen und Praxis*, Munich: Oldenbourg 2009.

Oliver Schulz, *Ein Sieg der zivilisierten Welt?*, Münster: LIT Verlag 2011.

Michael Schwartz, *Ethnische 'Säuberungen' in der Moderne*, Munich: Oldenbourg 2013.

Stephen M. Schwebel, *International Arbitration: Three Salient Problems*, Cambridge: Grotius Publications 1987.

Theodor Schweisfurth, *Sozialistisches Völkerrecht?*, Berlin: Springer 1979.
Völkerrecht, Tübingen: UTB 2006.

Iain Scobbie, 'Hersch Lauterpacht (1897–1960)', in: Bardo Fassbender and Anne Peters (eds.), *The Oxford Handbook of the History of International Law*, Oxford University Press 2012, pp. 1179–1183.

Ulrich Scupin, 'Völkerrechtsgeschichte', in: Hans-Jürgen Schlochauer (ed.), *Wörterbuch des Völkerrechts*, 2nd ed., Vol. II, Berlin: De Gruyter 1962.

Ignaz Seidl-Hohenveldern, *Völkerrecht*, 1st ed., Cologne: Heymanns 1965.
Völkerrecht, 2nd ed., Cologne: Heymanns 1969.

Ignaz Seidl-Hohenveldern and Torsten Stein, *Völkerrecht*, 10th ed., Cologne: Heymanns 2000.

Hugh Seton-Watson, *The Decline of Imperial Russia*, New York: Frederick A. Praeger 1952.

Mohammad Shahabuddin, *Ethnicity and International Law: Histories, Politics and Practices*, Cambridge University Press 2016.

Mohamed Shahid and Mohamed Khalid, *International Law and Politics of Intervention*, Delhi: Raj Publications 2003.

Stanford J. Shaw, *The Jews of the Ottoman Empire and the Turkish Republic*, New York University Press 1991.

Stanford J. Shaw and Ezel Kural Shaw, *History of the Ottoman Empire and Modern Turkey, Vol. II: Reform, Revolution, and Republic: The Rise of Modern Turkey, 1808–1975*, Cambridge University Press 1977.

Henry Shue, 'Limiting Sovereignty', in Jennifer M. Walsh (ed.), *Humanitarian Intervention and International Relations*, Oxford University Press 2004, pp. 11–28.

Brendan Simms and D. J. B. Trim (eds.), *Humanitarian Intervention – A History*, Cambridge University Press 2011.

A. W. Brian Simpson, *Human Rights and the End of Empire*, Oxford University Press 2000.

Christopher Simpson, 'Die seinerzeitige Diskussion über die in Nürnberg zu verhandelnden Delikte', in: Gerd Hankel and Gerhard Stuby (eds.), *Strafgerichte gegen Menschheitsverbrechen*, Hamburg: Hamburger Edition 1995, pp. 39–72.

Gerry Simpson, *Great Powers and Outlaw States*, Cambridge University Press 2004.

Jasjit Singh, 'India', in: Watanabe Koji (ed.), *Humanitarian Intervention – The Evolving Asian Debate*, Tokyo: Japan Center for International Exchange 2003.

Karen E. Smith, *Genocide and the Europeans*, Cambridge University Press 2010.

Louis Sohn and Thomas Buergenthal, *International Protection of Human Rights*, Indianapolis: Bobbs-Merrill 1973.

Peter K. Steck, *Zwischen Volk und Staat*, Baden-Baden: Nomos 2003.

Zara Steiner, *The Lights that Failed*, Oxford University Press 2005.

Cyrill Stieger, *Wir wissen nicht mehr, wer wir sind*, Vienna: Paul Zsolnay Verlag 2017.

Yannis A. Stivachtis, *The Enlargement of International Society*, Basingstoke, Hampshire: Palgrave Macmillan 1998.

Michael Stolleis, *Geschichte des öffentlichen Rechts in Deutschland Bd. 4: Staats- und Verwaltungsrechtswissenschaft in West und Ost 1945–1990*, Munich: C. H. Beck 2012.

Julius Stone, *Aggression and World Order*, Berkeley: University of California Press 1958.

Andreas Strippel, *NS-Volkstumspolitik und die Neuordnung Europas*, Paderborn: Ferdinand Schöningh 2011.

Kim Sung-han, 'South Korea', in: Watanabe Koji (ed.), *Humanitarian Intervention – The Evolving Asian Debate*, Tokyo: Japan Center for International Exchange 2003.

Mark Swatek-Evenstein, *Geschichte der 'Humanitären Intervention'*, Baden-Baden: Nomos 2008.

'Reconstituting Humanity as Responsibility – The "Turn to History" in International Law and the Responsibility to Protect', in: Julia Hoffmann and André Nollkaemper (eds.), *Responsibility to Protect – From Principle to Practice*, Amsterdam: Pallas Publications 2012, pp. 47–59.

Christian J. Tams, *Enforcing Obligations Erga Omnes in International Law*, Cambridge University Press 2005.

Christian J. Tams, Lars Berster, and Björn Schiffbauer, *Convention on the Prevention and Punishment of the Crime of Genocide: A Commentary*, Munich: C. H. Beck 2014.

Manesh Prasad Tandon, *Public International Law*, 11th ed., Allahabad: Allahabad Law Agency Publishers 1966.

Manesh Prasad Tandon and Rajesh Tandon, *Public International Law*, 20th ed., Allahabad: Allahabad Law Agency Publishers 1985.

Harold Temperley, *The Foreign Policy of Canning 1822–1827*, 2nd ed., Connecticut: Archon Books 1966.

Yves Ternon, *Der verbrecherische Staat*, Hamburg: Hamburger Edition 1996.

Fernandon R. Tesón, 'The Liberal Case for Humanitarian Intervention', in: J. L. Holzgrefe and Robert O. Keohane (eds.), *Humanitarian Intervention*, Cambridge University Press 2003.

Humanitarian Intervention, 3rd ed., Ardsley: Transnational Publishers, 2005.

Philipp Ther, *Die dunkle Seite der Nationalstaaten*, Göttingen: Vandenhoeck & Ruprecht 2011.

Ann Van Wynen Thomas and A. J. Thomas Jr., *Non-intervention: The Law and Its Import in the Americas*, Dallas: Southern Methodist University Press 1956.

Maria Todorova, *Imagining the Balkans*, 2nd ed., Oxford University Press 2009.

Valentin Tomberg, *Grundlagen des Völkerrechts als Menschheitsrecht*, Bonn: Götz Schwippert Verlag 1947.

Christian Tomuschat, *Rede zum 50. Doktorjubiläum*, Bonn: Bouvier 1988.

Human Rights – Between Idealism and Realism, 2nd ed., Oxford University Press 2008.

John Lawrence Tone, *War and Genocide in Cuba*, Chapel Hill: University of North Carolina Press 2008.

Ana S. Trbovich, *A Legal Geography of Yugoslavia's Disintegration*, Oxford University Press 2008.

D. J. B. Trim, '"If a prince uses tyrannie towards his people": Intervention on Behalf of Foreign Populations in Early Modern Europe', in: Brendan Simms and D. J. B. Trim (eds.), *Humanitarian Intervention – A History*, Cambridge University Press 2011, pp. 29–66.

D. J. B. Trim and Brendan Simms, 'Towards a History of Humanitarian Intervention', in: Brendan Simms and D. J. B. Trim (eds.), *Humanitarian Intervention – A History*, Cambridge University Press 2011.

Antonio Truyol Y Serra, 'History of International Law – Latin America', in: Rudolf Bernhardt (ed.) *Encyclopedia of Public International Law*, Vol. 2, Amsterdam: North-Holland Publishing 1995, pp. 818–823.

Andrei P. Tsygankov, *Russia and the West from Alexander to Putin*, Cambridge University Press 2012.

Manuel Tuñón de Lara, Julio Aróstegui, Ángel Viñas, Gabriel Cardona, and Josep M. Bricall, *Der Spanische Bürgerkrieg – Eine Bestandsaufnahme*, Frankfurt: Suhrkamp 1987.

Guy Vanthemsche, *Belgium and the Congo 1885–1960*, Cambridge University Press 2012.

Payappilly Itty Varghese, *International Law and Organization*, Lucknow: Eastern Book Company 1952.

Georgios Varouxakis, *Liberty Abroad, J. S. Mill on International Relations*, Cambridge University Press 2013.

Alfred Verdross, *Völkerrecht*, 2nd ed., Vienna: Springer-Verlag 1950.

    Völkerrecht, 3rd ed., Vienna: Springer-Verlag 1955.

    Völkerrecht, 5th ed., Vienna: Springer-Verlag 1964.

Alfred Verdross and Bruno Simma, *Universelles Völkerrecht*, Berlin: Duncker & Humblot, 1976.

    Universelles Völkerrecht, 3rd ed., Berlin: Duncker & Humblot 1984.

Hans Vest, *Gerechtigkeit für Humanitätsverbrechen?*, Tübingen: Mohr Siebeck 2006.

R. J. Vincent, *Nonintervention and International Order*, Princeton University Press 1974.

    'Grotius, Human Rights, and Intervention', in: Hedley Bull, Benedict Kingsbury, and Adam Roberts (eds.), *Hugo Grotius and International Relations*, Oxford: Clarendon Paperbacks 1990, pp. 241–256.

Wolfgang Graf Vitzthum (ed.), *Völkerrecht*, 4th ed., Berlin: De Gruyter 2007.

Sandra Voos, *Die Schule von New Haven*, Berlin: Duncker & Humblot 2000.

Bart Wallet, 'Dutch National Identity and Jewish International Solidarity: An impossible Combination? Dutch Jewry and the Significance of the Damascus Affair (1840)', in: Yosef Kaplan (ed.), *The Dutch Intersection: The Jews and the Netherlands in Modern History*, Leiden: Koninklijke Brill 2008, pp. 319–330.

Jennifer M. Walsh (ed.), *Humanitarian Intervention and International Relations*, Oxford University Press 2004.

Christian Walter, 'The US Intervention in the Dominican Republic–1965', in: Tom Ruys, Olivier Corten, and Alexandra Hofer (eds.), *The Use of Force in International Law – A Case-based Approach*, Oxford University Press 2018.

Dierk Walter, *Organisierte Gewalt in der europäischen Expansion*, Hamburg: Hamburger Edition 2014.

Michael Walzer, *Spheres of Justice*, New York: Basic Books 1983.

    Just and Unjust Wars, 4th ed., New York, Basic Books 2006.

Adam Watson, *The Evolution of International Society*, London: Routledge 1992.

Shand J. Watson, *Theory and Reality in the International Protection of Human Rights*, New York: Transnational Publishers 1999.

Malte Wellhausen, *Humanitäre Intervention*, Baden-Baden: Nomos 2002.

Jon Western, 'Prudence or Outrage? Public Opinion and Humanitarian Intervention in Historical and Comparative Perspective', in Fabian Klose (ed.), *The Emergence of Humanitarian Intervention*, Cambridge University Press 2015, pp. 165–184.

Andrew Wheatcroft, *The Ottomans – Dissolving Images*, London: Penguin 1993.

    Infidels, London: Penguin 2004.

Nicolas J. Wheeler, *Saving Strangers*, Oxford University Press 2000.

Stefan Wiese, *Pogrome im Zarenreich – Dynamiken kollektiver Gewalt*, Hamburg: Hamburger Edition 2016.

Lora Wildenthal, 'Rudolf Laun and the Human Rights of Germans in Occupied and Early Western Germany', in: Stefan-Ludwig Hofmann (ed.), *Human Rights in the Twentieth Century*, Cambridge University Press 2010, pp. 125–144

Andreas Wimmer, *Waves of War – Nationalism and State*, Cambridge University Press 2012.

Heinrich August Winkler, *Geschichte des Westens – Die Zeit der Weltkriege 1914–1945*, Munich: C. H. Beck 2011.

Geschichte des Westens, Von den Anfängen in der Antike bis zum 20. Jahrhundert, 3rd ed., Munich: C. H. Beck Verlag 2012.

Geschichte des Westens – vom Kalten Krieg bis zum Mauerfall, Munich: C. H. Beck 2014.

Rüdiger Wolfrum, 'Nationalsozialismus und Völkerrecht', in: Franz Jürgen Säcker (ed.), *Recht und Rechtslehre im Nationalsozialismus*, Baden-Baden: Nomos 1992.

'Preamble', in: Bruno Simma (ed.), *The Charter of the United Nations – A Commentary*, 2nd ed., Munich: C. H. Beck 2002.

Fritz Wust, Der gewohnheitsrechtliche Humanitätsgrundsatz im Völkerrecht, Dissertation, Nuremberg 1968.

Leni Yahil, *The Holocaust*, Oxford University Press 1990.

Maja Zehfuss, *Wounds of Memory*, Cambridge University Press 2007.

Max Zeuske and Michael Zeuske, *Kuba 1492–1902*, Leipzig: Leipziger Universitätsverlag 1998.

Karl Heinz Ziegler, *Völkerrechtsgeschichte*, 2nd ed., Munich: C. H. Beck 2007.

Rolf Zimmermann, *Philosophie nach Auschwitz*, Reinbek: rororo Taschenbuch 2005.

Danilo Zolo, *Invoking Humanity*, London and New York: Continuum 2002.

COLLECTIONS OF SOURCES

Wilhelm G. Grewe (ed.), *Fontes Historiae Iuris Gentium – Sources Relating to the History of the Law of Nations*, Vol. 3/1, Berlin: De Gruyter 1992.

Georg Friedrich von Martens and Frédéric Saalfeld (eds.), *Supplement au Recueil des principaux Traités*, Vol. VI, Part, Göttingen: Dieterich 1827.

(eds.), *Nouveau Recueil de Traites*, Vol. VII, Part 1, Göttingen: Dieterich 1829.

(eds.), *Supplément au Recueil des principaux Traités*, Vol. XII, Göttingen: Dieterich 1831.

(eds.), *Supplément au Recueil des principaux Traités*, Vol. XVI, Göttingen: Dieterich 1837.

Georg Friedrich von Martens and Charles Samwer, *Nouveau Recueil Général des Traités*, Vol. XV, Göttingen: Dieterich 1857.

Georg Friedrich von Martens, Charles Samwer, and Jules Hopf (eds.), *Nouveau Recueil Général des Traités*, Deuxième Séries, Vol. II, Göttingen: Dieterich 1878.

John Bassett Moore (ed.), *A Digest of International Law*, Vol. VI, Washington: Government Printing Office 1906.

Papers Relative to the Affairs of Greece, Protocols of Conferences Held in London, London: Harrison & Sons 1830.

Stephan Verosta and Ignaz Seidl-Hohenveldern (eds.), *Die völkerrechtliche Praxis der Donaumonarchie von 1859 bis 1918*, Vienna: Austrian Academy of Sciences Press 1996.

Index